A MAN FOR ALL SEASONS

A Man for All Seasons

MONROE SWEETLAND
AND THE LIBERAL PARADOX

William G. Robbins

Oregon State University Press   Corvallis

The paper in this book meets the guidelines for permanence and durability of the Committee on Production Guidelines for Book Longevity of the Council on Library Resources and the minimum requirements of the American National Standard for Permanence of Paper for Printed Library Materials Z39.48-1984.

Library of Congress Cataloging-in-Publication Data

Robbins, William G., 1935-
  A man for all seasons : Monroe Sweetland and the liberal paradox / William Robbins.
    pages cm
  Includes bibliographical references and index.
  ISBN 978-0-87071-811-3 (paperback) – ISBN 978-0-87071-812-0 (e-book)
  1. Sweetland, Monroe, 1910-2006. 2. Legislators–Oregon–Biography.
3. Civic leaders–Oregon–Biography. 4. Oregon. Legislative Assembly–Biography.
5. Democratic Party (Or.)–Biography. 6. Liberalism–Oregon–History–
20th century. 7. Oregon–Politics and government–1951- 8. National Education
Association of the United States–Biography. 9. Political culture–United States–
History–20th century. 10. United States–Politics and government–1945-1989.
I. Title.
F881.35.S94R63 2015
328.73'092--dc23
[B]
                           2015011484

Oregon State University Press
121 The Valley Library
Corvallis OR 97331-4501
541-737-3166 • fax 541-737-3170
www.osupress.oregonstate.edu

In Memory of Barbara Sweetland Smith
and
Floyd Smith,
Rebecca Sweetland,
and their families

Contents

Acknowledgments

Monroe Sweetland's name first surfaced in a graduate seminar at the University of Oregon in the late 1960s—and if memory serves me well—as a person associated with a romantic and radical political organization, the Oregon Commonwealth Federation. Sweetland's name resurfaced decades later when I attended a Pacific Northwest Labor History Association meeting in Portland and a friend identified him as the man who rose to ask a question from the back of the room. In subsequent visits to Portland I would occasionally see him in the vicinity of the Park Blocks near Portland State University, white cane in hand and usually in the company of a graduate student. Sweetland, who suffered from macular degeneration, had been legally blind since the early 1990s. Then, shortly after Sweetland's death in 2006, my longtime friend Steve Haycox (University of Alaska, Anchorage) urged me to write his biography. I begged off, already heavily invested in a big research project on insurgent movements in the American West. But the enormity and amorphous nature of that venture prompted me to consider something more definitive, a problem that brought to mind the *Peanuts* character, Lucy, who was reading a book—"A man was born, he lived and he died. The End." With that heady sentiment in mind, I typed Sweetland's name in a computer search line and found page upon page of links!

My research into Monroe Sweetland's life involved family members, friends and working associates, librarians, archivists, scholars, designated drivers, and more. Early in the project, Mary Ann Campbell, then the librarian at the Oregon Historical Society (OHS) in Portland, suggested the possibility of temporarily loaning the large collection of Monroe Sweetland Papers to the Oregon State University Archives in Corvallis. Such a move would save me travel expenses to Portland at a time when funds to support research were disappearing in the wake of the Great Recession. Oregon State University archivist Larry Landis was receptive, and with the full cooperation and assistance of OHS archivist Geoff Wexler, the documents were moved to OSU's Valley Library. Working through the Sweetland Papers in the winter and spring of 2009, I benefitted from the lively and helpful archival staff—Larry, of course, and Elizabeth Nielson, Karl McCreary, and Tiah Edmonson-Morton. David Robinson, director of OSU's Center for the Humanities, provided office space for my daily treks to and from campus. To the archivists, librarians, and others, I am grateful.

Monroe Sweetland's daughters, Barbara Sweetland Smith of Anchorage, Alaska, and Rebecca Sweetland of Lake Oswego, provided helpful contact information about Monroe's longtime associates, especially Reynaldo Martinez of Incline Village, Nevada, who traveled with Monroe when the two worked for the National Education Association as legislative consultants in the western states. Rey, who had unbounded respect for Monroe and regaled me with stories of their work together, later became chief of staff to representative and then Senator Harry Reid, his high school classmate from Searchlight, Nevada. Rey loaned me three boxes of his files detailing his long friendship with Monroe, including important documents related to their collective effort in the Southwest to develop support for the federal Bilingual Education Act of 1968.

Verne Duncan, former Oregon superintendent of education and state senator, shared witty observations about his friendship with Monroe, including when the two traveled together campaigning for the same Oregon Senate seat in 1998. Stan Federman offered valuable perceptions about Sweetland, but especially about his wife Lil, when they edited and published a weekly newspaper together, the *Milwaukie Review*. Federman turned the financially troubled newspaper into a thriving business before moving on to the Portland *Oregonian* for a long career as a columnist. He remembered Lil as tough-minded in the *Review* office and a great cook. Federman and his wife Laurie were married in the Sweetland's spacious living room in Milwaukie. I am also indebted to Eliza Canty-Jones, editor of the *Oregon Historical Quarterly*, for publishing three articles about Monroe's experiences in the Pacific during the Second World War and making available the digital images appearing in the journal.

Others also provided valuable insights about Monroe. William Lang, Portland State University professor emeritus in history, interviewed

Sweetland and told me that Monroe generally liked people and they, in turn, enjoyed him. Grant Schott, who traveled with Sweetland to numerous political events, cherished his stories about local and national political figures. Schott, who is transcribing the interviews of Howard Morgan—a contemporary who worked with Sweetland in the rise of Oregon's Democratic Party in the 1950s—offered interesting commentary on the two very different personalities. Jeanne Magmer was another who provided transportation for Sweetland from his residence at Willamette View Estates in Portland to meetings elsewhere in the city. She remembers Monroe convincing her to volunteer as a precinct worker for the Democratic Party.

Barbara Sweetland Smith, who passed away in March 2013, shared with me her rich trove of correspondence with her mother and other documents important to Lil's professional career with the federal government. Barbara, a trained and published historian, cared passionately about her father's biography, but always agreed that the historian's project was to follow wherever the documented evidence suggested. I am appreciative of her sage observation. Rebecca Sweetland, her younger sister who grew up in San Mateo, California, afforded insights to the Sweetland home when Monroe was traveling the western states and to Washington, DC, on behalf of the National Education Association. The San Mateo home provided easy access to NEA's nearby Burlingame office and the San Francisco Airport. Rebecca put me in contact with Les Francis, who headed NEA's Youth Franchise Coalition in the campaign leading up to the age-eighteen vote (the adoption of the Twenty-Sixth Amendment) in March 1971.

Tom Booth, a friend of many years and associate director of the Oregon State University Press, guided a sometimes impatient author through the review and production processes. Marty Brown, marketing manager of the press, reviewed various designs for the book cover and agreed that an action image of Sweetland was preferable to a photo portrait. I also want to acknowledge several acquaintances at Corvallis's Circle Boulevard Beanery who occasionally asked about my morning scribblings in the coffee shop— Walt, Luree, Chuck, George, Bill, Hugh, Earl, and John. Finally, and most important, my best friend of forty years, Karla, has always supported my passion for doing history.

Abbreviations

ACLU	American Civil Liberties Union
ADA	Americans for Democratic Action
AFL	American Federation of Labor
ASU	American Student Union
BPA	Bonneville Power Administration
CTA	California Teachers Association
CIA	Central Intelligence Agency
CIO	Congress of Industrial Organizations
ESEA	Elementary and Secondary Education Act
IWA	International Woodworkers of America
JACL	Japanese American Citizens League
LID	League for Industrial Democracy
OCF	Office of Production Management
OCF	Oregon Commonwealth Federation
NAACP	National Association for the Advancement of Colored People
NEA	National Education Association
NSL	National Student League
ROTC	Reserve Officers Training Corps
SLID	Student League for Industrial Democracy
UN	United Nations

Introduction: The Story of an American Liberal

Monroe Sweetland's life story spans America's political spectrum from the 1930s through his retirement years, a virtual tour through the nation's political and social landscapes during the last half of the twentieth century. Through seven decades, he was partner and witness to the economic collapse of the Great Depression, the unparalleled violence of a nation at war, ten years of fast-paced and important work with the National Education Association and, through the postwar years, the divisiveness of Cold War politics (culminating with the Vietnam War). His experiences illuminate the wrenching transformation of American political culture as the nation struggled with racial and economic inequalities, circumstances that motivated much of Sweetland's civic labor. His attraction to what he perceived as the righteous cause led to lifelong memberships in the American Civil Liberties Committee, the National Association for the Advancement of Colored People, the Urban League, and the Japanese American Citizens League.

With the parchment on his college degree from conservative Wittenberg College barely dry, the twenty-year-old Sweetland headed off to law school at Cornell University in the autumn of 1930, where he would board with his namesake uncle, a lawyer and local judge. His desire to pursue a legal profession, however, was ephemeral, giving way to radical, activist politics, including meeting renowned socialist and perennial presidential candidate Norman Thomas in New York City. Before the year was out, Sweetland was involved in antiwar activities on the Cornell campus and had joined the socialist League for Industrial Democracy. Because he neglected his studies, at his uncle's urging Sweetland enrolled in the Syracuse University Law School in the fall of 1931. To the inquisitive Sweetland, however, extracurricular activities always proved more attractive—opposing compulsory military training programs on college campuses, supporting striking miners in West Virginia coal fields, introducing socialist principles to students, and meeting Lillie Megrath, his future wife.

Those youthful years with the League engrained in Sweetland's psyche a profound commitment to democratic principles and equal rights for all Americans irrespective of class, race, or creed. Those formative years forged working associations with some of the more prominent progressives of the day, including, besides Norman Thomas, Roger Baldwin, founder of the American Civil Liberties Union; A. Philip Randolph of the Brotherhood of Sleeping Car Porters; and prominent CIO leaders Sidney Hillman, James Carey, Philip Murray, and Walter Reuther. Those individuals and many others were important to Sweetland's activities for three decades—notably, his efforts to modernize Oregon's lethargic and moribund Democratic Party and his work as a state legislator to enact civil rights and labor reform measures. Disappointments of the moment never dissuaded the always optimistic Sweetland, who moved on to new challenges and opportunities to advance causes related to economic justice, access to the ballot box, or cheap and affordable education.

Politics was his lifeblood, and Sweetland proved himself a skilled political operative in the best sense of the phrase. He worked expertly behind the scenes to promote the just cause, the appropriate candidate, or progressive tax measures. Although he aspired to higher objectives, his strategies and approaches were sometimes contradictory and personally conflicted—supporting the candidacies of Lyndon Johnson and then Hubert Humphrey in the 1968 presidential election on the basis that they were important to promoting civil rights and educational reforms—while ignoring the horrors of the violence of America's intervention in Vietnam. It is also fair to say that as he aged he tended to support the most liberal among *establishment* candidates. A thoroughgoing radical as a youth, he would have nothing to do with the equally radical Students for a Democratic Society of the 1960s, even vilifying young antiwar demonstrators as the irrational, nihilist, and irresponsible Left.

Despite those inconsistencies, Monroe Sweetland genuinely liked people, irrespective of political affiliation. During the later years of the Great Depression, he supported various policies of two prominent Oregon Republicans, Senator Charles McNary and Governor Charles Sprague. McNary, who was Senate minority leader in the late 1930s and Republican vice-presidential candidate in 1940, came to Sweetland's defense when conservative Democrats and labor leaders attacked his appointment to the federal Office of Production Management in 1941. In similar fashion, when Sweetland served as head of the leftist Oregon Commonwealth Federation during the late 1930s, he formed a sense of mutual respect with Governor Sprague and paid tribute to him on important civil liberties issues. The Japanese American Citizens League eventually honored both men for their efforts in defending the rights of Japanese Americans during and after the Second World War. And most notably, while critical of Mark Hatfield's fiscal policies, Sweetland developed solid working relations with the young Republican when the two served in the Oregon House and Senate during the 1950s. When Oregon voters elected Hatfield governor in 1958, Sweetland escorted the governor-elect to his swearing-in ceremonies in the capitol rotunda in January 1959. There were many others, including liberal Republican Verne Duncan, who became good friends with Sweetland late in life.

When Monroe and his wife Lillie Megrath (m. 1933) made the move to his birthplace in Oregon in 1936, he established friendships and working relations with political liberals Richard Neuberger and Wayne Morse that would last, with some distractions, for the remainder of their lives. Beginning with the nonaligned, collectivist-inspired Oregon Commonwealth Federation in 1937, he worked with other progressives to unseat reactionary, anti-New Deal Democratic governor Charles Martin in the 1938 primary election. In that effort he attracted the attention and support of progressives in President Franklin D. Roosevelt's administration that further upset conservative Democrats in Oregon. As a left-liberal activist before and after the war, Sweetland led the resurrection of the state's Democratic Party, an organization lacking imagination, vitality, and a touch with common people.

Monroe's ventures into the newspaper business after the Second World War were purposeful, to afford an income for the family and to provide a forum for promoting progressive social and economic policies and the leisure to pursue politics. The sine qua non to successfully operating a newspaper was his wife Lil, who oversaw the back shop and the daily operations of the three newspapers the Sweetlands published between 1946 and the early 1960s. But she was no victim of an overweening spouse, telling her daughter Barbara in the mid-1950s that she loved the work. Monroe's intense focus on politics complicated the newspaper business, contributing to carelessness with bookkeeping and expense accounts and repeatedly straining the family's finances. On more than one occasion, those financial problems led to strained relations with friends who had invested in the publishing ventures. To Monroe, however, the medium was important, providing a discursive platform for progressive politics.

After leaving Oregon and the newspaper business in 1962, the Sweetlands traveled abroad, lived in Indonesia for a year, and then returned home in 1964 to different vocations—Monroe as a legislative consultant with the National Education Association (NEA) working out of Burlingame, California, and Lil as a labor specialist with the federal government in San Francisco. Monroe thrived in his new organizational environment, taking on challenges that would move the giant NEA bureaucracy in new directions. During his ten years of fast-paced and important work with NEA, he served as a facilitator with Mexican American educators in the Southwest to garner federal support for bilingual education programs for schools with large numbers of non-English-speaking students. That collaborative enterprise led to congressional passage of the Bilingual Education Act of 1968. His other major achievement with NEA involved the hard-fought three-year campaign for the age-eighteen vote. Young people, who did most of the door-to-door canvassing, cite Sweetland's seminal role—as a sort of pied piper—in extending the vote to young people.

Reynaldo Martinez, Monroe's colleague with NEA (and later, longtime chief of staff to Nevada senator Harry Reid), cites Sweetland's skills as a public speaker and his rapport with local politicians as the reasons for his successes with NEA. Sweetland's NEA superior, Martinez recalls, let "him travel the western United States in his own unorthodox manner. Monroe didn't follow protocol, he already knew the major political players as friends." Sweetland also did his best to protect the agency's budget, with Martinez remembering Spartan meals and cheap motels during their travels about the American West.[1] When the journey concluded, according to daughter Rebecca, Monroe returned to the family home in San Mateo, usually with a gift for her and always a game of gin rummy with Lil. Through all the frenetic traveling on behalf of NEA—to Washington, D.C., testifying before congressional and state legislative committees, Monroe remained remarkably healthy. He retired in 1975 only because he had reached NEA's mandatory retirement age of sixty-five.

Beyond his accomplishments in the Oregon legislature, Sweetland had a long history of working with party liberals at the national level. Following the war and after his election to the Democratic Party National Committee, he became friends with rising Democratic Party luminary, Minneapolis mayor Hubert Humphrey. In the key presidential election of 1948, he joined Humphrey and others to place a strong liberal-rights plank in the Democratic Party platform, a move that led southern Democrats to walk out of the convention and form the Dixiecrat Party. Those events provided part of the story to President Harry Truman's famously narrow victory over Republican Thomas Dewey in the November election. And therein rest the ambiguities to Sweetland's political liberalism.

The political maneuvering before the 1948 election is a story that reveals, in stark terms, the positioning of liberals—many of them affiliated with the ultraliberal Americans for Democratic Action (ADA)—in an emerging Cold War consensus in which anticommunism became an irresistible force in shaping domestic politics. The narrative begins with Henry Wallace, Franklin Roosevelt's vice president during his third term (1941–1945) and a holdover secretary of commerce in Truman's cabinet. When Wallace gave a speech at New York's Madison Square Garden in September 1946 warning that American hostility toward the Soviet Union would lead to another war, the president summarily fired the former vice president. Wallace, who had urged cooperation and respect for each nation's spheres of influence, became editor of the *New Republic* and, in late 1947, declared his candidacy for president in 1948 under the Progressive Party banner. That declaration put him at odds with anticommunist liberals Hubert Humphrey, CIO officials Walter Reuther and Philip Murray, and most ADA board members (including Sweetland).

Liberals, who once revered Wallace, now reversed course and castigated the former vice president, accusing him of being a charlatan and soft on communism. For the left-liberal Sweetland—a socialist, antiwar noninterventionist in the 1930s—Wallace's candidacy threatened the Democratic Party's chances of winning the presidency in November. His fear—widely shared among liberals—was that Wallace would draw significant numbers of Democratic votes and give the election to the Republican candidate. Sweetland's newspaper editorials in opposition to Wallace enhanced his status with liberals on the Democratic National Committee. He was at one, however, with a large contingent of liberals who enthusiastically supported the social-welfare policies of the New Deal and then, in 1947 and 1948, began to purge from their ranks those who favored accommodation with the Soviet Union.

Humphrey, Sweetland, and their ADA cohorts were exemplars of the liberal paradox: a sizable group of political progressives willing to silence dissent in the name of national security, supporting federal and state efforts to demonize anyone suspected of following the communist line. In the emerging Cold War consensus, Henry Wallace, a noncommunist, accused of being insufficiently rigorous in the fight against communism, was the liberal's favorite target. "The complicity of the liberal class" in attacking Wallace, former *New York Times* correspondent Chris Hedges writes, was a product of insecurity, since many of them had been politically to the left during the Great Depression.[2] Sweetland's support for the death penalty of Julius and Ethel Rosenberg for passing secrets to the Soviet Union, his opposition to admitting the People's Republic of China to the United Nations, and his support for a strong military presence in Europe and the Pacific were striking departures from his life as a pacifist and civil libertarian during the 1930s.

There is still more to Sweetland's midlife establishmentarian politics. In the critical presidential election of 1968—with Vietnam as the horrifying spectacle of American interventionism gone awry—Sweetland was noticeably reticent about the riots and unrest at home and the violence rained on the Vietnamese people. His views during this period parallel that of liberal union leader Walter Reuther, who could be critical of the Vietnam War but, according to historian Jefferson Cowie, was "leery of allying with the anti-war cause animating the nation's youth . . . for risk of breaking with [President Lyndon] Johnson and Humphrey, in whom he saw the promise of the next leap forward in domestic reform." Speaking to a Democratic Party gathering in San Mateo, California, in early March 1968, Sweetland argued that foreign policy crises such as Vietnam were transitory and would not be the most critical factor in the fall election. Like Reuther, he insisted that it was important for the "standard bearers of the liberal cause" to focus on education and racial problems that would "lay the basis for peace among all peoples."[3]

Sweetland's evolution from antimilitarism to hardened Cold Warrior was diametrically opposite that of his erstwhile mentor, Norman Thomas, who remained an outspoken critic of American intervention abroad during the postwar years. The transition in Sweetland's ideological predisposition becomes more understandable when one considers his opposition to communists in leadership positions in the Oregon Commonwealth Federation. His correspondence also reveals that his appointment to the federal government's Office of Production Management in July 1941 was related to the agency's need for a committed anticommunist to head the sensitive job of mitigating labor-management conflicts in strategic defense industries. The same can be said for when he became director of the newly fledged CIO War Relief Committee in January 1942—the large industrial union's leadership (Philip Murray, James Carey, and Walter Reuther) wanted the committee head to be someone with solid anticommunist credentials.[4]

The incongruity of Sweetland's fervid anticommunism during the Cold War stands in sharp contrast to the decades-long attacks persistently charging that he was a closet communist or at least sympathetic with communist objectives. When he landed the federal job, Oregon's American Federation of Labor officials objected to his appointment, charging that he had tolerated communist domination of the Commonwealth Federation. Long after the demise of the Commonwealth Federation and long after his experiences working in Washington, D.C., in the early 1940s, Sweetland's friend Nathalie Panek explained to journalist Charles Royer (later mayor of Seattle) Sweetland's skill in keeping communists from influential positions in the federation. In similar fashion, liberal labor union leaders supported his appointments with the Office of Production Management and the CIO War Relief Committee because of his anticommunist credentials.

As a state legislator, first in the Oregon House (1953–1955), and then two terms in the Senate (1955–1963), Sweetland was the standard-bearer for liberal causes, sponsoring legislation to prohibit discrimination in public accommodations and advocating progressive income taxes. In the Senate he guided legislation establishing Portland State College as a major metropolitan institution, and he was the principal driving force in creating Oregon's community college system. He made two abortive campaigns for secretary of state, losing to friend and rising Republican star Mark Hatfield in 1956, the winner's closest margin of victory in any election. When Hatfield was elected governor two years later, Sweetland ran again in 1960, this time against Hatfield's appointed successor, Howell Appling. He lost the election by a sizable margin when John Birch Society members distributed hundreds of leaflets on election eve in the Portland metropolitan area and elsewhere charging Sweetland with having extensive communist ties during the 1930s.

Despite such disappointments (including his failure to land an appointment with the incoming John F. Kennedy administration in early 1961), the always positive Sweetland moved on to new opportunities, attending the World Assembly of Teaching Organizations in New Delhi in the summer of 1961, courtesy of the NEA. He subsequently spent an event-filled year as a visiting professor at Padjadjaran University in Bandung, Indonesia, in 1963, and then returned stateside with his family to more politicking and eventually the position with the NEA. His lifetime accomplishments were wide-ranging, extending from his insurgent, antiwar activism of the 1930s to his unsuccessful campaign—as a legally blind candidate—for the Oregon Senate in 1998. When he moved to a retirement community in Southeast Portland in 1998, he reputedly told a friend that he appreciated the single-floor dwellings, because it was easier to navigate the floors to canvass residents on election issues. Unusually positive in his relations with others and never dwelling on immediate frustrations, Monroe Sweetland remained to the end of his life an eloquent and persuasive proponent of the greater public good.

1

The Formative Years

"Politician at 11," headlined an article in the *Detroit News* on a Sunday in April 1924. Beginning "A little child shall lead them," the Constantine, Michigan, dateline recounted the story of young Monroe Sweetland, who used postcards to call into session the town's hitherto nonexistent Democratic Party caucus. Circulated without a signature to Democratic voters in the heavily Republican town, the postcards attracted several Democrats to the meeting, who forthwith posted a list of candidates for city and township offices. When it became known that the young son of Dr. George and Mildred Sweetland was the source of the postcards, the St. Joseph County Democratic Club invited the boy to be guest of honor at its annual Jefferson Day banquet.[1]

Monroe Sweetland's civic-mindedness resurfaced later that summer when he attended the nearby Kalamazoo Boy Scout camp and then journeyed to Boston with the scout band to visit historic sites and to perform a number of concerts. The group spent a week in Boston, visiting the government navy yard and giving a concert aboard the historic ship, *U.S.S. Constitution.* In addition to the celebrated vessel, the scouts toured through some of Boston's most iconic landmarks: Harvard University, the Paul Revere route, the Lexington and Concord battlefields, the James Russell Lowell and Henry Wadsworth Longfellow homes, and the Old North Church. The *Constantine Advertiser-Record* reported that Monroe returned with "a fine collection of souvenirs, and a fund of interesting stories."[2]

Other than his childhood dabbling in adult politics, there were few indications in young Sweetland's life of a budding public persona. Despite those few openings to a larger world, the Constantine of Monroe's boyhood was insular, rural Protestant, and Republican, with one Catholic and one Jewish family, a few African Americans, and little ethnic diversity. Only six miles north of the Indiana border, Constantine was nestled in the midst of southern Michigan's most productive farmland. Although he completed first grade elsewhere, Monroe would spend the remainder of his public school years in Constantine's only school building. With a population of 1,277 in 1920, the village's downtown included several brick buildings with turn-of-the-century Victorian architectural styles—Gothic, Italianate, and Greek Revival.[3] A quiet, peaceful community for a boy interested in the outdoors, it would stand in sharp contrast to the people and places in Sweetland's adult life.

Monroe Sweetland was born to Mildred (Mark) and George Sweetland on January 20, 1910, in Salem, Oregon. Monroe's father was a prominent football coach at Willamette University and working toward a second medical degree. Monroe's mother, Ethyl "Mildred" Mark, was born to James O. Mark and Mary Jane Hoover Mark who had emigrated from Ontario, Canada, via Detroit to Ramsey County, Dakota Territory, in 1882. Biographical sketches of "prominent old settlers" of the territory listed Mildred as the oldest child in the Mark family, with two younger siblings, Alice and Ada. James Mark was evidently a successful farmer in Grand Harbor township, the size of the Mark's farm at 640 acres.[4]

George Sweetland traced his ancestry to immigrants who arrived to Dryden, Tompkins County, New York, shortly after the village was incorporated in 1803. Among George Sweetland's five siblings, two were intimately associated with Monroe Sweetland's life: Monroe Marsh Sweetland (b. 1860, d. 1944), and Libby Jane Sweetland (b. 1869, d. 1958).[5] George Sweetland was educated at Dryden Academy and then Union College in Schenectady and Hobart College in Geneva, both in New York. The athletic Sweetland was a running back in football and a catcher on the baseball team at Union College. At Hobart, where he spent the school year 1896–1897, he was named an "All-Time Lettermen." George followed an uncle and an older brother, John, to Michigan, where both were physicians. George enrolled in Grand Rapids Medical College, the University of Michigan's new medical school, and then enlisted as a medical corpsman with the outbreak of the Spanish-American War. Sweetland completed his medical degree following the war and took a job teaching and coaching football at small Ishpeming High School on the Upper Peninsula. He coached the Ishpeming team to state championships in 1901 and 1902. One contemporary noted that Ishpeming's success was due to "the skill of their coach, George Sweetland."[6]

George Sweetland then moved to the University of North Dakota in 1904, where he coached football and served as athletic director for four years. His winning percentage of .906 as football coach remains the highest in the university's history. In Grand Forks, he met Mildred Mark, a student at the university enrolled in commercial courses. George and Mildred were married in 1907 in Hood River, the small Columbia River community where her parents had recently settled. The Sweetlands moved to Salem, Oregon, in 1908, where George coached and was athletic director at Willamette University. At Willamette he established a reputation as a "daring innovator" whose teams played "razzle-dazzle" football. When the small Willamette school defeated the much larger University of Oregon football team in 1913, Willamette officials named the football grounds Sweetland Field.[7]

At Willamette George Sweetland completed an internship at the local hospital and earned a second medical degree at Willamette Medical School. In the midst of those successes, he returned to his alma mater, Hobart College, in 1915 as football coach and athletic director. With his growing family—Ada Louise was born in 1912—George moved to Geneva, New York, and in his second season the Hobart football team went undefeated. Circumstances intervened again, however, when his brother John, a physician in Constantine, was killed in an automobile accident in 1916. George, who decided to take up his brother's practice, moved the family to Constantine.[8]

Constantine's location in St. Joseph County along the meandering St. Joseph River provided a distinctive small-town environment to nurture a young inquisitive boy. In the days when rivers served as superhighways, St. Joseph County was reputed to have more navigable streams than any other Michigan county. Like other historic communities in southern Michigan, Constantine's residents relied on rivers for travel and waterpower. White settlers first pushed their way into the ancestral lands of the Potawatomi Indians in southern Michigan in the 1830s following the completion of the Erie Canal in 1825. The numerous Native American villages that once stretched for miles along the St. Joseph River were largely gone by the 1860s. Platted in 1831 and incorporated in 1837, Constantine followed the pattern of other small towns in St. Joseph County as an agricultural center.[9]

Extensive prairies and wetlands covered southern Michigan, the latter serving as habitat for waterfowl and beaver, fox, mink, and muskrat. Long before the Sweetlands settled in Constantine, the commercially valuable forests had been logged, wetlands drained, and the prairies turned into productive cropland. Among the natural features that remained in 1916 were low-lying swamps with hardwood trees, marshes, and bogs, ideal habitat for a profusion of wildlife. Young Monroe would become conversant with the flora and fauna of riparian areas and lowlands in St. Joseph County, a familiarity that would lead to a lifelong interest in botanical species. By the outbreak of the Civil War, the huge influx of white settlers had introduced dramatic changes to the St. Joseph watershed. With most of the pre-Civil War population settling in its southern counties, Michigan territory's population of 86,000 in 1835 rose to 212,000 in 1840 and more than 590,000 by 1860.[10]

Southern Michigan's open prairies were ideally suited to agricultural crops such as corn, soybeans, oats, and hay. At some point during his boyhood, Sweetland began working traplines from late fall through the winter and into early spring. In an irregular diary covering 1922 and 1923, he recorded trapping skunks, muskrats, and mink and believes he saved about $1,000 through his efforts. His father established a savings account for Monroe at the local bank, and if he needed spending money, he requested it through his parents. He mixed running traplines with playing in the Boy Scout band and reporting on high school activities for the weekly *Constantine Advertiser-Record*. He also split and piled wood for the home furnace, tended office for his father, picked strawberries in season, weeded the family garden, and did yardwork for Emily Comstock, the local reporter for daily newspapers in Three Rivers and Kalamazoo.[11]

Comstock, whose correspondence with Sweetland extended until her death in 1958 at the age of eighty-one, was widely acknowledged as the voice of Constantine during her long life. She hired Sweetland to mow her lawn, weed the garden, and, when he obtained his driver's license, drive her to meetings and on errands. A Republican committeewoman, she carried on a lifelong banter with Monroe that lasted through his election to the Oregon legislature in the 1950s. When Ms. Comstock was away from home during Sweetland's senior year in high school, he wrote news items (published in the daily papers under her name). If Constantine was insular, Miss Emily

(Left) Monroe Sweetland (age 5) and sister Ada Louise (age 3), October 1915, on the William Smith College campus. George Sweetland, their father, coached football for one year at Hobart, the male counterpart to Hobart and Smith Colleges. (Courtesy of Susan Baroz, Ada Louise's granddaughter); (right) A current photo of the George and Mildred Sweetland home in Constantine, Michigan. (Courtesy of the Constantine Township Library)

provided an intellectual voice of reflection on local matters and beyond. A "'humble' Christmas greeting" to Monroe in the late 1930s captures her narrative spirit:[12]

> The little old town was never so beautiful at Christmas as this year. Candles in the windows, trees laden with gifts and beaming with lights, carols sung everywhere symbolized so much of peace and joy that one wondered if the over sea stories about bombs and sunken ships and destitute men and women were not all a horrible nightmare from which one would awaken.

Sweetland attended the Constantine Public School from 1916 when he entered the second grade until 1926 when he graduated from high school (he skipped grade eleven). When he left the Constantine school system in 1926, he was a very young-looking sixteen years old. Although he had traveled to Boston and Washington, D.C., to his maternal grandparents' home in Oregon's Hood River Valley and to his father's birthplace in Dryden, New York, he was by no means a worldly person. His senior high school diary, however, opens a window to the life of a very busy teenager—practicing for plays, socializing with friends at movies and dances in Constantine and the nearby towns of Three Rivers, Sturgis, and Centerville. Sweetland possessed a legal Michigan driver's license from the age of fourteen, and the diary entries include frequent references to his father's remonstrances about his late hours: "Tuesday, Jan. 12, 1926. Up at 7:00—Dad raves per custom about my being out so late on a school night.[13]

Growing up amid the fecundity of southern Michigan's waterways and wetlands shaped Sweetland's interest in flora and fauna for the rest of his life. In diary entries spanning the months from January to June 1926, Sweetland wrote frequently about gathering wild plant material for commercial purposes, obtaining watercress from Curtis Creek near Constantine and taking the edible plant to Elkhart, Indiana, to sell, a drive of some twenty-five miles. When he failed to find watercress on another day, he still returned home with wintergreen and flowers. A diary entry for May 6, 1926, reads: "Up at seven—packed my dandelions and got some watercress . . . struck out for Elkhart with my products—Sold all the dandelions and most of the watercress." On another occasion he went "to the Pine woods after Flowers—got lots of them—Ladies' Slippers, etc."[14]

That teenage interest in wild plants included more than the world of commerce. On one Sunday morning he decorated his local Lutheran church "with wild crabapple blossoms. . . . "Tres Jolie vraiment!" (very nice really). In another entry he wrote that he was appointed to the flower-decorating committee of his church. And the next day, to the pine woods again "and got a lot of flowers." On occasion he helped a neighbor woman gather flowers: "got a lot—Even a few Pink moccasins—Orchidacae [sic]." On Memorial Day, May 30, 1926, arranged "my flowers into what seemed to be a very fine boquet (sp) and went to the cemetery." Sweetland also decorated the local Congregational Church for high school commencement in June for his graduating class.[15]

At times young Sweetland's daily musings—veiled in teenage pseudosophistication—direct humorous barbs at his hometown. When a vaudeville troupe toured through Constantine with a bear in tow, the show caused "great consternation in our fair but unsophisticated burg—especially among the younger generation." And then there was Olga Scoville, the love of his life and the subject of the most entertaining entries in the diary. Olga, a year behind Monroe in school and very smart, lived in the countryside and took the bus to school. With a group of friends one evening Monroe suggested to a classmate that it might "be fun to trade women." His diary account that evening: "Oh-Ashes to Sackcloth on my ineptness. Olga was peeved and refused to speak to me." When he drove her home, she announced: "I will never be seen with you again." He signed off the entry, "An Awful Night." He made a commitment the next day, however, to avoid hurting "my cause with Olga"; the day following the vow: "Succeeded today in endurance test." After a few days, Monroe mused: "I don't know how long I can stand it without Olga." But he ended with another mark of success: "Avoided the crime most beautifully today." Within two weeks he noted a long talk with Olga: "We're on beautiful terms again. Hope it stays that way." Four days later: "Home with Olga at 11:00—parked in Smith's cabbage patch for an hour—The Aurora Borealis were wonderful. . . . Good day—better evening."[16]

Olga drifts away from the diary entries as Sweetland's small senior class of fourteen students readied for graduation. The following dates and entries catalogue some of his reflections.

> June 2: "School again—many tears shed by effeminate seniors over the fact that there is but one day left to them in their H.S. careers."
> June 3: "Last day of High School for me! At last I'm through— rather unusual feeling."
> June 6: "Baccalaureate—It was held in the M.C. Church and Huldne preached rather punk."
> June 10: "Worked at the Congregational Church all morning decorating for Commencement tonight. Spent most of the evening at it too. At 7:15 we all assembled at the church. . . . There were 14 of us. . . . I read the class will. To bed at 11:00. It's all over at last"

A class "Retrospectus" of the accomplishments of Constantine's graduating class of 1926 listed Monroe's nickname as "Doc." Sweetland was advertising manager and played the role of Baldwin Beverly in Harry L. Newton's *All on Account of Polly: A Comedy in Three Acts* (1915). He was also in the cast of May Hewes Dodge's *Cynthia's Strategy: A Musical Comedy* (1922). Both performances took place in his senior year. He also participated in *Oration*, in 1925, and *To Make the World Safe for Democracy* in 1926. His graduating classmates voted him "Most Popular Boy."[17]

At several points in his long life, Sweetland attributed his social and political values to his sixth and seventh grade teacher, Miss Loretta Sprang, one of the few Democrats in Constantine. He told a *Eugene Register-Guard* reporter in 1959 that Miss Sprang was a Woodrow Wilson Democrat who supported the League of Nations and other liberal causes of the early 1920s. And, most unusual for the small town, Loretta Sprang took a summer tour through Europe and returned to her classroom with gifts (an Italian carving for Monroe) and fascinating stories of life across the Atlantic. In his senior-year diary, he referred to visiting briefly with Miss Sprang: "She was my seventh grade teacher and I was very glad to see her again." His worldliness, according to daughter Barbara, rested in part with George Sweetland who "was very community-minded and . . . had no racial intolerance."[18]

Two local African American widows—Mrs. Byrd and Mrs. Williams— profoundly influenced Sweetland's ethical values and thinking. Early in his high school years, the elderly women asked Sweetland to pull weeds in the garden and around their small cottage. During the succeeding months, Sweetland became friends with the elderly women (both in their seven- ties)—to the point that they would loan him copies of the *Chicago Defender*, the most influential black weekly in the United States. A voracious reader, Monroe began devouring the newspaper, including its advertisements. Most important to his inquiring mind, the *Defender* presented a view of contem- porary America in sharp contrast with the *Chicago Tribune*, the newspaper his parents subscribed to. "I learned a lot from those women, much more that I can ever tell you," he told an interviewer later in life. His working expe- riences for Mrs. Byrd and Mrs. Williams—and his reading of the *Defender*— broadened his social and political consciousness before he left for college.[19]

Following the suggestions of his mother and father, Monroe joined the United Lutheran Church and as a teenager became active in the Sunday evening meetings of the Luther League, eventually serving as president of the chapter. In a seventh-eighth grade diary entry he referred to a trapping mishap: "Went to Sunday school. In the afternoon we went out back of Browning's and Duke [his dog] killed a big black [skunk]. I went to church and Luther League and smelled so skunky I didn't stay."[20]

It was through the Luther League and Lutheran pastor Reverend Wheadon, however, that Sweetland and a classmate made connections with conservative Wittenberg College in Springfield, Ohio, and visited the institution just before his June graduation. After "a very interesting trip" to Springfield with Reverend Wheadon, Monroe joined another student, John Davey, to see an evening movie and then have a long chat with other students until midnight. The next morning he played tennis and witnessed the laying of the cornerstone for a new chemistry building in the afternoon. At the cornerstone ceremony, he met a young woman acquaintance from

Monroe Sweetland (circa 1929) when he
was a student at Wittenberg College, now
Wittenberg University. (Courtesy of the
Oregon Historical Society)

Columbus, Ohio, who invited Monroe to join her family for dinner. The
evening then segued to a campus play, "'Robin Hood,' which I enjoyed tre-
mendously." The Constantine visitors returned home bereft of significant
intellectual excitement.[21]

To satisfy Wittenberg's entrance requirements, Sweetland enrolled
in Western State Normal School in Kalamazoo shortly after graduation.
Although Kalamazoo was only thirty-six miles north of Constantine, he
rented a room in a boardinghouse and enrolled in English and chemistry
classes. The summer session at Western State offered a different slice of life:
meeting students of all ages, experiencing loneliness, engrossing himself
fully in studying for the first time, and being exposed to a learned English
literature professor. Sweetland's diary entries record boredom, studying,
attending classes, and, on one evening at a local circus: "It was good I suppose but I wasn't especially thrilled." While he was less certain about the
chemistry class, he enjoyed the American Prose course—"the instructor, Dr.
Slosser is wonderful."[22]

Founded in 1845 as a training institution for Lutheran ministers, with
programs rooted in the classics—Latin, Greek, moral philosophy, and religion—Wittenberg added science to its curriculum in the 1880s. The college

joined the mainstream of American higher education in the early twentieth century when its courses extended to the arts, music, and science. Following his father's wishes, Monroe enrolled in the fall of 1926 as a pre-med major but soon shifted his focus to the social sciences. At Wittenberg he worked as a journalist, wrote for the campus newspaper and annual, played trumpet in the college band, and honed his skills as a public speaker participating on the college debate team. He joined the Phi Kappa Alpha fraternity, serving as its president during his junior year, and chaired the organization's recruiting committee, traveling the state of Ohio looking for students "who would make good prospects for the house."[23]

The high point of his involvement in the larger world of politics at Wittenberg was Democrat Al Smith's 1928 campaign for the presidency. On a campus with few Democrats, Monroe was the nominal leader of the campus Al Smith club. He remembered that the only significant Democratic official in Springfield supporting Al Smith was Salley James, an African American lawyer. But it was Sweetland's work doing precinct organizing in the city's slums with members of the Al Smith club that were his most lasting memories of the 1928 election, leaving the young college student with a profound interest in a truly democratic polity and a commitment to racial equality. Those encounters provided him with valuable "practical experience for later political . . . activity."[24]

Only one letter survives from his four years at Wittenberg, a short note from a coed, Janet—who addressed Sweetland as "Honey"—as she was packing for the summer while Monroe was going through graduation ceremonies. "If I don't see you again to say good-by, I want to tell you that I was happy last night for the first time in months." As she listened to the student band playing "Onward Christian Soldiers," she reminded him that he was "coming down to New York often." She signed off, "Good-by dear, and God bless you."[25] Although he would be in New York City that fall, there were no further meetings with Janet.

2

The Making of a Public Person

When Monroe Sweetland headed to Cornell University law school in the autumn of 1930, the United States economy was in free fall, with escalating unemployment and rumors about troubled banking institutions. Although the full-blown banking crisis awaited the end of the year, the storm signs ran the full gamut of the American economy. With European nations experiencing difficulties, what had been dubbed "the depression," historian David Kennedy writes, "was about to become . . . known to history as the Great Depression." This was the burgeoning new reality that Sweetland faced when he moved to Ithaca, New York, in late summer 1930. His family had arranged for him to board with his uncle, Monroe Sweetland, a well-to-do widower with no children, who hoped his nephew would eventually take over his law practice. Uncle Monroe, a respected lawyer in Tompkins County, was George Sweetland's oldest brother and a graduate of Albany Law School and Cornell Law School.[1]

Without the trappings of the Lutheran Church hovering over him, life at Cornell unveiled "a whole new world" to young Monroe. He encountered people with fresh ideas—a British laborite lecturing on literature and campus leaders involved in antiwar activities. To the inquisitive Sweetland, what took place outside law school quickly proved more attractive than his studies—especially campus socialists who were critical of both the Democratic and Republican parties. After meeting renowned socialist Norman Thomas that fall, he joined the League for Industrial Democracy (LID) as a student member.[2]

One of his first activist friends was Al Arent, editor of the student newspaper, the *Cornell Daily Sun*. A Jew from Rochester, New York, Arent was politically liberal and one of several friends who would move on to distinguished careers. When Cornell administrators planned a war memorial for alums who had died in the First World War, Arent and Sweetland petitioned to list Hans Wagner, a German national and Cornell graduate, among the roll of soldiers who had lost their lives on the battlefields of France. "And we won the thing," Sweetland recalled later in life. The *Cornell Daily Sun* commentary on the event would have been close to Sweetland's heart: "Cornell undergraduates have progressed beyond the bitter nationalism of past generations and reflect a new spirit of international understanding."[3]

Midway through his first year, Sweetland had become acquainted with most campus leaders and important "political factions on other campuses." Sweetland and other League student members used events such as the Cornell War Memorial as a forum for opposing compulsory military training programs (ROTC) on college campuses. Sweetland also became friends with Dan Eastman, son of the prominent radical writer, Max Eastman. With Eastman, Sweetland helped integrate Jews into his old fraternity, Phi Kappa Alpha. Sweetland also took advantage of a rich parade of speakers visiting the Cornell campus, including the brilliant British socialist intellectual Harold Laski, who taught at the London School of Economics.[4]

Sweetland's emerging radicalism appears to have been practical, realistic, and fundamentally political. Although he was aware of Karl Marx and Friedrich Engels, he was not a student of Marxist literature, nor was he interested in the intellectual underpinnings of socialist thought. "Current issues," he reflected, "seemed to be [more] important." His critics—"the heavy thinkers of both the Socialists and Communists"—chided him for being too political. Monroe was blunt in an autobiographical sketch: "I could never be a Communist because I liked elections too much." The radicalized Sweetland, however, "was running fast" as a "left wing socialist," interested in important political issues of the day.[5]

Although his extracurricular experiences at Cornell were riveting, he neglected his law studies, with the dean cautioning him to spend less time on politics and more on his academic work. Sweetland suspected that the dean had talked with Uncle Monroe, because his uncle later suggested that he transfer to Syracuse to get away from "a lot of questionable influences." He made the move to Syracuse in the autumn of 1931, where he would be

(Left) Monroe Sweetland hitchhiking, unidentified news clipping, circa 1933–34. (Courtesy of the Oregon Historical Society); (Right) Lil (Megrath) Sweetland and Monroe Sweetland, July 14, 1934, Westport, Connecticut. (Courtesy of the Oregon Historical Society)

removed from Cornell influences (and, his uncle believed, free from social-ist influences).[6] As it turned out, Syracuse provided an even larger stage for the young activist and is where he would meet a young woman who was more than his equal in fighting civil and economic injustice.

The fortuitous meeting at Syracuse University with two undergraduates, Lillie Megrath and her twin sister, Violet, marked a signal point in Sweetland's life. Monroe met Lil at a woman's cooperative house, a place "full of strong supporters" for progressive causes. In a very brief time, they became fast friends, with Monroe remembering Lil as "tough . . . a strong person" who "was very important on campus." Shortly after he arrived, Sweetland and a group of activists attempted to form a Liberal Club, similar to chapters on other college campuses affiliated with the League for Industrial Democracy. When Syracuse University vice chancellor W. P. Graham turned down the application, students simply moved the club off campus. The Megrath sisters' radicalism is evident in the Liberal Club's inexpensively produced publication, *Challenge: Voice of the Syracuse Student Liberal Club*. Its maiden issue invited readers to work for "an America stripped of starvation, race prejudice, the profit motive, slums, wars, and oppressed workingmen."[7]

If Lil was busy on the Syracuse campus, Monroe was moving in ever-larger geographies of activism—to the Midwest, New York City, and other venues for the League for Industrial Democracy. Through the rec-ommendation of Norman Thomas, Sweetland was named field secretary/organizer for the League in late 1931, a position that opened when Paul Porter left to recover from tuberculosis in Saranac, New York. Accepting the position put Sweetland on the road for nearly three years, hitchhiking and taking buses and trains to distant places to organize campus affiliates for the League. He initially agreed to a salary of $22.50 a week, a figure later reduced when Sweetland became adept at hitchhiking and staying in campus cooperatives.[8]

Sweetland withdrew from the Syracuse University Law School before final exams, fall semester 1931. Although he would make one more abor-tive effort to finish law school, the attractions of the political arena always interfered with life in the academy. With escalating unemployment and social problems in industrial economies, Sweetland was serving as the League's roving national organizer at an auspicious moment in the nation's history. Across America, blighted countrysides, urban shantytowns, and thousands of homeless men riding the rails were visual symbols of the realities of the Great Depression. At the onset of election year 1932, more than ten million people were out of work, an estimated 20 percent of the nation's workforce, while still others labored at reduced hours or worked for lower wages. "Unemployment," David Kennedy writes, "loomed not as a transient difficulty but as a deep, intractable problem that showed no sign of abating."[9]

The student activism that emerged out of the rubble of collapsing mar-kets differed from the student movement of the 1960s. Sweetland's friend Joseph Lash described student politics in the 1920s as "mostly a movement of inquiry and study rather than a movement of action." And then "came the Depression" when the mood in the country and on campus turned to "the politics of doing something about the problems immediately in front of us." One catalyst was the formation of the New York–based National Student League (NSL) in December 1931, an organization seeking more aggressive approaches to reform.[10] As Sweetland traveled the nation, the leadership of the Socialist Party and the League for Industrial Democracy, and campus radicals, turned their energies to the fall elections in 1932.

As field organizer for the League, Sweetland developed great admiration for Norman Thomas,[11] LID's executive director and Socialist Party candidate for president in 1928. In the critical presidential election of 1932, Sweetland and Joe Lash campaigned vigorously for Norman Thomas, identifying with the socialist leader because his ideology derived from Christian theology. "More than I ever realized," Sweetland recalled, "mine was too." The socialist leader, who was popular among college-age students, carried most of the campus polls protesting "against the vision of Roosevelt as a rich New York aristocrat." In his speaking engagements, Thomas urged students to move toward "a more positive and aggressive program for the world." Thomas told readers of the *Challenge* in the spring of 1932 that economic realities were contributing to the "growth of a college graduate proletariat." In the fall elections Thomas garnered 884,885 popular votes, the largest Socialist Party vote since 1912.[12]

In the fall of 1931 Sweetland gained the attention of New York governor Franklin Roosevelt when he conducted a straw poll on prospective presidential candidates for the 1932 election. On a return trip from Oregon, where the family visited his mother's parents in Hood River, Monroe polled relatives and friends, gas-station attendants, hotel clerks, and others along their route of travel to learn their presidential preferences. If there were errors in his poll, Sweetland told the *New York Times*, they likely favored Republicans, because "all our relatives and friends are 'dyed in the wool' Republicans." Monroe and his polling assistants—his mother and his sister—were divided in their preference for Norman Thomas, Hoover, and Roosevelt.[13]

The random poll favored Governor Roosevelt, with President Herbert Hoover and 1928 Democratic nominee Alfred Smith trailing far behind. Of the 649 people canvassed, sixty-eight were undecided, with a scattering of other votes. In addition to the *New York Times*, the Helena (Montana) *Daily Independent* and the Constantine (Michigan) *Daily Advertiser* published the poll results. Sweetland also sent the results to Governor Roosevelt, who found "the poll of great interest" and shared it with a *New York Times* reporter who used it in an article. If the governor could find the clipping, he promised to send it to Sweetland "in case you did not see it." The contact with Roosevelt may have been self-promotion on Sweetland's part, because he later asked Roosevelt for a copy of his original letter (which the governor supplied).[14]

It was Sweetland's work with the League for Industrial Democracy, however, that would establish associations and friendships that would last a lifetime. Foremost among this group was Joseph Lash (1909–1987), who authored the Pulitzer Prize–winning biography, *Eleanor and Franklin* (1971). During Sweetland's tenure with LID, Lash was the League's executive secretary and editor of its newsletter, *Student Outlook*.[15] Mary Fox (1893–1978), a graduate of Vassar who taught in progressive schools in Chicago and Brooklyn, worked in LID's New York City office. Fox was responsible for recruiting field organizers, editing the League's magazine, the *Unemployed*, and overseeing scheduling issues. During the Second World War, like Lillie Sweetland, she worked for the War Labor Board in Washington, D.C. By that time, she was married to well-known labor writer John Herling. Mary Fox remained close friends with both Sweetlands for the rest of her life.[16]

Dallas-born George Clifton Edwards (1914–1995), graduate of Southern Methodist University with a master's degree in English from Harvard, was another League associate. Edwards worked with Sweetland as a field organizer, traveling through the South and northern manufacturing and mining districts. Edwards left for Detroit in 1936 in search of ideas for a working-class novel. After a stint on an assembly line, he became an organizer for the United Auto Workers union (UAW) and then headed its welfare department. Edwards subsequently was elected to the Detroit City Council, studied law, enlisted in the Army, and was admitted to the Michigan bar, where he distinguished himself for many years. President Lyndon Johnson appointed him to the United States Court of Appeals for the Sixth Circuit, where he served until retirement in 1985.[17]

Paul Blanshard (1892–1980) was another League representative, loosely described as the organization's education director in the late 1920s. With Norman Thomas and Harry Laidler, Blanshard was instrumental in hiring Monroe Sweetland for the field-organizing position. A secular humanist committed to social and economic justice, Blanshard published essays in the *Nation* exposing working conditions in Southern cotton-textile mills. His most important book, *American Freedom, Catholic Power* (1949), an incisive critique of the Catholic Church on church and state issues, brought him opprobrium from the church and Catholic communities in New York and Boston.[18] Mary Hillyer (1902–1965), who later became Paul Blanshard's second wife, was another lifelong progressive. Reared in Kansas, she moved to New York City in 1920 where she met Norman Thomas and became involved with LID. Hillyer worked in the New York office during Sweetland's time with the League, managing its lecture series and promoting peace and civil rights issues.[19]

Stuart Chase, a cum laude graduate of Harvard, was one of the keenest minds to pass through the League's national staff. Chase joined the Federal Trade Commission (FTC) in 1917, where he investigated and exposed accounting irregularities in the meatpacking industry. A brilliant scholar with a gift for making economics accessible to the public, Chase collaborated with economic philosopher Thorstein Veblen to study ways to enhance administrative and fiscal integrity in government and business. He participated with LID for several years, serving as treasurer in the early 1920s, and authoring five pamphlets with the organization between 1922 and 1937, including the classic *Rich Land, Poor Land*. Like Paul Porter, Chase moved on to a distinguished career, serving as informal advisor to the Roosevelt administration, advising the United Nations, authoring books on planning, and optimistic to the end of his life that publicizing scientific research for the general public was a positive good.[20]

Shortly after becoming the League's field organizer, Sweetland realized the enormity of his responsibilities and convinced LID's policymaking board to appoint another coordinator. The board hired George Edwards, who had attended the League's summer workshop and served on the editorial board of the *Student Outlook*. As a member of the editorial board, Sweetland also wrote articles for the journal. From the beginning of his association with the League, he was also aware that communists were attempting to influence progressive movements. Shortly after he left Cornell, the campus Liberal Club convened a regional conference that turned into heated exchanges between LID and the communist-influenced National Student League. The principal speakers were socialist Paul Blanshard and independent communist Scott Nearing. The *Cornell Daily Sun* reported that Blanshard advocated "an evolutionary revolution" while Nearing supported "a more direct overthrow of the present system."[21]

The open dueling between LID and student communists intensified during the next three years, causing schisms among the League's leadership, its support staff, and eventually convincing Sweetland to resign from the organization. While Sweetland's correspondence indicates that he was always en garde about communist influences, he was equally passionate about promoting revolutionary socialism. Sweetland felt at home with British socialist A. Fenner Brockway, editor of the *New Leader*, who wrote Sweetland in 1933 about the difficulties of effective working-class action in England. Communists were the only group united on a national basis, he explained, and there was danger in agreeing with their agenda. Brockway feared that British communists wanted to "swallow" other progressives. "We are not going to be swallowed."[22]

Leftist politics during the 1930s was in a constant state of flux between dogmatic socialists and those willing to pursue wherever inquiry might lead. As social and economic chaos spread across the land, the rapid growth of communist factions presented a dilemma to socialists of all stripes. The Depression changed everything, Joseph Lash remembered, especially "a greater readiness on the part of students to take to militant activity." The rise of fascism in Europe strengthened the arguments of communists and weakened socialist objectives of achieving reforms through democratic means.[23] Because of socialist support for Norman Thomas in 1932, the League sought to bring "people who voted for Thomas into permanent LID chapters." In a tribute to the tireless energy of Monroe Sweetland and George Edwards, Lash noted, the effort had "a good deal of success." In truth, the Thomas campaign, once marginalized on college campuses, gave leftist students an alternative voice.[24]

As student activism grew, Sweetland's travels took him through a broad swath of the nation, from New York City to Los Angeles and college towns large and small. He also participated in League summer schools in New York City. Lillie Megrath, Sweetland's wife as of October 1933, wrote for the *Student Outlook* and, with Mary Fox, organized the initial "Training School for Students" in the summer of 1934. The curriculum featured discussions by Roger Baldwin, civil liberties; George Marshall, the labor movement; David Lasser, unemployment; Mary Fox, techniques of propaganda; and George Streator, "The Negro and the Labor Movement." Students were assigned to local unions, conducting surveys of unemployment, and were to "take an active part in . . . city wide demonstrations or protests that are held during the summer."[25]

Student Outlook published a lengthy report on League activities on college and university campuses in 1934. Titled "Agitate! Educate! Organize!" the summaries were obviously the work of field organizer Monroe Sweetland. The report was fronted with a photograph of Sweetland hitchhiking, arm and thumb extended—amid a rural Colorado backdrop—with highway signs indicating distances to Fort Collins (9 miles), Denver (75 miles), and Laramie, Wyoming (57 miles). The title of the article also reflects Sweetland's lifelong philosophical commitment to political work—educate and organize. Sweetland visited the University of Denver in March 1934, where he reported an active LID chapter with weekly meetings, speakers, and tours of mines, slum areas, and prisons. Sweetland moved on to the University of Washington, Whitman College, and Washington State College, where he led a conference on "Youth and War."[26]

At the University of Tennessee, Sweetland and Howard Frazier,[27] a local African American student, visited a dormitory where they engaged in a "bull session" with residents. After Frazier and others left, a student from across the hall returned and wanted to know about Frazier's identity. "Why," he remarked, "I didn't know that Negroes could be as educated as he was." Sweetland next traveled to Greensboro, North Carolina, where "yankee exploitation and southern prejudice meet" to attend the first LID conference south of the Mason and Dixon line: "This was not an interracial conference; but it is idle to say that a group of Negro and white students can come together in a Jim Crow town, and not have the problem of race prejudice uppermost in the minds of many. That subject was an undercurrent to every matter discussed."

Northern delegates realized the enormity of the race question when they read local press reports of the conference. White labor representatives and college professors "were named with the appropriate Miss or Mr. before their names." Other prominent people—the wife of a well-known African American college president and the associate editor of the *Crisis*—were absent those customary salutations.[28]

On occasion, Sweetland's travels placed him in the midst of riotous campus students. With newspapers warning that the League was a communist-front organization, Sweetland and his peers occasionally had to navigate through thickets of reactionary students. The most notorious incident took place at the University of Wisconsin when fraternity brothers, many of them athletes, summarily removed Sweetland and three associates from a meeting and tossed them into Lake Mendota on the evening of May 15, 1935. A university dean, George Sellery, later wrote that fraternity-athlete behavior contradicted Wisconsin's tradition of tolerance and freedom of expression. The rioters reputedly acted when a frustrated Monroe Sweetland complained about repeated interruptions to his talk: "This is the first time I ever addressed a bunch of rowdies." With that remark, according to Sellery, "the riot was on."[29]

Two days later university president Glenn Frank convened a university-wide convocation. Although the president insisted the gathering was to affirm freedom of expression and would not be a protest, several speakers—including George Sellery and Sweetland—spoke out strongly against vigilante behavior. Dean Sellery called the episode "the most disgraceful thing ever perpetrated at the university." Sweetland, who was addressing issues related to fascism at the disrupted meeting, told the gathering of some 1,200 students and faculty that his intended address "was illustrated with far more eloquence than I had at my command by the event." [30]

Sweetland was twenty-three years old when he visited Knoxville, Tennessee, and Greensboro, North Carolina, and another birthday had passed when Madison students threw him into Lake Mendota. Although his college experiences campaigning for Al Smith in the poorer sections of Springfield, Ohio, made him aware of America's great dilemma over race, his cross-country travels for LID pounded home the race question as never before. By the summer of 1934, his awareness of the ugly underbelly of American society was set in stark relief from his benign upbringing in largely homogeneous Constantine, Michigan. The people he associated with during those formative years of his life—Paul Blanchard, Mary Fox, Mary Hillyer, George Edwards, Joseph Lash, George Streator, Walter White, and above all, Norman Thomas—were progressives on issues of race and class. Their influence on the young field organizer is evident in Sweetland's lifelong support for equal rights for Japanese Americans, African Americans, Hispanics, and other minorities.

The splintered and militant American left increasingly affected Sweetland's work as field organizer. Although communists were making inroads among the American left, those gains were most significant among college students affiliated with the National Student League. Robert Cohen refers to the emergence of a vibrant student movement in early 1932 as the "Springtime of Revolt," an activism centered in the NSL-led student effort to aid striking miners in Harlan County, Kentucky. Although other groups were involved, including students affiliated with LID, the communist-supported NSL garnered national attention. Lash, who was assaulted by deputies on the student trek to Harlan County, was impressed with the political will of the NSL and the unifying effect the trip had on both student organizations. More than any other agency, Cohen argues, the NSL's aggressiveness revitalized LID and gave it a presence in the national spotlight.[31]

In the midst of growing student activism, the NSL and LID accelerated their cooperation on several fronts, including opposition to war. Responding to NSL criticism that they were too closely allied with senior LID officials, the students founded their own publication in 1932 and began identifying themselves as the Student League for Industrial Democracy (SLID) in 1933. Both student organizations sponsored an antiwar gathering, "The National Committee for the Student Congress Against War," in Chicago in December 1932. Convened on the University of Chicago campus, the congress cautioned students about "the events of 1917" and the role that science and technology played in developing poison gas and other chemical weapons. "Can you permit a recurrence of these shameful acts of intellectual prostitution?" the program queried.[32]

While the Roosevelt administration was making news with a wave of emergency reform legislation during its "First Hundred Days" in the spring of 1933, students at Oxford University in England set off an international peace movement when the university's debating society adopted a pledge to refuse to "fight for its King and country." The Oxford Pledge created a storm of reaction, including admonishments from the London *Times* and Conservative Party leader Winston Churchill. The Pledge quickly spread across British campuses, and American versions surfaced in the United States. Polling on American campuses indicated strong pacifist sentiment, much of it related to disillusionment with the First World War.[33] For the next few years, Sweetland took part in a variety of pacifist causes that were an important part of his life until Hitler's armies began marching through Eastern Europe.

The U.S. Senate's Nye Committee investigations (1934–1936)[34] into armaments-industry profiteering during the First World War accelerated antiwar sentiment. The NSL and SLID sponsored the first significant student antiwar movement in the nation's history, targeting campus ROTC training requirements. Self-serving economic interests, students argued, led to the United States declaration of war in 1917. Sweetland, who had supported anti-ROTC proposals at Cornell and Syracuse, promoted antiwar proposals during his visits to college campuses.[35] Cooperation between the League for Industrial Democracy and the communist-influenced National Student

League, however, always troubled Sweetland, putting him at odds with Norman Thomas, Joseph Lash, and others in the LID hierarchy. Although the NSL seemed "a typical communist front organization," according to Robert Cohen, students worried little about communists and paid more attention to organizing the unemployed and fighting for civil rights.[36]

In a lengthy letter to Sweetland in late December 1934, Norman Thomas offered personal insights about the student league's activities and its relation to other leftist political movements. He hoped Sweetland would tell audiences that SLID "never threw out any group of interested students." Instead, it was communists and the NSL that split with the student league. While he opposed a merger between the two student groups, Thomas thought there was opportunity for the two organizations to cooperate, especially if the NSL and SLID could avoid the communists' "tactics of misrepresentation." Thomas closed his comments with insights that stayed with Sweetland for the rest of his life:

> Your typical Communist in the N.S.L. is the kind of person who sees nothing inconsistent about asking my help, for instance, and then in the same breath abusing me for being yellow and God knows what else. That has happened to me more than once on the college campus. I do not want to generalize from personal experience but I do think that we can work better with the group by agreement on specific issues than when we, so to speak, sleep in the same bed with them.

Thomas insisted that the student league should not be under Socialist Party control. He trusted Sweetland's "tact and good sense" to convey this message to campus chapters.[37]

If Monroe Sweetland had an ideological father, that person would be Norman Thomas. Always pragmatic and seldom burdened with narrow dogmatisms, Sweetland's future association with the Oregon Commonwealth Federation and the CIO (Congress of Industrial Organizations) War Relief Committee, and his later efforts to modernize and energize Oregon's Democratic Party, focused on the politically practical, achievable policies of the moment. Like his mentor, Sweetland never lost sight of the larger social pursuits of equitable tax policies and a politics that advanced the diversity of American society.

Although Joseph Lash had differences with Sweetland, he agreed that cooperation with the National Student League entailed risks. The problem, Lash
recalled, was both organizations being involved in academic freedom and
ROTC fights requiring joint action. Merger between the two student groups
had been simmering since 1933, with young NSL communists lacking the
strident sectarianism of national Communist Party members. Both student
groups shared common adversaries—undergraduate indifference and campus administrators who wanted to suppress free speech. The critical global
situation, the rise of National Socialism in Germany and fascism in Spain,
further complicated matters between the NSL and SLID.[38]

The Student League for Industrial Democracy convened a major
national conference at Northwestern University in late December 1934.
Field organizers George Edwards and Monroe Sweetland bore witness to
the expansion of student chapters on college campuses during the previous year. Sweetland's tour through the western states suggested the vitality
of SLID. George Streator visited several black colleges in the South with
considerable success. But the key features of the program were heated discussions about amalgamation with the NSL. In lieu of recommendations
from the resolutions committee, delegates adopted Sweetland's substitute
proposal: "We look forward to the day when the Communist students have,
through our United Front activities, sufficiently gained the confidence of
other radicals so that we may work in the same organization without suicidal
internal conflict."[39]

West Coast chapters of the student league led the move to merge with
the NSL. Acting on behalf of the LID's senior office staff, Mary Fox sent a
"strictly confidential" memorandum to Sweetland in August 1935 outlin-
ing the suggestions of Norman Thomas, Joseph Lash, and George Edwards
about the potential merger. The memo asserted that the merged groups
should have "no final power or responsibility to the adult organization" and
should adopt a name independent of the SLID or the NSL. The LID board
offered to contribute the salaries of Sweetland, Joseph Lash, and George
Edwards to the new organization.[40]

Sweetland's long-standing objections to a merger were related to NSL's
ties to the Communist Party: "They have pretended to be a democratic
student-controlled organization, free from Communist Party domination. They have, in fact, been none of these . . . and every NSL organizer
is under the discipline of the Communist Party." In visits to NSL chapters

Monroe and Lil Sweetland, Boundbrook, New Jersey, shortly before their move to Oregon in late 1935. (Courtesy of the Oregon Historical Society)

around the country, Sweetland reported that locals were "officered by YCL [Young Communist League] or CP members." The NSL, he insisted, was incapable of acting independently of the CP. If the NSL cleaned its house of communist control, however, he would "heartily endorse amalgamation into one movement." In late summer 1935, Sweetland outlined his objections in notes scribbled on the back of a letter from Mary Fox, most of them citing the dangers of Communist Party influence in a merged organization. NSL influence carried the risk of Communist Party manipulation. With a merger, LID "would be clearly a dual organization, continuing [with] summer schools, college memberships, etc." LID would be more effective, he wrote, "by continuing its organization, and welcoming back the N.S.L."[41]

With words of caution from senior LID staffers, student leaders reached an accord with the NSL and agreed to present a proposal to their memberships during a Christmas-break convention at Ohio State University in Columbus. The joint recommendations included creating a new organization, the American Student Union (ASU). Robert Cohen contends that supporters envisioned ASU would "become a union of all progressive, anti-fascist students" in a single organization. When the organizers began planning for the convention, Hearst-controlled newspapers engaged in red-baiting, a tactic that prompted Ohio State University administrators to renege on their agreement to host the gathering. Seeking an off-campus venue, students secured the local YWCA for the event.[42]

The four hundred delegates assembled in Columbus on December 28 included 141 NSL students, 116 from the student league, and 170 unaffiliated representatives. Because NSL and SLID delegates had to approve the merger separately, the deliberations dragged into the second day while the student league determined a course of action. Sweetland led the opposition to the union, fearing that SLID would compromise its commitment to avoid war, because the NSL was "prepared to support 'progressive' or 'anti-fascist' war." When SLID balloted late in the afternoon, the results favored the merger 92 to 9.[43] The new ASU then met in full session to draft a platform that included a commitment to equal educational opportunity for all Americans, a pledge for racial equality, an end to racial quotas in college admissions, and opposition to the influence of wealth and property in American life. The most intense deliberations were associated with the Oxford Pledge and whether ASU would be committed to neutrality. SLID delegates were suspicious that NSL representatives wanted to abandon neutrality in favor of pursuing "progressive," anti-Fascist wars. Although delegates upheld the principle of the Oxford Pledge, debates over the Pledge would become more volatile as the question of collective security gained momentum in the face of Nazi aggressions in Europe.[44]

In a working tour of Pacific Northwest campuses in June 1935 (University of Idaho, Reed College, Linfield College, and the University of Oregon), Sweetland was quietly laying the groundwork to return to the place of his birth. In submitting his annual field report to the League for Industrial Democracy's New York office in late December 1935, Sweetland announced that he was "resigning as Organizer." Although he and Lil would be leaving for Salem, where he planned to resume law school at Willamette University, he promised to continue activities on behalf of socialism. His years as League field organizer reflected progress in the student movement from a discussion forum to "a self-governing organization with real esprit-de-corps." He praised Joe Lash's "splendid work" in turning *Student Outlook* into a first-rate journal and thought the summer schools were "the true measure of the significance of our work."[45]

Reflecting a half century later on the merger between SLID and the NSL, Sweetland was blunt: "We broke up. . . . I was at odds with my friend

Joe Lash and with most of the leadership. Thomas told me many years later that I was right about it, but I wasn't so sure . . . and I didn't wage a very good fight." In a brief campaign autobiography in 1960, Sweetland recalled that he had led the opposition to the merger even though the SLID and its student leaders favored amalgamation. Written in the third person, the document claims that Sweetland "refused to stay on as field secretary for the new organization" because of the merger. Although the Sweetlands were on their way to Oregon at the end of the year, his friendship with Norman Thomas and Joe Lash would carry over to his new work with the Oregon Commonwealth Federation.[46]

The newly fledged American Student Union enjoyed a turbulent, limited shelf life. Many years later Joseph Lash recalled the ASU's struggles with the Communist Party's popular-front maneuvering when the Soviet Union directed the Communist International to forge a Popular Front of collective security to protect against the growing threat from Nazi Germany. Lash indicated that ASU was the beneficiary of the Popular Front, because student members of the old NSL (who were less sectarian than the CP) could more amicably work with other students in a common cause. Lash also points out that Popular Front communists also changed their assessment of FDR and the New Deal, treating the administration as a progressive ally in the struggle to contain German advances. "It was great fun to be able to taunt the Communists with becoming reformists," he remembers, a partial payback for the days when communists "had taunted the Social Democrats."[47]

Because the Socialist Party followed Norman Thomas's pacifist leadership, socialists became increasingly isolated from the mainstream of American radicalism. Lash, who remained a socialist with the ASU, found himself moving "in the direction of FDR and the New Deal and in the direction of collective security." The clash between war and peace came to the fore at the American Student Union's annual convention at Vassar College in late December 1937. The atmosphere was rife with tension, especially following President Roosevelt's "Quarantine Speech" in October, in which he called for collective action among peace-loving nations to provide "a quarantine of those spreading the epidemic of world lawlessness." Although Socialist Party leaders denounced the speech, the ASU divided on the issue of peace because of its adherence to the Oxford Pledge and the collective security threat suggested in Roosevelt's speech.[48]

By the time of the Vassar convention, Joe Lash had resigned from the Socialist Party and was shifting his support to the New Deal. This put him at odds with supporters of the Oxford Pledge who held important leadership positions in ASU. Committee meetings leading up to the convention were rancorous. Several decades later, Lash remembered that Nazi and Fascist threats in Europe made a mockery of the notion "that all sides were equally responsible for any war that might break out and . . . that we would have no stake in the victory of Democracy." Because the American press was increasingly turning to collective security, the Vassar gathering received a great deal of publicity (and the attention of the Roosevelt administration). The outcome of the convention was an overwhelming affirmation of collective security and a repudiation of the Oxford Pledge.[49]

It is ironic to say that Popular Front maneuvering on questions of peace and war reflected Monroe Sweetland's personal ideological shift from unapologetic peace advocate to supporter for collective security. Although he was far away in Oregon at the time of the Vassar convention, Sweetland would soon be joining Joe Lash and others who were moving closer to the Roosevelt administration's halting steps toward collective security. His initial activities in Oregon, however, were supportive of peace initiatives and fighting against mandatory ROTC programs on college campuses. With German and Italian sponsored forces on the move in Spain and Japanese armies plundering China, Sweetland's passion for peace initiatives diminished with the passing months.

3

Toward a Cooperative Commonwealth

When the dust settled from the Northwestern University convention, Monroe and Lil were already en route to Oregon. The key attraction for Monroe was the world of progressive politics and returning to law school at Willamette University in Salem. The idea of returning to his place of birth had obviously been a point of discussion between Monroe and Lil for several months. Sweetland had followed the state's gubernatorial election of 1934, when farmer-labor groups supported independent candidate Peter Zimmerman, who lost a close race to conservative Democrat Charles Martin, a former Army general, by approximately 14,000 votes.

Oregon differed dramatically from the hustle and bustle of New York City. It was absent the association with progressive intellectuals, and there was no one with the stature of a Norman Thomas or the brilliance of mind of a Stuart Chase, Paul Porter, or Paul Blanchard. Portland's population was slightly more than 300,000 people, dwarfing the capitol city, Salem, with 30,000 residents.[1] Western Oregon was dotted with small towns and a timbered interior with narrow valley bottomlands. With its vast distances and dispersed settlements, central and eastern Oregon presented a strikingly different landscape. While Monroe would be fully engaged in political activity and studying law, adapting to the new environment would prove more difficult for twenty-four-year-old Lillie Megrath.

At the time of the move to Oregon, Sweetland's ideas about political economy embraced those of Minnesota's farmer-labor progressives and the principles of the Cooperative Commonwealth Federation (CCF) in the Canadian provinces of Saskatchewan and British Columbia.[2] Sweetland was interested in a range of cooperative ideas. Writing for the student league's publication, the *Student Outlook*, he cited Canada's fall elections in 1935 as an opportunity for farmer-labor progressives who were offering voters a choice beyond "the usual tweedledum and tweedledee of the Liberal (Democratic) and Conservative (Republican) parties." The two-year-old Cooperative Commonwealth Federation was "a class party," he argued, standing for "the abolition of capitalism and the establishment of socialism." Because of similarities between the political economies of Canada and the United States, Sweetland concluded that farmers and workers would succeed when there was "success across the line." The Canadian election, he believed, would be a powerful catalyst for the emergence of a parallel movement in the United States.[3]

Although law classes at Willamette University consumed much of his time, Sweetland became involved with the Oregon Committee for Peace and Freedom, whose objective was to rid the campus of compulsory ROTC. Joseph Lash, his friend with the League for Industrial Democracy, attempted to enlist Monroe to be an organizer for the Emergency Peace Campaign (EPC). A pacifist organization affiliated with the American Friends Service Committee, EPC operated out of the Friends headquarters in Philadelphia. Sweetland turned down the invitation "out of sheer frustration," telling his friend that he had already "been mixing too much politics and law and this time I want to do the one job first, so I'll be free for full attention to the other." He thought Lash might be interested, however, in his attempt to organize Willamette alums and students to honor former U.S. senator Harry Lane, a Willamette graduate, and one of six U.S. senators to vote against the American declaration of war against the Central Powers in April 1917.[4]

On another front, Sweetland informed the LID office about the formation of a Farmer-Labor Association in Marion County. He was also interested in the newly formed Washington Commonwealth Federation (WCF). On a visit to Seattle in March, he described the federation as a collection of "tag-end progressive and radical political fragments" that included Communist Party (CP) members. Despite its lack of cohesiveness, he thought it was a "radical . . . and politically potent" expression of the state's progressive politics. Most noteworthy was Sweetland's assessment of Howard Costigan, the federation's flamboyant leader, "the spectacular, well-informed radio spokesman of the Federation."[5]

At the home in Salem, Sweetland struggled to keep abreast of his law studies, while devoting his spare moments to honoring Harry Lane. He hoped to coordinate a tribute to Lane with the National Student Strike Against War scheduled for April 22.[6] Sweetland asked journalist Richard Neuberger—future Oregon legislator and U.S. senator—for information about Harry Lane: Was he a Willamette grad? His initiative came together quickly. The university's president agreed to dismiss classes on April 22, and with three or four Willamette students, Sweetland worked up a program for the day. They solicited letters from Nebraska senator George Norris, "only survivor of the heroic six," and Montana's Jeannette Rankin, the first woman to serve in Congress, who also cast a vote against the declaration of war in the House of Representatives. At this point Sweetland's views about war and peace reflected pacifist, noninterventionist, isolationist principles, sentiments that were pervasive among student progressives.[7]

The Oregon Committee for Peace and Freedom—with ties to the New York–based Committee on Militarism in Education (CME)—organized an initiative campaign in the late spring and early summer of 1936 to make ROTC drills voluntary rather than mandatory. Committee member Dorothy Shoemaker, a friend from New Jersey, asked Sweetland to become field secretary for the Emergency Peace Campaign, with funding to be funneled through the CME office in New York City. The immediate task in Oregon was urgent, organizing a volunteer force to gather 17,000 initiative signatures by July 1 to place the measure on the ballot. Writing for Monroe while he caught up on his law studies, Lil told Shoemaker that her husband would be attending summer school to advance his law program. Her own plans were to leave for New York in May "to spend the summer and perhaps more—it certainly will be good to get back home."[8] Left unsaid in Lil's April letter was the news that she was pregnant, with the baby expected in August.

Through late spring, Sweetland struggled to balance antimilitary and peace activities with law school. At the end of May he wrote to a socialist friend, "my days-of-judgment, that is, final examinations, come the next two weeks. I am absolutely swamped with work." Whether he was worried more about final exams, his affinity for political activity, or Lil's pregnancy is an open question. The languishing petition drive troubled him, especially the snail's pace of signature-gathering in Portland. In a letter to the Emergency Peace Campaign office in Philadelphia, Sweetland underscored the need for a full-time manager, outlined a budget for four months, and said that he was unwilling to undertake the job himself.[9]

While the Peace and Freedom Campaign struggled to gather signatures, Sweetland faced a more personal crisis—the family's finances were strained to the limit. His parents provided occasional support during his first year in Oregon—the loan of an automobile and tuition payments. Nathalie Panek, who became a close family friend and confidant, remarked decades later that Sweetland "had no money and things around the . . . household got a little bit grim at times for lack of it." Sweetland raised the issue of finances with Edwin Johnson, executive secretary of the Committee on Militarism in Education, asking for further clarification about his salary, expenses, and the extent he was expected to travel.[10]

Sweetland asked again about his salary in another letter to Edwin Johnson: "I don't like to have to bring up the point, but what with Lil and me having our first youngster this summer, I have to be able to keep abreast of our current expenses. Had you discussed salary? I'm ready to take your suggestion in the matter, and I think I know from long tribulation with the always-broke LID how to keep expenses down."

Johnson responded that his total budget would be $300, and that Sweetland was expected "to get along on a salary of thirty-five or forty dollars per week," a figure comparable to wages in the New York office.[11] Lil's earlier report that Monroe would be attending law school during the summer ultimately proved an empty husk, a point Sweetland acknowledged when he agreed to oversee the noncompulsory military training campaign. "As you know," he wrote Johnson, "I had all sorts of high resolution not to [take] part until the Law was over, but the situation is serious and the opportunity great, so I have succumbed. And I'm mighty glad of it, now that the decision is made." But he declined an invitation to join the executive board of the Workers Alliance of Oregon, explaining: "I cannot spread my very limited ability any wider than I have."[12]

With the Roosevelt administration making its first hesitant moves to halt the aggressions of National Socialism and fascism in Europe and Japanese advances in China, Sweetland saw the initiative campaign—making military training optional rather than mandatory—as "a referendum on the preparedness issue." Although most of the region's newspapers were "fighting us tooth and nail," Sweetland was pleased with the *Oregonian*'s strong support for optional ROTC training. To former Syracuse friends teaching at the Quakers' George School in Pennsylvania, he wrote: "There will be a good fight, and I know you would like to be here." In a note to Hayes Beall, a Willamette graduate with the National Council for Methodist Youth in Chicago, Sweetland thought it was critical to expose "Roosevelt's 'liberalism'" and "his anti-peace policy."[13]

Sweetland's whirlwind organizing and travels were successful. The campaign turned in more than 18,000 signatures before the July 1 deadline, with most of the effort concentrated in the populous Willamette Valley. During the final week, he "worked day and night . . . to get squads to work, and to keep them on the job." In his report to Edwin Johnson, however, he pointed to problems ahead: the Oregon State Grange had qualified three initiative measures for the November ballot, two of them addressing publicly owned utilities. The third initiative would establish a state bank. Although he supported all three measures, Sweetland feared the power trusts and promilitary conservatives would "call for a straight 'No' vote on all initiatives." Of the proposals before Oregon voters in November, two Grange initiatives were controversial, and many considered the state bank measure truly radical. The noncompulsory military training bill would prove equally problematic, with the *Oregon Journal* arguing that the initiative fit "The Red Plan." Although "good people and patriotic citizens" opposed compulsory military drill, the *Journal* believed they were mistaken in assuming that military training was a cause of war.[14]

To advance the noncompulsory initiative, Sweetland outlined a strategy to begin in September. In the interim, he planned to leave for New York on July 26—"I'll hitch-hike across"—arriving on August 2 or 3. In mid-July Sweetland wrote to New Jersey friends that there were positive signs at Reed College, because the campus included "an important concentration of some of our best workers." Before leaving for the East Coast, Sweetland received a letter from Edwin Johnson confirming that the Committee on Militarism in Education and the Emergency Peace Campaign would pay his expenses. EPC would provide $200 for Sweetland's July salary, a point that frustrated Sweetland when the EPC office sent him a check for $100. Distraught, Sweetland wrote New York that the campaign already owed him back salary, and that he was "desperately in need of what's due." While it might appear selfish to press his claim, he pointed out that "Lil will have to pay a hospital bill and I've counted on this to do it."[15]

Sweetland arrived in New Jersey to be with Lil when she gave birth to daughter Barbara on August 6. Before returning to Oregon, it was agreed that Lil and the baby would remain with Lil's parents. Once back in Oregon, Sweetland worked hard for the noncompulsory ROTC initiative, joining Richard Neuberger in debating American Legion officials in Portland on behalf of noncompulsory ROTC. The *Oregonian* followed the next day with an editorial refuting the charge that those who opposed compulsory drill were communists, pointing out that the accusers had lifted their arguments from Elizabeth Dilling's scurrilous book, *The Red Network*.[16] The *Oregonian* cited the names of prominent Americans in Dilling's book who were accused of being "subversive radicals": Interior Secretary Harold Ickes, Agriculture Secretary Henry Wallace, Labor Secretary Frances Perkins, First Lady Eleanor Roosevelt, and Oregon poet and essayist Charles Erskine Scott Wood.[17]

While Oregon voters overwhelmingly supported a second term for President Roosevelt in November 1936, they turned back all nine ballot measures, some of them by heavy negative majorities. The electorate defeated the Oregon State Grange's public power bills and the state bank initiative. In a letter to the *Oregonian*, Sweetland thanked the newspaper for its willingness to support "basic American civil liberties." He accused Portland's "red-baiters," especially the city's "Red Squad" of un-American behavior. "Official snoopery" and rumor campaigns had no place among a citizenry that believed in fair play.[18]

Although peace-related events consumed much of his time in 1936, Sweetland regularly attended Workers' Alliance and Grange meetings in Salem and worried that no one was pushing the Grange or the Oregon American Federation of Labor (AFL) toward independent political action. When progressives such as Roy Hewitt wanted to initiate a recall campaign against Governor Charles Martin, Sweetland opposed the move, agreeing with socialist friend Albert Streiff, who cautioned: "Permanent movements are not built on the spectacular. Hysterics is not history." Although relations between farmer organizations and the AFL remained problematic, Sweetland sought to bring the groups together on common issues.[19]

Because farmer-labor collaboration in Canada and the upper Midwest presented strategic models for progressive politics, Sweetland asked Howard Williams,[20] a major figure in Minnesota's Farmer-Labor Party, about effective approaches to political success.[21] In addition to organizing farmer-labor chapters at the county level, he wanted to infuse the groups with "conscious Socialists" to counter the "opportunism and personal ambition" of Richard Neuberger.[22] Although the journalist remained a friend and confidant until his death in 1960, Neuberger's sense of self-importance bothered many of Sweetland's associates, especially when Neuberger became a significant political figure.

The success of Oregon's farmer-labor movement was closely associated with the state's semi-dormant Socialist Party. Minnie McFarland outlined the attractiveness of a farmer-labor organization in a late June 1936 letter to Sweetland, citing the examples of governors Floyd Olson and Elmer Benson in Minnesota and Congressman Maury Maverick[23] of Texas, all supporters of "production for use." There were problems ahead for Oregon progressives, because many Grange and Farmers Union leaders opposed panaceas such as "production for use." As the brainchild of Wisconsin congressman Thomas Amlie, farmer-labor parties formed the American Commonwealth Federation in 1935 with the idea that it would lead to a new national party. For most Oregon farmers, however, the "production for use" principle seemed a dubious and dangerous idea.[24]

The ongoing discussions among Oregon's farmer-labor associations and independent progressives led directly to the incorporation of the Oregon Commonwealth Federation (OCF) in early November 1936. With the dubious "production for use" clause at the center of its ideological agenda, the corporate articles were largely educational in tone: "To educate farmers, industrial workers and other workers relative to their economic, social and political interests." The organizers borrowed liberally from older farmer-labor organizations, especially the Minnesota model. Sweetland's strategies are clearly apparent in the organizations and individuals represented in the initial filing—the Oregon State Grange, Oregon AFL, Oregon Farmers' Union, and notable progressives such as Willamette University's Roy Hewitt.[25]

Rural organizations, the Farmer's Union and the Grange, and organized labor provide much of the background to OCF. Although labor was well-represented at the founding convention, the Oregon State Grange and the Oregon Farmers' Union were arguably more committed to collective ownership principles. The organization's commitment to "education"—with a proviso for endorsing candidates for political office—reflected the policies of the national Grange and AFL, both of which opposed direct participation in politics. The Commonwealth Federation's founding members included Democrats, Republicans, socialists, communists, and Townsendites,[26] literally a nonpartisan alliance of progressives. The arrangement committee's minutes listed Monroe Sweetland as "organizer, OCF."[27] In the spring of 1937 Commonwealth's executive committee released "A Call To A Convention For Progressive Political Action"—inviting "liberal-minded" people to join with progressives to lay the groundwork for change in Oregon. The meeting would take place at the Portland Labor Temple, April 24 and 25, with Howard Costigan as guest speaker.[28]

Labor, farm groups, pensioners, the unemployed, student and youth groups, and miscellaneous other delegates were selected on a prorated basis. Trade unions were well-represented, with other groups having fewer delegates. The convention elected Stephenson Smith, a Reed College graduate and professor of English at the University of Oregon, as president of the organization. Monroe Sweetland, "organizer, OCF," was elected executive secretary, a position he would hold for the next five years. The convention also elected a board of thirty-three directors to represent the various caucuses. Commonwealth's platform listed the "public ownership of all natural resources, utilities, banks, and monopolies" as its first priority.[29]

The OCF platform supported pensions for the aged and unemployed, civil liberties, consumer protection, collective bargaining, across-the-board union wages, cooperative warehouses and marketing arrangements, free medical care for the poor, high taxes on large corporations, and "no sales tax." The platform supported a federal law banning lynching and promoted the "civil rights of Negroes and other racial minorities."[30] The reference to "civil rights of Negroes," born from Sweetland's extensive field experiences with the League for Industrial Democracy, reflected his influence in framing the OCF platform.

The *Oregonian* commented that "nothing seems to have been overlooked by the platform makers in the way of public beneficence, munificence, and magnificence." The convention expressed itself on another item close to Sweetland's moral principles:

"The establishment of world peace by an embargo on all war materials, and on all raw materials used for war purposes to fascist aggressor nations and by cooperating with all democratic peoples for the defense of international

democracy and peace." The only divisive item was Article X, a provision granting the board of directors the right to suspend (by two-thirds vote) any member or group supporting legislation or candidates for public office contrary to
Commonwealth principles. Oregon Federation of Labor delegates opposed
the measure because it challenged the autonomy of organized labor.[31]

The growing tensions between the national AFL and John L. Lewis's
Congress of Industrial Organizations (CIO) increasingly affected
Commonwealth's internal politics. This great schism in the American labor
movement revolved around strategies to organize all workers in common
industries, versus the traditional craft union approach of the AFL. When the
OCF held its convention in April 1937, AFL's national leaders had already
suspended ten CIO affiliates. To aggravate matters, the CIO had carried
out several successful organizing drives in major industries in 1936–1937.[32]
Those developments eventually affected progressive politics in Oregon and
introduced Sweetland to friendships and professional associations with
prominent CIO leaders.

Oregon's reactionary governor Charles Martin treated the OCF as dangerous to the common good, commissioning his personal secretary William
L. Gosslin and state police chief Lawrence A. Milner to bring public attention to communist influences in the organization. Gosslin was the first to
go public, charging that a Portland high school teacher had participated in
Commonwealth's April convention and that the Communist Party had organized the meeting. He made similar accusations against University of Oregon
professor Stephenson Smith. In a personal letter to the governor, Sweetland
protested retaliation against high school teachers or university faculty who
took part in Commonwealth's organizational meeting: "We deny that you are
entitled to use your high office as a political bludgeon," he wrote, warning that
OCF would "resist such fascist tendencies." If such threats originated with
the governor, they constituted "abuse of executive authority."[33]

Salem's *Capital Journal*, an outspoken opponent of Commonwealth,
gave traction to Gosslin's rumor-mongering, reporting his news releases
and providing editorial support. A letter to the *Journal* challenged Gosslin to
prove that the OCF was "a branch of the communistic party." The writer suspected that no group could meet and discuss politics "without being dubbed
radical or communistic by the governor's office."[34] Despite Commonwealth's
success in keeping communists from leadership positions, the accusations

continued until the dissolution of OCF in 1942. As Sweetland would learn, ill-founded charges of communism had a long shelf life. Although Governor Martin provided Commonwealth's leadership with cause for concern, his aggressive moves against OCF and other radicals provided an ideal target for the next election. The governor obligingly handed OCF plenty of ammunition, declaring in August 1937 that Commonwealth was a "gang . . . of young Jew[s] . . . communists, C.I.O.'s and crackpots."[35]

Governor Martin's spy network was deployed even before the first Commonwealth convention. Walter Odale, a special agent in Portland, provided the governor with the activities of the OCF executive committee and a list of the people endorsing the convention. Some executive-committee members were cited as members of or friendly to the Communist Party. Others were guilty by association, serving Commonwealth, such as Monroe Sweetland as "State Organizer OCF" and "organizer for the ASU" (American Student Union). Those endorsing the convention were vilified for their associations: "Communists claim they can rely on him"; "attended Communist meeting"; "one of the chief legal advisers of Communist Party"; "very active member of the Communist Party"; "active in various phases of Communist work"; "talks Communism from the pulpit"; and, for Peter Zimmerman, "subscribes to Communist literature and confers with Communist Party leaders on political matters." Most egregious of all was state police officer Milner's report to the governor: "The Communist Party issued instructions that the Governor of Oregon would be made the butt of all attacks by the various speakers during the convention."[36]

While the governor continued to snoop and gather information, Commonwealth confronted problems among its erstwhile labor supporters. Kelly Loe, Oregon AFL's public relations person, led the attack with a pamphlet circulated among union members in May 1937. Contrary to the convention's promoters, the pamphlet claimed that "manipulators," and "connivers," and communists controlled the proceedings at the convention, with OCF's leadership successfully deceiving "bona fide labor delegates" into supporting the constitution.[37]

Sweetland called Loe's allegations "red-baiting and heresy hunting." As for the Communist Party, Sweetland thought "the hysterical ranting of the ignorant or self-seeking" contributed little to the public's understanding of important issues.[38]

Despite problems with conservative AFL leaders, Sweetland and Commonwealth officials continued organizing OCF chapters beyond the Willamette Valley. In June 1937 the OCF began publishing a mimeographed circular, Oregon Commonwealth Federation News, with Sweetland contributing a regular column, "At the Front with Sweetland." In its first issue, the News highlighted a "Save Bonneville" campaign, including a caravan rally to Eagle Creek in the Columbia River Gorge. The purpose of the trek was "to carry the fight for public power to the great dam site" and to keep the distribution of Bonneville power out of the hands of the Army Corps of Engineers, fearing that the Corps would privilege private utilities in distributing electrical power.[39]

The public power issue was critical to rural Oregonians, with the federal government's Rural Electrification Administration (REA) in the process of bringing electrical power to rural America. Private utilities opposed REA (established in 1935), arguing that the government should not be competing with private enterprise. Oregon's electrical power debate was being played out on a large canvas, with many rural areas still without electricity. Governor Martin opposed REA and believed private utilities should control the distribution of Bonneville Power. While some members of the Oregon State Grange worried about the emergence of industrial unionism, most of its leaders continued to cooperate with OCF on a range of policy issues.[40]

Commonwealth News was delighted when eastern Oregon congressman Walter Pierce introduced a bill to keep the transmission of Bonneville Power out of the hands of the Army Corps of Engineers. With Bonneville Dam nearing completion in 1937, the Roosevelt administration brokered a congressional compromise establishing the Bonneville Power Administration (BPA) to handle the transmission and sale of electrical power. The president signed the Bonneville Project Act on August 20, 1937, creating the Bonneville Power Administration to market and transmit electricity and granting "preference and priority to the use of electrical energy to public bodies and cooperatives." The act left the operation of the dam facility to the Army Corps of Engineers.[41]

During its first year, Commonwealth focused on defeating Governor Charles Martin in the May 1938 Democratic primary. At its second biennial convention in December, OCF declared open warfare "against the tyranny of the 'Martin Reaction.'" Using a theme from the New Deal playbook, OCF

Nathalie Panek, center, on a voter-registration drive in Salem, Oregon, 1938. Panek was a longtime friend of the Sweetlands. (Courtesy of the University of Oregon Libraries)

accused "economic royalists" of attempting "to thwart the mandate of the people delivered in the 1936 elections." Oregon public officials had "conspired to defeat" Roosevelt administration policies and used the excuse of law and order to incite "vigilante violence against labor." Commonwealth sought alliances with like-minded citizens to join in a grand crusade—"The Defeat of Martin Reaction."[42]

When OCF met again in May 1938, delegates unanimously endorsed Democratic state senator Henry Hess for governor and Willis Mahoney, who lost a close race to Charles McNary in 1936, for Oregon's other U.S. Senate seat. Commonwealth endorsements included second district congressman Walter Pierce and third district congresswoman Nan Wood Honeyman. The daughter of Charles Erskine Scott Wood (renowned writer, lawyer, and raconteur), Honeyman was the first woman elected to Congress from Oregon in 1936. Responding to the OCF endorsements, Governor Martin referred to the Commonwealth gathering as a "convention of 250 nuts."[43] With his loose tongue and outlandish charges, the governor proved his own worst enemy.

As the primary neared, the *Oregon Daily Journal* regularly assailed OCF, quoting conservative union leader Kelly Loe's charges that Commonwealth's December 1937 convention "was completely dominated and directed by Communists." The gathering "provided ample evidence" that it was little more than "an adjunct of the C.I.O." The Oregon AFL publicist hoped that Commonwealth would "drain off and isolate undesirables from among citizens who still have faith in democracy." Despite Sweetland's conciliatory efforts, his hard work did little to moderate the tone of AFL conservatives, who now argued that Commonwealth was simply a poseur for the CIO.[44]

On the day before the primary election, Salem's *Capitol Journal* published a political cartoon, "Charge of the 'Hess-ians,'" depicting helmeted troops carrying guns, bayonets fixed, standing before a fortress-looking building. A figure labeled "Gov. Martin," with sword drawn, is standing in the arched doorway. In front of the troops, with names affixed to their hoods, is Harold Prichett carrying a CIO flag. Behind Pritchett are Sweetland, Stephenson Smith, Brian Carney, Ray Gill, and other Martin opponents. To the right is a commandant figure, "Capt. Hess." Behind the troop, urging them on with prods, are the figures of Nebraska senator George Norris and Interior Secretary Harold Ickes, both outspoken in their criticism of Governor Martin.[45]

Although there were few precedents for unseating incumbent governors in primary elections, Charles Martin proved an exception. While some considered Martin a New Deal liberal, Senator George Norris (a Republican) endorsed Henry Hess with a telegram just days before the election, calling the governor "a reactionary." Secretary Ickes also backed Hess with another telling assessment: "Martin is at heart no New Dealer." Hitherto a little-known state senator, Henry Hess emerged as the primary winner by 7,000 votes. As Martin's biographer Gary Murrell writes, "The governor's repudiation by the Roosevelt administration proved decisive."[46]

Hess's general election campaign for governor, however, proved ineffective. Sweetland complained that the candidate's staff lacked "able political generalship" and failed to send out campaign literature in a timely fashion. Republican candidate Charles Sprague, publisher and editor of the *Oregon Statesman*, defeated Hess handily by more than 55,000 votes in the November election. Although OCF attacked Sprague as an anti-labor conservative, Sweetland and the governor eventually acquired a profound respect for each other. When Sweetland telegrammed Sprague congratulations for his election victory, the gentlemanly governor-elect thanked Sweetland for his telegram: "The battle is over now so it is time to put the brick bats away in moth balls, though I suppose we will not forget where we have put them."[47]

Virtually all Commonwealth-backed candidates went down to defeat in the general election. Voters elected Republican Alexander Barry over

Democrat Willis Mahoney to fill the remainder of Frederick Steiwer's U.S. Senate seat,[48] and Republican Homer Angell denied a second term to incumbent Democrat Nan Wood Honeyman in Oregon's third congressional district. Democrat Walter Pierce, safely entrenched in his eastern Oregon seat, was the only Commonwealth-endorsed winner. Although only 20 percent of Commonwealth-backed candidates succeeded in the general election, Sweetland pointed out that 70 percent of its candidates in the primary elections were successful. Always prone to optimism, Sweetland told a colleague that many of Commonwealth's primary candidates were younger people.[49] The 1938 elections, nevertheless, revealed the slow process of modernizing Oregon's Democratic Party.

The late 1930s proved an especially tumultuous period for Oregon, with both national and international events shaping political discourse across the state. When the dust settled from the 1938 election, Oregon was still suffering from the ravages of the Great Depression and persistent high unemployment. Through the trials and tribulations of a struggling economy, however, President Roosevelt and New Deal relief programs were immensely popular in the state. Sweetland and Commonwealth supported innovative New Deal agencies such as the Works Progress Administration, which offered jobs to the unemployed. The Civilian Conservation Corps, the big federal dams on the Columbia River, and the National Labor Relations (or Wagner) Act of 1935 all appealed to Sweetland's sense of social responsibility. And he supported Section 7 of the Wagner Act, guaranteeing workers the right to organize and bargain collectively.[50]

There is little mystery about Sweetland's attraction to the CIO. The break with the craft-oriented AFL in 1938 occurred in the midst of successful CIO organizing in major industries—mining, automobile manufacturing, and waterfront workers. Sweetland's interests, however, ranged broadly: from public power to civil rights, national health insurance, old-age pensions, public housing, and unemployment insurance to a truly democratic politics. When he and Lil made the move west, he was a dedicated socialist, firmly believing that the United States should remain free of foreign entanglements. Developments at home and abroad would force his hand away from the Socialist Party to the liberal wing of the New Deal and eventually to cautious support for collective security.

4

Commonwealth, Communists, and Collective Security

From the beginning of Monroe Sweetland's Oregon sojourn, conservatives, the paranoid fringe, and opponents who sought to discredit his reform proposals were suspicious of his progressive politics. Conservative Oregonians questioned his antiwar activism, civil rights initiatives, and promotion of public power, and his support for progressive taxation, labor's right to organize, and the federal development of the Columbia River. In addition to the ranting of Governor Charles Martin, critics included conservative leaders in the Oregon Federation of Labor (AFL), especially after the emergence of the Congress of Industrial Organizations (CIO).

Adversaries repeatedly charged that Sweetland and the Oregon Commonwealth Federation (OCF) were closet communists out to capture the Democratic Party. It is testimony to the power of rumor and innuendo that this most liberal of public figures—who fought communists in the National Student League and elsewhere—would face similar allegations for three decades. Despite differences between AFL leaders and OCF, many rank-and-file union members found common ground with Commonwealth. One instance involved Initiative 317, an anti-labor measure on Oregon's ballot in November 1938 that directly challenged the National Labor Relations Act (Wagner Act) of 1935 and its regulatory agency, the National Labor Relations Board (NLRB). Employers resented the NLRB, because it had the power to investigate labor-management disputes and enforce the rights of workers to bargain collectively.[1] Supporters of Initiative 317, however, claimed that the measure would "protect the employee, the employer and the public in the case of labor controversies."[2]

The reactionary Associated Farmers of California, representing the state's largest corporate growers, began mobilizing farmers in Oregon and Washington in 1937 to oppose labor organizers and labor unions. Some Oregon merchants, the Eastern Oregon Wheat League, and large orchardists found the Associated Farmers message attractive. The association enlisted former Portland mayor George Baker to push the initiative and spent approximately $35,000 for radio time to push the anti-union message. In the face of this media blitz, Oregon's Democratic Party and most prominent politicians sat quietly on the sidelines. Speaking at an OCF dinner in August 1938, Sweetland dubbed the Associated Farmers "a semi-fascist organization," calling the initiative "the most vicious piece of legislation that has ever come before the voters of Oregon."[3]

Small farmers who identified farming and landownership with patriotism, historian Linda Gordon contends, bought into the Associated Farmers argument that communists would inevitably control labor unions. Charles Sprague's *Oregon Statesman*, however, called the anti-picketing bill "the most controversial" measure on the November ballot, because it was contrary to the principles of the Wagner Act. Moreover, it was unconstitutional, because most labor disputes occurred in industries engaged in interstate commerce. Employers, who thought the initiative would prohibit unions from picketing, could "be prosecuted under the Wagner Act." Voters should defeat the measure, the *Statesman* argued, because it would incite labor resentment rather than foster peace between management and workers. The *New York Times* remarked that Oregon was experiencing "the strange sensation of both major parties taking a liberal position" on an anti-labor initiative.[4]

"With the Democratic party on the sidelines," Commonwealth president Stephenson Smith observed, "reactionaries won their battle by default." In a paradoxical typographical error, Salem's *Capital Journal* remarked, "the anti-picketing bill was carried by a $50,000 majority." The passage of Initiative 317, journalist Richard Neuberger wrote, was "the most severe anti-labor law in America," threatening to reduce "unions to mere fraternal organizations." In Washington and California, where the Democratic Party opposed similar measures, voters narrowly defeated the initiatives. Because Commonwealth was involved in an expensive struggle to unseat incumbent governor Charles Martin in the spring primary and then to elect Henry Hess in the fall, Associated Farmers badly outspent the OCF in supporting the measure. The Oregon Supreme Court subsequently found the anti-labor measure unconstitutional in 1940.[5]

Long after Commonwealth's demise, Nathalie Panek remembered Monroe Sweetland's skill in preventing communists from dominating the organization. Although Sweetland had no objection to communist membership in OCF, he and other officials fought to prevent communists from dictating policy. Both Panek and Sweetland supported the strategy of working with communists when they shared similar objectives. "We had enough enemies," Sweetland recalled in an interview, "So we kept them in the Commonwealth Federation a year or two after our formation." Panek believed Commonwealth could work with communists when they shared common goals: "We didn't trust them but we thought it our job to beat them on the issues and we did." Understanding how communists behaved "came to different people at different times," she concluded.[6]

Although OCF leaders succeeded in limiting communist influences, the *Capital Journal* persistently attacked the organization for disloyalty and association with the Communist Party. The *Journal* described Commonwealth as "one of several Communist dominated political organizations working under cover to destroy American democracy." Harkening back to OCF's founding convention, it charged that Washington communists organized Commonwealth's meeting, picked the speakers, and framed its resolutions.[7] While Charles Sprague's *Statesman* and the Portland *Oregonian* were critical of OCF, neither paper indulged in red-baiting.

Issues of war and peace bedeviled Monroe Sweetland through the 1930s and early 1940s. Following the pacifist precepts of Norman Thomas, he opposed both American intervention in overseas conflicts and military preparedness at home. Those pacifist beliefs occasionally put him at odds with Commonwealth on foreign policy questions in the wake of Germany's aggressive moves in Eastern Europe and Japanese advances in Manchuria. Sweetland disavowed collective security, reasoning that the doctrine would lead the U.S. into war, a position that differed with a Commonwealth resolution supporting collective security against "fascist aggressor nations." The organization's small number of communists favored the resolution as well, because it implied that Hitler's Germany and Mussolini's Italy posed the principal threats.[8]

Richard Neuberger, who authored one of the earliest American exposés of the evils of Nazi Germany in 1933,[9] underscored Sweetland's problem— supporting New Deal domestic policies, while the Roosevelt administration was moving toward collective security. On domestic issues Sweetland was a thoroughgoing progressive, fighting "to raise the incomes of under-privileged groups"; however, Sweetland and Commonwealth's socialist factions, Neuberger wrote, leaned heavily toward isolationism, favoring "non-interference in world diplomacy." Collective security advocates who opposed the Sweetland group created differences that were volatile issues for Commonwealth.[10]

When the Soviet Union shocked the Western world and signed its infamous nonaggression pact with Germany in August 1939, the news stunned the anti-Fascist left in democratic nations. Many American communists followed Soviet directives, dropped collective security, and pushed the new party line of neutrality and peace with all nations. Addressing the state CIO convention in February 1940, Sweetland pointed to that "shivering September morn when Oregon's little Communist Party awoke to find that Hitler and Stalin had made up." Even more ludicrous was the Communist Party's new front in criticizing President Roosevelt and the Oregon Commonwealth Federation.[11] Sweetland, however, wanted the better part of both worlds—keeping Commonwealth free of Soviet foreign policy gyrations, while simultaneously defending communists' rights to participate in OCF affairs.

By the fall of 1939 Commonwealth meetings had become increasingly heated, with its board evenly split between collective security and neutrality. Communists continued to insist that, unlike Germany and Italy, the Soviet Union was not an aggressor nation. The Soviets bold move to join Germany in the partition of Poland and its invasion of Finland placed the Russian state squarely in the crosshairs of Western critics, including Sweetland. While he simultaneously criticized communists for following the Moscow line, Sweetland continued to support communist membership in Commonwealth as a civil liberties issue.[12]

Nathalie Panek's acerbic insights about working with communists "who profess belief in the same good cause and then change overnight when the foreign policy of another country changes," took on comedic proportions after September 1939 when party members distanced themselves from Commonwealth policies. Communist Party leaders in the Northwest first attacked OCF for red-baiting and then, in early 1940, turned their rhetorical fire on the Roosevelt administration and CIO's Columbia District Council of the International Woodworkers of America (IWA), accusing them of war-mongering.[13]

The IWA was a hotbed of dissension over the issue of communism, beginning with the union's first convention in December 1937 when Don Helmick criticized communist domination of policy decisions. Internal rancor in the IWA over communist influence caused the union's member-ship to decline until 1941 when noncommunists delegates defeated com-munist factions at the annual convention. In the midst of the Second World War, the IWA claimed approximately half of lumber industry workers in the American West and the great preponderance of lumber and logging union members in Oregon and Washington's Douglas-fir districts.[14] Helmick sub-sequently emerged as a significant leader in the IWA's huge Columbia River District.

Communist writers for Portland's *Labor Newdealer* accused Sweetland of attempting to divide the CIO. When Sweetland sided with IWA's anti-communist leaders after the Soviet-German nonaggression pact of 1939, communists adjusted their story and treated Sweetland and Commonwealth as tools of the capitalist class.[15] Sweetland aggressively countered in a news release, accusing the communists of being phony advocates of peace: "We must not trust any group, either inside the unions or outside, with American foreign policy if its primary allegiance is to the foreign policy of a foreign state. Our policies must be grounded on the interests of the American worker."[16]

When Commonwealth's board of directors voted to support the reelec-tion of President Roosevelt in 1940, its dalliance with Oregon communists continued. Following the partition of Poland, OCF condemned the imperi-alist aggression of Germany, the Soviet Union, and Japan with a resolution at the organization's sixth convention in December 1939. The resolution also made reference to "the continued abuse of colonial peoples by England and France." Because the Soviet Union had invaded Finland in late November, the overwhelming majority of delegates supported the condemnation of Russia as well.[17]

As the Asian and European continents descended further into a maelstrom of violence, the Roosevelt administration continued to grapple with a problematic economy. After a decade of bank failures, social turmoil, and a faltering economy, 14.6 percent of the labor force remained out of work in 1940.[18] The perpetually impoverished but maturing Oregon Commonwealth Federation kept a careful eye on state politics, lobbying progressive legislators to push reform proposals ranging from old-age pensions to socialized medicine. The OCF was also becoming more respectable, eventually serving as the conduit for federal patronage in Oregon.

As executive secretary, Monroe Sweetland stood at the center of action, using his friendships with the Roosevelt administration to advise on federal appointments in Oregon. Patronage, the low-hanging fruit for the party in power, slowly shifted away from Oregon's conservative Democratic Party to Commonwealth. OCF's initial federal plum involved temporary hiring for the 1940 census. Sweetland took the initiative, writing to census officials in Washington, D.C., inquiring if "the anti-New Deal State [Democratic] Committee will do it or whether the real progressive and labor elements will have a chance."[19]

As census assignments moved forward in the summer of 1939, New Deal administrators agreed to channel census appointments through the Commonwealth Federation. The U.S. Census Bureau named OCF board member and state senator Byron Carney to oversee the Oregon numeration. In a letter to former third district congresswoman Nan Wood Honeyman, Sweetland recommended OCF members Nathalie Panek, Ruth Haefner, and Moore Hamilton for other census administrative positions. Panek's application served as a model for the route to successful appointment. Describing herself as "a Democrat, and an ardent supporter of New Deal principles," she cited her board position with Commonwealth and her friendly relations with the Oregon Grange and state CIO leaders. Panek added that she had "the confidence of the liberal Democrats of the state."[20] When census officials approved her appointment, Panek wrote Sweetland that she had landed the census position: "I can't remember being so pleased about anything since Santa gave me my big doll when I was five." This time, she added, "You are my Santa."[21]

More than thirty years later, Panek recalled the significance of the 1940 census work:

Awarding of the 1940 census jobs to the OCF was a plum indeed. Monroe was like a starved kid looking at a plate of goodies. Jobs were still scarce—miserable little enumerator jobs were much sought after. Concessions were made to various regular Democrats and "friends," but real OCF members got goodies too. I became Assistant Director in 6 or 8 counties with offices in Salem. The Director quickly granted me the job of personnel. It was great to be able to give needed jobs to people who had labored so long with no payment. It was also necessary (and a pleasure) to weed out the Commies and, of course, I knew them. When we were attacked by the *Capital Journal* I could assert with confidence that we had none.[22]

From its inception, Commonwealth was active in promoting civil rights and civil liberties legislation. Its initial success was the repeal of Oregon's notorious criminal syndicalism law in May 1937. The revocation of the law followed the U.S. Supreme Court's decision in *De Jonge v. Oregon*, in which the court determined that Kurt De Jonge, a communist, was guaranteed the right of free speech and assembly when he participated in a protest against police raids in Portland's waterfront strike of 1934. Oregon's criminal syndicalism law, therefore, was unconstitutional. Commonwealth was less successful with a modest civil rights bill before the 1939 legislature that prohibited discrimination on the basis of race or religion in public accommodations. Committee hearings were raucous, with restaurant, hotel, and theater operators opposing the measure. The Oregon Senate eventually turned back the proposal.[23]

Commonwealth's position on civil liberties and civil rights was congruent in many respects with those of Governor Charles Sprague. Elected in 1938 and an opponent of the Associated Farmers' anti-picketing initiative, Sprague proved a friend to Commonwealth and especially to Monroe Sweetland. Referring to Sprague as "a principled conservative," Sweetland praised the governor when he vetoed legislation potentially harmful to free speech and civil liberties, especially to noncitizens. When the 1941 legislature passed a vaguely worded anti-sabotage bill to counter the Supreme Court's decision in the Kurt De Jonge case, Sweetland worked with the Oregon ACLU and Labor's Non-Partisan League to weaken the measure, fearing the governor would sign it into law. True to his growing reputation for defending civil liberties, Sprague vetoed the bill. "Any governor who would veto such a bill at times like this," Sweetland told Roger Baldwin, "does it out of principle and not out of political expediency." He urged the ACLU head to write the governor a letter of appreciation.[24]

"Social medicine" was another component of Commonwealth's progressive agenda. Although there is no direct evidence that Sweetland took the initiative in pressing OCF to take up the issue of public health insurance, his signature was on most of the organization's correspondence. New York senator Robert Wagner triggered a nationwide dialogue in 1939 when he introduced a measure to amend the Social Security Act "to make more adequate provision for public health" in the United States. Sweetland asked Wagner for copies of the bill, closing his letter with best wishes for "your efforts on behalf of a national health program."[25] During the next few months Sweetland gathered information on health-care legislation, asking correspondents for copies of bills that might be presented to the Oregon legislature. By the summer of 1939 Commonwealth's committee on "Social Medicine and Public Health" was exploring options to pursue in the 1940 election.[26]

With Commonwealth's health bill in final draft, Sweetland sought suggestions from the American Public Welfare Association and the American Association for Social Security.[27] The bill that OCF proposed to submit to the 1941 legislative session would amend the state's unemployment compensation law, require employer and employee contributions, and be limited to persons and families with incomes of less than $1,500. Commonwealth's strategy, according to Sweetland, was to test the legislative waters with no expectation that the measure would "be adopted by this conservative session." The next step would be to submit a revised bill as a statewide initiative.[28]

Bend representative Dr. J. F. Hosch introduced the health bill, HB 203. The measure gained a committee hearing and was reported out with a four to three "do not pass" recommendation. Once HB 203 was out of committee, however, the deviltry began, with Neuberger voting with the House majority to defeat the measure. When reports of Neuberger's vote reached Abraham Epstein of the American Association for Social Security, he wrote Sweetland: "That Dick Neuberger should not vote for the bill is indeed a surprise to me, but, then, liberals have stopped surprising me many years ago." Epstein published a short item about the Oregon health initiative in his monthly bulletin, *Social Security*, remarking that legislators who voted favorably "did not include Representative Richard Neuberger, well-known liberal writer."[29]

Neuberger responded to Epstein's criticism, explaining that he did not want to raise the public's hopes, because the bill provided no means of raising revenue. Epstein pointed to the falsehood in Neuberger's argument, because HB 203 included provisions for employer/employee contributions. Sweetland, in turn, sent a note to Epstein for publication in his monthly bulletin:[30]

> No vote cast by any member of the Oregon legislature during the 1941 session was more shocking than that cast by Representative Richard Neuberger against the Health Insurance Bill. Every other member of the liberal bloc supported the Bill. Not content merely to vote against the Bill, Mr. Neuberger gave the chief speech against it, thereby, marring an otherwise splendid progressive record.

Sweetland's insights to the American health-care system were remarkably perceptive. In April he took issue with a *Eugene Daily News* editorial faulting citizens for not giving proper attention to their health: "You failed to point out that the average American cannot afford to consult his doctor or dentist!" Although European countries had lower standards of living, they "have for many years taken good care of their people." In contrast, Sweetland argued, health care in the United States did not serve the public's need. He cited statistics indicating that maternity deaths in the United States were twice that for Sweden. He also pointed to the class divide in American health care, where infant mortality was five times higher among families with incomes under $500 than families with incomes above $3,000.[31]

The workup to the 1940 presidential election was fraught with minefields for progressives holding pacifist beliefs. Although Commonwealth continued to support New Deal social programs, President Roosevelt's increasingly interventionist moves against Germany and Japan troubled some OCF leaders. Sweetland, who supported a third term for the president, worried about Commonwealth's positions on war, conscription, and military preparedness.[32] After the German invasion of Poland on September 1, 1939, and the Soviet incursion into Finland two months later, Sweetland thought

Commonwealth's board of directors would continue its strong antiwar stand. To buttress his argument, he contacted Montana's progressive senator Burton K. Wheeler,[33] who favored a noninterventionist approach to foreign wars. Wheeler, who was quietly testing the waters for a presidential run, thought the United States had "nothing to fear from any foreign country or . . . any foreign ideology." The nation should consolidate its economic gains, "mind our own business and keep out of European and Asiatic wars."[34]

When Commonwealth voted overwhelmingly to support President Roosevelt for a third term, John Nelson of Wheeler's Helena office thought OCF had weakened itself, because Roosevelt might not be a candidate. Nelson asked Sweetland to recommend someone to chair a Wheeler-for-president campaign in Oregon to advise the Montanan about the May primary. Sweetland offered to help but cautioned that it was a mistake for Wheeler to openly oppose the president when "he is so acceptable to the great body of progressives as an alternative."[35] With no word to the contrary from the president, Sweetland consulted with CIO leader Sidney Hillman, a Roosevelt supporter, about Commonwealth's effort to place the president's name on Oregon's primary ballot. Despite communist opposition, Oregon's CIO unions supported Roosevelt. The situation in Washington and California was more complex, he told Hillman, because communists were relatively strong in the two states. Hillman's response to "Brother Sweetland" was unequivocal: labor would support the president if he decided to run again.[36]

When, with Roosevelt's approval, the mid-July Democratic convention nominated the president for a third term, Sweetland was relieved. Although he grumbled in letters to friends about military preparedness, he never wavered in his support for a third term. Remembering Nathalie Panek's lukewarm appreciation for Roosevelt, he admitted that "this conscription business has us all pretty much stymied."[37] Roosevelt's choice of Secretary of Agriculture Henry Wallace as his vice-presidential running mate, however, pleased Sweetland, who joined with other liberals in backing Wallace at the Democratic convention in Chicago.[38] When the ballots were counted in November, Roosevelt won a solid victory nationwide with 54.7 percent of the votes to Republican Wendell Willkie's 44.7 percent. In Oregon, Roosevelt tallied 258,415 votes (53.7 percent) to Willkie's 219,555 (45.6 percent).[39]

Although the documented record is spare, these were stressful years in the young lives of Monroe and Lil Sweetland. After Lil gave birth to daughter Barbara in New Jersey on August 6, 1936, she remained with her parents until early 1937 before returning to Oregon. The record shows that Lil (and occasionally Monroe) spent parts of the summer with Lil's mother, Florence, at Martha's Vineyard. From all indications, the family's finances were strained to the limit, a fact that family friend Nathalie Panek emphasized later in life. Another associate, Portland lawyer Gus Solomon, remembers that the impoverished and seemingly always hungry Sweetland would regularly stop by his office when he was in town, especially "if he didn't have anybody else to take him to lunch."[40]

Those circumstances placed strains on the Sweetland marriage. Friend and OCF associate David Epps closed an undated letter to Monroe (circa 1938) with a note: "Hope your family situation is improving." In the same correspondence, Epps reported that Commonwealth's funds were "scarce as per usual" and that he had referred a good accident case to Gus Solomon, hoping that he would "be helped some and indirectly we will prosper." Only days after the general election in 1938, Sweetland's mother died in Constantine, Michigan. In a letter to Epps, he reported his mother's burial and added, "the world has a pretty sombre cast this evening." His mother's death followed that of his younger brother, George, age nineteen, who died of polio in the summer of 1937. Worrying about his father, Sweetland hoped to "find some formula" to give his life further purpose: "He's a heart-broken, lonely, and—I now realize for the first time—old man."[41] Monroe, however, had more serious issues than his aging father, who would continue his work as a "country doctor" into the 1950s.

Not long after Lil returned to Oregon, perhaps frustrated with the family's finances or simply propelled by her own ambition to pursue professional work, she initiated a job search, visiting with Congresswoman Honeyman in Washington, D.C., in November 1937, inquiring about federal employment. Because government positions in Washington were few, Honeyman advised her to look for something in Portland.[42] Monroe told Honeyman that "if we can find something here [Portland] she will be more ready to consider it than [when] her hopes were to stay in Washington."[43] Between late 1937 and early 1939, Lil Megrath[44] apparently spent several weeks in Washington, with Congresswoman Honeyman reporting on one occasion that she missed Lil because she had been in a committee meeting. Lil's job quest appears again in November 1939, when Monroe informed Honeyman that Lil had attended a "Wages and Hours Training Course" in Seattle. A few days later he wrote again, complaining that he was "living at home with my orphan child and as much as I like her I think mother's place is in the home."[45]

Those exchanges suggest lengthy periods of separation. There is a likely possibility that Lil (and Barbara) spent several months with her parents in New Jersey. Lil's later employment resumé indicates that she held at least two federal jobs outside Oregon between 1937 and 1940, one with the National Youth Administration and the other with the U.S. Department of Labor. In a letter to Monroe in early 1940, Nathalie Panek added a humorous but caustic commentary on Lil's absence: "Give my love to Lil, et al. By the way, any progress with the Little Lady regarding Oregon? . . . If she only had the correct perspective, she'd know that she is what Oregon needs more of, and much more desperately than Washington or New York. Well, you work on her. . . . My arguments always wilt from under me."[46]

Ernie Norback, with the Los Angeles office of the new Wages and Hours Division[47] of the U.S. Labor Department, remembered "a vibrant young woman," Lillie Megrath, joining the Wages and Hours staff in the late spring of 1940. It was obvious to Norback, who became a close family friend, that Lil was forced "by the crunch of the Depression" to find employment far from home. "A stimulating conversationalist" with "superior intelligence," Norback recalled that she lived quietly and alone, saying little about her family life, except that "we knew . . . of her daughter (Barbara) being with Lil's mother back east and Monroe in Portland." Norback also remembered the grandmother and Barbara visiting Lil in Los Angeles at some point.[48] Monroe's meager income and his frequent absences from home placed child-care responsibilities with Lil, further burdening the marital bond.

As Commonwealth Federation's funding problems continued to worsen, Monroe wrote to OCF's Stephenson Smith in early September 1940 that the organization's situation had "reached desperate straits." He would, therefore, "have to [take] leave myself, long enough to earn some money, which will only serve to make things worse here at the office." While matters were going well politically, the "humiliating financial debacle" needed to be remedied.[49] Aware that Sweetland was personally in need, Hunter and Mary Scott—Oregon friends with the Sun Maid Raisin cooperative in Fresno— sent Monroe clothing items in the late summer of 1940. Thanking them for their "shower of abundance," he told the Scotts that he was going east for a month or two: "I have sunk deeper and deeper into the quagmire of debt and the only way I can get out is to let the sunshine of plenty play on said quagmire until it dries up."[50]

Monroe and Lil had been married two years when they made the move to Oregon in early 1936. During the succeeding years, he juggled political activism with another failed attempt to finish his law degree. The founding of the Commonwealth Federation, the political victories—defeating Democratic governor Charles Martin in the 1938 primary—were exhilarating moments for Sweetland and his progressive friends. The consequences, however, created discord in what was still a young and fragile marriage. In a remarkably candid letter while Monroe was serving with the Red Cross in the South Pacific in 1944, Lil provides part of the story about their struggles during those years:

> Darling – tomorrow is the 15th of October—11 years of connubial bliss—well 4 anyway—I get a cold chill when I look back on my behavior during much of our marriage—and realize how close I came to wrecking what has since come to be, for me, a very precious thing—I get honestly resentful sometimes of the manner in which I predicate everything I do on the fact that I am married to you— plans for the future—job possibilities—but mostly its very damn good—the most fun I have now a days is planning our life together "after the war."[51]

Monroe, who was reticent about personal issues, never acknowledged his part in contributing to their marital difficulties. Commonwealth's worsening financial troubles in late 1940 finally forced Sweetland to think seriously about leaving the organization. When Lil took a position in Boston with the International Ladies Garment Workers Union in early 1941, Sweetland wrote friend Eli Oliver—who provided counsel to Lil in her search for a position on the East Coast—that he was "unreconciled to this prolonged separation" and would leave the Commonwealth position so that he could "get into something so that we can be together."[52] The family's financial difficulties and his separation from Lil and Barbara prompted Sweetland to relocate to the East Coast. Monroe was emphatic about the move to

Washington, D.C., for a federal job in the summer of 1941: "We were very broke," he told interviewer Rick Harmon in 1985. "I was broke and hungry and Lil was upset" because of little income. He "was under pressure" to find a job and reasoned that the United States was "probably heading into a much more conspicuous part of joining the war in Europe."[53] It was inadvertent, but not by accident, that Eli Oliver would be a player in Sweetland's move to a federal job in mid-1941.

5

"Babylonian Captivity" and War in the Pacific

The nation's capital was abuzz with activity in the spring of 1941. With President Franklin Roosevelt's memorable Fireside Chat of December 29, 1940—that the United States "must be the great arsenal of democracy"— war orders from beleaguered European allies were helping to revive the American economy. The president urged the United States to act with dispatch, "so that we and our children will be saved the agony and suffering of war which others have had to endure." Embedded in Roosevelt's annual message to Congress, in January 1941, was a request for an appropriation of $7 billion to assist the Allies. Congress debated the measure, popularly known as Lend-Lease, and the president signed it into law on March 11.[1]

To efficiently carry out such initiatives, the Roosevelt administration revived the old First World War Council of National Defense in early 1941 under a new name, the Office of Production Management (OPM). The new agency was responsible for coordinating industrial production, streamlining the acquisition of material supplies, and providing a reliable labor force. OPM's immediate mission was "to develop and execute policies related to the production of defense material."[2] Monroe Sweetland's early association with Sidney Hillman and Eli Oliver would soon land him a position in the hastily organized federal agency.

When the president created the Office of Production Management, he appointed William Knudsen of General Motors director of the agency and Sidney Hillman associate director. Hillman's primary responsibilities were labor relations, building a sense of patriotism and esprit de corps for wartime production. Sweetland's friend Eli Oliver joined OPM in March 1941 as special assistant on labor problems. His appointment coincided with the establishment of a new Labor Division in OPM, with Hillman as head of the agency.[3] The president's purpose in forming the Office of Production Management was to counter the CIO's aggressive organizing among companies with large defense contracts. Labor militancy, Roosevelt's advisors warned, threatened defense production. To avoid the government's coercive labor tactics during the First World War, Roosevelt sought voluntary and cooperative approaches, appealing to the patriotism of workers to keep them on the job. His front man in this effort would be Sidney Hillman, who oversaw the Labor Division.[4] This was the labor-management universe that Monroe Sweetland entered in midsummer 1941.

Although Hillman formally invited Sweetland to join the Office of Production Management, Eli Oliver was his primary contact with the Labor Division. On OPM stationery in mid-July, Sweetland wrote Oregon Commonwealth official Clyde Wade that he had "succumbed temporarily to the federal maelstrom." His immediate associates would be Eli Oliver, Paul Porter, and Leo Perlis, people he had known for several years. He told Wade that he did not seek the job, "although it must look as though I'd walked out on you." The opportunity arose when Hillman's office traced his whereabouts to Patton Lake at his parents' summer cottage in southern Ontario where he was vacationing with Lil and Barbara. Even then, he traveled to Washington, D.C., and went "over the set-up with the big-shots and other friends." In a handwritten note at the bottom of the page, Sweetland added: "The salary is *ample* (!)." Two days after his letter to Wade, he resigned as executive secretary of the Commonwealth Federation, informing Stephenson Smith that he would return home "after my 'Babylonian captivity.'"[5]

While Sweetland was serving Babylon, he kept in touch with the sputtering and floundering Commonwealth Federation. Ralph Peeples filled the executive secretary's position for a time, and a few Commonwealth leaders carried on the good fight. In late summer 1941 the *Oregonian* observed that "Commonwealth has been strangely quiet since Mr. Sweetland is no longer with it." Portland friend Leonie Brooke wrote that OCF had lost its "vital leadership" when Sweetland left for Washington. "What OPM gained, Oregon has lost," she lamented. Alice Barnett (with her husband Wendell, founding members of OCF) complained that in Sweetland's absence Oregon politics seemed to be full of "small men in big places."[6] Commonwealth's grim prospects darkened in June 1942 when the International Woodworkers of America's (IWA) Columbia River District Council voted to disaffiliate with OCF. In late July the executive board voted to discontinue its activities "as a full-time political organization." While Sweetland regretted Commonwealth's demise, he believed that in the future another organization could follow OCF's model of progressive politics.[7]

Sweetland quickly adjusted to his responsibilities as a public relations liaison, journalist third class, with the Office of Production Management. His duties were to promote "labor's voluntary cooperation in the defense program," with special attention to "morale programs within defense industries." He was expected to organize regional labor conferences on "personnel and problems," focusing on labor issues in the western states. Salem's *Capital Press* applauded Sweetland's appointment to an important federal position but observed that the Commonwealth Federation would miss his "genius for organizing" and his skills in keeping the fractious organization on task. The *Press* reported that Sweetland ultimately planned to return to Oregon, where he would be "fighting for the underdog as usual."[8]

Among the denizens of small-town politics, the past has its rewards, where even modest achievement can generate its opposite in envy and resentment. When news of Sweetland's federal appointment hit Oregon newspapers, conservatives in organized labor and the Democratic Party went on the attack, questioning his qualifications for the job and his patriotism, and accusing Sweetland of being a poseur.[9] As might be expected, Sweetland's friends quickly came to his defense. Senate Republican minority leader Charles McNary wrote Hillman that "young Sweetland" was a person "of excellent character, reliable and industrious and in my opinion will render splendid public service in your organization." Democratic congressman Walter Pierce added that Sweetland was "a hardworking, able, and conscientious young man" who was "devoted to the public welfare and animated by a desire to do right."[10]

Records about Sweetland's employment with the Office of Production Management are spare—a few letters involving appointments in the rapidly expanding agency and occasional information about regional conferences that Sweetland organized.[11] OPM's activities escalated sharply throughout 1941, reflecting the growing commitment to provisioning the Allies after passage of the Lend-Lease law. A postwar study of the War Production

Board (successor to OPM) reported that Lend-Lease "stepped up require-ments for production facilities as well as for munitions," with the shortage of materials the most pressing issue. OPM's Labor Division was at the center of the crisis, tasked with assuring an adequate supply of workers. As its field offices multiplied, the number of OPM employees rose exponentially. With 1,886 personnel in March 1941, the agency listed 7,599 at the end of the year. At its peak under the War Production Board in early 1943, the organi-zation had more than 22,000 employees.[12]

Sweetland believed that Hillman valued his abilities as a conciliator "to work with both the AFL and CIO" to further war production. Wary of the strikes that took place when America declared war against the Central Powers in 1917, OPM issued news releases during the summer of 1941 underscor-ing the need for industrial peace. To achieve that objective, Hillman directed Sweetland to organize regional conferences involving both labor and man-agement officials. Ironically, the first one at Harvard University took place on Saturday and Sunday, December 6 and 7, 1941. The conference program, "Labor in National Defense," lists participants from Harvard's business and law schools and local and national AFL and CIO officials. Sweetland later penned a note on the front of the program: "(Conference organized by M. Sweetland for OPM—Pearl Harbor news arrived during Sun. PM session—Sweetland passed word to chm. (Dr. Cabot) who announced it to the aston-ished gathering)"[13]

Among Nathalie Panek's five decades of correspondence with Sweetland, her most riveting letter is one she wrote traveling by train "En Route to San Antonio on December 10, 1941" to accept a West Coast field position with OPM:

> The deluge has come and certainly in a different way than we had
> expected. . . . It is a world war now for sure, and not even Wheeler
> voted no. The prospects before us are so ugly that I shudder to think
> of them. One can be critical of past steps yet be unable to say no
> now. One of the disconcerting features of the last year or so is to
> have been wrong so many times—so many impossible things have
> happened. I think we will not be wrong in what we have said about
> the effect of war psychology on human beings. I am getting a double
> dose.

She grumbled about having to take "the long way home," but chalked the experience up as part of her education about the South. She added that Texas was "much larger than it has any excuse to be. It seems ugly and unpleasant."[14]

Even as Sweetland was considering a position with the CIO, he continued hiring personnel for the agency's new field offices—hence, Panek's trip to San Francisco. She was pleased that she would be "cracking a job" in San Francisco: "There is considerable satisfaction in getting what is euphemistically known as a man's job." When Sweetland told Panek about his pending job with the CIO (again, at Sidney Hillman's initiative), she applauded the move: "I'm puffed out like a pouter pidgeon [sic] fairly bursting to say 'I told you so'—nice going Sweetland." She mentioned Sweetland's father, who wanted Monroe to earn a law degree so that he "would have something 'to fall back on.' Good jobs," she mused, "seem to grow on trees for you."[15] Panek's move to San Francisco turned out to be transitory when Sweetland offered her an appointment as area director for the Pacific Northwest with the National CIO War Relief Committee.

The roots to Sweetland's move to the CIO National War Relief Committee originated in mid-January 1942, when CIO president Philip Murray's office approached him about assuming the director's position. Sweetland believed the committee would be important to CIO's national reputation; moreover, he would have "an even better salary than at OPM." The committee would handle CIO's war-relief effort: "British, Russian, Chinese, and domestic— take care of families, of NMU [National Maritime Union] sailors lost in these tanker sinkings, service CIO soldiers and sailors in the armed services."[16] The subtext to Sweetland's hiring was his ability to keep communists from meddling with New Deal domestic and foreign policy objectives, an issue similar to Hillman's rationale for his appointment to OPM. Because communists followed the Moscow party line, they found themselves increasingly marginalized in the CIO following the Nazi-Soviet pact of 1939. Philip Murray, United Auto Workers' Walter Reuther, and former United Electrical Workers head James Carey—all suspicious of communist intentions—were like-minded in the belief that Sweetland was the right person to head the War Relief Committee.[17]

The 1941 CIO convention in Detroit endorsed Murray's proposal to establish the CIO Committee for American and Allied War Relief. The committee was "to raise funds throughout the country to alleviate the misery of the workers and Peoples of those countries fighting Nazism and fascism."[18] The CIO's larger purpose in promoting social-welfare initiatives was to give organized labor greater legitimacy in the eyes of the public. Its rival, the much older trade-oriented AFL, had established the Labor League for Human Rights in 1938 to "help mobilize organized labor in its fight against tyranny and barbarism." A key objective for both committees was to gain union representation in the organizations they were funding: local war chests, community agencies, and the American Red Cross. Although the federal government urged the CIO and AFL committees to coordinate fundraising, the two big unions did not sacrifice their autonomy.[19]

The problem for the CIO (and Sweetland) was its member unions' deep-seated mistrust of public relief bureaus and social service agencies. In the past, the Red Cross had refused assistance to striking workers, fearful that such a move would antagonize employers, its largest contributors. United Mine Workers president John L. Lewis had denounced the Red Cross in 1939 for being "too near the wellsprings of American finance and those who set themselves up as being the American aristocracy." With War Relief Committee board members John Brophy and Irving Abramson, Sweetland took a personal hand in urging the Red Cross to place union members on its national and regional boards.[20] He also made certain that CIO unions gained recognition for their fundraising—to the chagrin of companies who believed they alone deserved credit because the funds were raised on their properties.

Sweetland spent the first months of 1942 staffing the national and twenty-three regional offices and hiring Charles Livermore as assistant director. He summarized the committee's work in July, calling the effort without parallel in American labor, "with no comparable experience to which to turn to for guidance." He thought the relief program would serve as a unifying agency for the CIO. Because the present staff, "working day and night for almost 5 months," was exhausted, he requested more people for the national office.[21]

The AFL and CIO war-relief programs marked the beginning of union participation in relief/community service activities on a grand scale. By the close of 1943, the CIO War Relief Committee had proven immensely successful, bringing in millions of dollars, with Charles Livermore working closely with agencies like the Red Cross to place union members on advisory

Monroe Sweetland speaking at a fundraising rally for the CIO War Relief Committee in 1942. (Courtesy of the Oregon Historical Society)

boards.[22] The fundraising totals for CIO relief funds were significant, testifying to the generosity of union workers. The total monies distributed for the years Sweetland served as national director (February 1942 to November 1943) indicate dramatic increases in allocations. From February of 1942, when Philip Murray appointed Sweetland national director, through the end of 1943 when he joined the Red Cross, the committee took in more than $2 million. But more important, the infrastructure was in place for the succeeding three years when collections soared to more than $8.5 million.[23]

Sweetland estimated that his staff of 120 people, scattered across twenty-three regional offices, raised approximately $61 million. Part of his responsibility, he noted, was to assure that funds did not support communist-backed projects overseas. One gnarly problem was the effort to channel relief money through the anticommunist Chinese Labor Association rather than the communist-controlled Eighth Route Army, the largest of the

Chinese communist armies fighting the Japanese. Sweetland's leadership in distributing funds intensified divisions in the CIO over the communist question. Following the war, those tensions prompted CIO president Philip Murray, closely allied with national Democratic administrations, to purge communist-controlled unions from the CIO.[24]

As organized labor's emissary to the Red Cross, Sweetland developed close ties with a few Red Cross leaders, including Robert Bondi, who asked in the fall of 1943 if he would be interested in serving overseas with the agency. After discussing the invitation with Lil, Sweetland announced that he would resign from the War Relief Committee. When the news circulated among friends and associates beyond Washington, the accolades rolled in. Ralph Blanchard, executive director of Community Chests and Councils, Inc., an affiliate of union war-relief agencies, wrote Sweetland about the "disquieting news" that he was leaving for the Red Cross, because "you have handled the situation in very statesmanlike and able fashion . . . and we hate to think of going on without you."[25] The November issue of CIO War Relief News[26] reported Sweetland's resignation, observing that under his direction, the CIO had "become the largest single source of financial support for the USO, British, Russian, and Chinese war relief in the world."[27]

In a "Hail and Farewell" column, the retiring director responded that he was leaving with regret:

> It is difficult for me to imagine that ever again there will be a staff so congenial and so wholly devoted to the job. For almost every member . . . it's been far less a job than a cause. . . . Throughout the country our people have worked selflessly day and night with all the fervor of an organizing drive—which indeed these early stages of the committee have been. They have been responsible for creating something new in labor relations; they have helped broaden the horizon of labor's activities, brought new prestige and respect to trade unionism.

Sweetland praised the regional offices for proving that workers' sentiments were deeply embedded in American society. In a personal letter to Sweetland, CIO President Philip Murray singled out the Relief Committee's public relations successes, which were "of inestimable value to labor."[28]

Former colleagues with the War Relief Committee confirm Sweetland's assessment of the agency's esprit de corps. Over the next months and years his associates underscored the camaraderie in the committee's Washington and regional offices. Hawaiian-born Japanese American Priscilla Yadad, who began working in the Washington office at the age of nineteen, wrote regularly to Sweetland, telling him of the comings and goings of staff members, especially those leaving for the armed services. Ethel Polk, from the Midwestern regional office in Indianapolis, sent Sweetland news about past associates. In a June 1944 letter, she praised Sweetland's article in the *International Woodworker*: "You even write charmingly, my pet. Seriously, it was good."[29]

There was a general consensus among Sweetland's friends that Leo Perlis, his successor as national director, presented challenges. Charles Livermore faulted Perlis's "profound lack of respect for theory and ideas" and his being "uncompromisingly opposed to freedom." When Livermore resigned to enlist in the Navy, he remarked that he could no longer tolerate the atmosphere in the office. With a penchant for gloomy introspection, Livermore provides a damning assessment of the management styles of both Perlis and Sidney Hillman: "Leo has that deadly Hillman touch—if it cannot be organized and bureaucratized it is useless." Since Sweetland's departure, Livermore reported, solicitations for funds were using "the shabbiest appeals to the most superficial kinds of self interests."[30] The enmity between Sweetland's friends and Leo Perlis continued to play out over the next several months, with Monroe serving as a confessional way station for people leaving the CIO War Relief Committee. Nathalie Panek wrote Sweetland when he was in the Pacific: "It's all pretty sad. You should have stayed, Sweetland."[31]

By the end of 1944 the War Relief staff was in disarray and the CIO executive board dissolved the committee and ordered Perlis to report directly to the board. "I should like to weep," Panek wrote Sweetland, "when I consider how Perlis has wrecked what Monroe built. . . . You were wrong to go Monroe. . . . And R.C. will give you no status with labor."[32] Dyke Miyagawa, who joined the Relief Committee's national staff before Sweetland departed for the Red Cross, wrote Sweetland that the committee's original staff symbolized the "ineffable Sweetland . . .the concept that leaves enough room in the ranks for *civilized* variants of political unorthodoxy."[33] Although the commendations about Sweetland's leadership of the War Relief Committee are rife with nostalgia, Leo Perlis's greatest difficulties were likely associated with the original staff that the affable and persuasive Sweetland brought to the committee. As a group they tended to view Sweetland as the pied piper for the noble and just cause, a person given to serving others and promoting ideals of equal rights and democratic decision-making.

As war raged across Europe and Asia, Monroe Sweetland, still predisposed toward pacifism, began searching for challenges beyond his responsibilities with the War Relief Committee. Although he had campaigned against U.S. intervention in foreign conflicts and opposed passage of the Selective Service Act in 1940, by the summer of 1943 he was considering a more personal part in the Pacific war. Nathalie Panek, with a premonition that Sweetland's observations were changing, added a postscript to a letter: "I was asked the other night if you are still a conscientious objector! I hedged—." She reflected that Sweetland had become increasingly ambivalent on the issue of pacifism after the bombing of Pearl Harbor and America's engagement in a two-ocean war.[34]

When American Red Cross officials offered him a field supervisor's position overseas, the invitation represented a dramatically new direction for Sweetland who had been a pacifist and a critic of the Red Cross. Sweetland later identified Robert Bondi as the official who urged him in mid-1943 to accept a Red Cross appointment with the expectation that he would be part of a northward military advance from India into occupied China. Sweetland entered basic training (a requirement for all Red Cross personnel serving in combat zones) in late 1943 and then headed for San Francisco and the Hawaiian Islands. He wrote a friend in November that he was going overseas with the Red Cross "to India or Burma, I hope." Once he was in Honolulu, however, the military scrapped plans for having Red Cross personnel as part of the China incursion. Given the option to resign, Sweetland requested an assignment in a combat zone.[35]

At the time Sweetland accepted the field director's position, the agency was in the midst of expanding its global operations to satisfy a congressional mandate to provide aid "to the sick and wounded of armies in time of war" and to act as a "mediator of communication between the people of the United States of America and their Army and Navy." At the high point of its commitment in 1945, the agency employed 39,000 people, with an additional 7.5 million volunteers. The American public—with significant contributions from the CIO and AFL—provided more than $784 million to support Red Cross operations. Of its four major programs, Services to the Armed Forces was the most significant, spanning three continents and most of the world's oceans. The agency's field directors (and assistant directors) numbered 3,520 in 1945.[36] As Sweetland quickly learned, a field director's desk could be in a headquarters building or in a tent on a makeshift flat surface.

The Sweetlands were living in a two-story rental house at 6800 Eastern Avenue in Washington, D.C., when Monroe joined the Red Cross. Through their long marriage, the most significant exchanges of correspondence between Lil and Monroe took place during his two years with the Red Cross. Lil's letters appear to be fairly complete, reflecting her husband's penchant for saving virtually everything. Of the extant letters, Lil's outnumber Monroe's about four to one, a remarkable testimony to his ability to preserve correspondence in the humid and turbulent environment of the Central Pacific. Elsewhere in the Sweetland collections, Lil's correspondence is spare, giving added significance to the wartime letters. Her writing reflects the full range of human feeling—delight in daughter Barbara and in her wartime job, fascinating insights about books and politics, frustration with some of Monroe's friends who stayed for a night or weekend, and witty stories about hosting weekend parties. She always offered affectionate musings about her absent partner:

Monroe mailed this cartoon clipping to Lil when he was serving with the Red Cross in the Central Pacific in 1944. (Courtesy of the Oregon Historical Society)

To Lil—
whom the artist musta known!)

"That's the beauty of our marriage ——
Bessie lives her life and I live mine."

When you start missing us, keep it up—you will be pleased to know
that I haven't been cold since you left—I have returned to my first
love—the heavy flannel pajamas with the feet in them.

In contrast, Monroe's letters were more informational and stylistically
less creative. Monroe may have been the "straight man" in their marriage,
grounded in the practical here and now, focusing on the conditional limitations of his immediate environment.

During the war Lil worked for the federal government, first with the
National Labor Relations Board and later the War Production Board. She
shared the house on Eastern Avenue with daughter Barbara, twin sister Vi
Shapiro, and Vi's son Mike.[37] In addition to managing a busy household and
holding federal jobs, Lil and Vi provided temporary lodging for friends and
acquaintances passing through Washington to new military assignments or
federal jobs. In brief, theirs was not a setting conducive to saving correspondence. Lil and Vi's professional work demonstrates that educated, activist
females shared vital positions in the workforce.

While he was in San Francisco, Sweetland had dinner with Nathalie
Panek, still with the War Relief Committee, and Doug Anderson, her companion and regional organizer for the CIO. During their conversation, Panek
convinced Sweetland to write articles for the *International Woodworker*, the
International Woodworkers of America's weekly CIO newspaper for timber and millworkers in the Pacific Northwest. Except for Lil, Panek—who
had a gift for biting wit and wry humor—proved to be a regular correspondent during Monroe's two years with the Red Cross. Her letter following
their San Francisco encounter included a story about a person she met, "a
dyed-in-the-wool CP and phoney as hell," and news about politics and their
Portland friend, Gus Solomon. She closed with words of advice: "keep your
fingernails clean, don't get fungus and don't eat strange fruit."[38]

Sweetland's route to his first duty station[39] included a stopover in Hawaii
and, finally, off to "a 'tough' assignment" at Eniwetok Atoll where he would
have "a chance to get out into an action zone." He boarded a military flight
in late March flying across several islands that had already witnessed fierce
battles and then to his destination, Eniwetok Atoll.[40] Contrary to his habit of
writing favorably about the places he visited, Sweetland described Eniwetok
as a shattered landscape, the fighting so violent that nothing was left "but

From right to left, Lil Sweetland, daughter Barbara (b. 1936), and nephew Mike Shapiro, the son of Lil's twin sister, Vi Megrath. The photo, circa 1944, was taken in a Washington, DC, park. (Courtesy of the Oregon Historical Society)

rubbish and sand," where "the hot sun beat down unmercifully." In the margins of a letter to Lil, he noted the precarious nature of their location: "This was the farthest American advance into Japanese territory, and we were surrounded by Japanese occupied islands—Ponape [also Pohnpei], Wake, Truk, Watje [Wotja], Ujelang [Atoll]."[41]

While in the Central Pacific, Sweetland kept his promise to Nathalie Panek, writing commentaries for the *Woodworker*. His articles addressed a range of issues: daily life for Red Cross workers, propaganda over Radio Tokyo, labor and the lumber industry at home, and the problems of reconversion to a peacetime economy. Workers in Northwest mill towns were reading his columns, because they occasionally asked about his duties. On one occasion, a writer reported that Nathalie Panek was urging workers to support the Red Cross. The writer asked, "How about telling us what's being done with our money. How about telling more about the Red Cross in the war?" Sweetland's subsequent articles appeared under subheadings, "My Red Cross Day," with stories about fishing excursions and lumber shipments to his base with familiar stamps: "Wauna, Weyerhaeuser, Mill 22, Moore's Mill, Pope & Talbot, Long-Bell."[42]

Labor and progressive politics were frequent refrains in his *Woodworker* columns. He expressed pleasure when Canada's Cooperative Commonwealth

(Left) J. Polan's pencil sketch of Monroe Sweetland somewhere in the Blue Pacific during the Second World War; (right) Lil Sweetland painting the family rental at 6800 Eastern Avenue in Washington, DC, during the war. (Courtesy of the Oregon Historical Society)

Federation swept the Saskatchewan provincial elections, offering an indication of what might be in store for that nation's federal election. He hoped Northwest labor would send representatives to Washington who would "join hands with progressives all around the Pacific" to rid the West Coast of those who exploited workers. He was optimistic that "real people who do the work" would cooperate across international borders to establish equitable trade policies and avoid "incidents like the shameful provisioning of Japan's war against China with our 'Jap squares' and scrap iron and oil just because Japan was able to pay premium prices."[43]

"These hand-to-hand battles for Guadalcanal, Tarawa, Kwajalein, Eniwetok, and Saipan," Sweetland observed, "were no-holds-barred, gruesome struggles." He suggested, however, that the behavior of some military personnel was providing fodder for Tokyo's propaganda machine. A recent *Life* magazine photo of an officer's girlfriend displaying a Japanese skull was only one example. Another incident involved a "trophy hound" who attempted to give President Roosevelt a desk ornament carved from a Japanese shinbone. He reported other accounts of watch fobs and necklaces made from Japanese teeth. His condemnation was sharp: "The shallow boasting in the American press, with photos of the morbid trophies" were inexcusable, ghoulish acts that threatened to prolong the war. "Even the appearance of race prejudice is a luxury we Americans cannot afford."[44]

After two months on Eniwetok, Sweetland thought he was getting along "surprisingly well with the officers," despite his close association with rank-and-file troops. The commanding officer was "an old-school democrat with strong aversions to officeritis," who impressed the men because he stood in the mess line and ate with the rest of the troops. Such behavior dovetailed nicely with Sweetland's passion for social democracy.[45] In other instances, servicemen praised Sweetland for being accessible and for his willingness to speak on equal terms with them.

In one of his letters to Lil from the summer of 1944, Monroe wrote about "a wonderful glorious night." An aide had just stacked "a high batch of letters on my desk tonight, 2 of them from you—your letter and a fat stuffed envelope from Washington just before you went to NY and your very delicious note from the Barbazon Plaza [sic]."[46] He was referring to an amusing letter that Lil wrote in late July from New York City's Barbizon-Plaza Hotel:

Darling—
Its high noon—and here I still sit in brassiere and pants. I've
completed the sacred rites—the shower, the hair brushing, the
painting of fingers and toe nails, the leg paint—so now I am a
bronzed, painted, high bosomed body beautiful with only my navel
(practically) as god gave it to me.[47]

Lil's Washington home front was personally more stressful than her husband's Red Cross assignment in the Pacific. Managing the household with her sister Vi and their children Barbara and Mike, a full-time job, and the comings and goings of friends and acquaintances proved taxing. To lessen the burdens of housework and child care, Lil and Vi hired an African American woman, Ellen, who lived with them. When Barbara and Mike traveled north to spend summers with Lil's mother on Martha's Vineyard, Ellen accompanied them. LeBaron Stinnett, who later came to live with Lil for nearly a year (with her son Jimmy), provides a striking description of Ellen's place in a seemingly chaotic household: "It's a circus—three children, three mommas and a dog—and of course, Ellen, who wends her serene way through all this confusion and is the only one who kept sane."[48]

In addition to expressions of affection for Lil, Monroe always asked about Barbara, her birthday, his frustration over an appropriate gift, "was it too grown up for her?" "Did she hear from Dad [Monroe's father]?

I wondered whether he'd remember." He asked about Vi's son Mike, and at times simply about "the kids." His father, still a practicing physician in Constantine, Michigan, was also in his thoughts. He was pleased when he learned that his widower father hired "Mrs. Slates, one of the abler, brighter village widows (perfectly safe, alas) to be his housekeeper." He referred to his father's "herculean decision," and hoped that his own letters had some influence in shaping his judgment. And always in his letters to Lil he asked for books, in one instance a second copy of Lillian Smith's *Strange Fruit*, because the original "must have been read by a hundred men."[49]

Before he left Eniwetok, Sweetland had a pivotal meeting with a young Japanese American interpreter that would become important to his civil rights commitments in later years. Frank Hachiya, a native of Hood River, Oregon, had been with Army forces in their invasion of the Tarawa Atoll and the Marshall Islands. At the conclusion of those campaigns, Hachiya stopped by Sweetland's Red Cross tent to say hello, and to get acquainted with a person who had connections to Hood River.[50] Caught in the spiraling web of war, Sweetland learned that Hachiya's mother and younger brother were visiting relatives in Japan when the Japanese bombed Pearl Harbor. After a period of waiting, his superiors ordered Hachiya to join with American forces in the invasion of the Philippines. He was badly wounded on Leyte Island in late December and died January 3, 1945.[51] Sweetland's correspondence for the next several years involved the long struggle to have Frank Hachiya's remains interred in Hood River.

Red Cross officials informed Sweetland that he would be returned to Honolulu for reassignment in late September 1944. Back on Oahu, the Red Cross offered him an assignment with the Tenth Army Division, an ominous choice as it turned out, because the Tenth would soon be involved in one of the epic battles of the Second World War, the invasion of Okinawa.[52] While he awaited the big event with the Tenth Army, Monroe recounted to Lil the deaths of personal friends in Europe and the Pacific. Lil's wintry letter before Christmas 1944 ("outside its trying to snow") recounted the German army's last ditch effort—the Battle of the Bulge—to drive through the Allied lines on the western front, making certain that the "European war will go on for several months." She wished that Monroe was home. "You have a kind of certainty, of good, that would be comforting to have about."[53]

Sweetland spent two or three short stays in Hawaii during his tour in the Pacific with the Red Cross. (Courtesy of the Oregon Historical Society)

Although both Lil and Monroe struggled with mood swings, for Lil, the crush of time (long working hours, attention to Barbara, and household chores) made daily life difficult. When she moved from the National Labor Relations Board to the War Labor Board in the summer of 1944, her new responsibilities added to those pressures. She was responsible for answering complaints, evaluating requests to reconsider board decisions, writing analyses, and recommending action. "It's a lawyers job essentially," she wrote Monroe, "at least what is normally thought of as a lawyer's job." Her new position was taxing and was taking a toll on her physical health: "Oh darling, if you could see what has happened to me—I look more than ever like your maiden aunt, skinnier than I've ever been since you've known me—102 lbs."[54]

Lil's household became more crowded early in 1945 when Vi and son Mike joined Lil and Barbara and LeBaron Stinnett and her son Jimmy. The full household gave Lil pause to wonder "how the 3 kids, 3 mommas arrangement will work out." With Mike and Vi in the house, however, this might "be the first step back to normalcy" and end her bouts with depression. In the next weeks, the daylight hours lengthened and finally daffodils bloomed in the backyard. "Spring," she wrote in February, "does seem really to be just around the corner—of course to you in your tropical—its never winter paradise—this can have no meaning."[55]

Several Sweetland friends visited or stayed the night at the family home. Charles Livermore stayed at "Headlong Hall," as he called it, when he had business in the nation's capital in April. In a letter to Monroe he likened Barbara ("Barbie") to Alice in Wonderland, a rapidly maturing child who "will really fill up a big place in your future."[56] Ethel Polk, War Relief's Midwest director, stayed briefly, writing to Sweetland about his maturing daughter Barbara who was reaching the romantic stage: "sitting in front of the fire, flushed after a too-hot bath, Lil braiding her pig-tails." Gazing into the fire and pausing to make certain the adults were listening, she whispered, "'Monroe's been gone so long now' with a catch in her voice, adding the exact length of time." Polk described the scene as "touching."[57]

The Tenth Army Division's major mission, the Battle of Okinawa, turned into an epic eighty-two day conflict that took the lives of more than 250,000 civilians and military personnel. The invasion of Okinawa, only 350 miles from the southern tip of mainland Japan, represented the first time Americans had fought on Japanese soil. The battle was even more tragic because 150,000 Okinawan civilians were killed. Only Stalingrad in Eastern Europe took more civilian lives. The Tenth Army—183,000 Army, Navy, and Marine personnel—lost 7,613 in the battle. In preparations for the attack, the United States Navy assembled some 1,300 ships off the Okinawa coast in late March. Although Okinawa was the final great battle of the Second World War, the bombing of Hiroshima and Nagasaki shortly thereafter has obscured its significance. Associated Press journalist Sid Moody summed up the Okinawa story in 1945: "Before Hiroshima there was Okinawa. Because of Okinawa, in considerable part there was Hiroshima."[58]

"In the Thick of It," Sweetland titled a delayed communiqué for the *Woodworker*. Operation Iceberg, the code name for the Okinawa maneuvers, began on April 1, with Red Cross canteens following the first troops ashore. The Red Cross also cared for men returning from battle zones, with officials reporting more combat fatigue cases on Okinawa than any other World War Two battlefront.[59] Sweetland reported at the end of May that combat had been in full force for a month and that he was busy moving eighteen agency offices to keep up with the repositioning troops. Although Island Command staffed the military hospitals, Red Cross personnel held most of the supervisory positions. His report cautioned that not all was well, because several Red Cross staffers had either resigned or requested transfer, "with few exceptions from men whose instability might have been determined when they were originally hired."[60]

And then it was over. The last Japanese had either surrendered or were slaughtered in what many deemed suicide toward the end of June. A few weeks later, the Pacific war itself ended when atomic bombs obliterated Hiroshima and Nagasaki. Red Cross work now shifted to processing returning Allied prisoners of war and civilian internees, a task that involved Sweetland for the next two months. In providing relief for prisoners, the American Red Cross cooperated with the British Red Cross Society and the Netherlands-Indies Red Cross Society. The agency provided assistance to approximately 14,000 U.S. prisoners of war and another 1,500 civilian internees.[61]

In a "what's mostly on my mind" letter in early July letter, Monroe revealed that he "would like to travel to mainland China before he returned home."[62] His question about the duration of his appointment and the prospect of visiting China put Lil "in a complete turmoil." She considered a "sporting" response—"this is a question that only you can decide"—but chose instead to say "the hell with ethical considerations—this is how I feel":

I want you to come home
a. I want to have a baby—in fact two
Babies—and time is fleeting
b. I hate—loathe—despise living
without you—wherever and however I
live I want to live with you.
c. I want to live the kind of life we can live together.
d. I want Barbara to know you and be influenced by you

She had put a lot of thought into "these simple bold statements—I'm not trying to be objective because god knows, I want you home with me—but I don't want you home if you'll be sorry."[63]

Monroe Sweetland left one remarkable remembrance of his Red Cross tour in the South Pacific, a twelve-page, single-space manuscript, "Hatred-Limited," his account of the recently liberated prisoners. The document, dated October 24, 1945, was written when he was leaving Okinawa. Consistent with his training in journalism, the document made liberal use of quotation marks bracketing the remarks of interviewees who spent time in Japanese prisoner of war camps.

"They call them 'RAMPS'—the Recovered Allied Military Personnel." Twenty-Two-Thousand, Four-Hundred-and-Ninety-Four of them. Day and night for 48 days we have been living with them as they begin once more to try their wings as free men, to eat American chow, to wear shoes that fit them and clothes that cover them.[64]

The liberated men—American, British, and Dutch—offered a preview, Sweetland believed, of attitudes that would prevail in the following months. Although some were reticent, most ex-prisoners expressed normal reactions to questions.[65] Some of the atrocity stories now being circulated in the states, Sweetland assumed, would be discredited when more information was at hand. In another sense, there was little doubt that Allied prisoners were "beaten, whipped, clubbed, starved, and in a few instances executed." The men reporting those stories added one important caveat: "They saw almost nothing done to Americans, even to the killings themselves, which they had not seen inflicted by Japanese superiors upon subordinates in their own ranks."[66]

Toward the end of the prisoners' evacuation from Japan, Sweetland met a few "stragglers" who spent time visiting "with Japanese families who had made them house guests when the war was over." Such incidents were contrary to the hatred that "the Japanese propaganda machine" had tried to instill in its citizens against the Americans and British.[67] Sweetland wondered how such stories would be woven "into the fabric of American postwar opinion?" Left to their own devices, he thought the ex-prisoners would tell of atrocities as well as the incidents of kindness that many of them experienced. He feared, however, that "domestic hate-mongers" would use the returning troops in their "revenge against all Japanese," but especially against Americans of Japanese descent. As one who was prone to see the potential for good, he believed Americans possessed a reservoir of compassion where "fairplay and good-will" would overcome race prejudice.[68]

Throughout his Red Cross service, Monroe shared with Lil information about purchasing an Oregon newspaper following the war to provide a forum for promoting progressive politics. Portland's Gus Solomon, who provided Monroe with information about small-town newspapers, warned that "the small towns in which daily newspapers operate are pretty conservative communities which hate and fear the New Deal and the CIO." One prospect, Monroe wrote Lil, appeared to be McMinnville, only a short drive from Portland or Salem and a "college town—rich, growing county (Yamhill)—county only slightly Republican (Dewey 5,600; FDR 5,000)—remarkably stable—more agricultural than lumbering, but some of both."[69]

Nathalie Panek was skeptical about Sweetland's newspaper ideas. She had "mixed emotions" about his returning to Oregon, believing that he was "cut out for 'bigger things.'" Although his presence in Oregon would make the state personally more attractive, Panek thought he would have greater opportunities elsewhere. "For all its beautiful trees Oregon is a pretty reactionary place," she wrote in November 1944. When Panek learned that Solomon was investigating a McMinnville newspaper, she expressed reservations about Sweetland's capacity to run any newspaper. "You'd never have time to run it—you'd be too busy on politics." She suggested that he seek a medium-salary position with the CIO. Because no one "has your savvy politically—I mean *no one*—why should you waste your time on a business." Besides, Panek fumed, "I hate McMinnville. Stinking, bucolic, reactionary little town." If he purchased a newspaper in McMinnville, "do you count on a cow and strawberries too? I will *not milk the cow*."[70]

Far away in Constantine, George Sweetland reflected on Monroe's experiences in the Pacific and thought they would prove useful, especially if he finished his law studies (which George offered to support): "As you grow older you will care more for home and quietness less for wandering." His advice—"keep the monthly checks coming in. Save now, sacrifice to the limit and you will later be happy." With the surrender of Germany and Japan, his father regretted that "President Roosevelt and Uncle Monroe" (his brother) could have lived to witness "the crushing defeat of the damned Japs and Germans." He was also very proud of Monroe's "efforts in this great struggle."[71]

Sweetland informed "the top office" in mid-August 1945 that he would help for a few weeks handling newly released prisoners, but that he wanted no part of the occupation of Japan. He advised Lil against signing a rental lease, "cause, darling, we're starting to live once more in Oregon in Jan 1946—." Because of the large number of liberated prisoners being processed through the Okinawa Red Cross camp, Monroe's letters were always hurried. In a September note to Lil, he referred to being on his way home by late October.[72] He thought it prudent to make a brief trip to Oregon to find a flexible rental, because they had no idea where they would be living. The search for a suitable paper would be a major part of his Oregon venture. Winding up the POW work, he told Lil, "is the best and most rewarding job I've ever done in RC—and believe me, I'm glad I was able to take over this big setup before I left."[73]

The absence of correspondence between Monroe and Lil has cloaked the details of Sweetland's return to civilian life in a veil of uncertainty. He apparently left Hawaii for the mainland in mid-November, visited Oregon, and then made his way to Washington, D.C., to rendezvous with Lil and Barbara. He left Washington on December 12 for Michigan to see his father in Constantine, telling Lil that his father had agreed "to stake me on the Salem venture" and was transferring $10,000,[74] which "should start us on both the paper and the house." There was a price to his father's generosity, however, "a stern lecture on our lack of ability to have money—he's pretty shocked that we have earned so much in 5 years but haven't any appreciable savings—my efforts to show him about our costs of living haven't convinced him—and only partly convince me!"[75]

Following the brief visit with his father, Monroe returned to Washington for Lil and Barbara and the long trip to Oregon. The Sweetlands' westward trek was part of a dramatic demographic shift that began with the onset of the Second World War and continued for several decades. Their homecoming took place in the midst of a dizzying pace of change in the state—urbanization, a rapidly diminishing farm population, and, most of all, a booming home construction industry that would power the state's economy through the 1970s. With modest capital support from his father and political friends, Sweetland would spend more than fifteen years in the newspaper business, an industry that permitted him (with Lil's significant assistance) to devote much of his time to politics.

6

Oregon Politics and the Newspaper Business

During his five years away from Oregon, Monroe Sweetland paid close attention to politics in the state of his birth. His most important political correspondents were Dean Wayne Morse of the University of Oregon Law School, Nan Wood Honeyman, former third district congresswoman, and lawyer friend Gus Solomon. The narrative thread of the incoming correspondence presented a bleak picture of legislative politics, with few progressives having electoral success. The struggle for control of the Democratic Party between conservative Democrats and insurgents from the defunct Oregon Commonwealth Federation persisted through the war years and beyond.

Despite Franklin Roosevelt's successes in the 1940 and 1944 elections, Oregon Democrats made no parallel advances. Republicans increased their hold on Oregon's congressional delegation and both houses of the state legislature. Lew Wallace, Democratic candidate for governor in 1942, was more conservative than Republican Earl Snell and garnered only 22 percent of the popular vote. Aged Democrat Walter Pierce, who lost his second district seat in 1942, was the last Democrat elected to Congress until Richard Neuberger defeated Guy Cordon for the U.S. Senate and Edith Green won Oregon's third congressional district, both in 1954.[1]

Among the Oregonians Sweetland corresponded with during the war, none would have a greater impact on state and national politics than Wayne Morse. In letters to Lil, Nathalie Panek, and Commonwealth friends, Sweetland frequently praised Morse for his liberalism and progressive politics. Although the two were casual acquaintances during the

Commonwealth years, they became friends when Monroe joined the Office of Production Management. Sweetland intervened with Secretary of Labor Frances Perkins in 1941 to keep Morse's name alive for federal labor mediation positions.[2] Morse resurfaced in a more significant way in Sweetland's life in late January 1944, when he wrote Sweetland that he would challenge Republican U.S. senator Rufus Holman in the Oregon primary. Morse thought his prospects would be "quite good" and that he would enter the race if he could garner the "financial support to conduct at least a skeleton campaign." In short order, Morse resigned from the University of Oregon law school and told Eugene neighbor Ruth Washke: "My hat's in the ring for the Senate race. I am probably jumping from the frying pan into the fire, but I can assure you there will be plenty of sizzling and I don't expect it to be my flesh."[3]

Some Oregon progressives, Nathalie Panek among them, were less than enthusiastic about Morse's Senate candidacy. "The theory is that he has to be nominated in the Republican primaries," she confided to Sweetland, "but I don't think he's persuading the Republicans and he is certainly making our [union] boys nervous." Panek refused to speak with Morse, because she was not keen on chasing "the great and near-great and reports of his uppity attitude doesn't warm up the project for me." In his effort to straddle the politics of an increasingly conservative Republican Party, Morse attacked the New Deal as a group "doped with the ingredients of totalitarianism." From Eniwetok, however, Monroe wrote Lil that, compared to his opponent, Morse was "on the side of the angels." And evidently he was, defeating the increasingly inept Holman in the primary 70,716 to 60,436. Morse was now free to pursue his progressive instincts in the general election against conservative Democratic nominee Edgar Smith, a wealthy wheat rancher.[4]

Although most unions, including Nathalie Panek's CIO, supported Morse, she remained critical, especially of Morse's "fulminations against federal control and regulation." The law-school dean, however, proved an adept campaigner, a riveting speaker and at ease with large crowds. He won wide applause when he rode his prize horse, Spice of Life, at county fairs and in the celebrated Pendleton Round-Up. He thanked Sweetland before the election for being "a grand friend," a kindness he would not forget. When the votes were tallied, Morse had won a resounding victory—269,095 to 174,140—carrying every county in the state and winning more precincts than any other successful Senate candidate in Oregon history. Most stunning of all, he garnered 9 percent more votes than the popular president at the head of the Democratic ticket.[5]

Fifty years after he returned to Oregon from the Pacific, Sweetland wrote a perceptive assessment of the state's politics in the immediate postwar period. Although President Roosevelt carried Oregon in each of his four campaigns, "the rest of Oregon's body politic throughout the '30s and '40s remained listless and conservative, captive of an entrenched Republican monopoly." But the Second World War had dramatically altered the state's demographic profile. African Americans who came west to work in the Portland shipyards stayed on after the war. Countless women learned new skills as wage laborers, and thousands of returning veterans, "children of the Depression," were coming home to take advantage of the G.I. Bill.[6] Although Republicans had dominated state politics, Oregon was in the midst of dramatic demographic changes that would eventually alter its political landscape. While the state's population increased 14 percent during the 1930s, the immigrants who flocked to the Portland shipyards in the early 1940s unleashed a trek of newcomers who numbered nearly half a million by 1950, an increase of 44 percent.[7]

Arriving in Oregon just after New Year's Day, 1946, the Sweetlands purchased the *Molalla Pioneer* and published their first issue of the small weekly on February 7, 1946. They promised to put "out a home town paper you will like" and praised Molalla—twenty-eight miles northeast of Salem—for its potential as part of "booming Oregon." The new publishers, who made their home in Molalla, wanted to strengthen the local educational system and help build the town's "business, social, cultural and religious life."[8] Although there are few details about the purchase of the *Molalla Pioneer*, it is striking how quickly the Sweetlands were able to acquire the newspaper and put out their first issue.

Sweetland and Felix Nash were listed as publishers, Monroe as editor, and Lillie M. Sweetland as editorial assistant. Published on Thursdays, the newspaper accepted letters about local news and opinion, but requested "no poetry, please." As Monroe readied the first issue, his father sent words of advice: "Be careful about your machinery. Work hard. Be one-hundred percent honest. Save. *Collect* your bills at once. Don't be partisan." This was heady counsel for the neophyte publisher, and counsel that would prove difficult to follow. The *Pioneer*'s editorials would be partisan, praising the

Monroe and Lil outside their rental home in Molalla, Oregon, 1946. (Courtesy of the Oregon Historical Society)

Oregon Farmers' Union and the Columbia Valley Authority, an effort to establish a clone of the Tennessee Valley Authority for the Columbia River drainage. A Lincoln's birthday editorial applauded the president for supporting racial equality and American laborers. Another described the American South as a "retarded part of our country."[9]

Sweetland's politics were evident everywhere in the *Pioneer*, urging citizens to support the Red Cross for its service to "men still in hospitals and overseas." With equal enthusiasm, the newspaper praised the USO (United Service Organization) for providing "meeting places, music, recreation, waiting rooms and reading tables" for American servicemen and women. Sweetland censured "bigoted Senators" for filibustering a Fair Employment Practices bill that would prohibit discrimination for reasons of race, religion, or national origin. The *Pioneer* sided with union loggers when lumber operators attempted to force workers to give up hard-won clauses in their collective bargaining agreements.[10]

At the foot of the Oregon Cascades, Molalla was part of a booming lumber and logging economy following the Second World War. Although agriculture had been the community's mainstay for decades, the flourishing construction industry after 1945 and the great stands of Douglas-fir in the Molalla River drainage invited investment in building logging roads and several small sawmills, and the expansion of larger operators such as

Weyerhaeuser and Pope and Talbot. Similar to other small towns in western Oregon, the log trucks that rumbled through Molalla daily were dynamic symbols of a thriving local economy.

As the 1946 general election approached, Sweetland predicted "impending doom" for Oregon's Democratic Party. The campaign of longtime friend David Epps for secretary of state failed to gain traction, and Republican incumbent Robert Farrell, Jr., a notorious Japanophobe, appeared en route to an easy victory. Republican governor Earl Snell was also expected to easily defeat his Democratic opponent, Carl Donaugh, the longtime U.S. attorney for Oregon. Responding to Sweetland's "impending doom" remark, labor leader Manley Wilson advised him to avoid being too discouraged. "After all you can't lose 'what you ain't never had.'"[11]

Wilson's call for patience and hard work as prerequisites for Oregon progressives to achieve electoral success proved accurate. Republicans made a clean sweep of all four congressional seats, Governor Earl Snell defeated Democrat Carl Donaugh, Robert Farrell easily turned back David Epps, and Sweetland friend, Ralph Peeples—former secretary of the Oregon CIO—lost his race for commissioner of the Bureau of Labor. Voters turned back Ballot Measure 8 to create a state old-age and disability fund, with only 26 percent of voters approving the initiative. Republicans won huge majorities in the Senate, 25 to 5, and in the House, 58 to 2. Although voters elected Manley Wilson to another term in the Oregon Senate, progressives had suffered a trouncing at the polls.[12]

Newspaper enterprises, first the Molalla Pioneer and then in 1947 the Newport News, were at the center of the Sweetlands' lives after their return to Oregon. Although he participated in Democratic Party politics in Molalla and Salem, Monroe's eyes were cast toward wider arenas of action. While he was hustling politics or financial support for their newspapers, Lil took responsibility for the Pioneer office—and more. On one occasion, she was reporter, photographer, and personal confidant, telling her husband about covering a horrific accident involving a car and a log truck in which two people were killed and four seriously injured. "The sight of dead bodies and much blood" was unnerving; she took photos with a Brownie camera, but thought the effort would go for naught: "I was shaking too much to focus well so they are probably flops."[13]

The Sweetlands purchased the *Molalla Pioneer* and its printing business for a down payment of $8,000, or half the full price. The inventory
included machinery to put out a small weekly, photographic gear, a rolltop
desk, typewriter, and miscellaneous items. After publishing the *Pioneer* for
less than two years, Sweetland had a buyer for the Molalla paper and was
engaged in purchasing and publishing the *Newport News*. The Sweetlands
joined with friends C. Girard "Jebby" Davidson and Dan Goldy to fund the
much larger enterprise. Both men were Democratic Party political appoin-
tees, Davidson as assistant secretary of the interior and Goldy as Northwest
regional manager for the new Bureau of Land Management (BLM) and its
western Oregon timberlands.[14]

The Newport purchases included the *Yaquina Bay News*, the *Newport
Journal*, and later the equipment of the defunct *Waldport Steelhead*. The
complex and ongoing negotiations involved Sweetland in a financial, time-
consuming juggling act, strained relations with his friends, especially Goldy,
and nearly drove the Sweetlands into bankruptcy. The purchase price for
the *Newport Journal* alone was $18,000, with $9,900 due no later than
December 1, 1947, and the balance (including interest) to be paid within
one year. With work proceeding apace to renovate the Newport printing
facilities, the prospective buyer for the *Molalla Pioneer* defaulted on the purchase, placing the Sweetland investments in jeopardy. In a letter to Davidson
and Goldy, Sweetland observed: "We can't complete the moving here until
we finish the sale there."[15]

Davidson and Goldy, who worked closely in the Interior Department
on regional issues, were keenly interested in the Newport venture. Goldy
first met Sweetland when the latter appeared on the University of Wisconsin
campus in 1935 as a recruiter for the League for Industrial Democracy.
Goldy, who wrote for the student newspaper, attended Sweetland's talk
and was eyewitness to the infamous incident when campus football players seized Sweetland and reputedly threw him into nearby Lake Mendota.
Goldy's column about the event subsequently appeared in college newspapers across the country. "That's how I met Monroe," Goldy told an interviewer later in life.[16]

With printing equipment scattered in two different Newport locations, the Sweetlands began publishing the *News* in early December 1947.
Although Goldy understood the difficulties they faced, he thought the first
edition of the paper was smart and nicely arranged. Because the *Pioneer*

was still on the market, he and his wife Rusty were apprehensive about Sweetland's effort at juggling "both balls at the same time." Goldy's letters always addressed fiscal matters, inquiring on one occasion if Sweetland had established "a Newport Publishing Company or a legal entity . . . which can give us a note?"[17]

The Goldy, Davidson, and Sweetland families were close friends, with Dan often addressing letters to "Monroe and Lil," and signing off on one occasion, "Love to Lil, and to Barbara, the assistant scribe of the Campfire girls." But he was also businesslike and brusque, inquiring regularly about the potential for selling the Pioneer, the layout and number of pages in the News.[18] It is apparent that all parties to the Newport venture were guilty of lax bookkeeping. Goldy frequently asked for business statements about the enterprise; the Sweetlands requested clarification about payments they were making on their balance sheets. In early January 1948 Sweetland complained about going through "a rugged month," with carpenters and electricians completing work in the print shop. He reported another flurry of activity in the sale of the Pioneer to an Alaskan buyer, but the deal never materialized.[19]

The failure to find a buyer for the *Molalla Pioneer* left the Sweetlands overextended and with little operating capital. They had outstanding notes due to the former *Pioneer* publisher, overdue payments for newsprint, and wage obligations for both businesses. In a February 1948 note to Goldy, Sweetland worried about the balance sheet and mentioned just being able to meet the month's payroll—with Lil putting "in a lots of night-time overtime" to keep everything afloat. To Crown-Zellerbach's credit department, he attributed his failure to pay monthly bills to the need to sell surplus equipment from the purchase of the two Newport papers and the failure to sell the *Pioneer*. "I am under terrific pressure here," he wrote, "and just haven't got enough operating capital on hand."[20]

Following several false sales proposals, Sweetland finally sold the *Pioneer* in April 1948 to a California publisher for $15,000. Goldy was "happily surprised at the price," but he and Davidson still wanted information about the excess equipment: had it been sold, has gross revenue increased, and "are we covering our current expenses?" Three weeks later Goldy repeated the same concerns, admitting that he and Davidson were "full of questions," but aware that Sweetland was busy "with the campaign and the newspaper."

(Sweetland was a candidate for one of Oregon's two Democratic National Committee positions in the May primary.) Despite questions about the Newport operation, Davidson assured him that their financial stake in the paper "should have absolutely no influence in what you say."[21]

Sweetland's decision—with Goldy and Davidson's support—to run for one of Oregon's two Democratic National Committee positions in the May 1948 primary brought additional stresses. Among the candidates, Portland tire dealer Mike DeCicco, a back-slapping glad-hander from an older-style politics, posed the greatest challenge. With a Democratic president and a solidly Republican congressional delegation, Oregon's two Democratic Committee persons would wield considerable power if the party retained the presidency in the fall election. Goldy thought a DeCicco victory "would be a complete calamity" for Democrats. With the support of former Democratic governors Oswald West and Walter Pierce and the endorsement of the *Oregonian*, Sweetland squeaked through with a margin of some 3,000 votes.[22]

The sale of the *Molalla Pioneer* did little to lessen Sweetland's financial problems. Goldy asked about progress on his advice, and credit offices continued to seek payment for outstanding bills. Sweetland finally reported the sale of surplus equipment to William Angel and Company for $5,900, with payment promised soon. He told Goldy about shopping for more advanced printing equipment and that he had hired a retired foreman to oversee work in the shop. As usual, Goldy asked detailed questions: "Have we actually sold the surplus equipment . . . or is the sale contingent on resale to someone else? The question arises from the fact that apparently we don't get paid immediately."[23]

Frank Hachiya, the young Japanese-language interpreter that Sweetland met on Eniwetok in the summer of 1944, resurfaced in Sweetland's life in the midst of his newspaper troubles during the spring and summer of 1948. Hachiya, a Hood River native killed during the invasion of Leyte, in January 1945, was buried in Grave 4479 in an Armed Forces cemetery in the Philippines. When Sweetland learned of Hachiya's death, he arranged a memorial service while he was in Honolulu awaiting the Okinawa invasion. Those attending included interpreters with the Army's intelligence sections and colleagues who were with him on Kwajalein and Eniwetok. In a letter to Hugh Ball of the Hood River News, Sweetland was pointed:

Our sadness at the loss of this rare friend is tempered by our
pride in his achievement. Hood River, too, can be proud, not only
because Frank Hachiya made a telling stroke toward victory in the
Philippines, but because it was in your Valley that he nurtured his
deep faith in America.[24]

Hachiya's father, Junkichi, who was in the War Relocation Authority's
internment camp at Minidoka, Idaho,[25] sent Sweetland a note expressing
his appreciation "for your graciousness during my recent bereavement." In
flawless penmanship, likely written by someone else, he informed Sweetland
about a local memorial service for his son with some four hundred people
present. Although Junkichi Hachiya was free to leave Minidoka, he was
uncertain about his future address. He was especially fond of the Hood
River Valley where he had spent thirty years of his life—"truly a beautiful
scenic spot, although the Legion has attached some shame to it."[26]

After his release from the Red Cross in October 1945, Monroe stopped
briefly in Genoa, Illinois, for a visit with Junkichi Hachiya who was working in a greenhouse. Although the "conversation was handicapped by the
language barrier," Sweetland remembered Junkichi asking if Hood River
people would be hostile if Frank's body were returned to his place of birth.
On the family's way through Hood River a few days later, Monroe spoke
with Hugh Ball of the *Hood River News*, who thought such an event would
be cathartic for the community and provide an opportunity for people to
"pay their respects for a Japanese-American neighbor." Those preliminary
conversations led to further discussions with Hood River's Ray Yasui, head
of the local Japanese American Citizens League (JACL), the exhumation of
Hachiya's body, and the shipment of his remains to Hood River.[27]

The memorial service at Hood River's Asbury Methodist Church on
September 11, 1948, brings Frank Hachiya's story full circle to the valley of
his birth. Two hundred Japanese American friends and another one hundred who knew him in some fashion were present to celebrate a remarkable
life. "Home with him," wrote *Oregonian* staff writer Leverett Richards, "came
the silver star with bronze cluster for gallantry in action he had bought with
his life in the Pacific." Gray-haired Junkichi Hachiya was there to accept the
flag that draped the casket. "This is still home to me," he remarked about the
place where he had lived for three decades. Sweetland retold the story of the
first memorial service for Frank in Honolulu where his fellow servicemen

celebrated his significance "at a time when Americans of his racial origin were still regarded with suspicion and robbed of all honor at home."[28]

Although Sweetland continued to work with the JACL on removing discriminatory restrictions on first-generation Japanese who were deemed ineligible for citizenship,[29] Frank Hachiya's family resurfaced periodically in the coming years. When Hachiya's younger brother, Homer, who was living in Yokohama, Japan, visited Oregon in August 1952, Lil and Monroe treated him to a trip to Hood River, the place of his birth. Homer traveled to his brother's grave site and renewed acquaintances with old friends during his brief stay. He told an *Oregonian* reporter that he and his mother did not learn of Frank's death until late November 1945 when they met Harry Takagi, an Army man from Hood River serving with American occupation forces in Japan. Three decades later, when Sweetland was living in retirement in California, Frank Hachiya (and Homer) would once again occupy a place in his life.[30]

Shortly after Hachiya's burial in Hood River, Sweetland expanded the Newport News from ten to fourteen pages to increase the percentage of advertising. By the end of the year, however, the newspaper's finances had reached a crisis when the Newport bank called for payment of the entire loan. That move set in motion a series of decisions that removed Sweetland from effective control of the newspaper. Much of this is revealed in a scolding letter from Dan Goldy addressing the reasons for the bank's decision, including its "disapproval of our editorial policy." The bank's legal argument, however, was the most serious: (1) sale of equipment without consultation, and (2) "failure to make regular payments on the note."[31]

Goldy was infuriated, telling Sweetland that failing to meet obligations for the bank loan "comes as something of a shock." In previous correspondence, he charged, "you had indicated that the one payment which had always been made on time was to the bank." After speaking with Gus Solomon, Goldy thought the situation could be rectified through more friendly banking partners. But the larger implications disturbed him. Failure to pay the bank note was "a kind of financial irresponsibility" that would lead to problems "from which we will not be able to extricate ourselves." He reminded Sweetland that he had promised weekly financial reports, and these had not been forthcoming. Goldy, who was traveling in the Northwest, suggested a meeting "this Friday" (three days hence) to clear the financial fog about "where we stand."[32]

Although the discussions that took place at the mid-December meeting are lost to the documented record, Sweetland named J. W. "Bud" Forrester general manager of the Newport Publishing Company in January 1949, a development that removed Sweetland from day-to-day operations. The agreement stipulated that Forrester was not to sell or purchase equipment without the company's consent. He was free to set editorial policy, except when the company's board directed otherwise, and was "to render the board of directors . . . a monthly financial statement." His salary of $50 per week would double when the business was profitable.[33]

According to the agreement, the Newport Publishing Company was capitalized at $25,000, with Monroe Sweetland, Lil Sweetland, Daniel Goldy, C. Girard Davidson, and Will Davis holding equal shares. When the business began to pay dividends, Forrester would be given $5,000 in stock: "The $5,000 in stock to be given to you shall be purchased by Monroe Mark Sweetland for the sum of $5,000 and shall constitute a debt of the corporation." In a letter to Davidson shortly after the agreement, Sweetland confirmed that Forrester found "that the financial picture is more grim than he had expected."[34]

Sweetland reported to Davidson that the company needed $2,000 "to meet pressing debts," and it was overdue in paying its withholding tax and other obligations. The accumulated debt, he noted, "has forced Lil and me to a decision on which we have dreaded to face." They had asked Gus Solomon to prepare the paperwork to transfer $5,000 of their stock to the company to put Forrester on a sound basis. "Dan is terribly upset," he noted, "and for plenty of cause, at the jeopardy into which we have put the investment he made." Sweetland admitted failing to properly assess the Newport opportunity and his ability to get results. For all the lofty principles upon which they launched the enterprise, he and Lil could no longer "involve any of you any deeper than has already been done." Even the stock transfer, "which is all we have to offer," would not be sufficient to pay all the bills. With the help of their stock, he was confident that Forrester and his staff "can get things operating profitably in due time."[35]

The Sweetlands moved to Salem sometime in early 1949. While Monroe adjusted to these new realities, Goldy provided feedback and support for Forrester and the Newport operation. He told Forrester and Gus Solomon that the company's greatest need, in Goldy's view, was to refinance the operation "to avoid the repetition of the situation with which we have been confronted in the past few months."[36] Although he no longer controlled the Newport News, Sweetland purchased the Oregon Democrat in June 1949, a vehicle to help in promoting the Democratic Party and to advance his work as Democratic National Committeeman. In a letter to Nathalie Panek, Sweetland told her about the move to Salem and that Bud Forrester was managing the Newport enterprise so that he could devote more attention to the Democratic Party.[37] He made no mention about their financial struggles.

From the time of Forrester's appointment as general manager of the News until its sale in September 1950, Goldy coordinated most of the Newport Publishing Company's financial affairs. It is also apparent that the company's debt problems were ongoing. When Ray Moe and financial supporters purchased the News in January 1950, the conditions stipulated that the buyers would inherit some indebtedness. Even then, the new owners were remiss in meeting payments, including $500 to John Ferguson, a Coos Bay creditor. In an apologetic note to Ferguson, Goldy explained that Moe had been "under the gun to pay off the accumulated accounts payable during the period of our ownership." In a letter to Moe, Goldy noted that the former owners of the News felt a "moral obligation" to see that Ferguson was paid.[38]

Davidson, Goldy, and Sweetland always mixed politics in their discussions about the financial status and direction of the Newport News. When Goldy and Davidson planned a trip to Oregon in late January 1948, Goldy asked Sweetland to arrange a meeting between Davidson and Democrats. Because the press would be asking Davidson questions, he asked Sweetland to prepare a few notes on issues "which you think Jebby ought to comment about and the general tenor of his comments." In the margins of the letter, he wrote "which might be helpful to the Demos." He also praised Sweetland's editorial criticizing Henry Wallace's decision to run for president as a third-party candidate. Davidson and Goldy were Truman supporters who were attempting to convince Idaho senator Glenn Taylor against joining Wallace as his vice-presidential candidate.[39]

Wallace's third-party candidacy in 1948 posed difficulties for Sweetland and other liberals who were longtime admirers of the former vice president. Sweetland's opposition to the third-party move marks his transition to mainstream political reformism. In addressing Sweetland's run for Democratic National Committeeman in the 1948 primary, the Oregonian complimented

Sweetland as the "best equipped with political savvy, personality and pro-motional vigor," but reminded readers that the former "admirer of Henry Wallace now can say nothing nice about the third party candidate."[40]

After President Roosevelt's death on April 12, 1945, three months after his inauguration for a fourth term, the president's liberal supporters were bewildered. Nathalie Panek wrote Sweetland that she would worry less if Wallace had been vice president, "but Truman! That seems impossible. I've seen him and I've heard him—he's a small man in very big shoes." As the coming months would prove, the "small man" worked his way through the presidency, sometimes by trial and error, gaining confidence with each passing month. Along the way he fired Wallace, who was commerce secre-tary, when the latter gave a speech in September 1946 to a Soviet-American friendship gathering in New York City arguing that the two nations should respect each other's spheres of influence. The political fallout that ensued prompted Truman to demand Wallace's resignation.[41] The dovish Wallace then became editor of the *New Republic* and moved quickly to establish him-self as a third-party candidate for president.

Wallace announced his third-party candidacy in December 1947, because it was widely believed that Truman had little chance of winning the November election. For those supporting Harry Truman as the Democratic Party standard-bearer, the third-party push was akin to consorting with the devil. Many former Wallace devotees now thought of him as the Antichrist, a fuzzy-headed liberal, or, as President Truman referred to Wallace and Interior Secretary Harold Ickes, members of a "lunatic fringe." The govern-ing board of Americans for Democratic Action wanted an open Democratic convention. While party leaders supported Truman's policies, they feared he would be a certain loser in November. The Sweetlands' friend, liberal jour-nalist James Wechsler, explained the issue: "Mr. Truman's place in history may be written in Mike Gonzales's ageless remark about a rookie ballplayer: good field, no hit."[42]

With editorials in the *Newport News* and *Molalla Pioneer*, Sweetland pointed to the fallacy of Wallace's Progressive Party campaign. A vote for Wallace would be a vote for conservative Republican senator Robert Taft of Ohio. Wallace would siphon votes away from Truman and give the elec-tion to Taft. A victory for the conservative Republican would damage the Marshall Plan and aid to Western Europe, "discredit American prestige,"

place government in the hands of big business, and "hasten economic collapse within this nation." Furthermore, Wallace was playing into the hands
of communists, who favored a Taft presidency. How, Sweetland asked, "can
any honest progressive still back this bird-dog for reaction?" [43]

Ancil Payne was another Oregon liberal who joined Sweetland in
opposing Wallace's candidacy. Payne, who would rise in the media world to
become head of King Broadcasting in Seattle, was ADA's Northwest regional
director during the 1948 campaign. In a visit to Lewis and Clark College,
he met with student leader Edward Gideon, urging him to support real
Democrats and "not trojan horses of the abortive third party movement."
Sweetland, who suspected Gideon might be a communist, consulted with
a person knowledgeable about "C-P elements" in Oregon and learned there
was no evidence that Gideon was a party member. [44]

Sweetland's long-standing opposition to communists in politics
weighed heavily in his opposition to Henry Wallace and the Progressive
Party. Because Wallace's foreign policy positions were friendly to the Soviet
Union, the American media charged that the campaign was riddled with
communists. Powerful and important friends from Sweetland's past held
similar opinions. Walter Reuther, president of the United Auto Workers
union, thought the Communist Party unduly influenced the Wallace campaign. Former *New York Times* correspondent Chris Hedges points out that
Wallace "was subjected to a vicious assault by the press and the liberal establishment," condemnations that "discredited and finally exiled [Wallace]
from political life." Historian James Patterson suggests that Wallace seemed
oblivious to the notion that communists were influencing his campaign. [45]

Because Democrats feared Republicans would easily defeat Truman,
they worried about his nomination. Two of FDR's sons, Elliott Roosevelt
and Franklin D. Roosevelt, Jr., initiated a move to draft General Dwight
Eisenhower. The *New Republic* urged Truman to drop out of the race. Dan
Goldy favored liberal Supreme Court Justice William O. Douglas. Other
prominent liberals—Connecticut's Chester Bowles, Minnesota's Hubert
Humphrey, Walter Reuther, and Florida senator Claude Pepper—initiated
a "Stop Truman" strategy. When Reuther, Humphrey, and other liberals
(including Sweetland) pushed through a strong civil rights plank at the
Democratic National Convention in Philadelphia (which Truman sup-
ported), the Alabama and Mississippi delegations walked out of the hall.
The so-called Dixiecrat rebellion led to South Carolina governor Strom

Thurmond's candidacy for president. Without the support of delegations from the Southern states, and in the absence of a liberal alternative, delegates nominated Truman as their standard-bearer.[46]

In preconvention maneuvering, Hubert Humphrey led the fight to adopt the findings of the president's Civil Rights Committee, which proposed legislation to end discrimination in employment, housing, health services, and public transportation. The report—"To Secure These Rights"—also recommended federalizing lynching as a crime and ending the poll tax. Because Humphrey and the ADA thought the president was moving too cautiously, they urged liberals to make the party's "moral position" clear. Democrats should not temporize with Southerners, but move forward on civil rights. To concede such issues, Humphrey contended, would strengthen their "reactionary Republican" opponents and the "Communist-dominated Third Party movement."[47] The convention adopted the Humphrey-led civil rights plank, and the president did likewise, issuing executive orders ending discrimination in federal civil service jobs and the armed forces.

Despite his decision to support Truman, Sweetland was pessimistic in the days leading up to the election. Because his weekly *Newport News* would be in press before Election Day, Sweetland's editorial has attributes of the *Chicago Daily Tribune*'s famous headline of November 3, 1948, "Dewey Defeats Truman." The *Tribune*'s front page featured a photograph of the victorious president, an impish smile on his face, gleefully holding the newspaper aloft. Sweetland's *Newport News* editorial reflected the author's disappointment: "History will mark Tuesday's balloting, with the election of Thomas E. Dewey to the Presidency, as the end of the Roosevelt Era." The editorial praised Truman's "valiant, bravely stubborn battle to keep high the banner of progress" and attributed his pending defeat to reactionary southern Democrats who "split away when President Truman rejected the white supremacy superstitions under which those gentry live." Communist Party support, with an "embittered Henry Wallace as their front man," would make Dewey the first president to be elected with less than 50 percent of the vote.[48]

Because the Molalla and Newport newspapers placed the Sweetlands' personal finances in crisis, Lil and Monroe survived through a variety of employment opportunities from the summer of 1949 until the purchase of the *Milwaukie Review* in the spring of 1954. In late spring 1949 Lil began

accepting contract work, the first providing campaign strategies for a public utility district in the city of Springfield. She was also seeking permanent employment with Oregon's new Fair Labor Practices Commission.[49]
Although he was no longer in charge of newspaper operations, Sweetland
still had a small income from the *Newport News*. While Goldy's correspondence with Sweetland ceased after the reshuffling of the *News* staff, Monroe
remained on cordial terms with Jebbie Davidson, a friendship that deepened when Davidson resigned from the Interior Department in 1950 and
relocated to Portland. The always gracious Davidson thanked Monroe and
Lil for their support and hoped he would have the opportunity "to repay . . .
the great obligation which I have to you all."[50]

By early 1951 the Sweetlands were living in Milwaukie, a suburb south of
Portland. With his base of operations at the Morgan Building in downtown
Portland, Monroe carried on his duties as Oregon's Democratic National
Committeeman and published the *Oregon Democrat*. To offer support for
Lil's job quest, Monroe wrote to mutual friend Ernest Norback who worked
for the Wage Stabilization Board. He cited Lil's ten years employment in fed-
eral jobs, including her time with the War Labor Board. But, he cautioned,
"she won't let me do anything through political channels to secure her
appointment," and she "doesn't want me to ask you directly." Norback, who
knew Lil when both worked in Los Angeles with the Department of Labor's
Wages and Hours Division in 1940, contacted Clark Kerr at the University of
California, Berkeley, recommending Lil for the new Wage and Stabilization
Board office in Seattle. Norback wrote Monroe, "She'd better apply at once."
His only regret—"I'd sure as hell like to have her on my staff."[51]

Norback's initiative bore fruit when the Seattle office of the Wage
Stabilization Board hired Lil as a supervisory industrial relations analyst
on August 22, 1951, at an annual salary of $7,240 (the board increased her
pay to $8, 360 the following April). The Seattle job entailed another separa-
tion for the Sweetland family, with Lil renting a small apartment in Seattle's
central business district. Barbara remained with her father in Milwaukie,
remembering that her maternal grandmother, Florence Megrath, may have
lived in the Milwaukie home. Florence, whose husband died in 1946, would
have been free to leave her New Jersey home to care for Barbara.[52]

In a letter to Oregon friend Austin Flegel in September 1951, Sweetland
called Lil's Seattle position "not the most ideal," but she hoped to transfer to
Portland before long. He told Flegel that he would be serving as a half-time

Lil, Monroe, and daughter Barbara, circa 1949–50. (Courtesy of the Oregon Historical Society)

public relations advisor with Alaska Airlines, helping the company expand its commercial and passenger services to Portland and the Northwest. After being aboard the airline's maiden flight between Portland and Anchorage, Sweetland expressed excitement about "Alaska and its possibilities."[53] The retainer with Alaska, however, would prove a mixed blessing, because the upstart company was frequently in arrears in its payments to Sweetland. Despite his busy schedule—traveling to Washington and elsewhere—Alaska never complained about his services. With his extensive political contacts in Alaska and the Northwest, Sweetland was likely ideally suited for the position.

With the 1952 primary season approaching, and expecting to run for another term as Democratic National Committeeman, Sweetland informed Alaska in February that he would need his monthly checks to fund his campaign. Winning the election with the extensive patronage that would follow would be important to the airline. His requests for payment continued through 1952 and into the spring of 1953, when Alaska finally regularized its payments. Burdened with responsibilities of legislative sessions and

Daughter Barbara, circa 1952.
(Courtesy of the Oregon
Historical Society)

publishing the *Milwaukie Review,* he asked in May 1954 that his agreement be terminated, offering, however, to assist with issues related to "Alaska statehood and Alaska development."[54]

These—again—were difficult years for the Sweetlands. The newspaper business thus far had been problematic. "Newport," Monroe admitted in a 1986 interview, "was not a happy experience." When voters elected him to the Democratic National Committee in May 1948, his life as a journalist became hectic. With Monroe's new responsibilities, Lil was the one who kept the newspaper functioning, writing articles, taking photos, and settling office disputes among employees. Although Monroe never admitted that Goldy had maneuvered his removal as publisher of the *Newport News,* there was little about the venture that was pleasant. "I was losing money, and—I didn't have any money to lose." He mentioned "an interim arrangement in Newport which was very shaky" but makes no reference to Bud Forrester taking over acting management of the paper. He told interviewer Rick Harmon: "It was a bad time."[55] His experiences with the *Milwaukie Review,* although not without problems, would be more successful and devoid of the animosity generated with the Newport enterprise.

7

The Mainstreaming of a Liberal Politician

When Monroe Sweetland began his second term as Democratic National Committeeman, he was already a well-known figure in state and national politics. Since 1948, he had energized the party's liberal base and earned the enmity of old-guard Oregon Democrats. Republicans still controlled politics in the state, but their stranglehold on state and congressional offices was eroding. Sweetland was an activist's activist, participating with the Americans for Democratic Action (ADA), the Oregon chapter of the National Association for the Advancement of Colored People (NAACP), the Portland affiliate of the Japanese American Citizens League (JACL), and the American Civil Liberties Union (ACLU) of Oregon. He had made his mark in national politics, joining liberal delegates at the Democratic National Convention in 1948 in pushing through a strong civil rights plank. He was firmly aligned with the national party's liberal wing—Hubert Humphrey, Adlai Stevenson, Paul Douglas, and others.

His political mantra—building a progressive political force in the state—dates to his experiences with the Oregon Commonwealth Federation. His strategy was to begin "at the bottom and build up strong and appealing legislative tickets." Only then was it prudent to move toward higher offices. When Democrats increased their numbers from four to ten in the Oregon Senate and from two to eleven in the House in the 1948 election, the new legislative session was notably different. One conservative Republican offered a puzzled commentary on this turn of events: "The saddest thing about Oregon's 1949 Legislature was the appearance of political partisanship. Our great tradition of non-partisanship maintained through many years lies shattered on the floor of the capitol." At the end of the 1949 session, Sweetland praised the accomplishments of the small "cohesive legislative minority." The longest legislative session in Oregon history to that date produced a functioning Fair Employment Practices Commission (FEPC), improvements in public housing laws, protections for state school lands from collusion in timber sales, and an increase in unemployment compensation. When Republican governor Douglas McKay signed the FEPC bill, he groused: "I don't believe in this sort of legislation, but everybody seems to want it."[1]

From the outset, Sweetland treated the disarray among Democrats as opportunity rather than misfortune. Oregonians, he insisted, were not conservative, but a people receptive to progressive politics. His most significant achievement as National Committeeman was Gus Solomon's appointment as judge of the United States District Court in Portland. Solomon, whose sizable legal practice was not very lucrative, acknowledged that his Jewish heritage and affiliation with the Commonwealth Federation were serious handicaps.[2] He also recognized that old-guard Democrats would present the principal roadblocks to his nomination.

Raymond Kell, Solomon's office partner, first suggested the District Court appointment to Solomon in the spring of 1948. Solomon initially thought it was a crazy idea—dealing as he was with a gauntlet of personal attacks, scrutiny of his legal career, and distractions from making a living. But Kell was persistent, indicating that it would be a big win for the progressive wing of the Democratic Party. Kell and Solomon agreed that Sweetland would be a willing advocate—and in an influential position, because the president was a Democrat and Oregon's congressional delegation were all Republicans. When Solomon discussed such an appointment with Sweetland, he told him that the nomination would have the support of Philip Parish, the editor of the *Oregonian*, and that Wayne Morse "would be very helpful."[3]

Because the Democratic National Committee (DNC) was central to any federal appointment, Sweetland provided important support for Solomon's candidacy. Sweetland was in frequent contact with William Boyle, DNC's executive secretary. He stressed to Boyle that Solomon's appointment would give "sympathetic understanding of the great legislation enacted during the past 16 years." To add credibility to the nomination, Sweetland assembled "an informal committee" of Democratic lawyers associated with the Grange, AFL, CIO, and the former head counsel of the Bonneville Power Administration. It was important, Sweetland added, that Solomon served as treasurer of the campaign placing President Truman's name on the Oregon ballot.[4]

Solomon's liberal friends provided valuable support for his pursuit of the federal district judge position. Sweetland, whose family occasionally spent weekends at the coast with Nathalie Panek and Gus and Libby Solomon, wrote Panek about Oregon's new judgeship position: "My candidate for the life job at $15,000 per annum is our familiar old friend-in-need, Gus J. Solomon." When President Truman used a recess selection to appoint Solomon to the position on October 21, 1949, Sweetland sent Panek newspaper clippings testifying to "one of the few recorded instances in politics where virtue actually had its reward."[5]

Oregonian columnist William Moyes thought the Solomon recess appointment "a hard blow" to conservative Democrats William Josslin and Walter Pearson, who both supported Earl Latourette. That Latourette "was not even being considered" testified to the conservatives' diminishing influence. While there were many "breast-beaters" claiming credit for Solomon's success, Moyes pointed out that "one man really did it—Sweetland." A companion editorial in the *Oregonian* emphasized the eroding influence of "old guard" Democrats in Oregon, thanks in part to President Truman turning to "the younger, more extreme new deal side of the Democratic Party."[6]

Democratic Party chair William Josslin proved a significant roadblock to the nomination, even when a poll of the party's central committee indicated a clear preference for Solomon. The real problem, Solomon wrote C. Girard "Jebby" Davidson, involved Josslin's bitterness "towards Monroe because he himself wanted to be recommended for the judgeship." Other than his problems with Josslin, Solomon told Davidson that he was not worried about his association with liberal organizations in the 1930s: "I certainly have no apologies for being a member of the ACLU and at the time I joined the Lawyers Guild," so did many others, including members of Josslin's legal firm.[7]

While Solomon was fending off attacks at home, Sweetland was cultivating ties at the federal level. He enlisted the support of Washington senator Warren Magnuson, a member of the Senate Judiciary Committee, informing him that Solomon was "Oregon's leading legal authority in the field of public power." Sweetland was also in contact with ACLU leader Roger Baldwin who provided him with files from the Dies Committee that exonerated the ACLU "of any Communist taint." At home, Solomon was more worried about the maneuvering of conservative Democrats who supported Earl Latourette than he was with frivolous charges that Josslin might dig up. "I would rather have an endorsement from you," he wrote Sweetland in early August, "than a thousand Pinkys."[8]

For all the praise Sweetland and his associates sent to Democrats in the nation's capital, the sniping about Solomon's left-wing activities continued through the summer and early fall of 1949. Ashley Greene and other conservative Democrats who supported Earl Latourette ultimately misplayed their cards. Fresh from his election victory in 1948, President Truman's decision to make Solomon a recess appointment in October 1949 suggests that state Democratic conservatives were no longer in step with national party leaders. Assistant Secretary of Interior Jebby Davidson let Sweetland know that Solomon's appointment "should make it much easier for us to get a united, liberal Democratic Party functioning in the state."[9]

Gus Solomon's route to the federal judgeship, biographer Harry Stein argues, was "longer, nastier, and more wearing" than the candidate imagined. Over a period of nearly eighteen months, Solomon and his supporters fought against old-guard Democrats who reached into the candidate's past to discredit him as a radical with ties to left-leaning organizations such as the National Lawyers Guild, Henry Wallace's Progressive Party, and hints of Communist Party membership. Former governor Charles Martin's Red Squad and its "spy files" from the 1930s were paraded before the Senate Judiciary Committee to highlight Solomon's perfidy. Following such fabricated testimony, the conservative, anti-Solomon *Oregon Journal* claimed in bold headlines that evidence linked Solomon to communists. Throughout Solomon's ordeal, Sweetland provided a steadying hand in the nomination fight.[10]

Monroe Sweetland's election as Democratic National Committeeman and Gus Solomon's appointment to the Federal District Court were important milestones in the ongoing struggle for control of Oregon's Democratic Party. "The battle . . . raged unabated," Robert Burton writes, "from 1946 to 1952, destroyed unity and temporarily rendered the party powerless in state politics." While they were accused of infighting and roiling party waters, insurgent Democrats were establishing a new, progressive brand of politics in the state—and restoring the viability of the two-party system.[11] This was especially unsettling to the party's anti-New Deal leadership, a group more conservative than Republicans who held statewide offices.

When the party named James Goodsell, a news reporter for the *Astorian Budget*, executive secretary in 1949, its Portland headquarters was unstaffed and housed only a few filing cabinets. The absence of functioning committees at the county and precinct level meant an enormous rebuilding job to revitalize the organization. Democratic liberals slowly began to rebuild, with Clatsop, Lane, and eastern Oregon's Baker counties leading the way. In Clatsop and Lane counties Robert Holmes and Charles Porter helped establish local chapters of the ADA, the nation's super-liberal organization. In Baker County, Al Ullman, a young businessman and real estate developer, began promoting a Columbia Valley Authority (CVA) and a proposed Hells Canyon Dam on the Snake River.[12]

In the fall elections of 1950, McCarthyism raised its ugly head in Oregon, with Democratic U.S. Senate candidate Howard Latourette leading the parade. Priding himself as "free from socialistic principles," Latourette accused Sweetland of favoring Republican incumbent Wayne Morse and torpedoing his Senate race. Liberals were following the Soviet line: "Step by step—first socialism, then enslavement through communism." Oswald West, conservative curmudgeon and former governor, indicted Sweetland for working in concert with "other red revolutionaries." In Oregon's fourth district, incumbent Republican congressman Harris Ellsworth described his contest with Democrat David Shaw as one between "Communists and fellow travelers and the rest of us."[13]

The 1950 election was another disaster for Oregon Democrats, with Republicans winning all four congressional seats and Democrats electing only Robert Thornton as attorney general. Sweetland told Washington reporter A. Robert Smith several years later that times were changing, because the Truman administration invested "time, money and effort in trying to help us." Moreover, when Latourette attacked Oregon's Democratic leadership, "most Democrats swung over to vote for Senator Morse." He believed Morse's liberalism put him "in serious trouble with the Republican rank and file," and that he would eventually move to the Democratic Party.[14]

Democratic Party infighting continued unrestrained through the early 1950s. Nicholas Granet, chair of the Multnomah County Central

Committee, charged that Sweetland's editorials in the *Oregon Democrat* were inaccurate and ignored the work of "average, traditional Democrats." Democratic state treasurer Walter Pearson joined the fray, calling for "harmony and cooperation" to avoid a repeat of the party's "very disastrous defeat" in the 1950 elections. "Slander and discord," he scolded, "will never win." In an ironic twist for one who thrived on dissension, Pearson asked party members to cooperate, to "forget petty jealousies and personal ambitions." Granet, however, made no call for party unity following the 1950 election; instead, he blamed Sweetland for the party debacle and admitted to Gus Solomon in a phone conversation that he voted for Republican Douglas McKay for governor.[15]

In an interview with the *Eugene Register-Guard* in 1952, David Epps provided insights to the "conflict between 'old line' and 'New Deal' Democrats." Epps put a different spin on the interviewer's question: "It's a struggle between the Portland boys who play politics for what's in it and people like Sweetland and a few others who think the Democratic Party ought to mean something." As for the "dearth of able candidates," Epps thought the issue would be rectified if younger progressives were able to gain control of the party and rid themselves of the old boys in Multnomah County who play "Chicago style" politics.[16]

Accusations of socialism, communism, and left-wing agendas are sprinkled across Sweetland's two campaigns for Democratic National Committeeman and his efforts with other liberals to gain control of party leadership positions. Sweetland's activism in the 1930s, with several degrees of distortion, had a habit of resurfacing when it was convenient for opponents to give events and organizations subversive meaning. His friend James Wechsler of the *New York Post*—a former communist—put the problem succinctly in his 1953 book, *The Age of Suspicion*: "We did not have the apprehension then that everything would be shadowed by the past and that we would have to spend the rest of our days defending or explaining or reciting plaintive recantations. The immediate problem seemed to be to make peace with ourselves rather than with society."[17]

Stiffening Cold War politics in Eastern Europe and the victory of the Communist Party of China in 1949 profoundly influenced Sweetland's positions on domestic policies. His correspondence, newspaper columns, and suspicions about questionable individuals appointed to state and federal offices increasingly reflected the views of a tough anticommunist. This was a dramatic shift from his pacifist, noninterventionist positions of the 1930s. A supporter of the Truman Doctrine[18] and Marshall Plan, the postwar Sweetland was wholly committed to internationalism, arguing that Robert Taft and the isolationist wing of the Republican Party were playing into the hands of international communism.

If Sweetland had an ideological home during the Cold War, it was vested in the ultraliberal, anticommunist Americans for Democratic Action. When a predecessor organization's membership lagged after the war, liberals James Loeb and Joseph Rauh (both friends of Sweetland) convened the inaugural meeting of ADA in January 1947 in Washington, D.C. Among those attending the event were several other Sweetland acquaintances: Leon Henderson, Marquis Child, Paul Porter, Walter Reuther, Jim Carey, David Dubinsky, Arthur Meier Schlesinger, Jr., Eleanor Roosevelt, Franklin D. Roosevelt, Jr., George Edwards, Hubert Humphrey, and Reinhold Niebuhr. Sweetland was named to ADA's first national board. At some point, Vi Gunther (nee Megrath), Lil's twin sister, became legislative representative and, finally, organizational secretary of ADA.[19]

One of the most telling junctures in Sweetland's evolution from pacifist, noninterventionism to full-throated, muscular internationalism rests in an op-ed piece he published in the *Oregonian* in January 1951. Responding to the newspaper's criticism of Herbert Hoover's speech, "Our National Policies in This Crisis"—where Hoover called for withdrawal from Europe and Asia and vigorous defense of the Western Hemisphere—Sweetland applauded the newspaper's censure of Hoover as necessary "to help keep our thinking steady in this heady, almost panicky hour." Sweetland called Hoover's address "the 1950 version of ostrich-isolationism," parroting the pure folly of the 1920s that "wrecked world peace" and enabled the rise of National Socialism in Germany and fascism in Italy. And then, in a ringing endorsement of the *Oregonian* editorial, he trumpeted: "we must now take the initiative in economic as well as military action," or we will "live on a fear-ridden island with inevitable disaster our only future."[20]

During the height of the Cold War, most American liberals were staunchly anticommunist, watchful of pro-Soviet sentiments at home and supportive of a strong military presence abroad. Hubert Humphrey, the "Happy Warrior," is representative of the younger generation of politicians who supported civil rights, environmental protection, progressive social and economic legislation, and federal support for education.[21] At the same time, Humphrey and other Minnesota liberals—Orville Freeman, Eugenie Anderson, and later Walter Mondale—led the move to purge the Popular Front (communists and communist sympathizers) from the Democratic Farmer-Labor Party in 1948. CIO labor leaders Walter Reuther and James Carey joined Humphrey and other liberal politicos in the fight against communist influences.[22] Before he was elected to the U.S. Senate in 1948, Humphrey was on the left wing of the Democratic Party, with domestic and foreign policy positions similar to those of Sweetland.

Fresh from his impassioned support for American internationalism, Sweetland took on other issues that divided liberals, including the opposition to admitting the People's Republic of China to the United Nations. He disagreed with Oregon Democratic chair William Josslin, who supported the admission of Red China to the world organization. Josslin's views did not reflect "the voice of the Democratic Party," Sweetland told a reporter. His dissent had the tone of a hardened Cold Warrior: "It would be disastrous to admit Red China now. Appeasement, or surrender to the Reds, would discredit both the United Nations and the United States."[23]

When "unnamed" sources began questioning the loyalty of federal employees during the height of the McCarthy hysteria, Sweetland was occasionally called on to provide information about his former colleagues with the League for Industrial Democracy (LID) during the 1930s. Chester Williams, a prominent educator, asked Sweetland in February 1951 to respond to a Loyalty Board "interrogatory" concerning their association in 1933 and 1934. Williams, who was working for the U.S. Mission to the United Nations, remembered discussions with Sweetland involving the merger of the student LID with the National Student League (NSL). Both of them, he recalled, were opposed because of the devious influences of communists in the NSL. Although this was the first time Williams had to respond to allegations that "characterized my activities as pro-Communist," he added that it would be wise for "us to be careful in our conversations to avoid reference to this matter."[24] Williams's worries testify to the widespread fear among liberals in federal employment about anonymous and unfounded rumors that threatened to derail individual careers.

Except for ambitious Republicans, few people accused President Truman of being a slacker when it came to communists. The president indulged in red-baiting against Henry Wallace's Progressive Party candidacy in 1948, and Truman furthered his anticommunist bona fides with the Truman Doctrine, the Marshall Plan, the Berlin airlift, and the Point Four program. It seems extraordinary, therefore, that Sweetland would appeal to Adrian Fisher, chief counsel to the Department of State, urging the president to deliver "a direct measure to the American people" about the importance of American world "leadership against Communism." Although Truman had already addressed the issue, Sweetland believed the president needed to underscore the nation's commitment in the fight against communism. He feared that "Communists might still be gaining in the world battle for men's allegiance."[25]

On occasion Sweetland questioned appointments to public agencies. This was the case with Ted Bloom, a young Minneapolis attorney seeking a federal job in Oregon. Because the position fell within the purview of Democratic Party patronage, Karl Rolvaag, chair of Minnesota's Democratic Farmer-Labor Party, asked Sweetland to look for such an appointment, adding that their mutual friend, Orville Freeman, had recommended Bloom. In response, Sweetland asked Rolvaag to inquire with Freeman about a report "that Bloom actively supported Henry Wallace in 1948. . . . As you and Orville know, it would completely chill my initiative . . . if he was actually a confirmed Wallace supporter or a supporter of that general point of view." Rolvaag reported that Bloom had been friendly with a "fringe group" but had never actively worked for the campaign. Moreover, Freeman thought Bloom had been naïve. Rolvaag said that he fully understood Sweetland's "hesitancy in actively supporting a Wallacite for a position in the Federal Government."[26]

The espionage trial of Julius and Ethel Rosenberg also figured into Sweetland's anticommunist calculus. When the Rosenberg's were found guilty and sentenced to death in March 1951 for passing atomic secrets to the Soviet Union, some liberals (with support from the Communist Party) launched a campaign to have their sentences commuted. The death sentence, critics asserted, was too severe. Klaus Fuchs, convicted on more serious atomic espionage charges, was sentenced in England to fourteen years in prison. Despite protests to the Eisenhower administration, the Rosenbergs were executed on June 19, 1953.[27]

Although he consistently opposed capital punishment—and sponsored a bill to ban the practice when he served in the Oregon legislature—Sweetland had little sympathy for the Rosenbergs or those appealing for a commutation of their sentences. Among those seeking to commute their death penalties was Reverend Mark Chamberlain of Oregon's Methodist Federation of Social Action. Based in Gresham, Chamberlain and a small cohort of social activists protested McCarthy-generated witch hunts during the 1950s and the Rosenberg's execution. In a letter to Chamberlain, Sweetland said he had no "sympathy with these traitors." Although he continued to oppose capital punishment, he found it "singular that out of the hundreds of capital punishment cases which might be selected, this particular unmeritorious one is taken to the bosom of your organization." Such efforts were "serving evil rather than constructive purposes." On other occasions Sweetland accused Chamberlain and the Methodist Federation of lending its good name to unworthy causes.[28]

Sweetland's attitude toward communists and communist-front organizations reflected the positions of many American liberals, people who were insecure because many of them had been involved with leftist politics in the 1930s. But their anticommunist phobia also involved, according to Chris Hedges, "a craven careerism and desire for prestige and comfort." At the national level, Minnesota senator Hubert Humphrey championed tough anticommunist legislation to protect himself from conservative attacks. Humphrey sponsored the Communist Control Act of 1954, a measure that declared the Communist Party a "clear, present, and continuing danger to the security of the United States." Humphrey's positioning, historian James Patterson argues, clearly indicates that "anti-Communist fervor was politically irresistible during these years." Sweetland's complicity likely reflected both political insecurity and a desire to protect himself from his own radical past. Ellen Schrecker writes that liberals found themselves in "a more politically exposed position." No longer positioned at the center of American politics, they had less room to maneuver.[29]

Through this period of heated anticommunist rhetoric, Sweetland attended to his responsibilities as Oregon Democratic Party National Committee man and worked closely with the state's central committee and its executive head, James Goodsell. While he worked well with Goodsell, that was not true of his relations with Multnomah County chair Nicholas Granet, who opposed most Sweetland initiatives. In May 1950, Granet sent a circular, "Machine Politics," to Democrats accusing "the Sweetland machine" of attempting to control the Democratic Party with its own handpicked candidates.[30] Even in the face of the election of liberal Democrats to state and federal offices, Granet, Thomas Mahoney, and Walter Pearson—Oregon's old-guard Democrats—would continue to pillory Sweetland's efforts.

Among Sweetland's opponents in the Democratic Party, none surpassed the invective of former governor Oswald West, who had supported Sweetland's run for Democratic National Committeeman in 1948. West stepped up his attacks in the spring of 1952 when he learned Sweetland was planning another run for the Democratic National Committee. In a widely distributed circular, the former governor attributed his previous support to his advancing years. He learned afterward that Sweetland had been registered as a member of the Socialist Party in Marion County in 1936, and "then came a greater shock (disaster)" when he read Elizabeth Dilling's *The Red Network*, a book that exposed "the Communist-Socialist world conspiracy." According to Dilling, Sweetland had worked as an organizer for the League for Industrial Democracy, an avowed communist organization.[31]

With Portland tire dealer Mike DeCicco making another run for Democratic National Committeeman, friends and newspaper editorialists came to Sweetland's defense. In a letter to Oswald West and another to the *Oregonian*, Leonard James excoriated West for citing Dilling's book as a reliable reference: "It's the first time I have ever heard of anyone of your status taking her seriously." He was surprised that Democrats "could be duped into believing any quotation from the Dilling diatribe," sixteen years after the book's publication. As an elder statesman in the Democratic Party, James accused West of joining the red-baiting attack on Sweetland.[32]

Minnie McFarland, a friend since Commonwealth days, chaired the Re-Elect Sweetland Committee. Other former Commonwealth associates supporting Sweetland included David Epps (Sweet Home), Helen Gilkey (Corvallis), Allen Hart (Portland lawyer with the Bonneville Power Administration), and J. F. Hosch (a physician, formerly from Bend, now practicing in Albany). The aged Walter Pierce also sent a letter to Democrats endorsing his reelection. Under McFarland's signature, the Re-Elect Sweetland Committee solicited financial help, highlighting the candidate as an "extraordinarily able and vigorous leader of our party."[33]

Sweetland's opponents—Granet, Pearson, and Mahoney—all supported Mike DeCicco's candidacy. Speaking to Douglas County Democrats a month before the election, State Treasurer Pearson preached harmony and told the audience that he "never attacked any *true* Democrat on a personal basis." He then proceeded to liken the Sweetland group to Russian Bolsheviks, where a tiny disciplined group gained control and ran the nation into disaster. Pearson reiterated that he was not speaking "from any personal standpoint" but in the interests of Oregon Democrats. "There is no room in our party for Communists or Socialists," he concluded. Sweetland, who was in the audience, said nothing during the event, but later told a reporter that Pearson had clearly linked himself with the Portland cabal of DeCicco and Mahoney and its disruptive tactics.[34]

The *Oregonian*, which had always treated Sweetland as a person of integrity, defended his record and urged voters to base their judgment on his achievements:

> One of the nastiest campaigns in this election is being waged
> against the Democratic national committeeman, Monroe
> Sweetland, whose enemies have descended to a new low in
> vituperation. If some of the material circulated could be believed,
> Mr. Sweetland should be hanged from the nearest limb. Mr.
> Sweetland was a Socialist in his student days, and that has been
> the takeoff point. We find nothing in his record, however, which
> is dishonorable or detrimental to the party he represents. His
> mistake, from the standpoint of his enemies, seems to be that he
> has revived the Democratic party in Oregon and gained some
> influence in Washington, D.C.[35]

In the May primary, Democrats gave Sweetland an overwhelming endorsement (Sweetland, 100,400; DeCicco, 46,100). In his previous campaign, he had won by a mere 2,800 votes statewide, with DeCicco carrying Multnomah County by 4,000 votes. Sweetland won every county in the state in 1952 and carried Multnomah County with a 2.5 to 1 majority. Sweetland's most vitriolic opponent, Oswald West, sent him a postcard acknowledging his win: "Congratulations upon the whopping vote you received in your race for Democratic National Committeeman." He added, "I didn't vote for either you or your opponent."[36]

Bob Frazier, editorial page editor of the *Eugene Register-Guard*, offered the most thoughtful sentiments, "the kind of letter no political writer should write. Hereafter I shall deny I ever wrote it." Sweetland's victory over DeCicco was significant, because "if Mike had won the Democrats of Oregon might just as well have thrown in the j—k." Frazier congratulated Sweetland and "Oregon Democrats, of which I am not one except in spirit." In a return note, Sweetland attributed much of his success in Lane County to "your handiwork." He thought his reelection was "a mandate for liberal policies and a liberal Democratic Party." [37]

What is surprising through the 1952 election season is the paucity of material in the Sweetland Papers related to his election to the Oregon House in the November balloting. Nominated in the Democratic primary through write-in votes, Sweetland narrowly won the traditionally Republican Clackamas County seat. The addition of another Democrat in the House, however, merely boosted the party's numbers to nine in the sixty-member chamber. Elsewhere the party fared poorly, losing both the second and third congressional districts, and secretary of state candidate Edith Green lost a close race to Republican Earl Newbry. Sweetland took quiet delight, however, in Tom Mahoney's defeat for reelection to the Oregon Senate and Walter Pearson's losing bid for another four-year term as state treasurer.[38] Sweetland's election to the House placed him alongside young Republican Mark Hatfield as another liberal voice in the legislature.

An exchange of correspondence with Jack Churchill, a Ph.D. candidate at Harvard University, offers insights to Sweetland's reflections on state and national politics following the 1952 election. Churchill offered suggestions for 1954 and 1956, especially "grooming someone" to run against Oregon's incumbent U.S. senator Guy Cordon. He suggested Neuberger as "the best man," especially if he "cultivated down state support."[39] Sweetland responded to Churchill's query about liberal Republican Wayne Morse, indicating that Morse had "no other future than to come into the Democratic Party before 1956." And in a refrain close to his working politics for nearly two decades, Sweetland advised Churchill that Democrats should "make 18-year old voting a part of our national program."[40]

If the office of Democratic National Committeeman gave Sweetland considerable influence in Oregon politics, the position presented similar opportunities at the national level where he had established himself as a significant player. He earned Hubert Humphrey's lasting friendship when he helped push through a civil rights plank at the Democratic Party nominating convention in July 1948. The move toward the 1952 presidential election, with seemingly open fields in both parties, presented a problem for all Democrats: reelecting President Truman, General Dwight Eisenhower's candidacy as a Democrat, versus the prospects of Tennessee senator Estes Kefauver or Illinois governor Adlai Stevenson.

Truman's candidacy quickly resolved itself when ADA's Vi Gunther told Sweetland in January that Truman would not be a candidate. The president promised to make a decision before February 6, according to Gunther, and he had made no effort to keep his name on the Minnesota primary ballot, where Hubert Humphrey was running as a favorite son. The ADA office, she reported, was doing its "damndest to stir up interest in Stevenson." Candidate Kefauver, she wrote, "appeals not at all to me." He was "terribly unorganized" and "had almost exclusively Dixiecrats (complete with coonskin caps)" when he opened his New York City office.[41]

With a Truman redux in his rearview mirror, Sweetland wasted little time jumping aboard the liberal's great hope, Adlai Stevenson, the cerebral and articulate governor of Illinois. He fired off a letter to the governor's assistant, Richard Nelson, informing him of the successful signature push in Oregon to place Stevenson's name on the primary ballot. Sweetland suggested Jebby Davidson as interim manager of the Oregon Stevenson for President Committee and asked if Stevenson would join Estes Kefauver as a speaker at Oregon Democratic Party's Jefferson-Jackson Day Dinner. "Everyone who knows both candidates agrees that the Governor makes a much better impression."[42]

In the weeks before the Chicago convention, the effusive Hubert Humphrey—always lobbying for liberal positions in the party platform—praised Sweetland's letter to Democrats for emphasizing the importance of choosing a liberal "who can ably represent our platform." On behalf of ADA, Humphrey suggested that Sweetland visit state delegations at the convention to gather support for a liberal platform. Vi Gunther assigned Sweetland a suite in Chicago's Congress Hotel to host meetings. "Someone like you, who is close to and known by all the organizational as well as the Congressional leaders," she thought, should have "his own hotel space."[43]

In carrying forth his ADA mission, Sweetland contacted delegates from western states to coordinate strategies on natural resources and statehood for Alaska and Hawaii. He expected greater difficulty in reaching agreement on the civil rights plank. Civil rights in the western states, he reminded California delegate John Despol, included Hispanic, Japanese, and Chinese citizens, American Indians, and African Americans. To Jack Arvey of Illinois, he cited the "reenactment of the civil rights formula of 1948" as a major objective. It was important to Asian policy and to "the Mexican and Oriental minorities of our region."[44]

In a note updating Hubert Humphrey on his preconvention effort, Sweetland reported that he was making a special endeavor to provide a "western accent to the civil rights fight, emphasizing the Mexican, Indian and Oriental minorities as well as the importance of civil rights in the Pacific area and Asia." He wrote Governor Stevenson, who had been avoiding the spotlight, urging him to declare his candidacy for president. Stevenson appreciated the "kind letter," but hoped, "literally praying on bended knee—that your designs will come to naught. Forgive me, but even the 'drooping Kansas sunflower' does not distract me from my job here, which continues to preoccupy all my time, attention and hopes."[45]

When the Democratic National Committee met on July 19, Sweetland joined a move to prevent Southern delegates from being seated unless they committed their support to the convention's presidential nominee. He also participated with a bloc of delegates—the Western States Conference—seeking approval of a "liberal" platform involving issues important to the region. The group designated Washington senator Warren Magnuson to carry the fight to the platform committee. The conference endorsed Sweetland's proposal to include a measure in the platform calling for an end to the Senate's "anti-Democratic" rules on filibustering, practices that allowed Southern senators to kill civil rights legislation through endless debate.[46] Sweetland's initiative did not make it into the platform.

Liberals who promoted Adlai Stevenson as a standard-bearer for liberalism may have been engaging in self-deception. To be sure, Stevenson was an internationalist, an assistant to Navy secretary Frank Knox from 1941 to 1944 and special assistant to Secretary of State Edward Stettinius in 1945, where he assisted with the organizational meeting of the United Nations in San Francisco and then served the United States delegation to the UN in various advisory capacities. Upset with corruption in his home state of Illinois, he ran for governor in 1948, winning with the largest margin in the state's history. Both business and labor praised his tenure for cleansing corruption from government and for being an able administrator. His campaign for president in 1952, however, differed little from Eisenhower's. He was a full-blown Cold Warrior, opposed public housing and "socialized medicine," and waffled on repeal of the Taft-Hartley Act. Historian James Patterson provides a fitting summary to Stevenson's candidacy: "liberal Democrats loved Stevenson—this is not too strong a verb—because he seemed to be everything that Eisenhower was not."[47]

Hubert Humphrey and other liberals, who wanted a civil rights plank in the 1952 platform, left Chicago empty-handed. To avoid another Dixiecrat walkout, delegates nominated Alabama senator John Sparkman, a conservative and segregationist, as Stevenson's running mate. With its customary litany of platitudes, the party platform committed Democrats to legislation that would act to "perfect existing Federal civil rights statutes and to strengthen the administrative machinery for the protection of civil rights." Irving Howe, founder of Democratic Socialists of America, cast a jaundiced eye toward Stevenson's campaign, concluding that his enthusiasts represented "Ikeism . . . with a touch of literacy and intelligence."[48]

When he left the convention, Sweetland was assured that Democrats were not "going to write Oregon off as expendable this year as they did in 1948." Monroe, who had traveled to Chicago with Lil, returned home "full of jubilation and high enthusiasm." He used those words in a letter to Stevenson to express his "eagerness to get to the big job between now and November 4." He added some housekeeping suggestions—appointing a party chair reflecting "your new leadership" and a more inspiring publicity unit. And then he offered a Sweetland staple: "more extensive concentration must be given the registration of voters."[49]

Despite the party's timid commitment to civil rights in 1952, Humphrey praised Sweetland for his work at the Chicago convention. Sweetland's travels around the West "bore fruit" in the "liberal victory at the convention," Humphrey exclaimed. Oregon's importance to the Stevenson campaign, however, proved problematic, with Stevenson's high command determining that he had little chance against Eisenhower in Oregon. Washington correspondent A. Robert Smith observed that party officials were not planning to spend time and money on Oregon's six electoral votes. And then in mid-October, Oregon senator Wayne Morse dropped a political bombshell, charging that Eisenhower had made "unconscionable compromises with

Monroe Sweetland, publisher and editor of the Milwaukie Review, 1959. Courtesy of the Oregon Historical Society)

the reactionaries in the Republican Party." When Morse announced that he would support Stevenson, an elated Sweetland told a reporter: "'Principle above politics' is Senator Morse's slogan and he is living up to it."[50]

As the campaign moved toward its November conclusion, Sweetland and Oregon Democratic Party chair Howard Morgan greeted Stevenson's running mate, Senator John Sparkman, at the Eugene airport. After a parade in Eugene, Sparkman traveled to Portland for more campaigning. The Democratic election season concluded with Hubert Humphrey making a visit to Portland. Although national polls predicted an Eisenhower victory, the results were striking, with Eisenhower winning 33.9 million votes to 27.3 million for Stevenson and winning the Electoral College vote 442 to 89. Eisenhower garnered 420,815 votes to Stevenson's 270,579 in Oregon. Despite the Republican win, campaign manager Wilson Wyatt expressed his gratitude to Sweetland for the politicking "done under your direction."[51]

After nearly twenty years of attempting to reform Oregon's political landscape, Monroe Sweetland's election to the legislature placed him in a position to directly shape public policy. During the next ten years in the House and Senate, he would pursue an array of liberal policies—maintaining the confidentiality of people on welfare, opposing anti-union, right-to-work legislation, preventing utilities from overcharging consumers, prohibiting discrimination in places of public accommodation, supporting civil rights in the workplace, banning discrimination in housing, liberalizing voting laws, passing an equal pay law (irrespective of sex), and supporting better pay for state workers. While Sweetland was carrying out his legislative responsibilities, he and Lil were also publishing the *Milwaukie Review*, a weekly newspaper that suffered fewer financial troubles than the Newport enterprise. In this new world of more stable finances and work expectations, Lil gave birth to a second daughter, red-headed Rebecca, on October 7, 1953.

8

The World of Legislative Politics

The Oregon legislative session of 1953 witnessed the appearance of a new liberal voice in the House of Representatives. From the opening bell until the legislature adjourned on April 21, Monroe Sweetland introduced and supported measures consistent with positions he had championed since his days with the Oregon Commonwealth Federation. There was a difference, however, because now he was an elected member of the legislature with responsibilities to his constituents in Clackamas County. He was no longer an interest group lobbying for or against particular bills—but rather an insider engaged in the rough-and-tumble world of politics. There were other dissimilarities. Where Commonwealth functioned with a degree of consensus on important issues, Oregon's Democratic Party was vastly outnumbered in both legislative bodies in 1953—26 to 4 in the Senate and 51 to 9 in the House.[1] Sweetland's already considerable reputation would be tested in an adverse political environment.

First among the hot-button issues before the legislature was House bill (HB321) requiring county welfare officials to make public the names and addresses of people on public assistance. Organizations such as the Oregon chapter of the American Association of Social Workers opposed the legislation, while county commissioners and most legislative Republicans favored the bill. Sweetland argued that such legislation was "part of a nation-wide effort to intimidate the helpless and indigent and to discredit the general program of public assistance."[2] At the county level, welfare commissions almost unanimously supported the measure, contending that children of aging parents were using the dependence clause in the welfare law to escape responsibility for supporting their parents. Sweetland made clear to his own Clackamas County Welfare Commission that he opposed public access to the rolls, because it was cruel "to make public the names of the old folks and families who are your unfortunate clients." He reminded the commission that the county protected citizens "who pay income taxes and have property on the rolls from the prying eyes of our neighbors."[3]

People receiving public assistance sent Sweetland heartrending letters, one woman writing that "through honest poverty and illness," she and her husband "happen to be on this roll." She could not understand "why we must have our names open for gossip and jealous neighbors as if we were on parole or as if afflicted with the 'Red Bug' of Communism." When the Joint Ways and Means Subcommittee held a hearing on the bill, some 350 people turned out in Salem, with critics charging that the measure was discriminatory and an invasion of privacy. A spokesman for the Oregon Farmers' Union denounced the bill as "an effort to intimidate persons entitled to assistance."[4]

When the bill passed both houses and was sent to Governor Paul Patterson for his signature, Senator Richard Neuberger raised a constitutional question about the welfare rolls as public records. How, he asked, does the bill's provision prohibiting newspapers and radio stations from publishing the names meet the requirements of Article 1, Section 8 of the Oregon Constitution that no law shall restrict the "right to speak, write or print freely on any subject whatsoever."[5] Because proponents worried that Neuberger might have a solid argument, the legislature removed the clause prohibiting newspapers and radio stations from publishing the lists, but included an amendment banning the use of welfare lists for political or commercial ends. Oregon's welfare program now mandated that children of parents on welfare should contribute if they were able to do so. While the measure was less punitive, Sweetland grumbled that deserving people "badly in need of help [would be] . . . kept off the rolls by pride and social pressure."[6]

An even more controversial issue before the session was a "right-to-work" bill that would drastically curb the power and influence of labor unions. Right-to-work measures proliferated across the nation in the wake of the labor-restrictive Taft-Hartley Law of 1947 and its controversial Section 14b, authorizing states to prohibit union shops (requiring employees to join unions as a condition of employment). States passing right-to-work laws imposed major barriers to union organizing. Oregon's House Bill 298, therefore, presented a significant threat to organized labor. As one of only nine

Democrats in the sixty-seat House, supporters of organized labor inundated Sweetland with letters asking him to do everything possible to defeat the measure.[7]

Bitter opposition from labor and some segments of the business community prompted the House Labor and Industries Committee to remove a clause in HB 298 that would have directly threatened union shops. The *Oregonian* called the move "a bow to expediency," acknowledging "that the union shop is firmly established—and sanctioned by federal law—and that outlawing it would cause serious discord, strikes, and loss of production." The *Oregonian* supported a provision in the bill prohibiting unions from using pickets to coerce employees to join unions, but the newspaper questioned the measure's constitutionality, because restricting picketing might be construed as abridging freedom of speech. A U.S. Supreme Court decision a few days later altered those dynamics when it upheld a ban on picketing in a right-to-work law in Virginia. Because there were direct parallels between Virginia's law and HB 298, the *Oregonian* did not believe the Oregon bill would infringe on the "legitimate organizational privileges of unions." In the end, labor lost its legislative struggle to defeat the ban on picketing in union organizing drives.[8] Although state and federal legislation would continue to erode union power, Oregon would never join the right-to-work states.

In the Oregon legislature, Sweetland had the opportunity to directly initiate and influence civil rights legislation. As executive secretary of the Oregon Commonwealth Federation, he had lobbied previous legislatures to pass laws prohibiting discrimination in restaurants and hotel accommodations. As a publisher and editor of newspapers, he consistently opposed discriminatory practices against Jews, racial minorities, women, and the lower classes. Speaking as an editor and businessman at Portland's Bethel Church in August 1950, he argued that "discrimination in public places is inconvenient and offensive in the daily course of business." It was outrageous that anyone would be turned away from a luncheon or the use of a conference room because of the color of their skin. Freedom, he insisted, was indivisible.[9]

Early in the session Sweetland joined in sponsoring Senate Bill 169, which provided all citizens with equal access to public accommodations in hotels, restaurants, movies, dance halls, swimming pools, and skating rinks. Otto Rutherford, head of the Portland chapter of the NAACP, spoke on behalf of the civil rights bill, as did Sweetland's attorney friends, George Dysart and Don Willner. Restaurants and hoteliers presented most of the opposition to the measure, with Lafe Compton of Coos Bay's Chandler Hotel telling Sweetland that such legislation would make it difficult for proprietors to maintain order in their establishments when people abused or abridged the rights of others. The legislation "will only stimulate race prejudice and be used to vent personal animosities as the result of minor grievances."[10]

In a testimony before a legislative committee, a consortium of lodging and beverage associations presented a brief opposing the measure. In states where such legislation had passed, "local pressure groups" had unfairly given the impression that the public wholeheartedly supported the bills. To avoid the onus of foisting such a decree on the people of Oregon, the lodging and beverage group urged that the bill should contain a clause "referring the matter to the people for their vote."[11] Although letters pro and con accumulated in his mailbox, Sweetland was optimistic that SB 169 would pass. Speaking before Portland's NAACP, Sweetland observed that the chances of success were better than at any time since 1914 when civil rights legislation was first introduced. While he was certain the bill would emerge from the Senate without amendment, he was less sure of the House.[12]

The civil rights bill cleared the Senate without a stipulation referring it to voters. In a supporting editorial, the *Oregonian* called SB 169 "fundamentally an educational measure," paralleling similar laws in California and Washington where "the bars of discrimination have been dropped in compliance with the spirit of the act." The debates in the House, however, were heated, with packed galleries representing the Urban League of Portland, the NAACP, and allied groups on one side, and restaurant and lodging interests on the other. The League of Women Voters arranged a special caravan to the state capitol to support the bill. House members subsequently approved the Senate version without amendment and sent it to Governor Paul Patterson for his signature.[13]

Edwin Berry, executive secretary to the Urban League of Portland, paid tribute to the many organizations and individuals deserving credit for the passage of the civil rights law. He singled out for special praise the Oregon Committee for Equal Rights and its chair, E. J. "Bill" Ireland, a Molalla businessman and personal friend to Monroe Sweetland. "Our state becomes a better and finer place because of this," he told the *Oregonian*. In a similar note to Sweetland, Berry noted that his hard work for the passage of SB 169 would be "long remembered." Governor Patterson signed the measure on April 29, making it illegal for public dining, lodging, and entertainment venues to discriminate on the basis of race, religion, or place of national origin. Although Portland Episcopal Church rector Elbert D. Riddick launched an initiative petition to refer the law to voters, the drive faltered and Riddick abandoned the effort.[14]

With three other Democratic legislators, Sweetland introduced House Joint Resolution No. 7 to place a constitutional amendment on the ballot to lower the voting age to eighteen. When the House committee on state and federal affairs hosted a Saturday hearing in Salem to solicit public input, students, teachers, and veterans groups turned out in large numbers. Sweetland pointed to the state of Georgia where eighteen-year-olds had the right to vote and to South Dakota where voters turned back a similar measure by only 260 votes in an election involving 300,000 ballots. Although the resolution failed to move beyond the discussion stage, Sweetland would be more deeply involved at the national level when the National Education Association made a major push for the age-eighteen vote in the late 1960s.[15]

Facing vastly superior Republican numbers in the House, Sweetland had proven himself a political force in the legislature. In the give-and-take of legislative maneuvering, he offered a powerful liberal voice for progressive measures related to civil rights, labor, and social justice. The *Oregonian* regularly sought his opinion on bills moving through the legislature. One of his strengths—reflecting experiences with the League for Industrial Democracy in the 1930s—was his ability to see Oregon issues in a broader national, even global context. Moreover, his responsibilities as Democratic National Committeeman placed him in contact with national policy agendas, and his association with ADA further sharpened and enhanced the liberal perspective he brought to legislative deliberations.

After the legislature adjourned, Sweetland traveled east to seek family support for another weekly newspaper venture, the *Milwaukie Review*. He wrote to newspaperman Steve "Bud" Forrester about his "embarrassing and difficult choice" of seeking assistance "from the family in the East." Sweetland learned about the sale of the newspaper from a print salesman who sold newsprint to the *Newport News*. Even then, the negotiations for the *Review* extended over several months when the cautious publisher, Ed Donnelly, was uncertain about an appropriate sales price. Before agreeing to the purchase, Sweetland carefully gathered information about the growing community of Milwaukie—the absence of a weekly competitor, a population "strongly Democratic," undeveloped industrial sites, adequate transportation systems, and the newspaper's building, plant and equipment, and staff. Donnelly—asthmatic, overweight, and advised to move to a dryer climate—was asking between $52,000 and $57,000, with $17,000 down and monthly payments of about $200. Sweetland stalled on the purchase, hoping that Donnelly would lower the price. If the purchase went through, he planned to publish the *Oregon Democrat* in the same plant and convert the "little magazine from a hard struggle to a positive asset economically."[16]

When the Sweetlands finally acquired the *Milwaukie Review*, the purchase involved considerable personal risk, involving Monroe mortgaging his interest in his recently deceased father's estate to the tune of $40,000. In scholarship information submitted to Mills College where daughter Barbara was a student, Lil explained that the reorganization of their new business explained the family's "abnormally low income." She listed their "combined gross income for 1954 at $2,955 from two sources, the weekly newspaper and her husband's nominal salary of $600 as a state legislator. In addition to Barbara, she listed her mother, Florence (who was living in their home), and sixteen-month-old Rebecca, as dependents. The purchase of the *Review* in March 1954 involved Sweetland acquiring the Prineville *Central Oregonian* from L. R. Batman and then exchanging that contract with Ed Donnelly for the *Review*. Both weeklies were now under new ownership—Donnelly, following doctor's orders, was in a drier clime east of the Cascades and Sweetland was the owner of a newspaper close to the center of Oregon's political influence and population base.[17]

There was more to the story of acquiring the *Milwaukie Review* than simply mortgaging Monroe's inheritance. Jebby Davidson, an investor in the Newport venture, provided interim financial support while the George Sweetland estate was being settled. Sweetland, who needed help meeting a $24,000 payment due on June 1, 1954, worked out an agreement whereby Davidson would receive secured *Milwaukie Review* bonds "for the difference between the amount you can pay and the $24,000." In the interim, Davidson congratulated Monroe and Lil for a copy of the *Review*, its appearance, "its substance, and even more, the number of ads." In a separate memorandum to a financial officer, Davidson revealed his faith in the new enterprise:[18]

> With reference to the assignment from Monroe, I assume the note is sufficient. Neither he nor I want this instrument of record and I am sure that everyone connected with the transaction realizes that the note which I hold from Monroe represents my advance to him for acquisition of the *Milwaukie Review*.

The Sweetlands assumed control of the *Review* on March 29, 1954, and published their first issue on April 1. Because of their proximity to Portland, the new owners of the weekly disavowed any competition with the city's two large-circulation dailies. As a "home-town weekly," their task was to report accurately the life of Milwaukie and its satellite communities. They believed it important "to foster and promote a conscious pride in our city" and to promote and foster its "values and virtues." The Sweetlands announced that the *Review* would be a mirror and sounding board for the community and asked citizens for their comments. They promised to strengthen Milwaukie's schools, churches, social organizations, and industries.[19]

From all accounts, the *Milwaukie Review* operation began efficiently; Lil managed the shop, and Ed Donnelly's small staff stayed on with the new owners. While Lil was at the *Review* office, her mother, Florence ("Nanna") provided day care for Rebecca. The *Review* also became a union shop, joining the Oregon City *Enterprise Courier* as the second unionized printing plant in Clackamas County. Annie Chambers, secretary of the Hotel and Restaurant Employees and Bartenders International Union trusted that there would be sufficient demand for printing work to repay the Sweetlands for their "efforts to secure the union label." Monroe told Chambers that the *Review* would strive to show "that labor and management can get along better by mutual agreement and mutual respect."[20]

The new Eisenhower administration sharply reduced Sweetland's patronage responsibilities, freeing time for attending to the dearth of Democratic office holders at home. Always on the alert for progressive young liberals, he had been corresponding since 1950 with two Harvard Law School graduates, Charles O. Porter and Donald Willner, who would be significant players in Oregon's Democratic Party. While he scoured the state for viable candidates in 1954, friends urged him to run for the state's third congressional seat, a sinecure for Republicans since Nan Wood Honeyman's defeat in 1938. Such a suggestion would require Sweetland to move from his home (and business) in Milwaukie, both in the first district. His most significant accomplishment in 1954 was finding viable and attractive candidates to run for the state legislature. The November election would show dramatic successes for the party across the board—in the legislature, in the congressional races, and in Democrats capturing a U.S. Senate seat for the first time in forty years.

Despite the seemingly bright prospects for Democrats in 1954, petty jealousies and personal ambitions threatened the party's chances (although this time liberals were at the center of the discord). In the midst of those machinations was Oregon Democratic Party chair Howard Morgan, who had targeted Edith Green for Oregon's third district congressional seat. When newspaper rumors circulated that Sweetland might seek the same office, Morgan caustically remarked to a reporter the irony that a Democratic Party official seeking quality candidates for the third district race should find the question answered when he stood before his shaving mirror. Whether Morgan's deliberate baiting rankled Sweetland is unknown; however, the national committeeman issued a simultaneous announcement: "I will not be a candidate for federal office this year." In a February letter to Senator Wayne Morse, Sweetland remarked about the congressional district races: "It looks like Henry Hess in the 3rd (much as I would have liked to have made the race, but have stayed out in deference to the wishes of Dick and Howard). No one yet against Norblad in the 1st—and it won't be me!"[21]

When Democratic National Committee chair Stephen Mitchell visited Oregon, he further roiled party waters when he urged Henry Hess to run for governor rather than challenge Green for the third district congressional seat. Hess, who was retiring as U.S. District Attorney for Oregon, told a reporter that he was still undecided about entering politics. The *Oregonian* suspected that state Democratic chair Howard Morgan encouraged Mitchell to intervene in the Oregon primary to assure Green's nomination. When Morgan was asked if he had influenced Mitchell's suggestion, he replied, "No comment." The *Oregonian* reiterated that Morgan strongly opposed Sweetland filing for the third district seat. Left unsaid again in Morgan's worries was the reality that the Clackamas Democrat's home and business were both in the first district.[22]

In the midst of this political jockeying, Sweetland ended further specu-
lation about his options when he filed as Democratic candidate for Oregon's
eleventh senatorial district, setting up a campaign against Republican
incumbent Howard Belton. Leading up to the May primary, Sweetland
and Morgan plumbed the state seeking good candidates for legislative
races. Sweetland reported in June that Democrats had achieved significant
successes and would present fifty-five candidates for the sixty-seat House.
Among the aspirants was Medford's Robert Duncan, soon to become a
major player in Democratic politics. On the Senate side, Democrats would
field thirteen candidates for seventeen open seats.[23]

After hinting that he would run for a major office, state senator Richard
Neuberger took the plunge to challenge sixty-seven-year-old Guy Cordon
for the U.S. Senate. Chair of the powerful Senate Interior Committee,
Cordon would be a formidable opponent for the articulate forty-one-year-
old Neuberger. In the primary elections, Democrats nominated Edith Green
for the third congressional district, with Henry Hess deciding to return
to private practice. Journalist and radio commentator Tom McCall, who
defeated longtime Republican incumbent Homer Angell in the primary,
would be Green's opponent in the fall. Newcomer Charles Porter would
take on incumbent Harris Ellsworth in the fourth district and Baker City
Democrat Al Ullman would challenge incumbent Republican Sam Coon in
the second district. Former Portland mayor Joseph Carson ran unopposed
to face Republican governor Paul Patterson in the general election.[24]

The Cordon-Neuberger campaign was one of the most closely
watched Senate races in the nation. The energetic Neuberger appeared to
take an early lead, spending much of his time speaking to audiences in the
southern Willamette Valley, southern Oregon, and communities east of
the Cascades. Republican polling in early October showed Cordon with a
slight edge and indicated that all four Republican congressional candidates
were leading as well. But the Senate contest dominated Oregon's political
news. Neuberger charged that Eisenhower-administration policies were
giving away Oregon's natural resources, with his criticism directed at the
administration's "partnership plan" (public/private cooperation) for river
development. Cordon defended his support for Idaho Power Company's
dam-building projects on the middle Snake River. At the dedication of
McNary Dam in October, President Eisenhower told the press that he
supported the reelection of "my good friend, Guy Cordon." When Vice

President Richard Nixon visited Oregon a week later, he referred to Neuberger as a "left-wing Democrat."[25]

The *Oregonian* noticed several "campaign curiosities" in the fall contests, its election-eve editorial pointing to the irony of former Portland mayor Joseph Carson (Democratic candidate for governor) climbing "into bed with his severest critics of a few years back, Monroe Sweetland and Richard Neuberger." An even greater paradox was Senator Wayne Morse, who once believed it an "ethical duty" to support Republican reactionaries, "out beating the drums for Democrat Neuberger." The editorial quoted the Eugene *Register-Guard's* William Tugman's worry about Oregon sending "two 'prima-donnas' to the Senate." The *Oregonian* also pointed to Neuberger's contradictions—once attempting to block construction of The Dalles Dam to save Celilo Falls and now supporting full development of the Columbia River.[26] And then to everyone's relief, the voters trekked to the polls.

Two days after the November 2 election, Portland's *Oregon Journal* headlined its final edition, "Neuberger Wins In Late Spurt." A photo shows an ebullient Richard Neuberger shaking hands with grinning Democratic National Committeeman Monroe Sweetland. With the support of independent Wayne Morse, who promised to caucus with Democrats, Neuberger's narrow win gave Democrats control of the U.S. Senate. His victory was auspicious for Oregon Democrats who had not elected a U.S. senator since Harry Lane in 1914. There were other Democratic successes in Oregon, chiefly Edith Green's narrow win in the third congressional district over Tom McCall.[27] In Oregon's fourth district, Republican Sam Coon won a close race over young liberal Democrat Al Ullman, and Governor Paul Patterson easily prevailed over Joseph Carson in the gubernatorial contest. Democrats made significant gains in the legislature, especially in the House where the party increased its seats from nine to twenty-five. Its successes in the Senate were modest—from four to six members—with Sweetland easily defeating Howard Belton. Another liberal voice moving from the House to the Senate was Republican Mark Hatfield.[28]

In his first news conference after the election, Neuberger remarked that Democratic gains in the House had "cracked the one party legislature in Oregon." With Wayne Morse's party affiliation still in limbo and the senator up for reelection in 1956, the *New York Times* speculated about Republicans who might run against Morse. Former governor Charles Sprague, a liberal

Republican, observed that if Morse filed as a Democrat, he would win. But it was the Oregon Democratic Party's significant gains that intrigued the *Times*. This was a "victory for a 'young Turk' group," especially "the three muske-teers"—Richard Neuberger, Howard Morgan, and Monroe Sweetland.[29]

In an interview published in the *Oregon Historical Quarterly* in 1994, Howard Morgan took outsized credit for maneuvering the Democratic Party's major victories in 1954. Morgan's claim to the contrary, people long familiar with Oregon's politics give most of the credit to Sweetland, a person not inclined to sing his own praises. For Sweetland, Democratic Party successes reflected years of hard work and pursuing liberal positions. "We are a party," he wrote in the *Oregon Democrat*, "which is in politics to achieve a program, and get-ting our men and women elected is only our starting point."[30] Among the party faithful, Sweetland's focus on issues of public power, equal rights for women and minorities, and fair wage and housing legislation invigorated the party with a sense of reason and purpose.

Eleanor Forrester—wife to Bud, who briefly managed the troubled *Newport News*—wrote for both Forresters in the aftermath of the November election to commend Sweetland for the way his "good efforts over several years have finally paid off."[31] Cornelius Bateson, who served in the House and later as head of the Oregon Health Division, attributed Democratic Party successes to Sweetland's decision "to stand for national committee-man and run the Mahoney-DeCicco gang out." Without that effort, "Dick would never have been a candidate." Bateson credited Sweetland with lever-aging precinct workers to do the hard work of getting out the vote. H.R. Glascock, a friend from the 1930s, applauded Sweetland for restoring "lib-eralism to the Democratic party in Oregon. . . . You have recruited first-rate new blood in place of the reactionary party leaders who had made the party a shabby and disreputable counter-part of the GOP. . . . I know of no one else in the state who could have done it."[32]

Those closer to Monroe, wife Lil and longtime friend Nathalie Panek, provided strikingly different assessments of the 1954 election. Panek, who was living in Los Angeles and between jobs in late 1954, wrote with "mixed feelings" when she learned Neuberger had defeated Cordon. She was proud of Oregon for trending Democratic but infuriated that no congressional seat came through for Sweetland. With her penchant for straight talk, she found it fascinating "that the biggest ego in the U.S. should be put by fate in such an ego-satisfying position." She was "glad, however, that Oregon has a Democratic senator." Panek thought Sweetland should have made a run for Congress in 1954 and urged him to run in 1956—"Please don't be a shrinking violet—go after it." While he appreciated Panek's advice, Sweetland reminded her that voters elected Edith Green from Portland's third district and assured her that she would be "a very good Congresswoman."[33]

Lil was ambivalent about the November election. In a letter to Barbara at Mills College, she praised the Democratic Party's fortunes, Neuberger's "breathtaking" victory, Edith Green's election, and "Monroe . . . beating even old Howard Belton, Mr. Republican himself in this Republican county." While she was proud of Monroe's success, the dirty campaign waged last spring "by some of our democratic friends, including as you know RLN,"[34] still offended her:

> Dick will make a good and possibly great U.S. Senator but I shall
> always remember, I hope without rancor, that he got there by
> planting one foot firmly on Monroe's neck and saying Down Boy
> or I won't play—perhaps "greatness" will make him less oblivious
> of the careers and welfare of others—I am amused that the dirty
> radical who would ruin RLN's chance of election was the top
> vote getter in Republican Clackamas county where everything
> in the book including the charge of "communist" was thrown at
> him—in Multnomah county for Congress with its heavy labor
> and democratic majorities there is no question . . . that Monroe
> would have done much better—however all that is water under
> the bridge and Monroe came through the whole experience with
> flying colors—and, like Monroe, with no ill will or even much
> remembrance of the incredible betrayal he suffered at the hands of
> his friends.

Lil's allusion—"planting one foot firmly on Monroe's neck"—referred to Neuberger's threat (delivered through Howard Morgan) that he would find a candidate who would beat Sweetland in the primary should he file as a congressional candidate. Because of his affiliation with the League for Industrial Democracy and the Socialist Party during the 1930s, Neuberger feared that a Sweetland run for Congress would invite charges of communism and radicalism upon the entire Democratic ticket. In an interview published in the *Oregon Historical Quarterly*, Morgan said he told Neuberger "if it comes to that, we can kiss the whole election good-bye because that will split the Multnomah County Democrats right down the middle." What followed was Morgan planting the story about the party official finding the "ideal candidate" while shaving one morning. Although Sweetland's name was never mentioned, Morgan told an interviewer nearly four decades later that it would have been impossible for Sweetland to seek a congressional seat "without acute embarrassment."[35]

There is a remarkably self-serving tone to Morgan's telling of those long-ago events. Despite taking full credit for engineering the Democratic victories, he remembered being "saddened, although greatly relieved" when Sweetland decided not to file as a candidate for Congress: "At a fairly heavy cost in injured pride and lost friendships," he told the interviewer, "Dick Neuberger had a free track to run on, and he was to make the most of it, with the considerable help of his friends and Wayne Morse." In Morgan's view, Neuberger would not have to rub shoulders during the campaign with a congressional candidate tainted with a radical past, and Edith Green could enter the Democratic primary without serious opposition. Morgan also took credit for the even greater Democratic successes in 1956, because Neuberger and Green "made possible those big gains in '56."[36]

In answer to Morgan's forty-year-old recollections about the 1954 election, Sweetland responded in the *Oregon Historical Quarterly* by citing "the great issues that stirred Oregonians in those years," an approach far more instructive that focusing on "personality conflicts among some of the principals." Adlai Stevenson's high-minded presidential run in 1952 attracted new people to the party who were "exposed to the spirited personalities of Dick and Maurine Neuberger, Gus Solomon, [and] Edith Green." His election as Democratic National Committeeman in 1948 and Howard Morgan's appointment as state Democratic chair in 1952 were important to the party's turnaround. The cadre of young liberal candidates "excited the enthusiasm of liberal farmers, logging and lumber workers, students, schoolteachers and educators." Sweetland acknowledged that strong personalities clashed during those years, but "on matters that count, on the transcendent political issues," Neuberger, Morse, Morgan, and Sweetland "were unambiguously allies."[37]

A copy of an anonymous letter to the *Oregon Historical Quarterly*, marked "never sent," provides strong support for Sweetland's critical role in

the successes of Oregon's Democratic Party. "Bewildered" at Morgan's interview, the writer thought time had fuzzed Morgan's memory, or perhaps he
was still unhappy over the loss of Sweetland's friendship, which was "mainly
of his own doing." When a person ages, the writer speculated, "there is a tendency to embellish a story at the expense of playing fast and loose with the
facts." Sweetland would do nothing to jeopardize a Democratic candidate,
the letter continued, and as Morgan knew, Monroe had "devoted his life to
the Democratic Party." That he would do harm to Edith Green's chances in
the third district "borders on insanity." The unsent letter admonished the
Oregon Historical Society for failing to publish both sides of the story in its
fall issue: "It was bad journalism—and Monroe deserves better."[38]

Wayne Morse's independent status continued to roil Democratic Party
waters. In a celebrated post-1954 election hiatus, Morse told the *U.S. News
and World Report* that he intended to run for reelection in 1956 as an independent. Sweetland, cited in the same article, told the interviewer that he
would support the senator only if he filed for reelection as a Democrat.
The party expected to nominate "the best and strongest candidate we can
find," and Morse would be their "overwhelming choice if he changes his
registration." Sweetland believed "the logic of the situation" would convince Morse to make the switch. "As long as the Democratic party stands
for the principles it does," Morse would feel at home. Neuberger differed,
telling *U.S. News* that he would support Morse in 1956 even if he ran as an
independent.[39]

The *Oregonian* reported that Democratic Party chair Howard Morgan
was upset because he had not been consulted about Sweetland's quasi-
ultimatum regarding Morse. Morgan argued that no responsible Democrat
would "have been thoughtless enough to confront Senator Morse with anything which might be described as an ultimatum." Morse followed his "independent" declaration with telegrams to Morgan and Sweetland, assuring
Sweetland that he was "not the least bit concerned by any such statement and
I assume that you had no intention of trying to embarrass me or injure me."
To Morgan, he declared his intention "to exercise an independence of judgment on the issue as to my party." He would never be partner to an arrangement where the Democratic Party would put up a weak candidate if he ran
as an independent—"such a proposal would have been politically unethical."
Shortly after the mid-November skirmish, Morse wrote Sweetland hoping

that all was "quiet on the western front and I trust that means that we may not only have a cease fire, but a permanent peace before too long."[40]

Less than a month after the public clamor about Morse's party status, some eight hundred Democrats convened in Portland's Columbia Athletic Club to applaud senator-elect Richard Neuberger for his election victory. State senator-elect Monroe Sweetland, who chaired the "victory dinner," told the gathering that November's election ushered in a new day for Oregon Democrats, who "campaigned as a team which they had never done before." Senator Morse, who sat next to Sweetland at the head table, complimented Neuberger for his win, signaling that "liberals in Oregon politics have challenged the monopoly of the reactionary Republican machine." Neuberger promised the assembly that "when 1956 comes two people named Maurine and Richard Neuberger . . . will be campaigning for the senior senator of the state of Oregon." Representative-elect Edith Green described the meeting as "a history-making occasion," marking the first time that two Oregon senators shared such a forum.[41]

Oregon's senior senator did not dally. After the holiday season, including a family wedding in South Carolina, Morse stopped off at the Lane County courthouse in Eugene on a trip home and changed his registration to the Democratic Party. Morse told a reporter trailing the small entourage (including Morgan) that "to continue in the [Republican] party would be to live a lie." Former governor Charles Sprague put it best in an *Oregon Statesman* editorial: "Senator Wayne Morse's decision to join the Democratic party and run as its candidate in 1956 was inevitable and at least consistent with his analysis of political realities."[42]

As Sprague and Sweetland contended, Morse's decision to file as a Democrat in 1956 was expected. His biographer, Mason Drukman, argues that Morse's dalliance "*was* an act, that Morse had no home except in the Democratic party, that he had no chance of winning as an Independent in 1956." The correspondence between Morse and Sweetland also suggests that the two remained friends. It should be noted that Morgan's "ultimatum" allusion appears only in his interview about Sweetland's statement. Sweetland poked fun at the use of the term in an earlier letter to Charlie Porter, referring to the "matter of the misnamed 'ultimatum.'" His greatest worries were Morse's reputation as a maverick. "I'm for the guy on his policies," Sweetland wrote to Porter in the fall of 1953, "and hope to Jefferson he won't get so squirrelly personally that we can't abide him."[43]

The 1955 legislative session ushered in a new political calculus for Sweetland, this time as an elected member of the Oregon Senate. Although Democrats were vastly outnumbered, Sweetland was now a veteran party official with significant ties to influential people beyond the state. At home, the *Milwaukie Review* was operating smoothly thanks to Lil's attention to detail, and the few words gleaned from her letters during those years suggest she loved the work.[44] Daughter Barbara was thriving as a sophomore scholarship student at Mills College, and family correspondence delighted in red-haired toddler Rebecca's growing vocabulary. In their Milwaukie home, Nanna provided day care for Rebecca, with the granddaughter later reflecting that she "always felt safe with her." Monroe turned forty-five years old in January 1955, and Lil turned forty-three two months later.[45]

9

Missing the Brass Ring

When the Oregon legislative assembly convened in 1955, it marked the beginning of four consecutive sessions that Monroe Sweetland would serve in the state Senate. Before moving on to other opportunities, he was easily reelected to the Senate and made two ill-fated efforts to win the office of secretary of state. Beyond Sweetland's personal world, the *Oregonian* observed in a New Year's editorial that people were healthier and lived longer than their parents and grandparents. "Never have the American people had more and enjoyed more than at this time." Automobiles were commonplace, and television brought "entertainment into the humblest home." There was still more to celebrate—shorter work days, longer vacations, and Oregon's labor markets were at peace, a sharp contrast to the recent strife in the lumber industry.[1] For sawmill workers and loggers it would be a good year, with the state's lumber production reaching an all-time high.

The *Oregonian* predicted a busy session for Oregon lawmakers, with some five hundred requests for bills to be considered, more than double the number for 1953. A looming legislative issue was raising sufficient revenue to meet budget demands. Loren Stewart, Cottage Grove lumberman and chair of the House taxation committee, predicted that an increase in taxes was likely. Although Republicans vastly outnumbered Democrats in the Senate (25 to 5), Sweetland again proved adept at working across the aisle on strategic measures. Mark Hatfield, who also moved from the House to the Senate, was named chair of the State and Federal Affairs Committee, and both served on the education committee.[2]

When Attorney General Robert Thornton's opinion in early January declared wiretapping legal, the *Oregonian* observed that the issue, "a touchy one at the national capital for a long time, now is with us at the state level." Based on a Eugene case in which police used wiretapped evidence to convict a man of contributing to the delinquency of a minor, Thornton declared that in the absence of legal prohibitions, such evidence was admissible in court. Because wiretapping was "not a criminal act in Oregon," he urged the legislature to consider the issue. As a longtime member of the American Civil Liberties Union (ACLU), Sweetland held that wiretapping violated an individual's right to privacy. As a consequence, he asked the legislative counsel to draft a bill "forbidding absolutely for all purposes . . . wire tapping or the recorded interception of telephonic messages . . . procured by wire tapping or other interception of private telephone conversations." Four legislators joined Sweetland as cosponsors—two Democrats and three Republicans.[3]

To build support, Sweetland sent copies of the bill to friends receptive to protecting the right to privacy. Senator Richard Neuberger thought it a worthwhile fight: "You ought to have a lot of fun with it." In a letter to Bud Forrester of the Pendleton *East Oregonian*, Sweetland asked for "editorial support in this important matter," assuming that Forrester agreed with the bill. Sweetland also invited noted civil liberties advocate E. B. MacNaughton, president of Portland's First National Bank, to speak in support of the bill during Senate committee hearings.[4] Witnesses who spoke at the hearings indicated support for making such practices illegal and forbidding prosecutors from using wiretapped evidence in civil and criminal trials. Sweetland argued that private detectives would make widespread use of wiretapping in divorce cases; moreover, thirty-eight states already had laws similar to the bill before the committee.[5]

Following the hearings, Sweetland sent a copy of the bill to ACLU's national office in New York City. With state legislatures meeting across the nation, he believed "the climate ripe for making progress against wire tapping." The New York office congratulated Sweetland for taking steps to protect the right to privacy.[6] In the end Sweetland and his bipartisan allies easily prevailed in the Senate, and the House approved the measure without amendment. When the governor signed the bill, the new law prohibited all tapping of telephone lines and radio communications, except for law enforcement officers, who were required to have court approval. The measure explicitly excluded extension telephones and people who listened to phone conversations on party lines.[7]

Although land-use issues would not reach fever pitch in Oregon for another decade, Sweetland received numerous remonstrances related to a zoning bill requiring only 10 percent of the freeholders in a district to petition for a change in land-use practices. The House approved the bill (HB 483) with little discussion and forwarded it to the Senate. The bill's opponents pointed to the undemocratic nature of the measure, as one petition noted: "Our democracy in this country is based on majority rule and 10 percent of the people speaking for the majority opposes the basic fundamentals of democracy."[8] While some of Sweetland's correspondents lived in wealthy neighborhoods anxious to protect their property values, others wrote about overcrowding in unincorporated areas, contaminated drainage ditches, and the safety of children. "Give this matter your more careful consideration," one woman wrote, and "consider it also from the viewpoint of a mother of five." Sweetland sent a circular to constituents, calling the bill "highly undesirable," because it allowed a small percentage of people to create chaos in a zoning district. He promised to amend the signature requirement to 51 percent. HB 483 died in committee during the waning days of the legislature.[9]

The 1955 session revisited the welfare laws that had consumed much of Sweetland's time during his previous term in the House. A Multnomah County circuit judge found the "relative responsibility" clause making family members responsible for the support of elderly, indigent parents unconstitutional. Sweetland, who opposed the original measure, joined in an effort to repeal the act, because requiring relatives to be responsible for senior citizens "was socially and economically wrong." Heartrending letters from constituents again deluged his office. One woman from Sandy, who had lived and farmed with her husband for sixty years—"worked real hard cleared lot land lot improvements raised a large family"—requested relief because they were not eligible for social security. She asked him to support legislation that would prohibit counties from attaching liens to the property of elderly citizens who were unable to pay their taxes.[10]

Despite such requests, legislators continued to seek punitive measures to resolve welfare support: (1) enforce prison terms for people failing to provide support; (2) allow district attorneys to initiate contempt citations for those in arrears; and (3) permit the state to make claims against a welfare recipient's estate. Although legislators deliberated those punitive measures into April, in the end they lessened the requirements of the "relative responsibility" clause.[11]

Sweetland backed another measure close to his politics: support for gender equity (equal pay for equal work). Senate Bill 2—the equal pay law—attracted widespread union support. The Senate unanimously passed the bill in February, the House approved the Senate version, and the bill was sent to the governor's office.[12] Both houses also approved a civil defense bill giving the governor broad powers to deal with emergencies should the state be subject to enemy attack. Bernhard Fedde, a lawyer and Sweetland friend, argued that the legislation was "part of the bomb hysteria under which we are suffering" and would only exacerbate international relations. Sweetland, leery of any governor holding such powers, remembered vividly how governors' offices acquiesced in the violation "in the war-time evacuation of the Japanese" from the West Coast. The Senate ultimately approved the bill granting the governor extensive powers in the case of an enemy attack.[13]

The most contentious issues before the Oregon legislature involved proposals for raising revenue, including a sales tax, an approach that Sweetland considered the most regressive of all revenue measures and had opposed since the 1930s. In a letter to the *Oregon Journal* in March 1955, he took issue with an editorial supporting a Senate resolution (SJR 4), restricting the use of Oregon's initiative and referendum.

Because the sales tax was "the most unfair of all taxes," SJR 4 was "an effort to put over the sales tax by destroying that part of the initiative and referendum law which is the people's best defense."[14] When the House taxation committee held hearings on revenue measures, Sweetland supported increasing the graduated income tax; a sales tax, he emphasized, contradicted standards of equity and fair play. A writer to Arthur Bone, editor of the *Oregon-Washington Farmer* union publication, applauded Sweetland's "incisive testimony against the sales tax." Although the push for a sales tax persisted through the remainder of the session, the Senate killed the effort after the House approved a 3 percent sales tax as part of the revenue bill.[15]

Oregon's fledgling urban institution of higher education—Portland State Extension Center—garnered legislative attention when lawmakers renamed the institution Portland State College in 1955, with authority to grant four-year degrees. Sweetland, who played an important role in turning the extension center for veterans into a major urban university, had been promoting the institution from the time the family settled in their Milwaukie home in 1952.[16] When an effort to establish a four-year college failed in the 1953 legislature, Sweetland reflected that "Portland State College had the arguments and the facts, but they just didn't have the votes." With Portland State Extension director Stephen Epler leading a well-organized campaign, the 1955 legislature moved quickly to make Portland State College a four-year institution and member of the Oregon State System of Higher Education. As the Portland state bill moved through the legislature, Sweetland congratulated Epler for his long and successful struggle—"most of us here consider you its Godfather and midwife and you should be its Patron Saint!"[17]

Although the Democratic Party had made great strides in the 1954 election, there were rumblings of discontent among its leadership about disorganization, a party in disarray, and a state chairman (Howard Morgan) who was abusing his office. While Sweetland seldom mentioned internecine party conflicts, he occasionally revealed his opinions on state and national Democratic politics to family and close friends. "Morgan has been behaving incredibly badly, fearful that he won't be given full credit for Dick's victory, and most resentful of me," he wrote to sister-in-law and brother-in-law Vi and John Gunther. Although he was embarrassed, he wanted to avoid getting into "this silly contest over 'credit.'"[18]

Morgan further roiled Democratic waters when he published a letter in the *Oregonian* in October 1955 questioning the integrity of New York governor Averill Harriman, a prospective Democratic nominee for president in 1956. Explaining that he was writing in "my entirely unofficial capacity as an individual voter and member of the Democratic party," Morgan's condemnatory letter listed Harriman's liabilities: (1) he was too old; (2) he had little support from rank-and-file Democrats; and (3) his appointment of Tammany Hall head Carmine DeSapio as New York's secretary of state would not be accepted "west of the Hudson River." In an accompanying editorial, the *Oregonian* delighted in the obvious: "The division among the Democrats, as witness Mr. Morgan's letter, is news that makes headlines."[19]

When news of Morgan's letter reached Harriman, the governor called the charges "utterly ridiculous." DeSapio, who had never heard of Morgan, thought he was "either a member or an associate of the Republican party.

. . . He could be a Trojan horse for all we know." Sweetland friend Jebby Davidson objected to a state party chair showing favoritism toward one candidate (Stevenson) so far in advance of the Oregon primary. In a letter to county Democratic chairs (with a copy to Morgan), Davidson criticized Morgan for "extremely bad political judgment." Morgan's disparaging remarks about a prominent Democrat made "it impossible, from now on, for him to carry on effectively the duties of that office." Wayne Morse's biographer Mason Drukman observes that, during Morse's first campaign as a Democrat in 1956, there were complaints that Morgan's leadership of the party "had become increasingly high handed." Those problems ended when Morgan left Oregon for a position with Stevenson's national campaign.[20]

After Democratic successes in 1954, Sweetland thought the prospects for 1956 were even brighter—with the expectation that the party would pick up a second U.S. Senate seat with Wayne Morse registered as a Democrat. Party leaders had reason to be optimistic about capturing the secretary of state and governor's offices as well. The chips began to fall in mid-January 1956 when Sweetland announced that he would be a candidate for secretary of state and would not run again for national committeeman. State senator Robert Holmes of Gearhart declared for the governor's office and Multnomah County sheriff Terry Shrunk, a liberal, chose to run for mayor of Portland. Sweetland believed the fall election would be an opportunity for Democrats to gain a majority on Oregon's important board of control (governor, secretary of state, and treasurer).[21]

Oregon's secretary of state contest would pair two candidates who had served nearly identical terms in the legislature. Thirty-three-year-old Mark Hatfield, dean of men and assistant professor of political science at Willamette University, had served two terms in the House and joined Sweetland in the Senate in 1954. During their time in the legislature, they worked in concert to advance civil rights legislation and the hot-button age-eighteen vote. Sweetland was realistic about his chances against Hatfield, telling Nathalie Panek "this will be a tough fight."[22] Sweetland ran unopposed in the primary, enabling his campaign staff to focus on fundraising and fine-tuning strategies for the November election. When the results of the May primary were tallied, Sweetland's campaign manager, Keith Burns, was pleased with his prospects in the fall. Monroe posted the most votes—199,928—of any candidate on the Democratic ticket. On the Republican side, Hatfield won the secretary of state nomination with 147,896 votes to his opponent William Healy's 88,710 votes. With the help of surrogates, Sweetland portrayed himself as a tribune of the people—supporting public power, minority rights, and the interests of the working class.[23]

The most vexing issue facing Sweetland was fundraising. When he attended a DNC meeting in Chicago, he spoke with United Auto Worker officials Walter and Roy Reuther about the problem in Oregon—the "tremendous appetite of the Morse treasury" for funds. When he returned to Oregon, he wrote Roy Reuther that his staff hoped that his campaign would warrant a "UAW investment." More than three months after the election, Sweetland's treasurer was still asking supporters for contributions to settle a $2,000 deficit.[24]

Although the candidates occasionally took swats at each other, the secretary of state campaign was absent significant acrimony. Sweetland took Hatfield to task for a GOP proposal to make Oregon's elected attorney general an appointed office. The attorney general was the "chief law officer of the states; he is not just the governor's legal advisor." Such a move would concentrate executive power "and take it away from the people."[25] When the *Oregonian* endorsed Mark Hatfield in early October, it referred to the secretary of state contest as "a clear test between a progressive Republican, Mark O. Hatfield, and a dedicated New Deal Democrat, Monroe Sweetland." The editorial favored Hatfield, because he was "conservative in fiscal and tax matters, liberal in the defense of civil rights and the improvement of social conditions." Sweetland deserved major credit for modernizing the Democratic Party and building close relations with organized labor, but his youthful background as a socialist and "later secretary of the far-left Commonwealth Federation" suggested that he would approach public issues "from a fixed, party-good standpoint."[26]

Salem's *Capital Journal*, Sweetland's nemesis from Commonwealth Federation days, berated him for his radical past and for practicing a politics of liberalism. Sweetland, like Senator Morse, had also switched political parties, in his case from a Norman Thomas socialist to a New Deal Democrat. The editorial pointed to his work as an organizer for the League for Industrial Democracy, "a militant left-wing socialist organization." The *Journal* noted that when Sweetland came to Oregon, he joined "the Oregon Commonwealth Federation, a left-wing group. . . . listed in *The Democratic Front* in 1938 by Earl Browder, then leader of the communist party in the U.S.A." The editorial was initialed "G.P.," very likely George Putnam, the longtime publisher who had recently sold the *Capital Journal* to Fred Mainwaring.[27]

Former Republican governor Charles Sprague's *Oregon Statesman* declared for Hatfield in mid-October, describing Hatfield as a young man destined "for great public service," who has sought to make the Republican Party forward-looking. Sprague praised Sweetland for rehabilitating the Democratic Party "powered by New Deal philosophy." As a campus radical from the early 1930s, Sprague was not convinced that Sweetland had disavowed his socialist past, because "he is still a rousing advocate of public power." Yet he had rid Oregon's Democratic Party "of some barnacles [and] he believes in clean government." If Sweetland were elected, however, Sprague feared that he would "use the office as an amplifier for magnifying propaganda of the left-wing stamp."[28]

Sweetland's *Milwaukie Review* offered recommendations for several offices, including an amusing suggestion for Oregon's secretary of state: "For those who like his point-of-view, we recommend *State Senator Monroe Sweetland*; for those who'd like to get the editor out of their hair we recommend *Monroe Sweetland*." The *Medford Mail Tribune*, Pendleton *East Oregonian*, and *Coos Bay Times* gave Sweetland ringing endorsements, citing his "warm regard for his fellow citizens and real devotion to the public good." The *Coos Bay Times* applauded Sweetland for being on the side of farmers, wage earners, and small business enterprises, a person who was firmly convinced "that his career was to serve his fellow man through the field of liberal government."[29]

A Democratic Day—And Ike's" the *Milwaukie Review* editorialized on November 8, the day following the election. Although returns were incomplete, Democrats had captured the governor's office, reelected Senator Wayne Morse as a Democrat, won three of four congressional seats, gained control of the Oregon House, and increased their influence in the Senate. In the secretary of state contest, the review continued, Monroe Sweetland "swept to big majorities in this area . . . but lost the state by a 1% margin to the personable young senator from Salem, Mark Hatfield." Sweetland won the large Portland-area counties—Multnomah and Clackamas—by narrow margins. In contrast, Mark Hatfield carried his home Marion County, nearly doubling his opponent's vote total (27,359 to 14,123). Two weeks after the election, the *Oregon Labor Press* pointed to the paradox in the balloting: "It is particularly ironic that Monroe Sweetland should be defeated in the election that gave the Democratic Party its greatest victory in Oregon history."[30]

The Hatfield/Sweetland campaign deepened the mutual respect that had developed during their years in the Oregon legislature. Sweetland's statement following the election confirmed that opinion: "I congratulate my friend Mark Hatfield on his opportunity for new service to Oregon [and] . . . for keeping his campaign on a friendly and constructive plane by which we avoided the destructive rancor which is often the bane of politics." He repeated the same message to weekly newspapers in Clackamas County, referring to Hatfield as "an able and appealing young man" who engaged in a hard-fought race "without the rancor and mud-slinging which is the bane of many political campaigns."[31]

Even in defeat, friends congratulated Sweetland for the Democratic Party's achievements. Jebby Davidson, elected Democratic National Committeeman in the May primary, praised Richard Neuberger, for winning the first major Democratic victory in 1954, and "the many years of hard work and sacrifice that Monroe Sweetland . . . devoted to the cause of good government in Oregon." Norman Nilsen, Oregon's Democratic Commissioner of Labor, commended Sweetland for "personal and financial sacrifices," his "unselfish devotion to the Democratic Party," and his success in getting gifted and qualified candidates to run for office. The explanations for Hatfield's successes were obvious—he was young, articulate, attractive, and he had a large campaign chest that his staff used effectively to put their candidate before Portland-area television audiences.[32]

The 1957 session of the Oregon legislature would prove to be a test in political compromise. With a Democratic governor, Democrats in control of the House, and the Senate evenly split with fifteen Democrats and fifteen Republicans, finding common ground on revenue bills depended heavily on Senate negotiations. Before the legislature convened in early January, Sweetland carried his party's bargaining chips to Republican leader Rudie Wilhelm, suggesting a compromise that would have conservative Democrat Walter Pearson serve as Senate president. A Democrat would also chair the ways and means committee and hold majority membership on the important taxation committee. Democrats based their reasoning on the proposition that voters had given the Democratic Party a mandate from voters "to try its hand and program in running State government."[33]

The Senate deadlock ended when Democrats put forward Boyd Overhulse, who was unanimously elected Senate president on January 24. Democrats took the chairmanships and majority memberships of key committees. Republicans would have "to accept a lamb's share of committee responsibility," the *Oregonian* declared. "Playing second fiddle in a Senate they have dominated since 1878 is not easy for Republicans to accept." For their part, Democrats believed they would need to be cautious in reforming tax policy, because a citizens' initiative could easily overturn the measure. The legislature, the *Oregonian* warned, must "approach its task with the foreknowledge that any tax program it devises may be killed aborning."[34]

Reflecting his abiding interest in public education, Sweetland was named chair of the Senate Education Committee and given another important assignment on the taxation committee. The success of one was closely tied to the other, because Oregon's beleaguered school districts depended on local property taxes and supplemental state revenue. Because funding problems were especially severe in districts with low property evaluations, Sweetland joined with his counterpart in the House to develop a new formula for distributing basic school support. A recommendation in Governor Robert Holmes's inaugural address, the "key district" strategy, would link local taxes statewide to the ability of Portland schools to fund adequate educational programs. The measure's sponsors, including Sweetland, argued that the proposal would equalize educational opportunity across the state according to need.[35]

In late March the Senate Education Committee approved the key district proposal (SB 64) on a narrow four to three vote, with geography, rather than political parties, explaining the split balloting. Those supporting the measure included Sweetland and Republican senators from Medford and Eugene and a Democrat from Roseburg. The minority—two Democrats and one Republican—were all from the Portland area. Portland was the wealthiest district and stood to lose the most from the formula if the legislature failed to raise sufficient revenue. Some Democratic legislators viewed Sweetland's efforts to push the measure through as a "force play" against another faction of the party. The *Oregonian* reported that economy-minded Democrats opposed such generous aid to education. Senator Ward Cook, a

Portland Democrat, contended that the bill would mean a sizable increase in Oregon's income tax.[36]

When the Senate passed SB 64 largely intact, the bill was subjected to a blitzkrieg of criticism during the next few weeks. Because the state lacked revenue to fully fund the bill, Portland schools stood to lose $4 million in support under the key district formula. School administrators in Portland and eastern Oregon attacked SB 64, observing that counties receiving revenue from Bureau of Land Management (BLM) timber receipts[37] in western Oregon would have an unfair advantage under the formula. The *Oregonian* accused supporters of using "pork barrel principles," noting that "there are more legislators from districts that stand to gain than from districts that would lose."[38]

As the most volatile bill before the legislature, the Sweetland-led effort to provide more funds for poor school districts survived but in sharply modified form. Led by Representative John Mosser, the House amended SB 64 to provide additional aid to poor districts while avoiding precipitous loses to the politically powerful Portland schools. The *Oregonian* thought the compromise "can be lived with," but it was scathing in denouncing those who supported the district proposal: "its principal spokesmen had been uncompromising and in some instances unprincipled." Although the final bill was "an acceptable compromise," the newspaper's tirade against the first significant effort to achieve equal funding to help poorer school districts was likely grandstanding before the home choir.[39]

On the revenue challenges before the legislature, Sweetland testified repeatedly in favor of raising the income tax. He differed with Democratic leaders—Governor Robert Holmes and Speaker of the House Pat Dooley—in calling for additional revenue. He proposed increasing dependency deductions from $500 to $600 and repealing the federal income tax exemption in filing state returns. While raising rates on higher incomes, his program would reduce taxes for incomes below $8,000. In a letter to a constituent, he called himself "the most vociferous legislative advocate of property tax relief." He urged private utilities to pay a fairer share of taxes, but the repeal of the federal income tax exemption held the most promise for raising revenue, "the one painless source of enough money to meet our needs."[40]

As the legislature moved toward adjournment in mid-May, the House passed a revenue measure bearing some resemblance to Sweetland's tax proposal. With their numerically superior numbers, House Democrats sent to the Senate a revenue package that increased personal exemptions and dependency from $500 to $600, increased state revenue on income brackets for those earning more than $7,000 a year, and reduced state taxes for people making less than that amount. The final bill included a 6 percent increase in the personal income tax and raised the corporate excise tax 17 percent. It did not repeal the federal income tax exemption. The measure promised to increase per-student funding from $80 to $95 for every census child.[41]

Predicated on a $9 million income tax increase, the House sent the governor a bill that included a complex formula for dividing the state school fund, the most bitterly fought measure before the legislature. The new distribution formula divided expenditures evenly among all school districts as flat grants per student. An additional 20 percent of state monies were intended as an equalization fund to assist poorer districts in financing standard educational programs. Speaking to the Portland City Club after adjournment, Sweetland termed the session "fairly successful," insisting that "Democrats had the issues as a mandate." Cecil Posey, head of the Oregon Education Association, praised lawmakers for passing "more favorable legislation for the public schools of Oregon than any previous session." He especially praised Governor Holmes and Senator Sweetland.[42]

The Milwaukie Democrat pushed activist policies in other ways, introducing a bill requiring lobbyists to register before pressing their influence on lawmakers. "Legislators and the public" had a right to know who the lobbyists were representing, Sweetland argued. The bill never made it out of committee. In another move that anticipated a successful effort in the 1960s, Sweetland and other legislators introduced a resolution calling for a constitutional amendment to legalize the public ownership of ocean beaches. Like the lobbying measure, the beaches bill awaited a more liberal mood in the Senate.[43]

With the end of the session, Sweetland looked forward to a summer of relaxing with his family and gearing up for the next election cycle. Because of his busy legislative schedule, he had sold the *Oregon Democrat* the previous March. Stan Federman, a California transplant who joined the *Milwaukie Review* staff in 1955, continued as general business manager with occasional editorial responsibilities. As senior editorial writer, Monroe weighed in on issues local, state, and national. Lil's efficient hand, as Federman later acknowledged, was always "practical" and important to running the paper.[44]

Daughter Barbara completed her junior year at Mills College in 1957 and took a summer job with the Public Health Service in Washington, D. C. The most riveting family event that summer was the theft of Monroe's 1956 Oldsmobile and its involvement in a crash on Union Avenue in Southeast Portland. Although the thief escaped, the *Oregonian* reported that campaign material from the 1956 election was strewn along Union Avenue where the accident occurred.[45]

Mark Hatfield, now holding down the secretary of state office, periodically joined Sweetland in public forums. When the local NAACP hosted an African American judge from Missouri to speak at the Vancouver Avenue Baptist Church, NAACP officials invited Sweetland to serve as master of ceremonies and Mark Hatfield to introduce the guest. In another October function in Portland, *Oregonian* columnist B. Mike reported an exchange between Hatfield and Sweetland in which Hatfield referred to a rumor that Sweetland would run for superintendent of public instruction in 1958 and that Republican candidate Martha Shull, "who has brains, ability, and beauty," would be his opponent. The never bashful Sweetland replied: "I'll tell you Mark, I got up against that combination in 1956 and I don't intend to take it on again."[46]

Because the end of the biennial legislature prefaced the next election cycle, during the summer and fall of 1957, Sweetland looked forward to a second term in the Senate and providing support for Oregon Democratic candidates. At the top of the agenda was Oregon's gubernatorial contest, an office that Robert Holmes had filled when he won election to the unexpired term of Governor Paul Patterson, who died in January, 1956. Popular with most Democratic leaders, Holmes was expected to be a strong candidate for reelection.[47]

Although he was still adjusting to the secretary of state position, Mark Hatfield was already casting an eye toward the governor's office. He dallied, however, telling Republicans in November 1957 that if state treasurer Sig Unander ran for governor, he would not be a candidate. When a poll of legislative Republicans revealed that most of them preferred Hatfield, he reconsidered his position and in mid-January 1958 declared his candidacy for governor. A fiscal conservative, he accused Governor (and candidate) Robert Holmes of increasing the state's budget and promised to reverse that policy, because it was "an open invitation to reckless spending." In the May primary Holmes easily defeated a Democratic challenger, and Hatfield beat

Unander and another Republican by what the *Oregonian* termed "a booming plurality."[48]

Seeking a second term in the Oregon Senate, Sweetland was unchal-
lenged in the primary and expected an easy path to reelection. The only
hitch in his campaign took place in mid-October when Clackamas County
Republican chair Don Quesinberry circulated a four-page brochure,
"Is Monroe Sweetland a Real Democrat?" The publication questioned
Sweetland's membership in organizations during the 1930s that the attorney general and others had deemed subversive. Sweetland called the charges
"demagoguery" and accused Quesinberry of reviving "smears used against
me in every campaign, based on alleged incidents a quarter of a century
ago." Clackamas County voters, he told a reporter, "know me pretty well." In
a letter to the *Oregonian*, a writer remarked that Sweetland "frustrated and
defeated the nearly-successful drive of the Henry Wallace radicals to seize
control of the Democratic Party of Oregon" in 1948.[49]

With Mark Hatfield fronting Oregon's Republican Party, Democratic
leaders knew that Robert Holmes faced a difficult reelection fight. In a visit
to Senator Richard Neuberger in his Washington office, Holmes acknowledged that he faced a tough campaign. Neuberger urged Democrats to
confront Hatfield with serious questions, because "he has never really been
associated with any fundamental cause—only a handsome face and glitter-
ing generalities." The *Oregonian* thought otherwise, declaring Hatfield "the
most exceptional candidate for governor in the nation this year." He excelled
as a speaker, an educator, understood government, and possessed "a clear-
cut goal of major service in public office." Although Robert Holmes was "a
cut above average," the *Oregonian* supported Hatfield.[50]

Oregon's 1958 election paralleled trends established two years earlier,
with Republican Mark Hatfield again demonstrating great popular appeal
with voters and Democrats making strides in congressional and legislative races. Sweetland's longtime friend David Epps, now state Democratic
chair, told a reporter that Hatfield had "won a terrific personal victory,"
while Democrats had gained control of both houses of the legislature. In a
striking turnabout from the evenly balanced Senate of the previous session,
Democrats now outnumbered Republicans nineteen to eleven, the first time
they had earned a majority since 1878. Although the margin in the House
had narrowed, Democrats still had a working majority.[51]

Monroe and daughter Rebecca (b. 1953), late 1950s, at their home in Milwaukie, Oregon.

Voters easily approved Ballot Measure 13—"Persons Eligible to Serve in the Legislature"—a bill that endorsed the right of teachers to serve in the legislature. The success of the hotly debated issue meant that Oregon would join thirty-two other states allowing educators to serve as lawmakers. In an October meeting of the Portland City Club, Sweetland told members that denying teachers the right to serve in the legislature was "rank," because lawmakers always voted on decisions directly affecting themselves. The *Oregonian* praised voters for having "confidence that lawmakers chosen from the profession will not abuse their dual public role."[52]

At the onset of the 1959 session, the Sweetlands were in the midst of personal transitions. Barbara, who graduated from Mills College, was a master's candidate at the Russian Institute at Columbia University, courtesy of a two-year graduate fellowship. Rebecca, who would be in first grade in October, was still loving the outdoors and "animals of all sorts" and coming home from school to Nanna's care. Rebecca remembers that unlike Barbara, who "grew up in Mom and Dad's lean years," she lived her childhood and adolescence "in Mom and Dad's rich years." Except for brief periods when Barbara was home from college, "I felt like I was an only child." However, hers was not a pampered and idealized childhood, because at the age of three she lost most of her hearing from medication to treat a fever. Her mother was devastated and "felt awfully guilty," while her father was quite the opposite. Because of her hearing loss, she missed out on her parent's political commentary. But, differing from Barbara's childhood, Rebecca recalls that she "lived in the same house the first nine years of my life."[53]

Lil, with major oversight for the *Milwaukie Review,* worked closely with Stan Federman in putting out the weekly and its supplement, the *North Clackamas Shopper.* Monroe continued to write editorials, although Federman wrote some columns reflecting the owners' guiding principles. When his legislative responsibilities lessened in May of 1959, Monroe turned his attention to presidential politics, in this case vesting his energies as never before in promoting the candidacy of Massachusetts senator John F. Kennedy. The next several months would prove to be some of the most exhilarating, challenging, and disheartening of his career.

10

Legislative Successes and "the fringes of this dirty game"

When Governor-elect Mark Hatfield strode to the rostrum in the capitol rotunda to take the oath of office on January 12, 1959, his escort, Monroe Sweetland, may have stunned the assembled lawmakers. Although they differed on fiscal policy, the two men had an abiding respect for each other.[1] During Hatfield's first term as governor and Sweetland's third term in the Senate, they jousted over school funding, public welfare, and the administrative restructuring of government. Following the swearing-in ceremonies, the new governor's inaugural address proposed wide-ranging changes in Oregon's government, recommendations that his escort would strongly oppose. At the top of his agenda was making the offices of attorney general, labor commissioner, and superintendent of public instruction appointive rather than elective. Hatfield also recommended changing the line of gubernatorial succession from the Senate president and speaker of the House to the statewide elective offices of secretary of state and treasurer.[2]

The reaction to Hatfield's inaugural address varied from hallowed praise to skepticism, depending on party affiliation. To Senate president Walter Pearson, the governor's proposals were "full of platitudes." Democratic Party chair Dave Epps thought Hatfield's "scintillating personality stood out," but he wondered how the governor would pay for such an ambitious program while urging economy in government spending. Sweetland praised Hatfield's "program of social and governmental improvements," but criticized his "Spartan tax policy" for being a drag on the governor's proposals.[3]

Among the governor's most contentious proposals was his recommendation that Oregon adopt the "Missouri Plan" for selecting lower court and state supreme court justices. Under the scheme, the governor would appoint judges from a list provided by a bipartisan "nominating commission." After serving one term, judges would then run for election on their own terms. While supporters argued that the plan would "improve the quality of the judges," Sweetland and others thought the change would threaten "our democratic processes." Portland attorney W. A. Franklin called the measure "a system to get the judges elected for life." With Democrats controlling the Senate Judiciary Committee, Sweetland predicted the death knell of the Missouri Plan. In mid-March the committee quietly tabled the measure.[4]

School funding, a perennial issue before Oregon lawmakers, was moving in the wrong direction, according to Sweetland. Speaking in the wake of the Soviet Union's successful launching of the Sputnik satellite, Sweetland argued that there was a dire need for executive leadership. Especially harmful to school support was a legislative move—Sweetland dubbed them "loaded dice election laws"—requiring 50 percent voter turnouts for passing bonds and levies. Teachers, parents, and administrators thanked Sweetland for his persistent stand in support of education, with Salem's Jean Roth writing, "We all must give up a little to provide for education." Opponents were relieved when the "loaded dice" proposals died in committee.[5]

With significant successes in the previous legislative session, the Oregon Education Association (OEA) and other public school supporters pressed for increases in teachers' salaries. In response to Anna Pratt of Nyssa, Sweetland thought the most critical issue was to "get the burden of school taxation off the necks of local farm and home owners." Those with higher incomes and corporations, he believed, should contribute more to the state's general fund. Stella Chlopek, a Bend teacher, pointed out that schools had only one source of local revenue, property, while the state could draw on many sources. The problem, Sweetland replied, was an economy-minded legislature.[6]

When Sweetland and Al Flegel, chair of the House Education Committee, arranged a joint committee hearing on the evening of March 23, an unprecedented crowd of some 1,500 people filled the capitol's basement hearing room (capacity 350) and spilled out into the corridor and up the stairs to the main-floor rotunda. Workers set up loudspeakers to enable those outside the hearing room to listen to testimony. Veteran observers called it the largest attendance at a committee hearing ever held in the state. As chair of the Senate Education Committee, Sweetland outlined an agenda to increase the state's contribution to local school districts to 50 percent. To fund his proposal, he would eliminate the deduction for federal taxes from state income taxes or restore the 20 percent reduction in the schools budget passed in the special session in the fall of 1957. Either proposition would bring the state's contribution to about 50 percent of local district operating costs.[7]

An *Oregonian* reporter covering the hearing highlighted funding public schools as one of the legislature's toughest decisions. Republican representative Shirley Field from Portland supported the 50 percent goal but wanted a broader tax on all incomes or a sales tax to fund increased expenditures. Senate president Walter Pearson suggested submitting a 3 percent sales tax to voters, arguing that the sales tax would relieve property taxes. Although Sweetland strongly opposed a sales tax, he agreed that local property taxes "cannot and must not rise." The hearing proceeded with various suggestions for achieving the 50 percent target.[8]

An optimist on most issues, Sweetland was on the losing end in the effort to increase support for public schools. Shortly after the legislature adjourned in early May, the *Oregonian* offered a blunt summary of its accomplishments:

> What the legislature didn't do in the field of education may be
> more important to many Oregonians than what it did. It refused
> to grant any additional state money for support of public schools.
> The Oregon Education Assn., the School Boards Assn., and other
> educators sought an increase of $35 per school child, more than 17
> million dollars a year, and would have settled for substantially less.
> They got nothing.

Ultimately, Sweetland's proposals foundered on the shoals of differences among economy-minded Senate Democrats."[9]

Although he lost the school funding fight, Sweetland succeeded with legislation to establish statewide community colleges. Such institutions, he believed, would enable students in small towns to earn lower-division college credit while living at home. Don Pence, president of Central Oregon College, the state's only community college, worked with Sweetland to gain state support for two-year colleges. Pence later complimented Sweetland for his work and looked forward to supporting "the proper development of these institutions." At Pence's request, Sweetland agreed to give the college's commencement address that June.[10]

Sweetland joined Bend representative J. Pat Metke in drafting a bill to establish fifteen community college districts in the state. The geographical spread of districts across the state invited protests from towns removed from locations of prospective community colleges. Residents of Gold Beach in Curry County objected to being placed in a district with the college located in Coos Bay. Sweetland responded that Curry County students would attend the Coos Bay institution in far greater numbers than they would the University of Oregon or Oregon State College. Legislators finally agreed to create community colleges in locations where the Oregon Department of Education approved a citizens' petition. The Sweetland bill included a funding proposal dividing support among the district, the state, and the basic school fund.[11] Sweetland's community college initiative was another mark in his advocacy for viable educational programs at all levels.

There were other personal victories, including Sweetland's initiative to establish a graduate degree of social work at Portland State College. Playing off the governor's inaugural address about the need for graduate education in social work, he pushed the proposal in the 1959 session, earning the support of social workers' organizations and the Governor's State Committee on Youth. The issues were complex—funding, selecting a dean, planning a curriculum, and recruiting a faculty. Although the legislature gave a thumbs-up to creating a Graduate School of Social Work, matters drifted into September when Senator Jean Lewis asked the chancellor's office about progress in planning the program. Chancellor John Richards assured Lewis that the state Board of Higher Education was moving ahead to hire a dean in light of expected appropriations in the next biennium.[12] Fulfillment would wait another two years.

Following Governor Hatfield's recommendation, the legislature made sweeping changes in personal income tax policy, approving a measure that Sweetland had proposed in the 1957 session—disallowing the deduction of federal income taxes when filing for Oregon income taxes. The legislature also adopted another Sweetland proposal, a new tax on inheritances expected to bring in more than $3 million annually. The *Oregonian* thought the revenue measures would bring in "just enough to pay the bills in the current

biennium." The economy-minded governor criticized the legislature's revenue program, but for different reasons. Hatfield charged Democratic leaders
with socking "the same taxpayers who have been hit so often and hard for so
many years," warning that a taxpayer rebellion could be avoided "only if we
in government administer with economy and efficiency."[13]

At the close of the session, Sweetland was widely recognized as the guardian
of public education, responsible for establishing the state scholarship commission and the community college system, and regularizing a retirement
plan for teachers. Governor Hatfield named Sweetland to represent Oregon
at the meeting of the Western Interstate Conference on Higher Education
in San Francisco, his second appointment to the gathering. The *Milwaukie
Review* frequently gave voice to public education issues, and Sweetland regularly addressed school and parent and teacher meetings and college assemblies on important education matters. The Oregon Education Association
(OEA) recognized his contributions in March 1960, naming him Education
Citizen of the Year.[14]

As the legislature adjourned, Sweetland's energies turned to support-
ing the presidential candidacy of Massachusetts senator John F. Kennedy.
But he was also casting an eye toward another run for the secretary of state
office. When Hatfield was elected governor in 1958, he appointed Howell
Appling, a political novice, to replace him. A graduate engineer from Rice
Institute in Texas, Appling moved to Oregon in 1946 and established a successful wholesale business selling logging equipment and farm machinery.
At the time of his appointment as secretary of state, he was also employed
as an industrial manager in Washington County.[15] Democrats, including
Sweetland, considered Appling a greenhorn, prone to uninformed errors,
and an easy target if he ran for election to succeed himself in 1960.

If Sweetland had come within a percentage point of defeating Hatfield,
he had every reason to believe that the office was his for the taking. He was
a seasoned politician, a riveting public speaker, and well known across the
state. When the *Oregon Statesman* issued a preliminary endorsement of
Appling in February, Sweetland wrote a personal letter to the editor likening
the newspaper's approval of Appling as equivalent to "endorsing an illiterate for university president." Democrats attacked Appling elsewhere when
he placed a statement in a League of Women Voters pamphlet urging his
"re-election" and using the phrase "if re-elected." Sweetland's supporters,

however, were aware that the contest would be difficult. Walter Dodd wrote Mike Katz, Sweetland's campaign strategist, that this would be a tough fight: "Appling is an ass, but possibly many people will not realize this."[16]

For Oregonians the most striking event of the early 1960 election season was the untimely and tragic death of Senator Richard Neuberger. Oregon's junior senator died on March 9, 1960, at the age of forty-seven after a two-year bout with cancer. Less than a year earlier, the talented and courageous journalist publicly acknowledged his illness in an article, "When I Learned I Had Cancer," published in *Harper's* (June 1959). Although the actual cause of death was a massive cerebral hemorrhage, those close to Neuberger were aware that his death was imminent. Governor Mark Hatfield, after some deliberation, appointed Oregon Supreme Court justice Hall Lusk to fill the remainder of Neuberger's term. Maurine Neuberger, who was denied the interim appointment, subsequently declared herself a candidate and won a full term on her own right in the November election.[17]

In the May primary, two little-known candidates provided only token opposition to Sweetland, who offered a sharp contrast to the incumbent, who repeatedly praised the free enterprise system, smaller government, and called for reducing taxes. Speaking to housing and redevelopment officials in Gearhart in early June, Sweetland praised "responsible, enlightened, and progressive government," insisting that "Government is not evil." He compared present-day "anti government calamity howlers" to "nineteenth century anarchists." Although they did not support violence, they used "weapons of denunciation and character assassination," undermining public confidence "in the social purposes of government."[18]

Appling's campaign touted its candidate's "fight against the Socialists and left-wingers." Addressing a Portland Rotary Club luncheon in August, Appling charged that liberals were "heading for state socialism and an all-powerful central government." Sweetland, who also addressed the Rotarians, was more accommodating: "Americans [were] . . . a nation in fundamental agreement rather than disagreement." When Arizona senator Barry Goldwater visited the Oregon Republican Party's annual summer picnic, he likened the Democratic Party platform to a "'manifesto,' as in Karl Marx and Friedrich Engels' 'Communist Manifesto.'" With Appling and Elmo Smith—who was running for senator against Democrat Maurine Neuberger—joining him on stage, Goldwater warned the gathering of some

Monroe Sweetland, Oregon secretary
of state campaign, 1960. (Courtesy of
the Oregon Historical Society)

twenty thousand: "If we ever give in to the siren call of Socialists who want
to pour us all in the same mold, then we're gone."[19]

Rumor and innuendo had always dogged Sweetland's campaigns—that
he was a radical leftist and not to be trusted with public office. That pattern
resurfaced with a vengeance in his second secretary of state campaign. As the
campaign moved into October, Oregon newspapers declared their support for
the secretary of state candidates. Eric Allen, Jr., the well-known editor of the
Medford *Mail Tribune*, supported Sweetland based on "temperament, ability,
experience, and by the respect he has earned over many years as a legislator . .
. and fair-minded politician." Appling's "low-brow politics" forfeited any claim
he might have for the office. The Eugene *Register-Guard*'s Robert "Bob" Frazier
endorsed Sweetland, criticized Appling for suggesting that Sweetland was "a
dangerous revolutionary with horns and a tail," whereas the Democratic candidate "has sold his own product and has been a gentleman about it."[20]

The *Oregonian* endorsed Appling for his fiscal conservatism in running
the secretary of state's office. Departing from its usually generous treatment
of Sweetland, the editorial referred to him as a "'knee-jerk liberal,' . . . slav-
ish toward organized labor," supportive of public ownership and bigger
federal programs. The most interesting editorial among Oregon's newspapers was Charles Sprague's *Oregon Statesman*'s support for Howell Appling.
Little-known when he was appointed secretary of state, Appling had been

Campaign poster, secretary of state campaign, 1960. (Courtesy of the Oregon Historical Society)

"a good watchdog over public spending" and deserved election to a full term. Because "the office is primarily administrative," if Hatfield's government reforms became reality, Sprague said, the secretary of state's job "will become chiefly ministerial." Although Sweetland enjoyed a sterling record in the legislature, especially in "defense of civil liberties," he would not be a "patient administrator of an office of declining importance."[21]

And then in mid-October Sweetland was the object of an incendiary attack, the circulation of a two-page leaflet, "Monroe Sweetland—His Real

Record." Some 50,000 copies of the leaflet were distributed across the state, some mailed, some handed out on street corners or delivered door-to-door, others passed out at political gatherings. In fourteen enumerated charges, the document accused Sweetland of being "chosen and trained by a Soviet agent to organize the infamous Oregon Commonwealth Federation." It listed Sweetland as a member of subversive organizations during the 1930s and added that the Oregon Committee for Honest Politics had documented evidence. Most hurtful to Sweetland was the accusation that "his distinguished and respectable father" had disinherited him "for his radical opinions and his subversive activities."[22] There was, of course, no disinheritance, and three decades of correspondence indicates a close relation between father and son.

The *Milwaukie Review* recounted the events that "changed the tone and pace of the [election] contest." Faced with defeat, the incumbent secretary of state and his supporters became desperate and turned to hitting "below the belt" to reverse public sentiment. First there was the misrepresentation of an address Sweetland gave at Linfield College. "Then on Monday night was slipped under the doors of all Milwaukie business houses a scurrilous personal assault on our publisher. It is libelous at almost every point, an utterly false and malicious document." Although the *Review*'s staff had carried on while Sweetland was campaigning, "we could not contain our resentment at the vicious turn taken by subversive elements who published these smears."[23]

Friends in powerful media outlets came to Monroe's defense, addressing the defamatory attacks without mentioning a name. Ancil Payne—working his way up the hierarchy of KGW/King Broadcasting in Seattle—wrote a four minute editorial, "Election Smears," to be delivered nightly on KGW radio and KGW-TV from November 4 to November 7 (election eve). In a note to Sweetland, he wrote: "First Editorial ever delivered on KGW/KING. Note date: I wrote it and it was in your behalf." Reading the script was the familiar voice of Tom McCall, a liberal Republican soon to make his own successful try as Oregon's secretary of state.[24] The KGW editorial addressed hate literature and the issue of "justice, decency and good government" and criticized the smear sheets' "unfounded charges and hateful attempts at character assassination." In the conclusion to Payne's script, McCall read: "Freedom is a fragile thing. Truth and freedom must be perpetually protected against the onslaught of lies, crazed emotional attacks or fanatic attempts to discredit."[25]

The eleventh-hour assaults on Sweetland as an unpatriotic radical rested in part with Howell Appling's public statements during his brief tenure in office. Unlike Mark Hatfield, Appling indulged in verbal assaults on liberal Democrats—a group not to be trusted with public office. In an early address to a Republican gathering in Klamath Falls, he urged party members to destroy "the false face of an unprincipled opponent who has masqueraded . . . as the friend of the so-called 'little man.'" Republicans, he told the gathering, should support free-market principles "as opposed to a socialistic organization of our economy."[26]

Political rhetoric has consequences, and the 1960 secretary of state campaign was costly for Monroe Sweetland. While Appling and Republican Party leaders denied any role in the extreme right-wing attacks, Appling's speeches and party news releases denigrating Sweetland as a socialist marked a sharp departure from the Hatfield-Sweetland contest four years earlier. Appling's firebrand oratory about socialism and free enterprise kindled a spark and likely spurred those with more extreme views to action. Although a Multnomah County grand jury issued indictments for political criminal libel (four people were arrested) three days before the election, the damages to Sweetland's reputation had been accumulating through weeks of relentless political attacks. On Election Day, Howell Appling marched to an easy win with nearly 55 percent of the vote.[27]

With the results apparent, Sweetland congratulated Howell Appling and expressed his "heartfelt gratitude" to his supporters for their hard work during the campaign. If victory proved elusive, "we tried our best and campaigned the only way I know how—on the issues and without malice toward my opponent." Edited out of the statement, perhaps at Lil's insistence, was a tribute to his wife's courage "in the face of extreme adversity in the closing days of the campaign. Without her loyalty, wisdom, devotion and courage, I would have been unable to campaign as vigorously or as conscientiously has [sic] I did."[28]

The postelection synopsis in the *Milwaukie Review* was headlined "Smear Effective." Calling the race the "most turbulent of the statewide campaigns," the *Review* observed that the "smear sheet was circulated principally in populous Clackamas and Multnomah counties." Although Sweetland did well in sizable downstate counties (Lane, Lincoln, and Coos), voting in the Portland metropolitan area clearly reflected the toll of the election-eve attacks. The *Review* quoted GOP chair Peter Gunnar who attributed the circulars to "fringe groups" beyond the party's control.[29] Among the letters of condolences was one from Nathalie Panek:

> I've managed to put off writing because I don't seem to know how to say that my heart is broken. It's not exactly rational but more than anything—more than Kennedy and the whole state—I wanted you to make it. I hope that the right-wing screwbats who gave you so much trouble have a chance to cool their heels in jail.[30]

The libel trials that took place in May and September of 1961 were a constant presence in Sweetland's life during a period when he was tending to his newspaper business, attempting to land an appointment with the Kennedy administration, and sitting through another session of the Oregon legislature. Multnomah County district attorney Charles Raymond indicted five people for political criminal libel, among them Reverend Claude Pike, a conservative radio commentator on KGON, and Homer Rogers, owner of the Freedom Book Store, specializing in anticommunist literature, both of them members of the Oregon Committee for Honest Politics. A sixth person was subsequently arrested in Washington County for distributing the handbill at a school meeting.[31]

Because he would be expected to testify, Sweetland began contacting friends from the 1930s to refresh his memory "about the struggles during those years." With a travel agenda that included the Kennedy inaugural, he contacted former associates Norman Thomas and James Carey and asked for an hour of their time. Portland attorneys Paul Meyer and Paul Hanlon, working pro bono, were busy contacting Sweetland friends from the Oregon Commonwealth Federation willing to testify about his strident anticommunism.[32] Two key people were longtime friend Nathalie Panek and Howard Costigan, the former executive secretary of the Washington Commonwealth Federation (WCF). Panek thought Costigan—a communist when he was with the WCF, but who left the party in 1939 when the Soviet Union signed the nonaggression pact with Germany—would be a good witness: "He's certainly experienced testifying and has nothing but good will toward you."[33]

After the failed prosecution of the person handing out handbills at the school meeting, Panek asked about the case against the principal defendants.

"This is a terrible ordeal for the Sweetlands," she noted. "A victory would be wonderful but defeat would be devastating—and Lil needs to get away for a while." For the next trial, she hoped "we can be celebrating a victory over the pea brains." The notoriety of the libel cases also attracted the attention of the conservative *National Review*, which supported the Oregon Committee for Honest Politics. The committee's efforts showed Sweetland's "connection with left wing groups throughout his life." The *Review* hoped the district attorney would fail in prosecuting "the desperadoes" with a "margin as devastating as the margin by which Sweetland was repudiated at the polls."[34]

The trial of the five defendants, scheduled to begin September 25, was reset for October, because the Sweetlands would be out of the country for much of September. When Lil and Monroe returned, the case concluded after extended negotiations when a single defendant, Homer Rogers, pleaded guilty to one charge of political criminal libel—that Sweetland's father had disinherited him because of his radical politics. Judge Arno Denecke delayed sentencing until after the 1962 general election with the proviso that all charges would be dropped if Rogers behaved properly. The district attorney then dismissed the libel charges against the other defendants. Sweetland welcomed the guilty plea as a personal vindication that the leaflets were untruthful.[35]

Because the case was settled within days of the Sweetlands' return from their world travels, it appears that Monroe wanted the issue behind him— that he was personally through with politics and anxious to move on to new challenges. "The GOP oriented *Oregonian*," Stan Federman argues, published a series of articles that helped put "an end to Monroe's political career in Oregon." After the 1960 campaign and its Red Scare ugliness, Sweetland "never fully recovered that previous marvelous passion he had for the political ring." Following the 1962 elections, Judge Denecke, who would soon be on the Oregon Supreme Court, ordered the suspension of Homer Rogers's conviction. The *Oregon Journal* reported Denecke's judgment that Rogers had taken no part in political activity and that "the record should be straightened up." A photograph of Freedom Book Store operator Homer Rogers, who was eighty-one years old, shows a tall, balding, bespectacled man in suit and tie, the symbol of conservative respectability.[36]

In a New Year's Eve editorial in the *Milwaukie Review*, Sweetland used the adjective "soggy" to describe the prospects for 1961. After seeing the reference in *Wall Street Journal's* business advice for readers, he determined that it might be "the prevailing mood of the New Year." Holiday shoppers were restrained, unemployment was high, and most of the jobless were unskilled workers. For Sweetland, that indicator meant the need for more educated and skilled workers better-equipped to hold onto their jobs, even in a down economy. The silver lining, however, was the new activist president who was "determined not to be trapped by a recession deepening into depression."[37]

Before vesting his energies in the 1961 legislative session, Sweetland made a concerted effort to secure an appointment with the Kennedy administration. He had, after all, expended considerable political capital in working for Kennedy's election to the presidency. There is more than a bit of irony in Sweetland's support for John Kennedy, because Minnesota senator Hubert Humphrey, Monroe's friend and ideological colleague since 1948, was also a candidate for the Democratic nomination for president in 1960. Humphrey and Sweetland had formed a philosophical bond in the fight over the civil rights plank at the Democratic Party Convention in 1948. Both were charter members of Americans for Democratic Action (ADA), and when Humphrey and his wife Muriel passed through Portland, they usually socialized with Lil and Monroe. There was still more: Lil's twin sister, Vi Gunther, was ADA's political secretary and, like other ADA members, supported Humphrey's candidacy.

Although Sweetland had participated at some level in presidential campaigns since 1928 and supported Adlai Stevenson's failed presidential runs in 1952 and 1956, he was far more involved—and at an earlier date—in the events leading to Kennedy's nomination in 1960. Precisely when Sweetland decided to back Kennedy is unclear, but the correspondence with Kennedy and his staff dates to May 1959. Long after the election, Sweetland claimed that he and John Kenneth Galbraith were "among the earliest . . . liberals to back JFK." Stan Federman claims that Sweetland "believed Kennedy was the shining knight the Democrats needed to recapture the White House."[38]

As Humphrey was gearing up for his first run for the White House, he wrote Sweetland in May 1959 asking for his advice: "You know the ins and outs of Oregon politics, so I will surely appreciate any observations or guidance you can give me." Humphrey was unaware that Sweetland had already contacted Kennedy advisor Ted Sorenson, a point the Massachusetts senator acknowledged in a note expressing gratitude "for the help and advice you gave to Ted Sorenson." Kennedy hoped they would "work more closely together in the future."[39] When news of Sweetland's dalliance with the Kennedy campaign reached ADA headquarters in New York City, Vi Gunther wrote Monroe that her colleagues were distressed that he would support the Massachusetts senator. While Kennedy's nomination would not be "an unmitigated disaster," she thought "it's taking a hell of a big chance" with someone who only recently had cultivated the image as a courageous liberal. Gunther quoted Humphrey's reaction when he learned of Monroe's decision: "How could Monroe not be for me—why we think alike on every issue. I'd be for Monroe for anything."[40]

Humphrey's pleading letter followed in short order:

> I hear that you have been coming out and speaking for Senator
> Kennedy. I just can't believe it. This is no reflection on Jack; he
> is a fine fellow. But really, Monroe, when we stuck up a ten-year
> record in Congress on the liberal issues that affect the Northwest, I
> believe that you will agree my record takes no second place. More
> significantly, I had always looked upon you as a close personal
> friend and political ally. We have campaigned together out in
> Oregon, and I did so when there was nothing in it for me. . . . What
> has happened? What is the magic touch of my friend Jack and the
> weakness of Humphrey?[41]

Friends near and far continued to express surprise that Sweetland had lined up with Kennedy. Sweetland acknowledged that most of his close friends were Humphrey supporters, but he expected Kennedy to benefit, especially from organized labor. Charles Press, a friend from East Lansing, Michigan, was "incredulous, distressed, disheartened" to learn Sweetland was supporting Kennedy. To Kennedy naysayers, Sweetland repeated his conventional argument that Humphrey could not win the general election. Only two Democrats could defeat Nixon—Kennedy or Adlai Stevenson— and "Kennedy is by far the most likely." Humphrey simply had not "registered enough with the people" to be successful in the present election cycle.[42]

When he visited Oregon in August 1959, Kennedy gave a spirited address to the Oregon AFL-CIO convention in Seaside, emphasizing his opposition to anti-labor legislation. His enthusiastic reception prompted the *Oregonian* to declare that Kennedy would do well in next year's presidential primaries. The newspaper noted that his audience appeal was obvious:

From left to right, Oregon Congresswoman Edith Green, Monroe Sweetland, Jacqueline Kennedy, Senator John F. Kennedy, and an unidentified woman, during a Kennedy campaign event in Oregon, 1960. (Courtesy of the Oregon Historical Society)

"sincerity, youthful vigor and good humor." The Massachusetts senator, however, had yet to prove that he was a fighter, "a major asset of Vice President Nixon." Kennedy thanked Sweetland after the visit and said that he would need his "persuasiveness" in the coming months.[43]

Although he had not announced his candidacy, Kennedy was laying the groundwork for the 1960 campaign. He spent time in delegate-rich California and made several stops in Oregon and Washington. Joe Miller—a University of Oregon graduate and self-styled "political junkie"—joined the Kennedy campaign in early 1959 to work the strategic states of Wisconsin, Oregon, and West Virginia.[44] Miller praised Sweetland for his "far-flung reputation among liberals" and thought he could be helpful to Kennedy beyond Oregon. In his travels about the country, he was often asked, "How's my old buddy Monroe Sweetland?" Sweetland told Miller he was working for Kennedy's fortunes in Oregon and was attempting to form "a national committee of liberals . . . for Kennedy." Shortly after this exchange, Sweetland introduced Kennedy when he made a whirlwind tour through Oregon between November 6 and 8.[45]

As the 1960 election season opened, Democratic candidates and their entourages began trouping to the key primary states—Wisconsin, West Virginia, and Oregon. After filing an affidavit in July 1959 that he would not become a candidate for president, Senator Wayne Morse entered the Oregon primary as a favorite-son candidate just before Christmas. Despite

Morse's declaration, Oregon's leading Democrats were either committed to Kennedy or Humphrey.[46] Although Morse campaigned feverishly with little money and no serious Democratic support, the other candidates never took him seriously. Oregon's May primary turned into a win for Kennedy with 51 percent of the vote. Favorite-son candidate Wayne Morse garnered 31.9 percent, and Humphrey, the closest among the major candidates, gleaned only 5.7 percent. Sweetland informed Kennedy that he won thirty-four of Oregon's thirty-six counties and added that he thought Morse was on a "vendetta," his hostility directed at Edith Green, Charlie Porter, and Sweetland for "disloyalty."[47]

The Democratic Party's nominating convention convened in Los Angeles from July 11 to 15. As a delegate committed to Kennedy, Sweetland was attending his fifth Democratic National Convention. Shortly before the delegates arrived in Los Angeles, Texas senator Lyndon Johnson, the powerful Senate majority leader, and perennial candidate Adlai Stevenson announced their candidacies. The Johnson and Stevenson entries, however, were no match for the well-organized Kennedy machine. With the first round of balloting completed, Kennedy emerged with more than 50 percent of the votes, the minimum requirement for nomination. All was well with Sweetland and friends until Kennedy chose Lyndon Johnson as his running mate. Liberals were outraged, with Sweetland expressing his dismay in a live television interview with NBC's Herb Kaplow. To a constituent who praised his "moral courage and personal integrity," Sweetland replied that in politics one could never "be sure what will work out for the best."[48] While Sweetland accepted praise for his remarks to Kaplow, he quickly accepted the ticket and believed Johnson would help sell Democrats to party conservatives.[49]

With the exception of Maurine Neuberger's resounding win to succeed her late husband in the U.S. Senate, Oregon Democrats did not fare well in 1960. Although Kennedy won narrowly at the national level, Democrats suffered defeat in most of the western states, except for California. Kennedy's victory, Sweetland's *Milwaukie Review* argued, should be attributed to his running mate, Lyndon Johnson, who held most of the Southern states for the Democrats "without compromising the strong platform commitments on civil right(s) and economic progress." Those who opposed Johnson as Kennedy's running mate "must eat their words and revise their estimates."[50] Sweetland was obviously tempering his criticisms in the face of the election victory.

Despite the onset of the 1961 meeting of the Oregon legislature, Sweetland turned his attention to landing a federal appointment with the Kennedy administration. As the earliest prominent Oregon Democrat to declare for Kennedy and the person who worked tirelessly to push his campaign in the state and elsewhere, Sweetland would seem an obvious candidate for a federal job. Oregon's Democratic National Committeeman, Jebby Davidson, wrote Michigan governor G. Mennen Williams—who had just been designated Assistant Secretary of State for African Affairs—about an assignment for Sweetland. He praised Monroe as Oregon's most respected leader in civil rights, race relations, and education. Davidson cautioned, however, that Sweetland would leave Oregon only if he was offered something "in his area of special interest." Title or rank was less important than "the nature of the job to be done."[51]

Sweetland wrote to Arthur Schlesinger, Jr., providing him with personal biographical information for the Harvard historian's forthcoming trip to Washington. Among his notes, Sweetland listed "first Democratic leader in Oregon to declare for JFK for the nomination (about May 1959)." If he were offered a position in the administration, he would take leave from the legislature. Sweetland contacted Kennedy staffer Ted Sorenson, expressing interest in education, scholarship, and race-related areas. He asked: "Is this the way to put my hat in the ring?" Sorenson responded that Sweetland's application was in "the proper channels with a strong recommendation."[52]

Other supporters made inquiries on Sweetland's behalf. Wayne Morse offered assistance, although it may have been pro forma, because Morse collaborated with Edith Green to obtain a seat on the Federal Power Commission for Howard Morgan. Morse, however, asked Sweetland "in confidence" if there were a particular job he was seeking. Hubert Humphrey was another who offered his services: "Seems to me you ought to be in this national administration. You surely deserve it in light of the hard work you have put in for Senator Kennedy." Sweetland interviewed with former congressman James Quigley, the new assistant secretary in the Department of Health, Education and Welfare (HEW) for a position with the "International desk." Back in Oregon, he wrote Quigley "that nothing in the Federal service had quite the attraction for me as the broad scope of Health, Education & Welfare." In the interim, he announced in the *Milwaukie Review* that he was taking a year's leave of absence to seek employment outside the state.[53]

Sweetland wrote Humphrey that "a note from you would be enormously helpful" for the HEW position. He also had what he considered a firm offer with George Weaver, a good friend from the 1930s and the new special assistant to the secretary of labor in charge of "international affairs." In a letter to Edith Green, he hoped that Howard Morgan would land the position with the Federal Power Commission (FPC). When Green received his letter, Morgan had already been named to the Power Commission. Sweetland quickly fired off a short note to Morgan congratulating him on his selection and apologized for Democrats who criticized his appointment.[54] This was a minefield for Sweetland, who had to walk a tightrope through Oregon's faction-ridden Democratic leadership in his quest for a federal appointment.

In truth, by early February the sands were running out for Sweetland's prospects. An undated, angry letter from Lil speaks volumes about the forces at play:

> I'm sorry I made you unhappy last night by the vigor of my reaction
> to the two possible appointments. But I was, and am, outraged.
> I've been in and around the fringes of this dirty game long enough,
> god knows, to fully realize that neither justice nor logic play roles
> in politics! But I am not yet so callous that I can accept with
> equanimity the failure of those whom you have served so well,
> and at so much sacrifice, to give you recognition with prestige and
> responsibility. I am very damn tired of frustration and hurt, and
> completely outraged (I repeat because it's the exact word) that
> men of no ability (Kelsay) and men who were outstanding for their
> efforts to defeat Kennedy (Morgan) could be rewarded with the
> highest appointments anyone in this state has or will receive. I know
> you don't share this personal, myopic view—and undoubtedly
> you are not "tough" or "positive" enough to bludgeon recognition
> or reward—but I am mad clear through to the marrow of my
> bones—[55]

Lil wrote the letter while Monroe was traveling on the East Coast. In early February the *Oregonian*'s Washington correspondent, A. Robert Smith, reviewed the realities of obtaining appointments with the Kennedy administration. The most influential regional people with influence in the White House were Washington senator Henry "Scoop" Jackson and Oregon congresswoman Edith Green. While Jackson handpicked the head of the Bonneville Power Administration (BPA), Charles Luce, Green chose Howard Morgan for the Federal Power Commission. "Jackson and Mrs. Green," Smith told readers, "are marked for commanding roles in the years immediately ahead." President Kennedy consulted with Green about important positions, including the FPC. Smith concluded with an assessment of Democratic Party factionalism in Oregon in which "Morgan has been prominent," but "he has always had Representative Green as a friend and ally."[56]

The HEW "international" position was the first possibility to fall through. In late February Sweetland was still corresponding with George Weaver, asking the special labor assistant if he should mobilize Sorenson and others on his behalf. Senator Morse wrote Weaver that Monroe would be happy to work with him. Morse reported that he had discussed Sweetland's prospects with Vice President Johnson, but came away with the impression that there was no chance of Sweetland landing an appointment on Johnson's Committee on Equal Employment Opportunity. The Oregon senator urged Weaver to consider Sweetland for a job on his staff, even if it were not one completely to his liking. Two days after Morse's letter to Weaver, Sweetland informed Morse that he would forgo a federal appointment for the moment.[57]

George Edwards, Sweetland's partner as an organizer with the League for Industrial Democracy, wrote finis to Sweetland's pursuit of a Kennedy administration appointment. A justice on Michigan's Supreme Court, Edwards recounted a visit to Washington and meeting Sweetland's in-laws, Vi and John Gunther. In a remarkably candid note, Edwards told Monroe that he thought Monroe's effort to land a job in Washington was a reaction to his political defeats in Oregon, and that Monroe had lost sight of his contributions. Then Edwards spoke to truth—that for both of them there may be "political limits and we may have to learn to live with them and within them." Although unsolicited advice was usually unwelcome, Edwards hoped he would be forgiven "when it comes from genuine affection and concern."[58]

The hiatus between the adjournment of the 1959 legislature and the convening of the 1961 session may have been the most hectic of Sweetland's event-filled life. He entered the new legislature with conflicted emotions— the exhilaration of John F. Kennedy's defeat of Richard Nixon for the presidency and the resurgence of the Republican Party at home—his loss to

Howell Appling, John Durno's win over Charles Porter in the fourth district, and Republicans narrowing Democratic majorities in both the House and the Senate. Moreover, many Democrats now in the legislature were conservative, one indication being the election of Democrat Walter Pearson as Senate president.[59] Added to these disappointments was the growing realization that the politics of federal appointments in Oregon and Washington were not in his favor.

As chair of the Senate Education Committee, Sweetland would be in the crosshairs of the three-volume findings of a legislative interim commission on education that addressed financing and distribution of state funding, school reorganization, and teacher tenure. Under the leadership of research director Tom Rigby, the commission recommended two of Sweetland's education objectives—a state contribution of 50 percent for school operating costs and equalizing funding across districts to provide every child with a uniform educational experience.[60] Although Governor Hatfield supported quality public schools, his fiscal conservatism and the conservative legislature indicated that increased state support did not look promising.

Another vexing legislative issue was tenure for teachers and some administrators. The Oregon School Boards Association was seeking to modify standards for teacher tenure after three years, providing performance and service were satisfactory. At the same time, the Oregon Education Association was pushing a bill to include small school districts hitherto not covered under the tenure law. But it was House Bill 1082, the stalking horse for weakening teacher tenure, that upset educational professionals. Speaking for his school's faculty, Richard Rosekang warned that school boards and administrators in smaller communities imposed "the most flagrant infringements on individual expression."[61] OEA executive secretary Cecil Posey added that principals would have difficulty carrying out their duties without job security. Because HB 1082 failed to include principals and vice principals, a Portland administrator urged Sweetland to oppose the measure.[62]

At Sweetland's urging, the Senate Education Committee tabled HB 1082. The *Oregonian* immediately accused the OEA of "shameful lobbying" and "disgraceful" and "stupid" campaigning. Despite a favorable ballot in the House (36 to 19), the Senate Education Committee's vote removed the immediate threat to teacher tenure. It was clear that, firmly committed to labor unions and worker protection since the 1930s, Sweetland would oppose any move to weaken teacher tenure. In the end the *Oregonian* praised the 1961 session, citing the "disinclination of the Legislature to adopt important changes in policies and activities of state government" and attributing its success to an experienced alliance of conservative Democrats and Republicans.[63]

Although the *Oregonian* boasted that conservative legislators kept liberals at bay, Sweetland could point to initiatives benefitting the long-range health of Oregon's educational system. His effort to establish a Graduate School of Social Work at Portland State College bore fruit when it received an appropriation of $167,685 in the 1961 session. More important for broadening educational opportunities across the state, Sweetland's community college proposal was gaining momentum, despite grumbling in some parts of the state. With the potential for federal aid for community colleges, Sweetland worked closely with representatives Edith Green and Al Ullman. In the absence of federal assistance, Sweetland wrote Ullman, Oregon's ambitious community college program would struggle, because construction programs in several parts of the state would suffer.[64]

In a *Milwaukie Review* editorial, Sweetland judged the 1961 legislature's achievements modest: "Just as water cannot rise above its source, the Senate coalition of ten Republicans and a few right-wing Democrats put a ceiling on progress exactly when Oregon needed to move forward." But Democrats "were able to checkmate" most of the coalition's major objectives—defeating harmful labor bills and both higher education and public schools fared well. Student scholarships and community colleges made major advances, and there were slight increases in funding for school districts. He was especially proud that Clackamas County would "probably use the new community college law within a few years." Sweetland's prediction proved prophetic; within a year Clackamas citizens had formed a committee to establish a community college district, a move that led to the offering of classes in Gladstone High School in the fall of 1966.[65]

The shuttering of the 1961 legislature marked a major transition in Monroe Sweetland's life. His decision not to seek reelection to the Senate is not surprising after the disappointing loss in his second campaign for secretary of state. The *Bend Bulletin*, now under the editorship of Robert Chandler, who succeeded Robert Sawyer in 1953, reasoned that Sweetland's bitter loss to Howell Appling "must have made him feel that the end of the political road was near." Referring to Sweetland as "our favorite Democrat," the *Bulletin* described him as "an able man and an articulate spokesman for . . . liberalism. He has been a man of integrity. His campaigns were always conducted on the highest level." The newspaper speculated that there would be "something in the future . . . which will put to the best use his restless energy and fine mind."[66]

That "something" would be a grand venture that he and Lil referred to as their World Tour, circumnavigating the globe to visit faraway lands— Japan, Indonesia, India, Israel, and points beyond. The long journey would eventually lead to an academic year appointment at Padjadaran University in Bandung, Indonesia, where Monroe would serve as a visiting professor of journalism and the family would travel through much of the island nation. And whether it was a visit to Tokyo, Java, or Jerusalem, Monroe always proved the astute observer.

11
Southeast Asia Calling

With the purchase of the *Milwaukie Review* and its weekly companion, the *Shopper*, the ever-optimistic Monroe Sweetland assured friends that the success of the enterprise had freed him to pursue politics on an expanded scale. Sweetland's old Achilles' heel of improperly kept account ledgers—mixing political expenditures with business costs—resurfaced in 1958 when Jebby Davidson, an investor in the enterprise, asked to have the *Review*'s books audited on a monthly basis. At Davidson's suggestion, the Sweetlands incorporated the business in the fall of 1958, with Davidson and Ancil Payne as company directors.[1] Davidson was a partner in the firm Frontiers-Oregon, Ltd., and Payne worked for the company.

Under Payne's signature, Frontiers informed Sweetland in May 1959 that loans to the *Milwaukie Review* dating to March 1957 were long overdue. "Since the date of your incorporation," Payne wrote, "no payment has been made . . . toward the reduction of the capital loans or the accrued interest." When the board of directors reviewed the company's operations in January 1959, they determined that the labor force was excessive and directed Sweetland to release his foreman. In a second letter, noting that the foreman was still employed, Frontiers insisted that the person be immediately dismissed to reduce operating costs. Writing for Frontiers, Payne informed Sweetland that the company needed to protect its securities in what it judged "an uneconomical operation."[2]

In a less formal cover letter, Payne told Sweetland to use Frontiers legal statement in releasing the foreman. There were other problems facing the *Review*, related to a forthcoming labor agreement involving retroactive wage increases. Payne urged an immediate board meeting to "face up to our problems." With the 1960 election season looming on the horizon, he wanted to see the *Review* "in a sound fiscal position" while Sweetland was campaigning—then he could claim that he had "properly managed a successful business." It would also help "from your own emotional and psychological viewpoint."[3]

Although Sweetland dismissed the foreman, the *Review's* problems persisted into the fall. Payne wrote again in October 1959 that, despite personnel changes, payroll expenses were up 12 percent for the "back shop" during the previous nine months. Charges for supplies had also inexplicably increased, and travel and auto expenses had increased to more than $300 per month. Payne asked the obvious: "Are you billing the Kennedy Committee for the use of your car?" He urged Sweetland to arrange repayment for expenses unrelated to the newspaper business. Even more alarming, Payne indicated that the *Review* was showing a loss for the calendar year of $812 through September, whereas last year's audit had shown a profit of $3,762. Payne's call for another board meeting resulted in retaining Stan Federman a month later to oversee the entire management of the enterprise.[4]

Federman revolutionized the efficiency and operations of the *Milwaukie Review*. "Who would believe it," he wrote Davidson five months after he took the job. "From a 'have not' outfit we have suddenly blossomed into a 'have'"—to the point that the business was "going to have a tax problem" by the end of the fiscal year. He and Monroe and Lil would be having a "'board' meeting" to determine how to reduce their monthly net for the remainder of the year. Federman attributed the turnaround to increasing efficiency in back-shop production, keeping a wary eye on purchases to avoid redundancies, and gradually raising the newspaper's abysmally low advertising rates. Federman also happily reported "we have no account over $25 that's more than 60 days old." Living in retirement in Milwaukie after a long and successful career with the *Oregonian*, Federman admitted that he arranged "huge increases in ad revenues, money they [Lil and Monroe] used to clear up debts and which provided Monroe with working capital for his politics."[5]

Stan Federman had been managing the *Review's* striking financial successes for about thirty months in June 1962 when he reported to Davidson that the recent fiscal year was the best "since Monroe bought it back in '54." In the midst of the *Review's* positive news, however, he warned Davidson about a serious advertising competitor, a person he referred to as "Clark":

"Were it not for the Clark competition we literally would be looking forward to 'easy street' . . . but, Clark is here, and he's not going to disappear. He's our problem . . . today, tomorrow and for as long as we're in Milwaukie." Federman then turned to the point of his letter:

> Monroe is the eternal optimist, always the rose-colored glasses, things will always work out, . . . "let's keep playing it by the ear." I don't think we can, Jebby; not anymore. It's time for a decision: we have in my opinion, three ways open to us: we can eventually beat him, . . . we can stay in there and slug it out on an even basis with him . . . or we can pull out.

The newspaper lacked the working capital to take on Clark, and it could not afford to lose more advertisers, because Clark was "constantly applying pressure to our current accounts." His recommendation to Davidson was to find "some eager beaver" with money and sell "while we still have a solid gross just behind us."[6]

"Monroe in his heart hates the idea of selling," Federman told Davidson, "so regardless of what I tell him, he sees everything eventually working out." He advised selling immediately "if we can swing a deal which will bring you and Monroe a price that makes it worthwhile." Federman believed he was being a realist; he had been in the newspaper game long enough to understand trends. He enclosed with his letter the addresses and phone numbers of newspaper sales organizations. "I'll let you be the gunner on it, Jebby."[7] Whether Federman or Davidson was the more persuasive, the Sweetlands sold the newspaper in September 1962. The sale of the *Milwaukie Review* and the *North Clackamas Shopper* indicates that the Sweetlands were anticipating major changes in their lives. Federman promised to stay on with the new owner, Idaho newspaperman Dale Johnson. The news release announcing the sale of the *Review* informed readers that Monroe's "work far away from Oregon makes unwise our continued proprietorship." The Sweetlands planned to keep their Milwaukie house, however.[8]

With the adjournment of the 1961 legislature, the Sweetlands embarked on a global tour that would take them to Japan, the Philippines, Indonesia, and eventually to New Delhi, India, where Monroe would be attending the World Assembly of Teaching Organizations, courtesy of an invitation from the National Education Association (NEA). In a letter to a friend in New Delhi, Sweetland described the trip as "the experience of a lifetime," especially for "a couple of provincials like Lil (my wife) and me." With the *Milwaukie Review* still under the capable management of Stan Federman, the Sweetlands' two-month journey would lead ultimately to a visiting professorship in Bandung, Indonesia. Daughter Barbara, who had married Harvard law student Floyd Smith in June 1960—with six-year-old sister Rebecca as flower girl—was living in Cambridge, Massachusetts. Rebecca, now seven, flew to Boston, and Barbara and Floyd took her to Martha's Vineyard where she would spend the summer of 1961 with Lil's mother.[9]

Before their departure, Sweetland contacted Portland friend George Azumano for advice about places to visit during their stay in Tokyo. Azumano wrote journalist friend George Somekawa in Tokyo seeking his counsel, including a request that was vintage Sweetland: "He is not interested in sight-seeing. He has a great interest in people and would like to talk to various persons regarding the political and social situations." Sweetland also corresponded with John Kenneth Galbraith, esteemed liberal economist and ambassador to India, who arranged hotel accommodations in New Delhi. Sweetland thanked Galbraith—an original board member of Americans for Democratic Action—and provided an itinerary of their travels.[10]

True to his affinity for journalism, Sweetland published a trove of observations in the *Milwaukie Review* about the places they visited. In Tokyo, George Somekawa treated the Sweetlands to a tour of the Japanese Diet and arranged a meeting with the speaker and deputy speaker of the lawmaking body. The Sweetland's stop in Manila provided "a treasure-house of memories for Americans"—they visited public buildings and memorial cemeteries and drove through small villages "where the basic life of the Islands is lived." In Hong Kong, the family observed their "first authentic 'ugly American,'" a man from Los Angeles. Alluding to Eugene Burdick and William Lederer's classic novel, *The Ugly American*, Sweetland thought the authors "could have used him as a model for one of their chapters in the book which jolted the American conscience two years ago."[11]

In a column written in late July, Sweetland described their seven-day visit to Indonesia, "the very Shangri la of the enchanted islands." Few Americans knew much about Southeast Asia and would certainly have failed a geography test. Of the nations in the region, Indonesia was the largest—ninety million people scattered through some seven thousand islands, spanning a distance wider than the United States across the equatorial Pacific. Sweetland described the ethnic and cultural makeup of the country, its colonial background as the Dutch East Indies, and Indonesia's importance to Cold War geopolitics. While the nation borrowed elements of American education and production, its people associated capitalism with Dutch colonialism "and talk about it loudly in their politics."[12]

Indonesia's neutrality in the Cold War intrigued Sweetland, especially after Soviet premier Nikita Khrushchev spent three weeks visiting the country in 1959. Sweetland cautioned that Indonesia's communist party supported President Sukarno's government but "awaits the right time for decisive action." With both China and Russia playing chess over smaller nations in the region, the Indonesia party's real focus was "big and vital Indonesia." If the party was successful," he wrote, it would deliver "Asia to their cause." Indonesians, however, were freedom-loving, and everywhere he and Lil traveled they met people "who like American ways, who want American friends and friendship."[13]

As the coming months would prove, Indonesia loomed large in Sweetland's thinking. His interests and commentaries about the nation were filtered through a Cold War ideological lens that juxtaposed Soviet and Chinese communism against the democratic, market economies of the West.[14] There was an obvious excitement among the Indonesian people— beauty and color infused daily life, with yard ways pleasingly landscaped and decorated with flowers, even among the poorest residences. Before leaving Djakarta, they met the American ambassador to Indonesia, Howard Jones. A holdover appointee from the Eisenhower administration, Jones was popular among Americans and Indonesians for performing a "difficult task in a difficult country." The Sweetlands were treated to a stay at the U.S. Embassy for the last part of their visit. Communist-inspired demonstrators had sacked the embassy grounds earlier, Sweetland explained, as a reaction to the assassination of Patrice Lumumba, the hero of independence in the Democratic Republic of the Congo. The rioters stripped furniture and fixtures from the spacious veranda and burned the debris on the front lawn.[15] Sweetland's assessment of the rioters' rapacious behavior reflected his tendency to attribute vile motives to ideologically driven incidents he disagreed with.

The Sweetlands' sojourn in India was different: "The sights and sounds and smells and even its explosive politics and spiritualism impinge on you from all directions." With Monroe's conference commitments in New Delhi taking up most of his time, the Sweetlands devoted early mornings and evenings and a day or two after the meeting adjourned to travel about the great city. They visited the opening of the Indian parliament and observed Prime Minister Jawaharlal Nehru parry with news reporters. Indians, Monroe reported, were fond of Ambassador John Kenneth Galbraith, despite the negative views of communists. Nehru's large and unwieldy Congress Party was "an uneasy coalition, already affected with old bones." While India was making great gains in economic progress and education, Sweetland observed that population increases were weighing on its successes.[16]

The principal object of Sweetland's trip, the eleventh conference of the World Confederation of Organizations of the Teaching Profession, attracted people from seventy-six nations. The keynote speaker, Prime Minister Nehru, told the gathering that the best-educated nations had failed in their greatest mission—achieving peace. Even those countries that had rid themselves of poverty were "full of hostility toward each other." Elsewhere at the conference, Sweetland observed other differences—American teachers saw themselves as professionals, whereas in most countries teachers considered themselves important segments of the labor movement.[17]

With their exhaustive stay in New Delhi behind them, the Sweetlands were off to the Middle East in mid-August, where they traveled through Iran, Lebanon, Jordan, and Israel. Monroe's views on the troubled region appear in the opening line of a *Milwaukie Review* column: "After a week of Arab indoctrination on the evils of Israel during our visits in Lebanon and the Hashemite Kingdom of Jordan, Mrs. Sweetland and I entered 'The Promised Land'" via Jerusalem. They navigated through barbed-wire and concrete roadblocks, but once on the sixty-mile bus trip to Tel Aviv, they saw olive and citrus orchards, vineyards, and overhead irrigation systems. Israel's beauty, however, could not hide the uncomfortable reality of conflict, "the rusting hulks of trucks and tanks blasted into wreckage in the Arab-Israel warfare of only a few years ago."[18]

Before returning stateside, the Sweetlands visited the "Eternal City" and had an opportunity to observe Pope John firsthand. After presenting their credentials in Rome, the Sweetlands made the trip "through the vineyard-decked Etruscan countryside" to the Pope's summer residence at Castel Gandolfo. The Pope's audience represented "every nation, every race"—women in beautiful saris from India, and Africans, Swedes, and

Germans.[19] From Rome the Sweetlands flew to Paris and then to London for a few days, including a train trip to Oxford. From London they were off to New York City on September 8 and rented a car for the drive to Martha's Vineyard, where Rebecca was still in Nanna's care. The family spent a day in New York City and another "crowded day of reports and interviews in Washington, D.C." They returned to Portland in mid-September just as the final settlement of the libel cases was released.[20]

Sweetland's loss in the secretary of state contest in 1960 and his decision not to seek reelection to the Senate put his career options in limbo. Lil and Monroe's extended stay in Indonesia in July 1961 provides only the faintest hint of future possibilities. After returning from their global journey, Monroe gave several talks in the greater Portland area on Indonesia. A *Milwaukie Review* editorial, "Let's Be Fair," published on December 21, 1961, offers another suggestion about Sweetland's growing interest in the island nation. The *Review* took the *Oregonian* to task for denouncing Indonesia's President Sukarno for his efforts to seize West Irian (West New Guinea) from Dutch control, because the Dutch agreed to transfer all its colonies to Indonesia when it became independent in 1946. The United States, he charged, should not identify itself with "dying colonial systems" but should support emerging nations to avoid having the Soviets accuse the United States of obstructing justice.[21]

Two newspaper items, one in the *Oregonian*, the second in the *Milwaukie Review*, indicate that Sweetland would be leaving to assume a new job. In January 1962 an *Oregonian* column revealed that Sweetland would be taking a year's leave of absence to pursue "an overseas assignment for some organization." Information about the new position, he told a reporter, would await word from the employer. A few days later Sweetland announced in the *Milwaukie Review* that Stan Federman would be the new editor of the newspaper "during my absence which is of indefinite duration." Sweetland's explanation was brief: "For several months I will take part in a program of orientation and study toward new duties which will take me out of the Northwest."[22]

The beginnings of Sweetland's new venture, the Indonesian-American Society, rest in correspondence and telephone conversations, between December 1961 and January 1962, and an oral interview with Sweetland in

1986. When Sweetland's Indonesian ventures were in the past, New York's Robert Delson claimed responsibility, "together with Monroe Sweetland," in organizing the Indonesian-American Society "and in procuring the cooperation and assistance of the Indonesian embassy." In his 1986 interview, Sweetland attributed the Society's beginnings to the American ambassador to Indonesia, Howard Palfrey Jones. Alexander Shakow, who joined Sweetland as an East Coast organizer for the Society, agrees that Jones may have urged Sweetland "to do what he could to help improve relationships." Sweetland initially contacted the New York–based Asia Society, an organization dedicated to promoting knowledge about Asia in the United States. Through Asia Society's executive secretary, Wendy Sorensen, Sweetland put together an unofficial board of directors leading to establishing the Indonesian-American Society in June 1962.[23]

Sweetland's initial strategy to link the Indonesian-American Society with the older Asian Society ran aground when Sorensen told him that Asia Society's budget could not sustain an office on the West Coast. Frequent trips between Los Angeles and San Francisco and flights to New York and Washington, D.C., in the early months of 1962 suggested a frenetic schedule for Sweetland. Focusing on the Society's budget, Sweetland began courting corporate donors, asking the executives of Lockheed Aircraft—"with a substantial stake in Indonesian development"—to fund programs to enhance U.S.-Indonesian relations. His request to the Bank of America included the caveat that the Indonesian-American Society was "a 'free' civilian agency of Americans, not controlled by either government but working closely with both. Its activities were non-political."[24]

During the first few months, Sweetland lived at Beverly House in Beverly Hills, California. The murky funding of Sweetland's early work with the Society raises suspicions about sources, because at least one member of the board of directors, Guy Pauker,[25] was linked to the Central Intelligence Agency (CIA) on Indonesian projects. Student board member Alexander Shakow remembers that Sweetland received no salary and does not believe he received funds from the CIA. Robert Delson, a radical New York City lawyer during the 1930s, was also heavily involved in promoting noncommunist governments in Southeast Asia after the Second World War. Delson was active in Indonesian-American relations and represented the Indonesian government in the United States. He worked with both ambassadors to promote favorable relations between Indonesia and the United States.[26]

At the Society's first official board meeting in Los Angeles (June 17, 1962), members amended the articles of incorporation and unanimously elected officers, including Sweetland as executive vice president and Guy Pauker as secretary.[27] After the Los Angeles meeting, Sweetland was off to Martha's Vineyard to meet Lil, Rebecca, and the Megrath clan. Society business, however, was closely interwoven with recreating. On Martha's Vineyard, home to "Eastern seaboard literati and eggheads," Sweetland met with the publisher of the *New Republic* and Roger Baldwin before leaving the island for Washington, D.C.[28]

When Sweetland returned to his quarters in Beverly Hills in late August, he wrote Shakow about his plan to leave the Society "as the principal organizer and factotum" early in the new year. Of those he had worked with the last few months, he hoped Shakow would succeed him. Although the Society had financial problems, he believed those would be overcome in the next months and remarked that Shakow's talents "were perfectly suited for Indonesia."[29] Although Shakow was uninterested in assuming Sweetland's responsibilities, he expressed frustration with the Indonesian field (both Indonesians and Americans). He worried that there were too many "ego people involved." He thought Wendy Sorensen and the Asia Society were merely passing on questions from various sources, especially about Guy Pauker serving as an officer of the Indonesian-American Society. There were questions about the Indonesian-American Society's finances, according to Shakow. While Sorensen thought Sweetland provided much of the money, others suggested "that the CIA or the like must be behind it."[30]

With California's Indonesian-American Society fundraising debacle behind him, Sweetland returned home in early February 1964 to ready for a year of teaching journalism at Padjadjaran University. He had made arrangements for this opportunity through his contacts with the Indonesian Embassy. Monroe, Lil, and nine-year-old Rebecca departed for Southeast Asia in late February, stopping in Japan, Hong Kong, and Singapore before reaching Bandung, Indonesia, in mid-March. They settled into a rental home, and Rebecca began attending a local English-speaking school. Monroe introduced himself to local Americans and busied himself with the Indonesian community and Padjadjaran University. In an informational letter to Indonesian president Sukarno he outlined his appointment as a guest lecturer at Padjadjaran University and explained that he had "no official status with the American government." Ambassador Howard Jones, he added, "has been continuously helpful to us." He reported that he had attended the opening session of the Provisional People's Consultative Congress and was impressed with the president's message.[31]

If Monroe pursued the high road, introducing himself to the Indonesian president, lecturing at Padjadjaran, and scouting other places to visit, Lil complained of inconsistent mail deliveries, because they seldom traveled to nearby Djakarta—"that steaming miserable city"—more than necessary. In a short note to Barbara, she reported Rebecca's success in attending the small English-speaking school. With her practiced eye for social insight, Lil added that the person heading the local American Association organization was a "prototype of the American clubwoman abroad," interested in promoting her own prestige among her fellow citizens for its "snob value."[32]

In an oft-related story, both Sweetlands enjoyed telling about one of the first trips in their Chevy Greenbrier Van.[33] Spending a short weekend at William "Bill" Palmer's villa in the mountains at Puncak Pass between Djakarta and Bandung, they awoke the next morning to find the Greenbrier high and dry—all four wheels stolen during the night along with the jack and other items. After friends loaned them wheels to bring the Greenbrier back to Bandung, Monroe reported that police had recovered "all their goods (and the perpetrators) in a nearby village."[34]

The gathering with William Palmer, a well-known representative of the motion picture industry, placed the Sweetlands in a social milieu with a man widely suspected of working with the CIA. In a meeting with President Sukarno in August 1963, Cornell Indonesian scholar George Kahin reported that the Indonesian head of state strongly suspected that Palmer was an intelligence agent. Jovial and well-liked by most Americans and many Indonesians, Palmer held weekend gatherings at his villa where, according to Kahin, "political gossip was intense" even if not well-informed about Djakarta politics. During their stay in Indonesia, the Sweetlands returned for other weekend retreats at the Palmer residence.[35]

From June through August, the Sweetlands traveled in the Greenbrier through Java and the big island of Sumatra. Lil described their trek—the Greenbrier packed with "bedding, pillows, tools, spare parts, thermos jugs, tinned food, toilet paper—and among non-essentials, Becky's new parrot, Kediri." The family passed through spectacular landscapes—"high, rugged jungle-snagged mountain passes over the volcanic ridge which bisects Java." Their accommodations were better than expected, especially the "hill stations" built in the mountains for the former Dutch colonials to relax. But there were common features everywhere—poverty, crowds of children, men carrying heavy loads, and women wearing apparel that varied from place to place.[36] Lil closed her letter with a story certain to resonate with friends and family:

> Those of you who are familiar (and you all are) with Monroe's impatience with traffic hazards and his desire to "get there," and who are also familiar with my unrestrained compulsions as a backseat driver—may have some idea of the atmosphere in the car as we thread our way, horn blowing, through a broken-field of yoked men, basket-balancing women, wide-burdened bicycles, horse carts, betjas, ox carts, trucks and occasional cars.

The Sweetlands' most consistent observation about their visit was Indonesia as a Cold War representation—the ubiquitous presence of the communist party, the Partai Komunis Indonesia (PKI). Even in remote Java villages, Lil noticed "the familiar red and white signs identifying the Party headquarters." Many of the Chinese-owned stores displayed the flag, along with an occasional photo of Mao Tse-tung. Although the PKI was popular beyond Indonesia's 2.5 million Chinese, the latter had borne the brunt of previous anti-Chinese riots. President Sukarno, pursuing a crude nonaligned politics between East and West, had survived a CIA-instigated rebellion in 1958, accommodated the powerful PKI, and instituted a practice of "guided democracy" in the aftermath of the turmoil. The incoming Kennedy administration, while continuing to support clandestine operations, improved ties through increased foreign aid and invited President Sukarno to Washington for a visit.[37]

Prior to Sukarno's White House visit in late April 1961, Kennedy strategists—including Secretary Rusk, CIA planners, and Ambassador Howard Jones—devised a strategy to resolve the West Irian situation with the Dutch and to offer a broad program of economic development.[38] Sweetland's arrival in Indonesia in the spring of 1963 coincided with stepped-up U.S. aid programs to the island nation. The Kennedy initiatives built on Ford Foundation grants to modernize Indonesia's infrastructure to achieve self-sustained economic growth and to undercut the PKI's influence. When President Kennedy's special envoy to Indonesia, Wilson Wyatt, was able to keep Sukarno from nationalizing American oil industries, Sweetland praised the emissary for building closer relations between Indonesia and the United States.[39]

With a close eye on Indonesian domestic affairs, Sweetland suggested that recent improved relations with Tokyo and Manila were evidence of a shift toward the West. To Arthur Schlesinger of Kennedy's White House staff, Sweetland confided that the PKI's influence was weakening because of its decision to side with China in its fractious relations with the Soviet Union. Despite Indonesia's "economic distress . . . apparent to all," Sukarno was a nationalist and certainly not communist in his leanings. Sweetland predicted that President Kennedy's trip to Indonesia in early 1964 would "open the gates to cooperation."[40]

In a letter to Alexa Saunders (with the Indonesian-American Society), Sweetland criticized America's "doomsday Cassandras" who predicted Indonesia's loss to the communist world. President Sukarno's initiatives were addressing the nation's economic problems, "vindicating those of us whose basic faith in Indonesians has been constant." Although communists remained "busy with their plans, in concert with their Peking pals," Sukarno was not playing into PKI hands. In a note to Indonesian ambassador Zarin Zain, Sweetland fretted over "the troubled times in the relationship between Congress and the President on . . . aid to Indonesian projects."[41] Sweetland's favorable assessment of Sukarno would change dramatically under a different Indonesian regime.

And then the shocking news of President Kennedy's assassination reached Bandung. A few days later Sweetland delivered a memorial address to American Association members, expressing "shock, grief, humiliation, disbelief, anger [and] outrage" at the president's death. As Americans living in a foreign country, his colleagues understood the implications of the president's assassination—"terrible for our Nation and for its relationships with other peoples." Americans in Indonesia were, nevertheless, grateful for the outpouring of sympathy from Indonesian friends "following the tragic news from Texas." Within two weeks he was writing to Hawaii's senator Daniel Inouye asking for help in shaping President Lyndon Johnson's positive views on Asia.[42]

During his last weeks in Indonesia, Sweetland lectured at Padjadjaran University and made trips to other universities on Java to deliver talks on journalism. Over one long week, he flew to Semarang, 374 kilometers (232 miles) east of Bandung to visit Diponororo University. From there he was off to Hasanuddin University in Surabaya, another 312 kilometers (193 miles) east of Semarang. In those visits he lectured on "The Standing of Journalism," a survey of classical journalism in the Western tradition, the rise of the modern newspaper industry, and the diminution of newspaper numbers in recent years. Among his "canned" lectures, "Hungry Teachers Cannot Teach," was especially appropriate to Indonesia where President Sukarno had recently doubled the base pay of teachers, "no easy task in an economy of scarcity."[43]

With her characteristic talent for explaining events, Lil told her mother about the family's annual holiday tree in their living room, courtesy of a friend who owned property in the mountains. Decorated with lights borrowed from another American, the tree attracted crowds of children. Although the family limited their personal-gift exchanges ("too much junk to lug home"), they received wonderful presents from Indonesian friends.[44] Otherwise, the Sweetlands were winding up their affairs in Bandung, obtaining exit permits and selling the Greenbrier. Lil was leaving behind difficult-to-find linens for their Indonesian friends. Many of the homeward-bound items were antiques not subject to duties. Monroe's university students—some of whom would write to him for years—feted him in a farewell gathering.[45]

The Sweetlands' return to the United States followed a circuitous route—Bangkok, Karachi, Cairo, Istanbul, Belgrade, Paris, London, and New York. From New York they stopped in Washington briefly before catching a United Airlines flight to Oregon. "It's great to be back," Sweetland told a reporter upon arriving in Portland. Responding to a question about Indonesia, he remarked that the "fierce drive of the Chinese Reds to dominate the Communist parties of Asia, and eventually the world" was Asia's great predicament. Although he would soon be moving toward a decade of political work with the National Education Association, Sweetland continued to lobby for AID programs for Indonesian journalism students.[46]

In his public appearances, Sweetland warned of the dangers of losing Indonesia to the Chinese communists. He told a Salem Kiwanis gathering that foremost among American problems was "Indonesian neutralism,"

President Sukarno's anti-American oratory, the large and vocal communist party, and the anti-Chinese demonstrations. He concluded with a personal version of the domino effect: If Indonesia fell to the Chinese communists, it would "swamp" smaller Southeast Asia nations, endanger the Philippines and Taiwan, and isolate Australia and New Zealand. When Indonesian-American relations deteriorated in the spring of 1965, Sweetland became more vocal in defending the U.S. presence in the island nation. The Peace Corps, he wrote the *San Francisco Chronicle*, had been magnificent: "We must never abandon the field to the Communists" or bend to anti-American rhetoric intended "to outrage U.S. opinion to the point of retreat."[47]

Indonesia's escalating anti-Americanism in 1964 and 1965 paralleled the spiraling violence in Vietnam as the United States began striking at Viet Cong guerilla forces in the south and, in March 1965, initiated a bombing campaign in the north. In the midst of rising violence in the region, Indonesia president Sukarno attempted to navigate between his powerful military and the PKI, the largest communist party in the noncommunist world. Under circumstances still hotly debated, young army officers staged a coup in Djakarta on September 30, 1965, seizing radio stations and killing six top generals. The coup was short-lived, however, as officers under General Suharto quickly moved to retake control of communications and accused the officers of acting in collusion with the PKI.[48]

What played out across Indonesia during the ensuing months—with the full support of General Suharto—was the massive liquidation of the PKI and anyone sympathetic to the party. Suharto demanded that "Communists be completely destroyed" and ordered the army to support lawless militias who, in conjunction with the army, killed somewhere between 600,000 and one million people between October 1965 and early 1966. Suharto and American officials (including Rand Corporation's Guy Pauker) hewed to the line that the PKI was deeply implicated in the coup. Subsequent research raised questions about such an analysis, because it relied heavily on a CIA study released three years after the September coup. Except for CIA operatives such as Pauker, there is no convincing evidence that communists were behind the coup.[49]

With the United States intervention in Vietnam intensifying, the Johnson administration quickly mended ties with Suharto's government. The new regime began demonizing China as well as the remnants of the PKI. Suharto solidified his power in early 1967 when the Indonesian legislature named him acting president, replacing Sukarno. More significant for Western interests, Indonesia declared itself open to investors, an objective that the nationalist Sukarno had discouraged. The *Oregonian*'s business editor Gerry Pratt referred to Sweetland "as an unpaid, one-man campaign manager for Indonesia." The government's recent guarantees that American investments would be protected, Sweetland argued in 1967, "removed the uncertainties that had slowed development under President Sukarno."[50]

A few years after Suharto's rise to power, Sweetland referred to "the dark Sukarno years," a sharp departure from his earlier views of the Indonesian leader.[51] For all his idiosyncratic mannerisms, most contemporaries viewed Sukarno as a nationalist, a leader similar to Jawaharlal Nehru, who remained neutral in the Cold War between the Soviet Union and the United States. For an American government focusing on counterinsurgency strategies to forestall communist takeovers in third world nations, nonalignment was intolerable. Sweetland's activities in Indonesia were predicated on saving the island nation for the West, an ideological position that meant accepting the Peace Corps and AID programs and opening Indonesia to foreign investors. Nationalists like Sukarno and India's Nehru often viewed foreign aid programs as intrusions on national sovereignty.

The Sweetland stay in Indonesia took place in the midst of the expanding American military presence in Vietnam and its spillover effects throughout the region. An avowed anticommunist since his days with the League for Industrial Democracy, Sweetland committed himself to full support of Cold War policies during the administration of President Harry Truman. By the time he was elected Democratic Party National Committeeman in 1948, his ideological predispositions were similar to other liberal Cold War internationalists who feared that wars of national liberation were communist inspired. By the 1960s, Southeast Asia and Vietnam were simply the most recent American efforts to contain the spread of communism. Indonesia, thousands of miles from Cold War conflicts in Eastern Europe and Africa, served as Sweetland's personal testing ground. As he learned more about Southeast Asia's realpolitik, he placed Indonesia's PKI within the larger Cold War struggle against communism. While the rhetoric of President Sukarno and his supporters became increasingly anti-American after the Sweetlands' departure, Monroe's ideological inclinations predisposed him to describe the nation's history to 1965 in terms of "the dark Sukarno years."

When the Indonesian bloodletting began in late 1965, Sweetland was fully engaged in a very different political venue with the National Education Association. Although Cold War values were a persisting influence in his life, their political implications were usually associated with events beyond the workplace—the Vietnam War, presidential elections, and the California and Oregon congressional delegations. And Henry Wallace-like heretics such as Senator Eugene McCarthy's challenge to Lyndon Johnson in early 1968 were still anathema to Sweetland. His job with the NEA, however, would be invigorating and challenging, dealing with issues on a much larger canvas than he had faced as a member of the Oregon legislature.

12
A New Life with the NEA

Through his many contacts with the Oregon Education Association (OEA), speaking before regional gatherings of the National Education Association (NEA), and his presence at the weeklong World Assembly of Teaching Organizations in New Delhi, Monroe Sweetland earned a reputation as a perceptive and articulate spokesperson for public education. His progressive positions on civil rights, the age-eighteen vote, and a host of related issues made him attractive to NEA. In the spring and summer of 1964 he opened discussions with James McCaskill in NEA's Washington office, recounting his lengthy experiences on behalf of public education and offering Oregon congresswoman Edith Green and Governor Mark Hatfield as references.[1]

Those efforts bore fruit in December of 1964 when Roy Archibald, head of NEA's West Coast Regional Office, offered Sweetland a position as legislative consultant for the thirteen western states, with responsibilities to oversee fieldwork and carry out legislative assignments. Sweetland was ideally suited for pursuing federal initiatives that would influence public education. Rey Martinez, his future colleague with NEA, points to the obvious: "Monroe had a national reputation before he joined NEA." He recalls that Archibald thought highly of Sweetland, "letting him travel the Western United States in his own unorthodox manner."[2]

Founded in 1857 to advance the cause of public education, the NEA had grown into a large and influential bureaucracy by the 1960s. With headquarters in Washington, D.C., the 900,000-member organization supported federal programs affecting public schools in the United States.

From his West Coast regional office in Burlingame, California, Sweetland would speak before state legislative assemblies, congressional hearings, and regional conferences on matters ranging from bilingual education to the age-eighteen vote. Along the way he landed some "big fish" (as a cartoon celebrating his retirement would show): passage of the federal Bilingual Education Act of 1968 and congressional ratification of the Twenty-Sixth Amendment to the Constitution lowering the voting age to eighteen.[3]

The Sweetlands move to California was strategic, related to employ-ment—Monroe with the NEA and Lil as a manpower specialist with the U.S. Department of Labor in San Francisco. The family rented a house in San Mateo, and Rebecca enrolled in the San Mateo school system, begin-ning the fifth grade at midyear. The new home was convenient to the San Francisco Airport, testimony to the fact that Monroe would be on the road throughout his decade of service with NEA. Sweetland joined NEA at an auspicious moment in modern American history, with the congressional passage of the Civil Rights Act of 1964. Lawmakers followed in 1965 with federal support for elementary and secondary education, Medicare and Medicaid, and the Voting Rights Act guaranteeing the ballot to all citizens. Each of those measures would be important to Sweetland's work with NEA. Most immediate would be the Elementary and Secondary Education Act (ESEA), a measure providing federal aid to schools, with a clause—com-pensatory education—supporting children from poor families.[4]

As one of his central missions with NEA, Monroe became involved with Mexican American educators and the problems that Spanish-speaking chil-dren faced in public schools. Another NEA initiative involved his sense of fair play—segregated teacher organizations in the Deep South. Sweetland had been aware of segregated educational organizations since at least 1961 when George Jones, executive secretary of the all-black American Teachers Association (ATA) approached him about soliciting members for the orga-nization in Oregon. Jones pointed out that "discriminatory differentials" also existed in states outside the South.[5] Because he was sympathetic to the ATA, Sweetland had written to William Carr, NEA's executive secre-tary, asking how he should respond to Jones. Carr's response was classic for an influential bureaucrat—he liked George Jones but believed Jones erred when he agreed to serve as executive secretary of the ATA. "Now that Negro teachers join the NEA, in approximately the same proportion as white teachers," Carr thought ATA would be of little use in the future.[6]

Although NEA argued that ATA had outlived its service as an educational organization, many rank-and-file African Americans were proud of the organization and feared that merger with the larger NEA would diminish their accomplishments. The NEA-ATA merger talks involved nasty exchanges. When ATA president J. Rupert Picott asked the NEA to extend scholarship offers to African American high school students to attend college, Carr objected. Another ATA leader chided the NEA for its "extended silence" on integration issues, and George Jones argued that partnering with NEA should mean "more than having Mahalia Jackson at a meeting."[7]

Although the U.S. Supreme Court's 1954 decision in *Brown v. Board of Education* initiated a new era of civil rights activism, the NEA moved slowly and chose to leave the initiative to federal courts and allow time to resolve discriminatory practices. During the heated integration battles in 1955 and 1956, NEA said little about the successes of integration. Its claims to being in the vanguard of integrating public schools and strengthening fair employment laws, voting rights legislation, and equal educational opportunity appear mostly in association memoranda many years later.[8] When Sweetland became involved with NEA policymaking early in 1965, however, the association began implementing policies to integrate the professional teacher organizations. Over the next few years the NEA was successful in integrating its professional teacher organizations in the Southern states.[9]

While the NEA and ATA were working through their merger agreements, Sweetland wrote to Roy Wilkins, executive director of the National Association for the Advancement of Colored People (NAACP), about voter registration drives in the South. Wanting to involve the NEA more directly, he asked Wilkins to help NEA develop a coordinated effort to register voters, believing that African American teachers in Alabama and Mississippi would provide the "opening wedge for broader registration objectives." Because NEA's "Fit to Teach—Fit to Vote" slogan would put the lie to literacy requirements for voting, he hoped the NAACP would join in forging a "favorable alliance."[10] When Sweetland urged NEA's executive committee to launch a voter registration drive in the summer of 1966, the committee demurred and took no action on the proposal.[11]

More immediate to Sweetland's mission with the West Coast office was his help in assisting poverty-stressed Mexican American communities seeking federal funding for bilingual education programs. At Sweetland's memorial service in 2006, his daughter Barbara Sweetland Smith remarked that her father always considered his background work leading to passage of the Bilingual Education Act the most significant accomplishment of his life. Contemporaries who worked with him during those years, especially Adalberto Guerrero and Reynaldo Martinez, agree that Sweetland was the prime mover and principal architect. Martinez, who often traveled with Monroe during these years, characterized the trips as "painful," because they "stayed in the cheapest motels and ate Spartan meals."[12]

The move to involve the federal government in bilingual education originated among Mexican American activist educators in Arizona, Texas, New Mexico, California, and Colorado. The NEA's West Coast office became involved when Sweetland began working with teachers experimenting with techniques to advance the education of Spanish-speaking students through bilingual approaches—instruction in both Spanish and English. Two major studies ignore those local initiatives. Writing in 1988, Rachel Moran cites the failure of state and local educators to tackle the problem and credits federal policymakers with addressing the issue. More recently John Skrentny (2002) argued that "the sources of these local initiatives are obscure."[13] A closer look at developments in Arizona and Texas reveals a different story.

Early in his tenure with NEA, Sweetland became involved with Mexican American educators in Tucson affiliated with the Mexican-American Regional Project. Among others, he met Adalberto Guerrero, a young Spanish-language instructor at the University of Arizona who began teaching at Pueblo High School in Tucson in 1958. The following year Guerrero taught a Spanish-language program for Spanish speakers with remarkable success. When he joined the Romance Languages Department at the University of Arizona, he continued teaching an accelerated course at Pueblo High School, further developing strategies to improve both Spanish and English proficiency among his students. "By 1965 the success of the program was patent," he remembered, "Students not only excelled in Spanish, but improved markedly in all other subjects."[14] Guerrero, who would become a valued Sweetland ally, provided practical, on-the-ground confirmation for bilingual approaches in teaching English to

Spanish-speaking students. Sweetland was the facilitator, arranging major regional conferences and eventually congressional hearings on bilingual education.

In southern California Sweetland worked with the Association of Mexican American Educators of California, centered in Los Angeles. With chapters scattered through the Central Valley and several in Los Angeles and San Diego, the organization sponsored workshops and curried the favor of friendly news reporters such as Jack Jones, who published a six-part series, "Revolt in the Barrio," in the *Los Angeles Times*. The association's 1966 meeting in Long Beach was a rousing success, with some 550 teachers and community resource specialists attending. In a follow-up letter to the executive secretary of the California Teachers Association (CTA), Sweetland praised Mexican American educators for "striking a responsive chord among California teachers of Spanish surname." Because there was a feeling among those attending the convention that CTA had done little about the problems facing Spanish-speaking children, Sweetland recommended that CTA upgrade its outreach to Mexican American educators.[15]

In mid-April 1966 Sweetland addressed the House Committee on Education and Labor, which was considering amendments to the Elementary and Secondary Education Act of 1965. ESEA had provided a legal channel for supporting bilingual education, with Sweetland obtaining funding for trial bilingual initiatives in Arizona and Texas. He applauded congressmen "who carried the day in 1965 for the Elementary and Secondary Education Act." As "landmark legislation," ESEA stimulated "state and local innovation and research," important to southwestern states with heavy concentrations of Mexican American families. Sweetland pointed to successes in school districts that made use of federal aid with striking successes, such as "the hiring of native speakers of Spanish to work with elementary and primary children as teachers, aides and visitors, on bilingual approaches to education."[16]

Two major conferences were critical to addressing the problems of Spanish-speaking children. The first, "Our Bilinguals: Social and Psychological Barriers-Linguistic and Pedagogical Barriers," convened in El Paso, Texas, in November 1965. Conference participants offered recommendations echoed in subsequent conferences and publications: (1) schools should offer "effective bilingual education program[s] from the first through the sixth grade; (2) in early grades some subjects should be taught in the Spanish language; (3) English should be taught as a foreign language; (4) literacy in Spanish should have first priority; (5) schools with large numbers of Spanish-speaking students needed well-trained and compassionate teachers.[17]

The release of the NEA-Tucson Survey Committee's report, *The Invisible Minority: Pero No Vencibles*, in the summer of 1966, represented the most significant research/publication during this period. Adalberto Guerrero provided background to the Tucson survey in a 2003 letter:

> Monroe Sweetland . . . had confided in Maria Urquides [Pueblo High School] that there was pending legislation which provided funding for successful innovative educational programs for minority students. Maria informed him about the special Spanish program and they agreed to form the NEA-Tucson Survey Team to determine if there were other similar programs in the Southwest which might be emulated. With $2,000 that Mr. Sweetland obtained from the NEA Department of Rural Education, team members Rosita Cota, Martina Garcia, Hank Oyama, Paul Streiff, Maria Urquides, and I did the survey and produced the report *The Invisible Minority*.[18]

Sweetland's handiwork is evident in the report—in the selection of the Thomas Jefferson epigram fronting the foreword, in the report itself, and in the initiatives taking place in southwestern states. The NEA-Tucson Survey Committee's acknowledgments included the Tucson Board of Education, the National Education Association, and "particularly Monroe Sweetland," consultant to the survey. The foreword praised NEA for working with teachers and school systems in developing "forward-looking solutions" to bilingualism. "The most acute educational problem in the Southwest is that which involves Mexican-American children," the report declared. Poverty, language, and cultural differences explained much about school failure.[19]

In addition to the language barrier, *The Invisible Minority* report declared that Mexican American children encountered "a strange and different set of cultural patterns" and teachers with little understanding of Spanish speakers and their cultural background. The report's recommendations included that instruction should begin in Spanish and English in early grades; English should be taught as a second language, with initial instruction emphasizing speaking, writing, and reading good Spanish; teachers should provide Mexican American students with pride in their ancestral culture; schools should hire more teachers and aides who speak Spanish; universities should train teachers in bilingual education; and states should repeal laws specifying English-only instruction.[20]

The Invisible Minority challenged the prevailing rationale for underachieving Mexican American children—that cultural background explained poor performance in the classroom. Guadalupe San Miguel, Jr., argues that the NEA-Tucson report offered an alternative explanation—discrimination and "non-accommodating school policies and practices" better explain underachievement. The report was radical, challenging the melting-pot hypothesis and proposing that assimilation give way to bilingualism and cultural pluralism. The NEA-Tucson report, San Miguel contends, "began the chain of events that eventually led to the enactment of the Bilingual Education Act of 1968."[21]

Because he was an inveterate collector of news clippings, Sweetland sent a swath of laudatory newspaper articles about *The Invisible Minority* to NEA's Washington office.[22] Washington administrators, in turn, put an ironic twist on recent events in the Southwest: the Tucson survey resulted "from unusual circumstances" and was "almost accidental." There was, of course, nothing "accidental" about the survey and its publication, because the Tucson committee and Monroe Sweetland planned the research and publication of the report. The Washington office admitted, nevertheless, that the survey team's initiative might "spark a chain reaction of efforts in behalf of all Spanish-speaking Americans."[23]

Shortly after publication of the survey, Sweetland drafted a tribute to Tucson's six years of experimentation with bilingual approaches for teaching Spanish-speaking children, methods providing a "workable bridge" to understanding English. Representing fourteen months of work, *The Invisible Minority* provided a blueprint for the future—providing encouragement to teachers fluent in Spanish and sympathetic to Spanish language and culture. To pursue those revolutionary proposals, Sweetland and the NEA began planning a symposium at the University of Arizona with U.S. senators Joseph Montoya (New Mexico) and Ralph Yarborough (Texas) present. Sweetland closed his tribute with Adalberto Guerrero's admonition: "We have been wasting our great resource of the bilingual potential of the Southwest."[24]

With Sweetland serving as facilitator, the Tucson conferees invited state and federal officials, educators and researchers, and Hispanic activists. The Third National Conference on Civil and Human Rights in Education— "The Spanish-Speaking Child in the Schools of the Southwest"—focused on implementing the findings of the Tucson survey. Convened in October 1966, the conference devoted most of its effort to bilingual education. Speakers reprised statistics revealing the low educational achievements of Mexican American students. Senator Yarborough praised bilingualism as the catalyst for raising the educational level and economic status of Mexican Americans. Senator Montoya applauded the potential of bilingualism for enhancing the ability of Mexican Americans to enrich two cultural worlds.[25]

Four hundred fifty educators and political leaders attended the Tucson gathering. At the end of the symposium, state teachers' representatives urged NEA to give its highest priority to developing "bilingual-bicultural curricula" for schools with large numbers of Mexican American children. Gilbert Sanchez, who assisted with the Tucson symposium, argues that the meeting reflected Sweetland's "efforts to high-light and implement the NEA-Tucson Survey Team Report." Dean E. Triggs, superintendent of schools in Ventura County, California, wrote NEA's Roy Archibald in mid-November: "Monroe did an excellent job at the Tucson conference," turning "the Mexican-American 'problem' into an asset."[26] The symposium report, *New Voices of the Southwest*, praised the conference speakers for treating *The Invisible Minority* as a call to arms. Sweetland garnered one photograph in the report, his name listed as one who worked "in preparing the conference." As Guerrero and Reynaldo Martinez would point out decades later, Sweetland insisted on staying away from the limelight in such events.[27]

Three months after the Tucson symposium Senator Yarborough introduced a bilingual education bill in the Senate. Alan Mandel and Gene Godley of the senator's staff joined Sweetland, Guadalupe Anguiano, and Armando Rodriguez in drafting the bill. The measure, S.428, amended the Elementary and Secondary Education Act of 1965 to assist public schools in establishing bilingual education programs. Section 702 of the legislation would assist school districts "to develop . . . new and imaginative elementary and secondary school programs to meet these educational needs." The measure authorized $5 million for fiscal year 1968, $10 million for 1969, and $15 million for 1970, with monies allocated on the basis of the number of Spanish-speaking students in each state. The original bill included programs "to impart to Spanish-speaking students a knowledge of and pride in their ancestral language and culture."[28]

While S.428 worked its way through Congress, Sweetland traveled the Southwest speaking to state-teacher associations and coordinating NEA appearances before committee hearings in the nation's capital.[29] California's congressional delegation provided strong support for S.428. Republican senator Thomas Kuchel, a cosponsor, reminded his colleagues that California was home to the largest number of Spanish-speaking children, 80 percent of them native-born Americans. Because the language barrier handicapped children, passage of the Bilingual Act would better train teachers to deal with problems in both Spanish and English. California representative Edward Roybal introduced HR 8000, directing the federal government "to provide bilingual educational opportunity programs" to school districts with large numbers of students for whom English was a second language.[30]

The hearings before the Senate Subcommittee on Bilingual Education convened on May 18 and lasted for five days. In calling his committee to order, Senator Yarborough praised the effort to redress the "injustice and harm" inflicted on Spanish-speaking children in the Southwest. He cited the 1960 census ranking Texas at the bottom, "with a median of only 4.7 years of school completed by persons of Spanish surname." Yarborough praised the "experimental educational projects" and conferences for suggesting a way to introduce Spanish instruction in the public schools.[31] Sweetland, Adalberto Guerrero, and NEA's executive secretary, William Carr, appeared on the second day of the hearings, with Sweetland addressing the failure of the educational system to provide "equal opportunity" to Spanish-speaking children. In the Southwest, ESEA funds had been devoted only to remedial reading programs. Sweetland cited specific needs—teacher aides conversant in Spanish; tutorial programs; improved liaison between schools and families; better libraries with Spanish-language books; and recruitment of Spanish-surnamed teachers. When Sweetland left the witness chair, Senator Yarborough remarked that Sweetland had been involved with bilingual education for several years and was a "national leader in this field."[32]

Guerrero, who was up next, introduced himself as a teacher at Pueblo High School and at the University of Arizona. Then he switched to Spanish for several moments; pausing, he switched back to English, observing that most of his audience was lost, because they were unfamiliar with Spanish. "This is precisely what happens to many of our students when they enter school," leaving them with the notion they are not as smart as their peers who understand English. Bilingual programs would improve student self-esteem and give them pride in their language and culture. They should be aware that they "have a very rich cultural background." He thanked Senator Yarborough for sponsoring a bill that had the potential to "provide more equitable educational opportunities" for students in the Southwest who had been "an invisible minority."[33]

A subcommittee of the House Committee on Education and Labor held hearings in late June on two resolutions (HR 9840 and HR 10224) to amend ESEA to include a bilingual component for its education programs. Sweetland, who appeared before both Senate and House hearings, described the opportunities for Spanish-speaking children in the American Southwest the "most signal failure" of the nation's school systems. The historic strategy of eradicating the mother tongue was "an unfortunate mistake." Instead of treating non-English languages "as a blight to be exterminated," bilingual approaches would "conserve the mother tongue and parallel it with effectiveness in English."[34] He underscored the importance of Spanish in the early years of school, because it provided a means to sustain a culture "and the pride and self-image of the Mexican-American student." The federal government deserved some responsibility for supporting bilingual programs, because teachers' aides fluent in Spanish would "improve communication in the classroom" and provide "a bridge between the counselors and the families."[35]

It is in error to assert, as some scholars have, that bilingual education was a political strategy absent of pedagogical theory. The findings in the southwestern states—dating *before* 1965—involving individuals such as Adalberto Guerrero and Maria Urquides puts the lie to such allegations. Florida's Cuban immigrant community and Ursula Casanova, one of their advocates, viewed the bilingual education initiative as an interloper, bereft of any substance about language learning. Ignoring the substantive research from southwestern states, Casanova belittled Yarborough's bilingual proposal as "a political artifact born not of knowledge, or even of expressed need, but of political maneuvering perhaps heavily laced with a sense of social responsibility."[36] People like Adalberto Guerrero and Maria Urquides, who were working with impoverished and illiterate Spanish-speaking children in the Southwest, indicate otherwise.

In the months following the congressional hearings, NEA sponsored conferences in key southwestern cities, and legislative supporters held hearings in the politically strategic states of Texas, California, and New York.[37] Although congressional support seemed strong, liberal Senator Yarborough's enemies, most of them Texans, opposed the bilingual bill. President Lyndon Johnson and conservative Democratic governor John Connally were against the measure. The compromise bill that emerged from the conference committee included all children deficient in English: "For the purposes of this title, 'children of limited English-speaking ability' means children who come from environments where the dominant language is other than English." The Senate and House passed the measure and the president signed it into law in early January 1968.[38]

If the Bilingual Education Act raised expectations among Mexican American educators and activists, tightfisted administrations and congresses sorely tested their patience. The increasing costs of the Vietnam War restrained spending for all social and educational programs. Although the bilingual measure authorized spending $15 million on the program in its first year, Congress appropriated no funding. Between 1969 and 1973, congressional appropriations fell below authorized funding levels. Congress had authorized up to $135 million for those years, but appropriated only $35 million. Rachel Moran argues that the 1968 legislation may have been more important in encouraging states to enact their own bilingual education measures. In addition, several states repealed their English-only instructional laws.[39]

Caught in the midst of parsimonious state and federal governments, Sweetland spent the succeeding years lobbying Congress to increase appropriations, citing the bilingual education law to draw attention to "the failure of our schools to deal competently with the Spanish-speaking child." Senator Yarborough and a few southwestern congressmen praised Sweetland for his yeoman work in shepherding the bilingual legislation into law. Speaking to NEA's 1968 convention in Dallas, Yarborough recalled

Sweetland asking him to speak at the Tucson conference in October 1966 on behalf of bilingual education. With Sweetland's assistance, "we saw that bill, that idea, written into law last year." The legislation, Yarborough reflected, "would still be a dream, and not a law that we can fight for" without the hard work of the NEA.[40]

In the workup to the Bilingual Education Act, Sweetland enjoyed the support of conservative Republicans, including California senator George Murphy, who proved a stalwart in urging the Nixon administration to fully fund the law. In January 1969 Murphy requested an appropriation of $30 million for the next fiscal year, his letter citing the "appalling statistics" of the high dropout rate for Mexican Americans. California's other senator, Alan Cranston, and the state's congressional delegation also supported Murphy's petition.[41]

Under Sweetland's name, NEA's West Coast office issued a news release in January 1969 criticizing southwestern states for leaving their responsibilities for bilingual education to the federal government. The most alarming failure was the inability of school districts "to provide successful teachers for children from Spanish-speaking homes." In a letter to Ernest Garcia, president of the Association of Mexican American Educators, Sweetland underscored the importance of full funding under the Bilingual Act—"after all, it is largely a California issue."[42] Speaking in the House of Representatives in April 1969, California congressman Edward Roybal pointed to the abysmal funding for the program—$30 million authorized and only $7.5 million appropriated. With the Bilingual Act set to end in 1970, the successes of pilot programs would be lost if the program was not extended. Despite Roybal's worries, the program survived with slowly increasing appropriations in the next few years. In fiscal year 1972 Congress authorized $80 million and appropriated $24 million to local school districts. Writing for the *Saturday Review* in April 1972, Jeffrey Kobrick reported that Title VII served only eighty-eight thousand of an estimated five million non-English-speaking children; bilingual education, he feared, would wither without federal assistance.[43]

When the five-year funding cycle for the Bilingual Education Act was up for renewal in 1975, the program had expanded to $70 million in appropriations and benefitted 375 school districts with some 200,000 students. However, there were more than five million students in the United States with limited proficiency in English. In the fight to reauthorize the act, Democratic senators Joseph Montoya, Edward Kennedy, and Alan Cranston amended the law to provide an official definition for bilingual education—teaching students both in their native languages and English and including instruction in the student's native culture.[44]

Through the first half of the 1970s, Sweetland continued to advance the cause of bilingual education. When a vacancy occurred on the Bilingual Education Advisory Committee (a component of ESEA Title VII), he wrote New Mexico senator Paul Fannin urging the appointment of Adalberto Guerrero to the committee. Guerrero, "who had much to do with the genesis of the Act itself," belonged on the committee. Sweetland himself served as a member of Maestros Para Manana (Teachers for Tomorrow), a California organization assisting Mexican American high school youths in finding jobs and completing college applications. A roadblock to bilingual programs in California was Governor Ronald Reagan, who refused to sign a bill for "bilingual and bicultural education" school programs. The governor told the California Senate in August 1972: "I believe it is imperative that California's children obtain proficiency in the use of the English language."[45]

Bilingual programs increasingly came under attack through the 1970s. Among the critics was *Washington Post* writer Stephen Rosenfield, whose September 1974 column expressed fear that Congress had "radically altered the traditional way by which immigrants become Americanized." If Congress reauthorized the legislation, Rosenfield worried that schools would no longer serve to assimilate "foreigners to a common culture." New Mexico senator Joseph Montoya, a sponsor of the original bill, responded that it was difficult "to imagine a statement founded less on fact and more on fright." Rosenfield's criticism ignored that a person's "language and cultural heritage is something of value."[46] An increasingly conservative Congress, however, gained credibility over the next two decades, with attacks on bilingual education as part of a larger assault on property taxes, school funding and busing, and affirmative action. Because of its bicultural component—imparting pride in their mother tongue and cultural background—bilingual education was a special object of conservative censure. California, once the pacesetter in innovative education, fell to conservative forces with two ballot measures: Proposition 13 to limit property taxes (1978), and Proposition 227, the English for Children proposal, which passed with more than 61 percent of the vote in 1998, effectively ending bilingual education in California.[47]

When Congress passed No Child Left Behind, President George W. Bush's major school reform in 2002, legislators terminated Title VII of the Elementary and Secondary Education Act. The measure ended most bilingual programs and expanded funds for intensified English-language instruction. Writing for the journal *Rethinking Schools*, James Crawford published an obituary for bilingual education: "Its death was not unexpected, following years of attacks by enemies and recent desertions by allies in Congress." Adalberto Guerrero, Sweetland's friend from the first light of bilingual education in the 1960s, told the *Arizona Daily Star* in 2011 that history was repeating itself, with opponents of bilingual education promoting the same failed pedagogies of the past. Their objectives were always to deny teaching Mexican American children their language, history, and culture. The eighty-one-year-old Guerrero told his interviewer: "We have the right to instruct our children in a manner that reflects us."[48]

As the bilingual education campaign was winding down in late 1967, Sweetland urged NEA leaders to begin looking at the age-eighteen vote as a way to bolster support for "beleaguered state and local schools." He believed eighteen- to twenty-one-year-old citizens would "be far more supportive of schools than their elders." Lowering the voting age also had the potential to bring "a massive infusion of new pro-education voters into the body politic." In a memo to Dirck Brown in NEA's office in November 1967, Sweetland suggested that he would push the issue with NEA's legislative committee and with the student NEA.[49] As the next months indicated, the NEA would move cautiously in pushing the age-eighteen franchise.

Shortly after the United States adopted the Twenty-Sixth Amendment to the Constitution, Monroe Sweetland rummaged through his old Oregon files and discovered documents related to a failed age-eighteen vote campaign from 1946. If he had searched through files from the late 1930s or his years with the Red Cross, he would have found additional material for lowering the voting age. Always operating at the limits of permissibility for citizen access to the ballot, he supported same-day registration and liberalized restrictions on absentee voting. The interesting feature to his old files, he wrote National Education Association's (NEA) Rosalyn Hester in June

1971, "was how identical the arguments were for and against 18 year voting even in the tranquil years immediately following World War II."[50]

As a member of the Oregon House in 1953, Sweetland proposed a constitutional amendment to lower the voting age to eighteen. Although the Republican-controlled assembly pigeonholed the measure, the issue was not a partisan one. The chair of the Republican National Committee, Leonard Hall, spoke in favor of lowering the voting age in May 1953, with both President Eisenhower and Vice President Richard Nixon joining in support. In his State of the Union address in January 1954, Eisenhower recommended lowering the voting age to eighteen. During Sweetland's first term in the Oregon Senate, he joined Republican Mark Hatfield in sponsoring a bill to lower the voting age to eighteen. The Senate approved the measure, but it failed in the House.[51] With his time-tested commitment to lowering the voting age, Sweetland was ideally suited to lead NEA's nationwide initiative for the age-eighteen vote.

With escalating opposition to the war in Vietnam, resistance to the military draft, and increasing unrest on university and college campuses, the nation's youth were fragmented among mainstream, liberal, and militant solutions on issues of war, race, and economic equality. With its huge and diverse population, California was the poster child for much of the social turmoil of the 1960s. Beginning with the "free speech" movement at the University of California, Berkeley in 1964, the emergence of the Black Panther Party in 1966, and continuing with mobilizations against the Vietnam War, California was the epicenter of protest and unrest.[52]

When Sweetland addressed the California Legislative Assembly in January 1968 in support of lowering the voting age, he told legislators the issue was urgent, because political decisions had not kept pace with the "greatly increased concern of American youth in the social and political questions of our time." He urged the Assembly to "acknowledge the product of your excellence in education by bringing youth into full participation in your public decisions." Although lowering the voting age would not quell all the "long, hot summer disorders," it would offer "peaceful alternatives, and would de-fuse and de-emphasize direct action and violent conduct."[53]

Among California's legislators, Sweetland developed a close working relationship with George Moscone, a young state senator who led the effort for the age-eighteen vote. Moscone collaborated with Assemblyman John Vasconcellos in the spring of 1968, with both introducing constitutional measures to lower California's voting age to eighteen. The Senate defeated Moscone's bill when it failed to receive the required two-thirds votes for constitutional amendments. Although he hoped to give Californians an opportunity to vote on the constitutional measure, Moscone told Sweetland that he intended to return in 1969 with similar legislation.[54]

Sweetland moved cautiously in early 1968 to develop a strategy—appropriate to NEA's membership—for pursuing the age-eighteen vote. He began with a question to an NEA colleague that needed emphasis: *"Do we educators really believe that the end result of our work with American youth through the 12th grade prepares them for the responsibilities of U.S. citizenship?"*[55] In pursuit of that objective he carried on more than six months of lobbying with NEA's larger state delegations to build support for a resolution endorsing the age-eighteen vote. His correspondence with state NEA affiliates extended from late 1967 and continued up to the eve of NEA's annual convention in Dallas, Texas, in early July 1968. Despite his meticulous work to build a consensus for lowering the voting age, approximately one-third of the 8,000 delegates voted against the resolution. Writing to Douglas Cater, President Johnson's special assistant, however, Sweetland reported that the NEA was mandated to press the age-eighteen vote with Congress and the states.[56]

As NEA's lead in the youth voting effort, Sweetland devised a strategy to bring the issue to the attention of state and federal lawmakers. The initiative—the Youth Franchise Coalition—grew out of the Dallas convention when Sweetland began soliciting financial backing for an ad hoc committee comprising a broad range of organizations to pursue the age-eighteen vote. By September 1968 the committee began preparing a strategy to push for the age-eighteen vote in Congress. Sweetland told Democratic senator Edmund Muskie of Maine, chair of the Democratic National Committee (DNC) that the coalition would place young people in the forefront of the campaign.[57] Although both political parties supported lowering the voting age, Republicans favored state-by-state initiatives while Democrats supported a constitutional amendment. Sweetland urged Muskie and the DNC to provide "central direction and push" to the campaign. Minnesota's Democratic congressman John Blatnik brought the party differences to public attention when he introduced an age-eighteen constitutional amendment in the House.[58]

The Youth Franchise Coalition garnered sufficient support from its cooperating partners to open an office in NEA's Washington headquarters in January 1969. The NEA appointed Les Francis, a young activist working for the California Teachers Association, to hire staff and serve as director of Project 18. In recounting his experience, Francis described Sweetland as the "Pied Piper to our band of young activists" the person who "worked tirelessly to put NEA's muscle behind Federal aid to education, bilingual education, civil rights, and the 18-year-old-vote."[59] Sweetland continued his frenetic organizing, traveling, and speaking before state legislatures. He urged NEA to gather facts about young people: How many states held eighteen-year-old defendants responsible under criminal law for debts and civil liability? What was the age of consent for marriage in states? What percentage of eighteen- to twenty-year-old men and women were married?[60]

Launched at a meeting in Washington in February 1969, the Youth Franchise Coalition was clearly a Sweetland initiative. Its "Statement of Purpose" reflected his long-standing argument that access to the ballot was fundamental to a democratic society. The missing ingredient, the statement declared, was a national campaign to press the issue before the public. The coalition, therefore, would "mount a massive educational program" to insist that Congress pass a constitutional amendment to lower the voting age.[61] Sweetland wrote new DNC chair senator Fred Harris to give more attention to state voting laws, because many of them disenfranchised the young and poor. He cited Texas, where voter registration closed at the end of January for the November election. Democrats should recognize the "election-winning impact this can have for us."[62]

Sweetland devoted considerable energy to California's age-eighteen vote campaign. In letters to newspapers and in testimony before legislative committees, he drew attention to the negative effects of depriving 18- to 20-year-old youths the franchise. When California's Constitutional Revision Commission approved lowering the voting age to nineteen, Sweetland knew that Governor Ronald Reagan, who opposed the measure, lacked legal authority to veto constitutional amendments. He pointed to polls indicating majority support for the age-eighteen vote. In a letter to the *San Francisco Chronicle*, he urged Californians "to bring young adults into full citizenship."[63] Testifying again in April 1969 before the California Assembly, Sweetland told lawmakers that lowering the legal age for voting would "help defuse the nihilists and direct actionists" and support those who believed in "orderly processes of decision-making." California should lower the voting age and cease feeding "the flames of hostility and recrimination." Arguments opposing voting by young people, he contended, "are almost exactly the arguments heard fifty years ago against voting by American women."[64]

There were warnings in some states of a backlash threatening to derail the effort, especially campus antiwar protests involving violence and other disorders.[65] The national effort to lower the voting age, *San Francisco Examiner* columnist George Crocker argued, was a cynical Democratic move to expand the party's base (after a Gallup poll revealed that it would help Democrats more than Republicans). It was a lie to say that the present generation of young people were the best educated in the nation's history; this was a simple-minded trope to justify money spent on education. Crocker rejected the noisome non sequitur—"if they are old enough to fight in a war, they are old enough to vote." Democracies were fragile and subject to dangerous excesses. In America's case, its excess was to bestow the suffrage on people "for whom the vote is an instrument to make fools of themselves and a wreck of their country."[66]

Sweetland fired off a rejoinder following Crocker's screed citing the op-ed column as unintentional support for lowering the voting age. "Crocker's intense hostility" toward young people reflected "the conceit of the old guard," he charged. His windy rhetoric mirrored narratives similar to those opposed to women's suffrage and extending the franchise to racial minorities. It was the height of arrogance to claim that democracy tends to bestow the right of "suffrage on persons unprepared to exercise it wisely." Young adults who bore important responsibilities—holding jobs, paying taxes, and serving in the military—should have a voice in decisions directly affecting them.[67]

Frustrated with the California legislature's ambivalent signals, Sweetland appeared again before an assembly committee in December 1969, addressing "collateral issues" related to lowering the voting age—the committee chair had declared that he would not put a measure to voters unless it was "clear how other statutory references to age might be affected." If California lowered its voting age to eighteen, Sweetland declared, other age-related statutes would "remain unchanged." He warned that "malingering on this issue" was playing into the hands of "cynical enemies of self government." He charged legislators with being the principal roadblock to lowering the voting age, allies of the witless left whom Sweetland described as "enemies of the American way."[68]

In the midst of cajoling California legislators on lowering the voting age, Sweetland traveled regularly to the nation's capital to push for a constitutional amendment to lower the voting age. His correspondents included senators, cabinet members, and congressional committee chairs.[69] Working with legislative representatives, governors, and state NEA leaders, Sweetland solicited information on progress in lowering the voting age. Oregon secretary of state Clay Myers sent Sweetland a news release supporting lowering the voting age to nineteen, a measure appearing on the Oregon ballot in May 1970. As the election approached, Governor Tom McCall indicated that citizens were angry over antiwar demonstrations and violence at Portland State University and the University of Oregon. Among the approximately seven hundred letters he received, nearly all of them urged strong measures against disruptive students. "These aren't the usual crank letters," the governor declared, but represent "the depths of people's feelings." McCall, who supported the referendum, expressed surprise about the letters: "I've never seen anything like them in my life."[70] McCall's direct and candid habits would soon make him the object of criticism.

To publicize the effort to lower the voting age in Oregon, Earl Blumenauer, a senior at Portland's Lewis and Clark College, organized and directed the state's "Go 19" campaign to support the measure on the May ballot. Sweetland visited his home state two weeks before the election, praising Blumenauer for an "excellent campaign." He thought Governor McCall's remarks were ill-advised and insensitive, especially because he (Sweetland) supported Blumenauer's campaign.[71] When the ballots were tallied, Oregon voters had rejected the referendum 62 to 38 percent. Blumenauer cited voter reaction to campus violence as the major factor in its defeat. "Bitterness is my gut reaction," he told a reporter. Several young people blamed Governor McCall's statement following the violence at Portland State for pushing undecided voters into voting no. The *San Francisco Examiner* remarked that Oregon's election results reflected "majority adult opinion in this country." That observation proved erroneous when the House of Representatives easily passed (272–132) a

Senate-approved federal statutory bill in June 1970 to lower the voting age to eighteen.[72]

A skeptical President Richard Nixon signed the measure into law and immediately urged courts to challenge its constitutionality. The measure, to take effect on January 1, 1971, would grant the voting franchise to eleven million young people. A second provision of the law extended the Voting Rights Act of 1965 for another five years. Despite his reservations about the constitutionality of the clause lowering the voting age, Nixon signed the measure, emphasizing its importance in extending voting rights to African Americans. The president directed Attorney General John Mitchell to expedite a court test of the voting-age provision and urged Congress to act on the constitutional amendment being debated in legislative committees.[73]

Although the federal statutory measure to lower the voting age awaited a court decision, Sweetland advised state legislative leaders to enact parallel measures to lower the voting age to avoid "the prolonged, expensive and difficult method of formal Constitutional amendment."[74] The U.S. Supreme Court added confusion when it determined in December 1970 that only Congress had the constitutional power to establish the legal age to vote for president and members of Congress. The decision cleared the way for eighteen-year-olds to vote for president and members of Congress in 1972, but left states the right to set age qualifications for state and local elections.[75] Advocates of a blanket legal age for voting now devoted their attention to amending the U.S. Constitution.

Sweetland predicted to Oregon secretary of state Clay Myers that Congress could save "us all from the swamp of endless constitutional amendments in the states by presenting a clear-cut Federal Constitutional Amendment within a few weeks."[76] Amalia Toro, an elections attorney in Connecticut, agreed with Sweetland that it was better to amend "the federal constitution restoring the nation to a single voting age by lowering the voting age to 18 for all elections." Confirming Sweetland's prediction, Congress voted in March 1971 to send a constitutional amendment to the states. The wording of the measure was straightforward:[77]

> Section 1. The right of citizens of the United States who are 18 year of age or older, to vote shall not be denied or abridged by the United States or by any state on account of age.

Section 2. The Congress shall have power to enforce this article by appropriate legislation.

Oregon Congresswoman Edith Green, a Democrat, who became increasingly conservative as she gained seniority in the House, was one of only nineteen to oppose the amendment.[78]

In the rush to approve the amendment, Minnesota and Delaware voted within an hour after the U.S. House approved the measure, sharing the distinction of being the first states to ratify the amendment. Tennessee, Connecticut, and Washington followed in quick order. Oregon ratified the amendment on June 4, becoming the thirty-second state to approve, but by only a narrow 15 to 14 majority in the Senate. When North Carolina endorsed the measure on July 1, it became the thirty-eighth state to approve the Twenty-Sixth Amendment to the U.S. Constitution; it was the shortest time that states had ratified an amendment.[79] Although Sweetland thought there were more substantive arguments for lowering the voting age than "Old enough to fight, old enough to vote," the extraordinary casualty rates in Vietnam among troops under the age of twenty-one served as a powerful counterpoint.

Following his success with the Bilingual Education Act, Sweetland's three-year push for the age-eighteen vote would rank as his second major accomplishment in his tenure with NEA. His associates were well aware of his wide-ranging, behind-the-scenes organizing with NEA's state affiliates in the measure's success. At a July 4, 2011, gathering in Washington, D.C., celebrating the fortieth anniversary of the ratification of the Twenty-Sixth Amendment, John Wilson of the Youth Franchise Coalition praised NEA for making the age-eighteen vote a reality and acknowledged Sweetland as "the driving force" in its success. In a personal memoir, Les Francis, who headed the coalition during its early months, was equally emphatic: "Monroe Sweetland . . . more than any single American" made possible the enfranchisement of young people.[80]

As Sweetland neared NEA's mandatory retirement age of sixty-five (he would turn sixty-five on January 20, 1975), he began laying the groundwork for life beyond the agency that he had served for ten years. Still in excellent health and from all indications enjoying the multifaceted tasks associated with his job, there is no indication that he had tired of his frenzied travel schedule or his frequent appearances in legislative hearing rooms. While he was moving into retirement, politics—at the center of his consciousness all of his adult life—would continue to be an important presence, especially with changing presidential administrations. He would promote, unsuccessfully as it turned out, Washington senator Henry "Scoop" Jackson, a liberal on domestic policy but a Cold War hawk, for the presidency in both 1972 and 1976.

13

The Politics of Turmoil

The summer of 1964 dawned hot and troubling in American politics. Still fresh from their year in Indonesia, the Sweetlands settled into their Milwaukie home while Monroe busied himself with speaking engagements on Indonesia and turning his attention again to the rough-and-tumble world of politics. With no significant Oregon elections on the horizon, state Democratic Party officials girded themselves for the upcoming national convention in Atlantic City, New Jersey, in late August. In the interim, Oregon Democrats focused attention on their own state convention in Coos Bay. One flash point for both the state and national conventions was a looming challenge to seating the all-white Mississippi delegation in Atlantic City. David Aberle, a prominent University of Oregon anthropologist, pressed Sweetland to convince Oregon Democrats to seat the integrated Mississippi Freedom Democratic Party delegates, ridiculing the claim that Mississippi's regular delegates represented the voters of the state when "most Negroes and many whites are prevented from registering."[1]

Supporters of the Mississippi Freedom Democratic Party, in Oregon to gather support, urged Sweetland to speak in favor of a Freedom Party resolution to be introduced at the state convention. Oregon Democrats convened in Coos Bay for three days in early July, with much of their attention on Senator Wayne Morse's resolution calling for the United Nations to adjudicate the American conflict in Vietnam. Sweetland, who spoke to the Mississippi question, adamantly opposed seating the regular delegation because they refused to support President Johnson in the November election.[2]

After Morse's blistering forty-minute speech charging that the United States had "no right to act unilaterally in South Viet Nam," delegates voted overwhelmingly to support the senator's resolution. The party then passed a second resolution requesting the national convention to seat the biracial Mississippi Freedom Democratic delegation. Sweetland noted that Mississippi's exclusion of blacks from politics was an old story; it was past time, he remarked, for the national party to take a stand. Reginald Robinson, a field director with the Student Nonviolent Coordinating Committee, reminded the Oregon Democrats that New York, Massachusetts, Wisconsin, and California had already declared support for Mississippi's Freedom Democrats.[3]

Worried that Oregon's delegates would fail to keep their vow to support the Mississippi Freedom Democrats, former fourth district congressman Charles Porter circulated a series of proposals delegates should support in Atlantic City. Where Porter listed support for Mississippi's "Freedom Delegation," Sweetland scribbled in the margin, "advice of convention sufficient." Sweetland was also mum on supporting Morse's recommendation that the United States cede responsibility for the Vietnam conflict to the United Nations. Neither were there notations on Sweetland's copy of Porter's memo praising Senator J. William Fulbright's proposal that the United States explore closer relations with China and Cuba.[4] The national convention and its aftermath would show that Sweetland, like many Cold War liberals, was tempering his criticism of American intervention in Vietnam because of Johnson's presidential campaign.

The dispute over the Mississippi delegation would provide Oregon Democrats with a prominent forum in Atlantic City. As delegates were leaving for Atlantic City, only three delegates—Sweetland, Democratic National Committeeman Norm Stoll, and Robert Straub—responded favorably to Porter's request that they reaffirm their commitment against seating the regular Mississippi delegation. Third district representative Edith Green and second district representative Al Ullman, members of the credentials committee, refused to commit themselves until they listened to evidence. Porter told a reporter there appeared to be "opposition or apathy to the resolution passed in Coos Bay."[5]

On the eve of the Atlantic City convention, reliable sources reported that President Lyndon Johnson was neutral on accommodating the Freedom Party's demands. If he supported the regular Mississippi delegation, he would antagonize party liberals in the North and African Americans every-where. In the end, the controversy was placed in the hands of the credentials committee. With two forceful members on the committee, Edith Green and Al Ullman, Oregon would have a prominent role in determining the out-come. From the outset, Green proposed to seat both delegations and divide Mississippi's twenty-six votes evenly. She insisted that if the regulars were seated they should take a loyalty oath to support the party's nominee. In sharp contrast, Ullman offered nearly a full plate to Mississippi's regular del-egation—twenty-four votes and two for the Freedom Democrats.[6]

Although Green's politics were trending conservative as she gained seniority in Congress, she was in the forefront in denouncing the Mississippi "regulars." Unlike Democratic Party leaders who feared damaging the par-ty's chances in the South, Green characterized Mississippi Democrats as a party that "has tried to prevent people [from] voting by murder, bomb-ing, beating people, and all kinds of threats and intimidations." While the credentials committee juggled its political bombshell, the *Oregonian*'s Herb Lundy compared Harry Truman's campaign in 1948 with Lyndon Johnson's effort in 1964. The *Portland Reporter* observed that Truman "told hard-nosed southerners to jump overboard if they didn't like it," and defeated Dewey without the South. President Johnson, in contrast, was attempting to mastermind a power play to prevent "any defections from his personal and inherited power structure."[7]

The credentials committee ultimately hewed to Congressman Ullman's proposal—seating two delegates from the Freedom Party as voting par-ticipants and all of the regular Mississippi delegates who signed a pledge to support the convention's choice for president and vice president. When the Mississippi Freedom Democratic Party rejected the so-called compromise, it heightened African Americans' mistrust of white liberals. Mississippi's equally angry all-white delegation, with some Alabamans, also walked out of the convention. Although Ullman called the end result "a great moral vic-tory," the compromise was a resounding defeat for the Freedom Democrats and their supporters. The negotiations, conducted behind closed doors with expected vice-presidential nominee Hubert Humphrey carrying the presi-dent's heavy mail, added further embarrassment for the would-be vice presi-dent. Although Green was dissatisfied with the final proposal, she conceded that it was better than seating the regular Mississippi delegations with no strings attached. Speaking to an *Oregonian* reporter, Sweetland agreed with

Ullman that the compromise was a moral victory, "a severe chastisement of the Mississippi establishment."[8] Conceding to the realpolitik of the credentials committee underscored the paradox, the dilemma of American liberals who would compromise fundamental principles in the interests of power.

With the vantage of hindsight, the 1964 presidential campaign takes on a different tone and meaning. Despite the Johnson administration's covert initiatives in Southeast Asia, Republican candidate Barry Goldwater's aggressive foreign policy rhetoric made him an inviting target for Democratic strategists who wanted to demonize him as a reckless, war-mongering candidate. "Extremism in the defense of liberty is no vice," the Arizona senator's stentorian voice echoed across the San Francisco Cow Palace when he accepted the Republican nomination for president on July 16. The Democrats successfully used his statements—along with aggressive television advertisements—to portray Goldwater as dangerous. Despite the administration's plans for further mischief in Vietnam, Democrats paraded their nominee as the peace candidate. Johnson promoted this view in a letter to party activists, characterizing the election as one between "peace and freedom, . . . a turning point in our national life."[9]

Vietnam, which would soon consume the energies of the Johnson administration, did not create the disorder at Atlantic City that it would four years later in Chicago. Nevertheless, Women Strike for Peace warned against "recurring crises" threatening to destabilize a world divided "into armed camps threatening mutual destruction." Norman Thomas, Sweetland's mentor from the 1930s, urged the platform committee to reconsider its position on Vietnam where "our intervention seems progressively to be losing rather than winning the support of the masses of the people"[10] There is no indication that Sweetland was speaking forcefully against American initiatives in Vietnam at this juncture.

After Johnson's landslide victory in November, rumors circulated among Oregon Democrats that Maurine Neuberger would not run for reelection. With Neuberger increasingly unhappy in the Senate, especially in her relations with Wayne Morse, and remarried to a Boston psychiatrist, Democratic Party leaders feared they would lose the seat, because Governor Mark Hatfield was expected to be the Republican challenger. The leading Democratic candidates appeared to be third district congresswoman Edith

Green, fourth district congressman Robert Duncan and, in San Mateo, California, doing battle for the National Education Association (NEA), Monroe Sweetland. No Democrat was willing to take the plunge, however, until the formidable Green decided on a course of action. Given his two failed secretary of state races and especially the ugly 1960 contest in which Howell Appling easily out-polled him, Sweetland's interest in running for the U.S. Senate is puzzling. It was also widely known among friends that the 1960 campaign still weighed heavily on Lil.[11]

Lorna Marple, a longtime Democratic Party activist in Portland, put the question to Sweetland bluntly. Although no longer active in party affairs, she remained a "dispassionate observer" with decided views about candidates. Marple characterized the Oregon Democratic Party as "weaker, more demoralized, and the voters more indifferent" than at any time since Sweetland first ran for national committeeman. Marple then addressed the purpose of her letter. She was upset when she learned through Lil that Monroe was considering a run for Neuberger's Senate seat:

> Monroe, you know no one was less fitted to be a candidate's
> wife than Lil. She loves too much and takes things too hard. You
> cannot possibly be serious about putting her through that again?
> Everything that was dragged out before will be dragged out again.
> . . . I don't have to tell you that the Hatfield people have unlimited
> funds and are going to put everything into his campaign to get him
> into the Senate.

Marple conceded that Monroe was the most qualified person to be in the United States Senate, "trouble is, you wouldn't go, and while nothing is certain, that is pretty close to it." The purpose of a good friend was to speak truths, not "as you might like to hear them."[12] Marple's letter did little to dampen Sweetland's interest in reentering elective politics.[13]

The watchful waiting for Congresswoman Green's decision continued into early 1966 when Mike Katz, Sweetland's close friend, relayed Oregon's latest political gossip in early 1966—"Edith's decision is still up in the air." Her friends were advising against running; however, if she did put her hat in the ring, Katz thought Sweetland could easily take the third district seat. At the end of the typewritten letter, this handwritten postscript: "Flash!!! Edith just announced at the City Club that she would not be a candidate for the U.S.

Senate." Green's decision to remain in her safe congressional seat extended Sweetland's interest in the Senate race. In a personal note to the Indonesian ambassador, Sweetland described his prospects: "With Congresswoman Edith Green out of the running, I could have the Democratic nomination for Mrs. Neuberger's seat in the Senate." But the expected Republican nominee, Mark Hatfield, would be hard to beat, "and only a serious fumble on his part will defeat him."[14]

Sweetland's conundrum intensified when a group of prominent Democrats approached him to declare for the Senate race. Sweetland was the state's most prominent Democrat after senators Morse and Neuberger and Congresswoman Green, and the group noted that he gave Hatfield his closest run in Dwight Eisenhower's landslide election of 1956. The Democrats cited the significance of Sweetland's "extraordinary vote-getting ability in Oregon Democratic primaries" and his "influence on the Washington scene, both with the White House and in Congress." To this strong party support, Sweetland responded that he enjoyed his work with NEA and until recently "had no intention of resuming political activity in Oregon."[15]

Despite the enthusiasm of party leaders, a few progressive friends floated red flags. Writing from Gaston, Oregon, Thomas Roe reminded Sweetland that he should demand "a campaign fully underwritten before agreeing to get into such an important race." Hatfield made certain he had "financial guarantees" before declaring, and despite his problems with labor, it would be difficult to "get the necessary FACTS across to the voters." Nathalie Panek, executive director of the American Cancer Society and living in Los Angeles, reminded Sweetland that "all the pundits agree that Mark Hatfield will make it." While Sweetland was her favorite "candidate for everything," she thought a campaign against Hatfield would be "a hopeless cause." To make a good race, he would need "solid pledges of money." Panek was adamant: "I really wish you wouldn't go for it. Another defeat would be heartbreaking. I hate to see you go through with it."[16]

From another segment of the political spectrum, Robert "Bob" Frazier, the conservative editor of the *Eugene Register-Guard*, cautioned Sweetland against "coming back to Oregon and getting his feet in the water." In an early February editorial, "Wrong Man," Frazier accused Democrats of "trying to sweet-talk" Sweetland into becoming a candidate. The reluctance of other Democrats to run for the U.S. Senate suggested "that the party may be looking for a sacrificial goat. Mr. Sweetland is too nice a man for such a sacrifice."

In a brief note to Sweetland with the editorial tear sheet attached, Frazier added: "Whether our advice is or is not heeded, you know that we meant every word."[17]

If Sweetland were to leap into the senatorial fray, Vietnam would provide sharp contrasts between the candidates. Governor Hatfield had joined Senator Morse in sharply attacking America's escalating position in Southeast Asia, whereas Sweetland was supporting the Johnson administration. Sweetland put off a decision until mid-February and then announced that he would step aside if fourth district congressman Robert Duncan became a candidate. Should Duncan refuse to make the race, he told the *Oregonian*, he might reopen his candidacy. Duncan, he noted, was a "hard-hitting and effective" congressman and would be a "champion of the Kennedy-Johnson policies, which mean so much to Oregon."[18]

A few Oregon journalists found both Duncan's and Sweetland's views on Vietnam unacceptable. Arthur H. Bone, publisher of the progressive Oregon-Washington Farmers Union in Salem, told Duncan that he would "either go fishing or support Hatfield, rather than vote for a Democrat who supports our immoral Vietnam policy." Bone predicted that Hatfield would win easily "if you run on that kind of platform." The big problem was China "which the United States has attempted to isolate." He urged Duncan to read China scholar John K. Fairbanks's writings as a counterpoint to Secretary of State Dean Rusk, who likened China to Hitler's Germany. Bone sent Sweetland a copy of the letter, urging him to "stand with Morse" to negotiate a way out of "the Vietnam mess" if he decided to run.[19]

A potential Duncan candidacy pointed to difficulties ahead. The *Oregonian*'s Harold Hughes observed that Duncan would place Vietnam at the center of a primary fight, because former state Democratic chair and Bonneville Power Administration official Howard Morgan told him "there will be an active primary campaign" if Duncan became a candidate for the U.S. Senate. The issue was Vietnam, Morgan told Hughes, and "I don't particularly like what I've been hearing." Supporters of Johnson's Vietnam policies, according to Hughes, were urging Duncan to run, believing he provided a sharp contrast with Governor Hatfield. When a Democratic National Committee (DNC) poll showed Duncan with a 4 percent lead over Hatfield, Morgan warned again that he would enter the primary if Duncan continued to support the administration's Vietnam policy.[20]

Because the DNC poll suggested a large crossover of Republican voters against Hatfield, Duncan announced that he would seek his party's nomination, a decision that would invite open warfare between liberal hawks and liberal doves. Although he would enjoy the support of many Oregon Democrats, there were significant dissenters in Howard Morgan, Charles Porter, and Senator Morse. Sweetland congratulated the candidate and promised that he and Lil would pony up cash for the primary, the race "more difficult to finance." Referring to events dominating the evening news, he thought the press would overemphasize "the Vietnam issue," because it was the nature of the news media to stress "the most controversial, even if not the most important, of the issues." He warned: "All your eggs must not be in the Viet Nam basket."[21]

If Oregon's Democratic primary for the U.S. Senate was a referendum on the Johnson administration's Vietnam policy, the result was a resounding affirmation for military intervention. Duncan carried every county, winning statewide by a two-to-one margin. The fall election, with significant national implications, presented a much greater challenge against the handsome and well-funded Hatfield. Stan Federman captured the mood of the campaign in an extended piece, published under the pseudonym Stan Berger, in the Americans for Democratic Action quarterly newsletter, *ADA World*. For the nation at large, he wrote, the chief point of interest was "the supporting cast of top actors," Senator Wayne Morse, a Democrat, backing Hatfield, and retiring senator Maurine Neuberger supporting Duncan. Oregon's Republican newspapers, Federman noted, were "unwontedly cool toward the Governor and are holding back on the accustomed 'rave reviews.'" Although Vietnam was the primary issue between the candidates, they also differed over domestic policy and Hatfield's support of Barry Goldwater in 1964. Whoever wins the Oregon election, Federman predicted, "the Senate of the United States will henceforth be constantly aware of his presence."[22]

As the campaign drew to a close, Duncan stuck to his script—if Americans failed to deter communist aggression in Southeast Asia, China would be the real victor. In his April 2011 obituary of Duncan in the *Oregonian*, Jeff Mapes paraphrased the candidate's warning that the central issue was "whether Americans will die in the buffalo grass of Vietnam or the rye grass of Oregon."[23] Duncan hammered relentlessly at the Chinese communist threat, whereas Hatfield urged negotiation to resolve the Vietnam

Lil Sweetland standing before the Harry S. Truman House in Independence, Missouri, early 1970s. (Courtesy of the Oregon Historical Society)

dilemma. The balloting on November 9 turned into a solid win for Hatfield, who tallied 348,639 votes to 325,810 for Duncan. The *Oregonian*, a supporter of the Vietnam incursion, insisted that the vote "was not a referendum on the war in Viet Nam," conceding, however, that the war "clouded the campaign and unquestionably reduced Governor Hatfield's margin."[24] The 1966 elections ushered in a resurgent Republican Party nationwide, including Tom McCall's election as Oregon's governor. With violence in Vietnam spiraling out of control, the election cycle two years hence would prove even more volatile.

Following his usual practice, Sweetland congratulated Mark Hatfield for winning Oregon's U.S. Senate seat: "You've done very well indeed in the years since we discussed our futures on a drive to Seaside—some 13 or 14 years ago." He was proud that Republicans "in a different mold can now send you to the Senate and Tom to the Governorship." Sweetland was even more generous in a letter to McCall (who supported the American presence in Vietnam): "I suspect we will find ourselves in agreement some 95 % of the time, as always, and that I will not be among your principal hecklers!" He was proud that Oregon politics operated "a few grades above the standards" for the rest of the nation. He wished McCall well and hoped Democrats would "support your progressive advocacies and oppose you only when you fall short."[25]

Except for a brief flirtation with public office long after his retirement, Sweetland's interest in Oregon's U.S. Senate seat marked his last significant electoral enterprise. His work with NEA initiatives—bilingual education and the age-eighteen vote—fully engaged his time and energy through the late 1960s. However, he continued to voice his opinion on politics, especially at the presidential level. Events in Southeast Asia greatly exacerbated political tensions in 1968 when the National Liberation Front (NLF), the communists' political arm in South Vietnam, launched widespread attacks against South Vietnamese and American forces on January 30. Known as the Tet offensive, the NLF and North Vietnamese assaults were a sharp setback to President Johnson's and General William Westmoreland's assurances that there was "light at the end of the tunnel" in the military conflict. When he made a trip to South Vietnam in the aftermath of Tet, trusted CBS anchor Walter Cronkite predicted the "bloody experience of Vietnam is to end in a stalemate."[26]

With Minnesota's eloquent antiwar critic Senator Eugene McCarthy challenging Johnson for his party's nomination, the Southeast Asian war loomed large in election-year politics. After McCarthy made an impressive showing in the New Hampshire primary on March 12, the president stunned the nation two weeks later when he announced: "I shall not seek, and will not accept, the nomination of my party for another term as your president." Johnson's Sunday evening declaration opened the gates to a host of candidates, including Robert F. Kennedy, now a U.S. Senator from New York.[27] Hovering in the background was perennial candidate—now vice president—Hubert Humphrey. Although Sweetland was no longer part of the Oregon delegation to the Democratic National Convention, he fully supported Humphrey's candidacy.

Despite Sweetland's romance with John Kennedy in 1960, Hubert Humphrey had always figured in Sweetland's political calculus. In a letter to ADA's Joseph Rauh in June 1967, Sweetland stressed that his "respect and appreciation of HHH has grown, not diminished, as the years go by. He would make a great president, and he just may." As for President Johnson, "Viet Nam aside, [he] has been far better than any of us could have hoped." Although he supported Robert Kennedy on most issues, he deplored those who "leapt to the RFK standard on the Viet Nam issue alone."[28]

It is worthwhile to reflect on Sweetland's political bearings on the eve of one of the nation's most tumultuous years. In a remarkable address to the Crystal Springs Democratic Club in San Mateo, California, on March 5 (before Johnson's withdrawal), Sweetland laid bare his political soul before a "belligerent" audience of McCarthy supporters. He began with a recitation of his own credentials:

> Because I am a decade or two older than the average among you, I have political experience in combat back to the depression years when I was a college student supporter of sit-down strikes, racial integration and campus anti-war demonstrations and "strikes," and have an early record of conflict with the ROTC and efforts to get the military off the campuses. All of my adult life has been spent in one part or another of the labor movement, in journalism and in practical politics.

During the current election year, he told his listeners, "effective liberals" would be supporting the Johnson-Humphrey ticket to defeat Republican conservatism. Those who insisted there were no differences between the two major political parties were "escapists and romantics . . . condemned to ineffectiveness."[29]

Sweetland predicted that, despite the discordant tone of present-day politics, Democrats would go to the polls in November united, "the standard-bearers of the liberal cause." On the Vietnam question there were too many "Monday-morning quarterbacks," critics claiming to have all the answers about a proper course of action. But there was no point in pursuing further this "terrible experience," because Vietnam was not even the major issue before the electorate. To focus only on Vietnam ignored factors more important to the future such as education and racial problems. Although international disagreements were difficult, they "come and go." It was important for Democrats to focus on domestic policies that "will lay the basis for peace among all peoples."[30] Even with the vantage of hindsight, Sweetland's assessment of the political landscape in 1968 seems myopic, a bankrupt liberalism, an ostrich-like inability to acknowledge the searing impact of Vietnam on American politics.

The divisiveness of the Vietnam War was played out in messy forums involving American liberals. The ADA exemplified those divisions when it endorsed Eugene McCarthy shortly before the spring primaries. After Johnson's decision not to seek reelection, ADA's Joseph Rauh sent a circular to members soliciting support for McCarthy, because there now might be "hope that we may end the Vietnam War." Liberals should "act on their convictions," Rauh argued, and "support a platform of genuine liberal positions on foreign and domestic policies." Ending the war would open the way to rebuilding the country, ending unemployment, raising people out of poverty, abolishing race discrimination, and establishing a "democratic foreign policy."[31]

Repeated commentaries that liberals had lost faith in Hubert Humphrey prompted Sweetland to survey the founders of ADA who were still living, to determine their preference for the Democratic nomination for president. The results, he found, indicated overwhelming support for Humphrey. Central to Sweetland's concern in what he described as "a dynamic year—tragic, convulsive, frightening," was Humphrey's nomination as the Democratic candidate for president. The assassinations of Martin Luther King in April, Senator Robert Kennedy in June, and continued violence in American cities made election-year politics even more volatile. With no delegate position in the convention, Sweetland appealed to Humphrey headquarters in Washington, D.C., for tickets: "Will our HHH organizations have some available?"[32]

Sweetland was not a fan of Eugene McCarthy, the New Left, or radical movements beyond the pale of the Democratic Party. His correspondence and public addresses on behalf of the age-eighteen vote indicate his disdain for Students for a Democratic Society, the Student Nonviolent Coordinating Committee, and the Black Panther Party. Granting young people the vote, he argued, would lessen the appeal of nihilists and those who believed only in direct action. His ideological friend Nathalie Panek expressed her contempt for the events at the Democratic National Convention in Chicago in a postconvention letter: "I am terribly hostile towards McCarthy and his alleged 'children.'" She also wondered where ADA, which had declared for McCarthy, "will go from here?"[33]

The assassination of Robert Kennedy for all practical purposes assured Humphrey's nomination. But it also revealed his difficulties—as vice president, he was linked to an administration pursuing the most unpopular war of the twentieth century. His campaign was disorganized, and his biographer Carl Solberg points to "his fatal dependence on the president." Those elements became glaringly apparent in the aftermath of the Kennedy assassination. Republican standard-bearer Richard Nixon told *Time* magazine's Simon Fentriss: "Humphrey's problem, one that he can't escape, is that he carries on his back the past. He is the candidate of the past no matter how much he tells about his programs and the future." As for Eugene McCarthy, the candidate expected to assume the banner of the fallen RFK, he retreated from the public eye and ceased to campaign. And when he returned, Solberg notes, "he was a ravaged man, looking and acting as if he thought he was responsible for Kennedy's murder."[34]

Historian Jefferson Cowie captured the essence of the conflicts rending asunder the Cold War liberal coalition:

> The vice president was the embodiment of institutional liberalism, the darling of organized labor, the choice of the powerful, the deal makers' man, the recipient of the legacy of Vietnam at exactly the moment when the establishment was under siege.

Forty years after the Chicago Democratic Convention, columnist Haynes Johnson, who covered the affair for the *Washington Star*, remembered the hot, humid weather, the city's taxi drivers on strike, and electrical service operating unpredictably. The convention took place, Johnson wrote, in the wake of "heartbreak, assassination, riots and a breakdown in law and order that made it seem as if the country were coming apart, . . . destroying faith in politicians, in the political system, in the country and its institutions."[35]

The nominee worsened his prospects in an interview with Roger Mudd of CBS News as conventioneers were leaving Chicago. Humphrey told Mudd that the demonstrations "were planned, premeditated by certain people in this country that feel all they have to do is riot and they'll get their way. They don't want to work through the peaceful process." Humphrey denounced the "obscenity, the profanity, the filth that was uttered night after night in front of the hotels." To young people, biographer Solberg contends, Humphrey "was both ridiculous and infuriating." From the ashes of Chicago, however, Humphrey nearly pulled it off, losing the popular vote to Nixon by 31,785,480 to 31,270,533. In the Electoral College Nixon prevailed with 301, to 101 for Humphrey and 46 for George Wallace.[36]

Hubert Humphrey was fifty-seven years old in 1968, Monroe Sweetland fifty-eight. Their parallel careers as crusading liberals on civil rights, economic policy, social justice, and a host of related issues placed them at the forefront of public policy most of their careers. Humphrey, Solberg argues, had been "ahead of public opinion" most of his life and suffered defeat in 1968 "because he had fallen behind American attitudes and public opinion." Although he fell short of Humphrey's stature in political accomplishments, Sweetland was similar in temperament, liberal to a fault, and democratic to the core. While Sweetland did not have an overweening president looking over his shoulder, his views paralleled Humphrey's on most issues.[37] And like Humphrey, Sweetland was partner to a fractured liberalism repudiated at the polls in 1968.

In an oral interview at the Oregon Historical Society two decades after the events of 1968, Sweetland acknowledged grudgingly that Humphrey's nomination alienated young voters because of his close association with the Vietnam War. Rick Harmon asked Sweetland if he and Humphrey symbolized an older-style politics that did not resonate with young people:

> Oh, sure. Yes I did, because I was a supporter of Hubert Humphrey.
> I remember even going to a Democratic meeting and giving a
> speech in support of the policies of Lyndon Johnson. But, of course,
> I exempted some of the military adventures and emphasized . . . his
> great contributions in the field of electoral reform, of civil rights,
> and of education.

Harmon pressed Sweetland on how he handled his feelings about the war:

> I didn't ever really cope with it. . . . It was a mess, it was terrible.
> . . . Here I am, basically a pacifist, against war at any level, any kind,
> and here's a president of my party, leading us into the Vietnam
> adventure.

Although bipartisan decisions led America to Vietnam, Sweetland still found the subject painful. When Harmon remarked that he remained loyal to the party even though a Democratic president was escalating the conflict,

Sweetland responded that he would "never have considered leaving the party."[38]

Although Sweetland continued to voice his views in subsequent presidential campaigns, the fractious 1968 election marked his last significant role as a participant. As legislative counsel for NEA, he tracked the organization's education objectives with presidential aspirants in 1972 and 1976. Even with Hubert back in his old Senate seat in 1970, Sweetland began promoting Washington's Democratic senator Henry "Scoop" Jackson's presidential prospects in late 1971. Writing to Bill Connell of Humphrey's staff—with the expectation that Humphrey was no longer interested in the presidency (he was wrong)—Sweetland wanted to promote Jackson's candidacy but worried that the Washington senator was still "hooked on his military-industrial complex commitments."[39]

Neither the Humphrey nor Jackson campaigns gained sufficient movement in 1972 to derail the momentum of Senator George McGovern. Humphrey waged a sterling, if disorganized, campaign, losing the critical California primary by the narrow margin of 5 percent. With the exception of Alabama governor George Wallace, Jackson was the most dogmatic aspirant for the presidency in 1972, supporting a strong defense and urging the United States to confront Soviet expansionism. Sweetland's old friend James Wechsler of the *New York Post* dismissed Jackson as "a symbol of the sterile slogans of another era, ... the faithful representative of every interest and ideologue that sees mankind doomed to another decade or more of the balance of terror and preparedness as the only national salvation." Jackson also trivialized young radicals as "intolerant extremists who have come to despise America and who would destroy the Democratic Party if they took over." Their candidate, George McGovern, was "'the chief traveling salesman' of the New Left establishment."[40] Although he floundered in 1972, Jackson would return four years later as a more formidable candidate.

Sweetland was busy pressing Jackson's candidacy well before the 1976 election. At the halfway point in the presidential election cycle, the *Daily Astorian* identified Jackson as a "super-hawk," unacceptable to liberals. Editor J. W. Forrester, Jr., Sweetland's former newspaper associate, charged that Jackson was a hard-liner, who always demanded more military spending to the point that he would "pile overkill upon overkill." Voters would be wise, Forrester continued, to seek a more liberal candidate such as Representative

Jerry Rubin, radical anti-war activist of the 1960s, with Monroe Sweetland, attending a conference on 1930s and 1960s radicals in 1978. Location unidentified. (Courtesy of the Oregon Historical Society)

Morris Udall of Arizona. Sweetland rejected Forrester's characterization of Jackson as conservative. "The only source you cite against your neighboring Senator is that he is a 'hard-liner' in dealing with the Soviets and Chinese." Jackson, he countered, "stands tall in every State and in the councils of the world."[41]

In California Sweetland worked with longtime acquaintance Howard Costigan to build a Jackson-for-president campaign. Costigan, who had come full circle from his Popular Front days of the 1930s, worried that Jackson's efforts to curry favor with the "New Politics" crowd would damage his reputation with centrist Democrats. Jackson needed to repair his relations with AFL-CIO head George Meany, Costigan warned, because with George Wallace in the race, he would need the blue-collar vote to secure the nomination.[42] It is ironic that the two former firebrand leaders of the Washington and Oregon commonwealth federations were now working to nominate a Democratic hawk for the presidency.

Jackson's second effort to seek the Democratic nomination for president foundered on the shoals of flawed campaign strategies and the candidate's personal shortcomings—he lacked television appeal. His biographer Robert Kaufman compared Jackson's weaknesses with Jimmie Carter's successes: "Candidate Jackson had a poor strategy, bad luck, and made many mistakes.

Candidate Carter had an excellent strategy, first-rate luck, and ran a nearly flawless campaign." A few days after Jimmy Carter won the Pennsylvania primary, Jackson flew home to Washington state and announced that he was no longer an active candidate for president.[43]

Monroe Sweetland had traveled a broad ideological landscape between his activist days in the 1930s and his accommodationist positions with the Democratic Party's power structure after 1950. On issues of war and peace, he downplayed international horrors if conflicts involved Cold War maneuvering among the United States, the Soviet Union, and the Peoples Republic of China. He discounted the brutality of the Suharto regime in Indonesia, especially when the new government opened trade relations with the United States and its allies. Sweetland supported the Johnson administration's policies in Vietnam, believing to the end that the president would find a way to broker a resolution to the conflict. He never understood the intensity of the antiwar movement and the toll it exacted on the American body politic. His letter to Robert Duncan in March 1966 when the latter announced his decision to run for the U.S. Senate—that Vietnam would not be the most important issue in the campaign—speaks loudly about his inability to appreciate the intensity of the growing opposition to the Vietnam quagmire.[44]

Epilogue: A Fruitful Life

With his retirement documents filed with the National Education Association, Sweetland left office in mid-January 1975. NEA's West Coast Regional Office delayed his formal retirement dinner until May 1975 when a large group of NEA staff gathered at the Hyatt House in Burlingame. In addition to accolades praising his work with NEA, the highlight of the Saturday evening affair was a slide show featuring Norman Lubeck's artistically creative cartoons portraying Sweetland's significant achievements.[1] With his old boss Bob Archibald providing commentary, the images traced Sweetland's career in Oregon politics, his work as a newspaperman, and his part in the emergence of Oregon's Democratic Party. One image shows Monroe, Lil, and Rebecca migrating south to California in 1964 with ocean-going gray whales. Another has Sweetland with his arms around the capitol building in Washington, D.C., "Monroe's natural environment." Two cartoons important to his accomplishments use fish representations: (1) "His first big catch was Bilingual Education"; and (2) "Then—with good timing and the right kind of lure, he landed the great blue marlin—the 18-Year-Old Vote." One of the last images shows Sweetland behind a desk with piles of paper: "What else is in store for Monroe now?"[2]

When Monroe Sweetland retired from the National Education Association in 1975, the United States was withdrawing its forces from Vietnam. By the time of his death on September 6, 2006, the nation would be fully involved in military ventures in Iraq and Afghanistan, and presidential candidates would already be jockeying for position in the 2008 primaries. After leaving NEA, Sweetland lived through five more presidencies, eighteen years of Republican and twelve years of Democratic administrations. Those were eventful years for Sweetland, who continued his engagement

Norman Lubeck, a graphic-arts
designer, created these cartoons
in honor of Monroe Sweetland's
retirement in May 1975. (Courtesy
of the Oregon Historical Society)

His first big catch was Bilingual Education.

Then --
with good timing
and the right kind
of lure, he landing the
great blue marlin --
the 18-Year Old Vote.

with precinct politics, even when his family convinced him to move to
nearby Willamette View Estates in early 1998. His final move was to Oatfield
Estates early in 2006, a residential community comprising homes with small
suites and common dining and living areas.[3]

While Monroe was shifting into different challenges, Lil continued on with
the U.S. Department of Labor in San Francisco, and Rebecca, who graduated from San Mateo H.S. in 1971, was finishing her undergraduate degree
at Chico State College the year of his retirement. As for Monroe, he was fully
prepared to move on to political work—as he said in an oral interview—to
"spend my declining years writing letters to the editors." But he soon returned
to an avocation that he pursued sporadically in Oregon—gathering and
shipping wild botanical greenery to distributing houses in midwestern and
eastern cities. He would make new friends in this enterprise, travel through

Barbara Sweetland Smith and Rebecca Sweetland, early 1970s, San Francisco. (Courtesy of the Oregon Historical Society)

new semiarid environments in search of exotic plant and shrub material, and realize only modest rewards for his efforts. It was the journey, however, that mattered, gaining knowledge about new flora and venturing into unknown environments in search of the unexpected.

Not long after his retirement, Sweetland's long association with the Japanese American community surfaced again when he received word that Hood River native Frank Hachiya, who died on Leyte Island in early 1945, would be receiving yet another posthumous honor. The Defense Language Institute in Monterey, California, was taking steps in 1979 to dedicate the central building in its new Asian language complex in Hachiya's honor. Sweetland, who had lost contact with Frank's brother, Homer, wrote Ray T. Yasui in Hood River, asking about Homer's whereabouts. Yasui consulted with older Issei in Hood River and located a person who had an address for Homer's mother, Shizuko Hachiya, in Japan. Yasui, who remembered that Homer at one time had been with the U.S. Army in Washington state, requested forwarding information from Mrs. Hachiya. In the interim, Sweetland made an inquiry through the U.S. Embassy in Tokyo that bore immediate results: Homer was working at the Yokosuka Naval Base. A phone call from the embassy to Homer elicited a brief letter, thanking Sweetland for the honor to be conferred on his brother.[4]

Frank Hachiya served in the Military
Intelligence Service in the Pacific during
the Second World War and was killed on
Leyte Island in the Philippines. (Courtesy
of the Defense Language Institute,
Monterey, California)

The dedication of the Monterey Defense Language Institute building
in May 1980 was a gala affair. Monroe and Lil Sweetland drove to the coast
from their home in nearby San Mateo. Monroe and California representative Leon Panetta spoke at the event. Homer Hachiya and Commander Koe
Nishimoto of the Veterans of Foreign Wars Department of Oregon were
also in attendance. Nishimoto, who had grown up in the Hood River Valley,
was a childhood friend of Homer Hachiya. After the ceremonies, Nishimoto
wrote Sweetland, amazed at the coincidence of attending the dedication as
"the State V.F.W. Commander but also a friend of the family and being from
Hood River." Nishimoto, whose family looked after Frank's headstone at
Hood River's Idlewilde Cemetery, confessed that "it means more to all of us
now. It is a feeling of great pride to all Japanese in this valley." He was pleased
to meet both Lil and Monroe. "We have read so much about you and what
you did for the Hachiya family."[5]

After Lil retired from her position with the federal government as a manpower specialist in 1979, she volunteered regularly at San Mateo's Chope
Hospital until she became ill in 1984. Monroe's deteriorating vision began
when doctors at the University of California in Berkeley discovered mela-
noma in his left eye. Subsequent radiation treatments eventually caused
him to lose sight in the eye. Rebecca, who graduated from Aragon High
School in San Mateo in 1971, earned a bachelor's degree in social welfare

and corrections at Chico State in 1975, a master's in social work (1980) at Portland State University, and then a doctor of jurisprudence at Lewis and Clark's Northwestern School of Law.[6]

Although she had requested no funeral or memorial services, Lil's death in April 1985 brought an outpouring of letters, phone calls, cards, flowers, food, and personal gifts from friends and associates. The list of those who contacted Monroe was lengthy and included an eclectic group of people from Oregon, California, and elsewhere—congressmen, senators, governors, executives, and Jerry Rubin, the antiwar activist and counterculture figure of the 1960s and 1970s. Among all the correspondents, Ancil Payne, longtime family friend and head of King Broadcasting in Seattle, wrote the most moving memory of Lil, capturing her indomitable spirit, her ability to be "critical without being accusatory." While Monroe was always "filled with enthusiasm and optimism," Lil was more "reserved and quizzical," challenging and sometimes confrontive. Payne confessed that he usually didn't like such mannerisms, but in Lil "I did." "She might have been bitching in her own inimitable way, but she was always there. Critical but never unsupporting."[7]

When Sweetland founded Western Wilderness Products from his San Mateo home, the business mirrored his earlier Oregon Wilderness Products enterprise. His interest in plant material and its commercial value, however, dates to his high school years in Constantine. During the early 1950s, struggling with financially troubled newspapers, he sold Christmas greens in midwestern and eastern markets, the modest income for "Christmas money, holiday money, that sort of thing."[8] In a second Oregon Wilderness Products enterprise in 1961, he shipped greens to Honolulu, Seattle, and Baltimore. He also consigned five hundred pounds of blue-berried desert juniper to Philadelphia in a Teufel Nursery railcar filled with holly. He included a case of Douglas-fir tips for the distributor to examine as a potential "handsome spray" for Christmas.[9]

Western Wilderness Products—the larger operation of his retirement years—involved dried floral material gathered in California's semiarid backcountry. The new venture had originated "by accident" when Monroe and Lil took a trip through Mexico to Guatemala. On their return, as was his custom, he filled the back of the car with attractive botanical specimens. Because he was "a strict amateur . . . in identifying plants and trees and flowers," he showed his cache of brown pods to a local florist who was interested in their commercial value. When he learned that the plant's provenance was in San Diego, Orange, and Ventura counties in southern California, he obtained Forest Service permits and began making gathering trips on weekends and selling the material to the local florist.[10]

From these beginnings, Sweetland's business expanded until he was hiring people to handle the gathering, hauling, storage, and shipping of dried floral materials. These were seasonal and occasional workers whom he appears to have trusted implicitly. Letters from some of the employees testify to Sweetland's compassion for people with troubled lives. Sevie Allen's letter of December 1985 was typical, from one who owed Sweetland "friendship, loyalty, kindness and about $600." Allen wrote from an alcoholic rehabilitation dormitory in Fort Lauderdale, Florida, where he had voluntarily committed himself to cope with his disease. Although they might never meet again, he wanted Sweetland to know "that it was you that made me face this turning point." After his release, he hoped to land a job and send Sweetland money to clear his debt.[11]

Patrick Cox was another alcoholic—"clean and sober for a little over 2 years" after having served time in jail—who contacted Sweetland shortly after his return to Milwaukie. After his release, Cox obtained a job and was in a position to make "steady payments to repay what I stole from you." He recalled what he "learned about nature, plants, trees, life, and yes, even politics" working with Sweetland. Monroe wished him success in landing a job that would make use of his computer skills" and thanked him for being able "to pay back already a good chunk of your debt." He wanted to know more about his job and asked if he were married—"with your skills and intelligence I feel sure you will stay on top from now on."[12]

On another occasion, San Mateo County's probation department asked Sweetland about the activities of Curtis Alan Hall. Sweetland cited his acquaintance with Hall since his hiring in the late 1970s: "Curt is an alcoholic, and his whole life seems to revolve around his week-end drinking bouts"; nevertheless, Curt was an "honest and intelligent, congenial" person to work with. Sweetland stood "ready to assist your counseling in any appropriate way."[13] Richard Williams wrote to Sweetland about wandering the West after leaving Western Wilderness Products and then returning to his parents' Oklahoma farm. He remembered Sweetland as "a great example of endurance" and included a check for fifty dollars "which you gave me in

After he retired, Monroe Sweetland formed Western Wilderness Products, a firm engaged in gathering plant specimens from California's arid backcountry and shipping them to eastern brokers who traded in natural decorative products. (Courtesy of the Oregon Historical Society)

exchange for future work that I was not able to complete." Another former employee wrote Sweetland in 1995, telling about his nearly completed degree in biochemistry. "In my somewhat emotionally stunted way," he wrote, "[I] considered you one of the best friends I have ever had." He had cleaned up his personal life "(if you know what I mean and I think you do) which leaves me a lot more time and energy, as well as a clearer mind."[14]

The Western Wilderness Products business expanded to the use of warehouses for storing, sorting, and shipping dried floral materials. Listed among "Desert Products" and "Larger Display Commodities" were agave (from Mexico), golden anise, wild grapevines, Mono willow trees, mountain lilac, and varieties of pine cones. Sweetland may have gathered agave, chiefly Mexican in provenance, in Mexico's Baja Peninsula where he collected on occasion. Although he may have used other warehouses, in early 1991 his letterhead stationery listed his home address as his office and a site in nearby East Palo Alto as the location for his warehouse.[15]

Those familiar with Sweetland's lifelong struggles with fiscal ledgers will not be surprised that Western Wilderness Products confronted similar problems. Delinquent unemployment insurance payments, confused accounts with clients, and on one occasion an incident with a fraudulent collection agency created some of the confusion. Terrie Marconi handled the company's bookkeeping in the early 1990s, including exchanges with California's Employment Development Department. In February 1992 Marconi returned a Western Wilderness Products check because it was supposed to cover an ongoing "accruing balance." One year later she returned the firm's payroll records to Sweetland, thanking him for the opportunity to work with his company. She added a note to the state's Employment Department announcing that she would no longer handle payroll taxes for Western Wilderness Products.[16] Monroe's retirement benefits from NEA were good, and family members suspected that he used those funds to keep Western Wilderness Products afloat. Lil had complained about the company losing money, and Rebecca concluded the company was a "money losing proposition."[17]

When his vision had deteriorated to the point that he could no longer drive, Sweetland relied on friends and associates to take him on gathering expeditions into the California interior. Mike Tassone, a friend and occasional employee, piloted Sweetland on several collecting outings, remembering with delight their running dialogue about politics, literature, and Sweetland's life story. As late as January 1993, Sweetland wrote enthusiastically about his "outdoor business," an enterprise that he expected would "taper off in reasonable time." At this point, he was operating from a sprawling ranch and outbuildings near Moss Beach less than a mile from the Pacific Ocean.[18]

The end for Western Wilderness Products came abruptly in May 1994 when Sweetland informed the owner of the ranch property that he intended to discontinue his business and terminate his monthly tenancy; his eyesight limitations posed a burden to continuing the business. Although the business might continue under new ownership, he was uncertain whether this would materialize.[19] Although the timing of his move to Milwaukie is unclear, he was settled in his new home by October.

Sweetland's retirement years were filled with friendships old and new. Nathalie Panek, the Sweetland's friend since the 1930s, kept in touch with the family, visiting them when she traveled to San Francisco from her home in Los Angeles, where she directed fundraising for the American Cancer Society. Panek, who went through several failed relationships over the years, married James Patton, the longtime leader of the National Farmers Union (NFU), in November 1972. Jim Patton first met Monroe during the insurgent farmer-labor movements of the 1930s. Affiliated with left-wing New Dealers, Patton worked as an aide to Pennsylvania's secretary of agriculture when he retired from the NFU. Both Jim and Nathalie attributed their relationship to Sweetland—Nathalie: "It all started with your having breakfast with Jim [at the Democratic convention] in Miami. You sent me his card. I wrote, he wrote, etc. and that's that. We are very happy." Jim: "Eureka! I found my girl. . . . Nathalie and I are agreed that you will be our special house guest."[20]

Panek, who teased Sweetland that he "should have the honor of giving the bride away," left her position with the American Cancer Society, sold her house, and moved to Washington, D.C., "lock, stock and barrel." The couple was married on Jim's seventieth birthday, November 8, 1972, celebrated the event at a private home amid eighty guests, and then honeymooned in the Virgin Islands. Nathalie's account of the wedding and its aftermath reveals a life strikingly different from the hardscrabble single parent the Sweetlands knew during the late Depression. She and Jim enjoyed a reception at an exclusive Capitol Hill home and then "an impromptu dinner for ten at the Rive Gauch in Georgetown, . . . a favorite hangout of the Kennedys."[21]

Their honeymoon in the Virgin Islands was equally elegant. From a balcony overlooking the ocean on St. Croix, Nathalie wrote of the pleasant view of the water "in shades of blue and green." They would be home by the weekend to their "two bedroom, two bath fairly spacious apartment with a view of the Nation's capitol, in a highrise in Southwest Washington about a block from the Potomac River." The area was a slum when she lived there in the late 1940s but was "very nice now." Security was evident everywhere in the apartment building, and when she and Jim left on their honeymoon, they set the alarm for their apartment. "Should anyone try to enter—all hell breaks loose."[22]

Using her husband's surname, Nathalie kept in touch with Sweetland in the ensuing years, giving voice to the world of politics and passing on news about friends. Informed of the death of Priscilla Yadad, she asked Monroe, "Wasn't she the lovely young girl who worked for CIO War Relief and went with Charlie Livermore? So beautiful and sweet."

Nathalie always provided commentary on contemporary politics, predicting that the Republicans could not defeat the Democrats in 1976, "but the New Left can do it for them.[23] In another note contemplating their move west, she complained about inflation and rising interest rates: "When even Arthur Burns declares our country in peril, it is hard to know what to do— maybe dig a storm shelter."[24]

The Pattons visited the San Francisco Bay Area after Monroe's retirement looking for a home but left discouraged when they failed to find a mutually satisfactory house and location. When Jim finally left his position with the Pennsylvania Department of Agriculture, the couple settled in Menlo Park and partnered in a cooperative strawberry farm. The exchanges between Nathalie and Monroe end in the late 1970s. Jim Patton died in 1985, with Nathalie living another seven years, passing away in the summer of 1992. Her son David provided the capstone to his mother's life in a letter to her friends, describing her marriage to Patton as "one of the nicest things that ever happened to her." After his passing and some health problems of her own, Nathalie moved to Bellingham where David taught psychology at Western Washington University. Although his letter provided "only bare and incomplete geographical details," what was important to his mother were the "very dear friends she shared experiences with along the way."[25]

Before Sweetland returned to Milwaukie, the Portland *Oregonian* regularly acknowledged Sweetland's role in the Democratic Party's emergence as a significant player in state politics. Stan Federman was the friendly columnist of many of the articles.[26] One of the more amusing was Jonathan Nicholas's column acknowledging an *Oregonian* gaffe in February 1986 referring to "the late" Monroe Sweetland. It happened that Sweetland was passing through Portland and read the report of his recent death. Experienced in dealing with faux news reports, Nicholas wrote, "Sweetland gently eased into his Mark Twain mode to inform us that reports of his demise had been greatly exaggerated." The surprisingly spry Sweetland told Nicholas: "But then, I've always been controversial. So it's perfectly appropriate that people would disagree on the issue." Besides, Sweetland said, notice of his death may have been a Republican plot.[27]

His return to Oregon in 1994 placed Sweetland again in proximity to family and old friends. In a circular letter to longtime acquaintances, he found it comforting "to slip back into the familiar routines of the Portland environment." With Lil's old 1975 Datsun and "a congenial driver," he was able to make personal visits. And despite his diminished vision, he managed

to navigate the metro area's public transit system and renewed his membership in the City Club of Portland. The Club acknowledged his return in its
monthly bulletin, recounting his life story as political activist, newspaper
publisher, state senator, political consultant to the NEA, and his floral enterprise. After living in the San Francisco Bay Area for thirty years, Sweetland
had moved into a new chapter as "a selfless public servant." The bulletin's
editor asked Sweetland what sustained him through sixty years of public life.
His response was unapologetic: "I'm an eternal optimist."[28]

With the assistance of friends, he wrote members of Congress on
pressing issues of the day, including a letter to California senator Barbara
Boxer, praising her "heroic efforts" to call attention to Oregon senator
Bob Packwood's inappropriate dalliances with several women. Packwood's
behavior pointed to the need for more women in the Senate and validated
the efforts of Emily's List to place more women in public office.[29] When
Leon Panetta joined President Bill Clinton's staff, Sweetland regaled him
with remembrances of their several meetings, especially when Sweetland
and his NEA colleagues intended to ask him to switch from the Republican
to the Democratic Party—only to learn that Panetta had already made the
change. Their paths crossed again during Panetta's first run for Congress
when Sweetland provided support for the campaign, and a third encounter
took place in 1980 when they both spoke at the dedication of a new building
at the Monterey Defense Language Institute in honor of Frank Hachiya.[30]

Occasionally friends from the past confessed to Sweetland about their
less-than-stellar financial circumstances. Oregon's former fourth district
congressman Charles Porter wrote in June 1996 about "politix *and* my own
search for a way out of fiscal swamps." He asked Sweetland for suggestions
about "remunerative employment, however humble." With their children
out of the family home, Porter and his wife were putting the house up for
sale. He added words of admiration for Sweetland's "solid philosophy, calm
and ever-cheerful, seemingly selfless ('seemingly' because I know you've
mastered the formula for not letting life's endless trials get the better of you)."
Harvard-educated Charlie Porter, one of Oregon's most prominent civil lib-
ertarians, who fought for three decades (with ultimate success) to have a
huge concrete cross removed from public property atop Eugene's Skinner
Butte, was seventy-seven years old and still struggling to make a living.[31]

Sons and daughters of former colleagues frequently contacted Sweetland during the autumn years of his life. Lisa Bentley—daughter of Lorna Marple, a liberal Democrat and civil rights activist during the 1950s—wrote Sweetland in 1997, apologizing for missing him during a recent visit to Portland. She remembered her mother's great pride about working with Sweetland on civil rights and Democratic Party issues. Sweetland responded, relating the latest news about Oregon's NAACP and the Bonneville Power Administration where her father worked. He provided news about Barbara and daughter Rebecca's position as head of Beaverton's mediation office.[32]

Among the friends from his California years, Mike Tassone kept in touch, exchanging letters about his personal ambitions as a writer and the potential for a collaborative project with Sweetland involving Captain Jack (Kientpoos), the renowned Modoc Indian leader whose band of sixty-six fighters held off as many as six hundred U.S. Army troops from late 1872 to the spring of 1873 in northern California's lava beds. With access to the wealth of materials in the Oregon Historical Society, Sweetland gathered documents and books and encouraged Tassone to "put together a dramatic monograph in a short period of time."[33]

Tassone, who appears to have been a procrastinator, dropped the Modoc project, writing Sweetland that he was burned out with school but had formed a group of friends who were "evolving into an art movement." His cohort—"writers, poets, teachers, thinkers"—gathered weekly for "drinking wine and discussing politics." To support himself, Tassone chauffeured clients, including Charlton Heston, columnist Herb Caen of the *San Francisco Chronicle*, comedian Steve Martin, and recent presidential candidate Steve Forbes. Tassone's interest in writing for a living was still alive, although plans were on hold until he finished school.[34]

Sweetland thanked Tassone for the "great semiannual report" and regaled him with news of the recent visit to Portland of President Clinton and Vice President Gore, with Portland Democrats giving the visitors an enthusiastic and spirited welcome. Many men, he observed, were anti-Clinton, but women favored the president by a two-to-one margin. He was continuing to enjoy the "Indian summer" of his life but had to reckon "with the pangs of mortality"—citing the death of his good friend Jebby Davidson. He closed with advice for Tassone: "I still want you to achieve greatly, so I have to hope your drive does not become blunted by *your endless preparations* (italics added).[35]

Tassone's last letter to Sweetland cast a somber tone on his personal life. "We've known each other a long time," he observed, recalling a visit to Sweetland on Sweetland's birthday in 1989. His life had "changed drastically in the last three months." Attending a month-long retreat in Joshua Tree National Park had "helped to crystallize a lot of things for me." After a three-year relationship, Tassone had broken up with his girlfriend, moved back to his mother's house, and withdrawn from school. The catalyst was his ambition to write, "so that is now what I am living." His first project would be a book reflecting his discussions with Sweetland on their many travels about the California countryside. He expected to cover some of Sweetland's biography "as revealed to me" and would include "threads of politics and American Indian history and philosophy."[36] Tassone's presence in Sweetland's life fades in the absence of further correspondence.

After living in a Courtney Road apartment for two years, Sweetland moved into his old residence on Kellogg Lake in the spring of 1996. By this time the house had been divided into upstairs and downstairs apartments, with Monroe occupying the first floor. At some point daughter Rebecca began managing her father's affairs, paying utility and housekeeping bills and asking Monroe not to make expenditures on the house or grounds without her written authorization. She cautioned that she would be unable to budget repairs if he failed to leave those decisions to her. Rebecca appreciated his willingness to help but wanted Monroe to keep her informed of required maintenance. She prefaced her note with a bit of satirical humor: "This letter, and its enclosures, has all your little heart desires: historical ego memorabilia, money, authority to live in the house of your desire, and much more!"[37]

Over the next few months Monroe and Rebecca worked to have the 120-year-old house, one of the oldest in the city, placed on the National Register of Historic Places. When the family filed for the historic listing, the home was already a "contributing" building within a larger historic district. The family applied to have the house upgraded to "significant," a designation providing greater protection against condemnation. A consultant for Milwaukie's Historic Review Commission declared the house important for "the events that have happened there," including dignitaries who were hosted in the Sweetland's living room: John F. Kennedy, Hubert Humphrey, former New York governor Averill Harriman, and countless numbers of

Oregon political notables. With the approval of the Oregon State Historic Preservation Advisory Committee, the house was upgraded to significant historic status.[38]

Longtime friend Stan Federman recalled the Kellogg Lake home and its spacious living room when he first traveled from Los Angeles to Oregon to interview for a position with the *Milwaukie Review*. He remembered Lil and her mother plying him with food and, many years later, "being introduced to a new delicacy" whenever he dined with the Sweetlands. But his best memories were reserved for "the old living room. . . . no living room was ever more lived in . . . and Lil was always trying to pass food upon us." Among the people he met in the living room were presidential candidate Hubert Humphrey and his entourage. Federman was also proud that he and his wife Lorrie were married in the Sweetlands' friendly living room.[39]

After returning to Oregon, Sweetland made friends with Verne Duncan, a neighbor, liberal Republican, and Oregon's former four-term superintendent of public instruction. The two developed "a great friendship," Duncan remembers, and because navigating Portland's public transit system was difficult, Duncan drove Sweetland to the weekly meetings of the Portland City Club. Duncan and his wife Donna began sharing dinners with Monroe at local restaurants, where discussions would range across their common interests in history and politics. The friendship deepened in 1997 when Clackamas County's Republican Central Committee passed over Duncan and recommended three little-known conservatives to fill a vacant state Senate seat. Democratic governor John Kitzhaber, with a supporting letter from Sweetland, appointed Duncan to the unfinished term.[40]

Verne Duncan's well-known moderation invited challenges from conservatives when he announced that he would run for a full four-year term in 1998. Two conservative challengers emerged for the District 12 Senate position, Dick Jones and Jesse Lott, with the latter spreading rumors that his nationally known cousin, Mississippi senator Trent Lott, would travel to Oregon to support his election campaign. With no viable Democrat filing for the seat, and fearing that Lott might win the primary, Democrats convinced Sweetland to file for the seat. This set the stage for a unique campaign between good friends, one a moderate Republican, the other an "unabashed liberal."[41]

When Sweetland stepped forward at the state capitol to file as a candidate, a reporter asked why he was filing, at the age of eighty-eight. The new candidate replied: "You can never retire from citizenship." "Back for another hurrah," headlined Vince Kohler's article in the *Oregonian*, referring to Sweetland as "the grand old man of Oregon liberalism." When he filed, Sweetland told Kohler that he "felt the adrenaline coming up" and that he was ready for the contest. As to questions about his age, he replied with a chuckle, "I'm not as old as Strom Thurmond, whoever he is."[42]

As the party's de facto candidate, Sweetland took his nomination seriously, campaigning across the district, often traveling with his liberal Republican opponent Verne Duncan. Sweetland's campaign literature cited his "proven 50-year track record of leadership for education," pointing to his successful effort for Oregon's community college system and his "decades of fighting for working families." In the November election voters sustained Duncan in his Senate seat by 18,324 (58 percent) to 13,391 (42 percent) for Sweetland.[43] Duncan's popularity in the district, and Sweetland's age and absence from the state for thirty years, explains the difference.

These were auspicious years, filled with honors, birthday celebrations, and—of course—political labor. After two decades in retirement, Sweetland continued to receive awards for his achievements in education and institution-building. One significant honor—his part in Portland State University's (PSU) emergence as a major metropolitan university—highlighted Sweetland's legislative support for the institution. When he was elected to the Senate in 1955, Sweetland cosponsored a bill establishing Portland State College as a full member of the Oregon State System of Higher Education. With Sweetland chairing the Senate Education Committee, the college made additional strides in the 1959 and 1961 sessions—expanding classroom buildings, establishing a Graduate School of Social Work (1960) and Graduate School of Education (1961). Those accomplishments were widely attributed to Sweetland's meticulous work as chair of the Senate Education Committee.[44]

Libby Solomon (wife of deceased Federal District Court Judge Gus Solomon), local attorney Keith Burns, and Myron "Mike" Katz initiated a move in 1993 to have Portland State University honor Sweetland for his efforts. With the significant support of Katz, a Sweetland associate since 1952, the effort bore fruit when PSU awarded Sweetland its Presidential Citation of Merit at its graduation ceremonies in June 1995. The award honored Sweetland as "legislator, publisher, civil rights advocate, world traveler,

Portland State University's commencement, June 10, 1995, where Monroe Sweetland was awarded the institution's Presidential Citation as one of the university's founders. Portland State also hosts the Monroe M. Sweetland Endowed Community Leadership Scholarship to honor Monroe's contributions to education.

and Portland State University's foremost educational citizen." University President Judith Ramaley told an *Oregonian* reporter that PSU "could have no finer guardian in its first critical years than Monroe Sweetland." Mike Katz told the reporter about efforts to endow a $50,000 scholarship "to worthy and needy" students in his honor. The Monroe Sweetland Scholarship Fund far surpassed expectations: beginning with a corpus endowment of $21,311 in 1997, it grew to $80,870 in 2001, $90,576 in 2004, and $114,000 in June 2012.[45]

In another richly deserved honor, the ACLU Foundation of Oregon presented Sweetland with a Civil Liberties Award in December 1994. Mike Katz, who submitted the principal nominating letter, remarked that Sweetland supported civil rights in Oregon "long before it became fashionable or acceptable." Katz recommended Sweetland to the ACLU awards committee on the basis of his long record of "distinguished political leadership in the fight for human rights." He cited as one of Sweetland's most courageous acts his opposition to the internment of Japanese Americans during the Second World War. The ACLU award—handed out at a banquet at Portland's Governor Hotel—recognized Sweetland's leadership in pursuing civil rights.[46]

Among the ongoing celebrations, the most lively and rewarding was the Oregon Democratic Party's Monroe Sweetland Appreciation Banquet held at Portland's Benson Hotel on the evening of November 8, 1997. Featured speakers included Sweetland's contemporary and former state Democratic Party chair Howard Morgan, Congresswoman Darlene Hooley, Congressman Earl Blumenauer, and Tom Bruggere, the party's nominee for Oregon's U.S. Senate seat. Colorado governor Roy Romer, chair of the Democratic National Committee, was the distinguished guest speaker. Former congressman Charles Porter, who was unable to attend, sent a note expressing his appreciation for knowing "Monroe as a friend for more than 47 years." If Sweetland decided to retire, "his kind heart and keen brain will continue to inspire and inform Oregon Democrats to ever greater civic accomplishment." [47]

One highlight of the evening's festivities was a memo distributed to all those attending, "Top 10 Reasons Monroe Sweetland is a Revered Democrat." The witty list included:

- Attended the first White House coffee with Thomas Jefferson.
- Only Democrat not running for office who has his own driver.
- Remembers when sleeping with the President meant attending a Cabinet meeting.
- Knows where Jimmy Hoffa is buried.
- Fought to make Trial Lawyers chase ambulances using American cars.
- Likes being called "Liberal" because it's a dirty word.
- Still talks to Eleanor Roosevelt once a week.[48]

In a late but even more deserving tribute, the National Association for Bilingual Education (NABE) honored him with its Ramon L. Santiago President's Award in 2003. The honor recognized his "tireless work . . . on behalf of our nation's limited English proficient children." The association would pay his expenses to the annual meeting in Albuquerque, New Mexico, where Sweetland would be presented the award on February 4, 2004 (shortly after his ninety-fourth birthday). Adalberto Guerrero, who worked closely with Sweetland in framing the strategy leading to passage of the Bilingual Education Act, was principally responsible for recognizing Sweetland's achievements. In a note to Angel Noe Gonzales of the NABE awards committee, Guerrero emphasized that "Sweetland, more than anyone else nationally, is responsible for the enactment of the Bilingual Education Act." In a letter to Sweetland, Guerrero regretted that his "invaluable contributions were not recognized and, in fact, are unknown to most people in Bilingual Education." Among the supporting documents in the award packet was Texas senator Ralph Yarborough's tribute to Sweetland as "the first person to call my attention to the need for this bill and the great impetus it would give to bilingual education in the United States."[49]

News of Sweetland's NABE award reached high places, including Nevada senator Harry Reid, the Democratic majority leader of the United States Senate. In a brief address to his colleagues, Reid honored Sweetland on the eve of the NABE gathering, as the individual responsible, "more than any other person," for passage of the Bilingual Education Act. The act made it possible for children in the American West "who are native speakers of Spanish" to learn English and about their own culture in a friendly environment. Sweetland convinced the NEA to support the initiative and arranged for witnesses to attend congressional hearings. "Without his efforts," Reid concluded, "it could not have passed." Although there were struggles ahead, the Senate majority leader hoped that "we never forget the contributions of Monroe Sweetland and others who helped pass the legislation of 1968."[50]

After his move to Willamette View in 1998, and later for a few brief months at Oatfield Estates, friends who visited Monroe occasionally wrote his dictated letters and read works of poetry or other literary genres. California-born Bob Davis, who spent his professional career in Seattle with the Family Life Insurance Company, moved to West Linn, a short distance from Milwaukie, in 2004. Because two of his cousins had lost their sight, he volunteered to read to elderly people who were vision impaired. Davis, who met Monroe shortly before Sweetland's gala ninety-fifth birthday celebration, began reading to him, writing letters for him, and driving him to meetings and doctor appointments. Davis remembers that the two spent at least two days a week together. They bonded early on when they learned that both shared common experiences in the Marshall Islands during the Second World War as well as the invasion of Okinawa in April 1945—Davis with the U.S. Army and Sweetland with the Red Cross.[51]

Mike Katz was a close political friend of Monroe's from the time Katz arrived in Portland in 1952 to the early 1960s when the Sweetlands left for Indonesia and then moved to San Mateo. They resumed their friendship when Monroe returned to the Portland area in late 1994. Katz, who coordinated Sweetland's memorial service, knew his close associates—Jebby Davidson, Dan and Rusty Goldy, Gus Solomon, Walter Dodd, and Nathalie Panek. Katz remembered Monroe as a person who loved to attend meetings, especially those of a political nature. This was especially true during his secretary of state campaigns when he would travel statewide to meetings in a multitude of small towns while most of the votes were in the Portland metropolis. At Sweetland's memorial service, Katz suggested that the most appropriate epitaph for his headstone would be that he died en route to a meeting. Katz insisted that Sweetland never became conservative with the passage of time, remaining true to liberal principles of unrestricted access to the ballot, full civil rights for all Americans, and equitable taxation policies.[52]

Fred Neal, who moved to southern Oregon with his parents in 1953, recalls that his first reckoning with politics was the election of 1960. After finishing law school, he joined the ACLU and became active in civil liberties issues in Oregon. When Sweetland returned to Oregon in the mid-1990s, Neal joined Mike Katz in pushing for Sweetland's civil liberties award in 1996. Because Monroe was virtually blind, Neal offered to read for Sweetland, a proposal that set in motion a decade of reading and friendship. Neal thought it important for Monroe to digest material beyond the piles of personal correspondence on his desk. What ensued between the two was engagement with poetry, biography, nature writing, romantic literature, and literary magazines. Neal enticed Monroe to join his reading group, where members discussed various works of literature. What Neal remembers best are "Monroe's stories," reminiscing—always—about politics. Despite his age, Monroe was a "very gregarious" person, outgoing, always enjoying political banter.[53]

Monroe Sweetland was nurtured amid the slow-moving life of southern Michigan, a largely flat agricultural landscape intersected with small streams. After graduating from high school, he left this bucolic setting for Wittenberg College in Springfield, Ohio. When he was twenty years old, he was off to the faster-paced intellectual environment at Cornell University. From Ithaca he began making frequent trips to New York City where he met the socialist Norman Thomas, who mentored Sweetland about the evils of discrimination, racism, and class inequalities. Through most of his long life, Sweetland carried those principles into the public domain—with the

Oregon Commonwealth Federation, the federal government, the CIO, the newspaper business, the Oregon legislature, and in his various missions with the NEA between 1964 and 1975.

A pacifist during the 1930s, Sweetland made a decision in the midst of the Second World War to join the Red Cross, a modified pacifism that underwent further adjustment when he supported a robust American military posture during the Cold War.[54] Despite his ambivalent liberalism over ventures such as Vietnam, Sweetland was an eternal optimist, moving on to the next struggle, the next contest, the next challenge.[55] A tireless spokesperson for democracy, he was optimistic to the end that people were capable of controlling the machinery of government for the greater public good.

Always the engaging conversationalist, during his retirement years Monroe regaled friends with stories of bygone political struggles, memories largely free of recrimination and anger. In the midst of turmoil and bad behavior in state and national politics, Sweetland was confident that rational liberal policies would democratize and humanize social and political institutions. While most Americans today may not share that vision, in his heart of hearts, Monroe was incapable of believing that there was any erosion to America's promise. With his friends and associates alike, Sweetland was rooted in the real world of success and failure, of admirers and detractors, but he never lost faith that rational good will would prevail. That mood, that sense of buoyancy, inspired others, perhaps no one more than Rey Martinez, his traveling companion with NEA: "There is hardly a day goes by that I don't think of Monroe. Every fiber of his being is seared in my memory. I never walked with a greater human being."[56]

Moral paradoxes and contradictory behavior characterize aspects of Sweetland's long and fruitful life. While his friends thought his disposition consistently sunny and cheerful, with members of his family that was not always the case. Among the wonderful times she had traveling the California backcountry with her father, Rebecca remembers instances as a child when he would be frustrated and brusque with his hearing-challenged daughter. In the family home Monroe was very much the "man of the house," according to Rebecca. He did no food preparation and little housework.[57] And yet the men who traveled with him on botanical-gathering excursions remembered him as a tough and congenial outdoorsman.

Despite his personal shortcomings, Monroe's memorial service at Portland State University in September 2006 proved the antithesis of

Monroe with Reynaldo Martinez, his friend and traveling companion, who assisted Monroe with conference organizing and other projects in the work-up to the federal Bilingual-Education Act of 1968. (Courtesy of Reynaldo Martinez)

William Shakespeare's immortal line in *Julius Caesar*: "The evil that men do lives after them, The good is oft interred with their bones." Mike Katz opened the ceremonies with the remark, "Monroe Sweetland had to be one of the most decent persons on the planet." Kate Sweetland-Lambird, Rebecca's daughter, recounted how she visited her dying grandfather before she left for Gettysburg College. Because he was sleeping, she wrote him a letter thanking him for teaching her to dance, "to debate with knowledge to back up my arguments, to have a sense of humor about life and live each day in service to others." Third district congressman Earl Blumenauer remembered Monroe's advice during the campaign to lower the voting age: "His unique magic was in helping people understand the gift of political participation." Daughter Barbara remembered her father for "his optimism, his boundless faith in democracy, his consistent effort to empower people." She then introduced a young family member, who led everyone in singing Monroe's favorite song, Woody Guthrie's "This Land Is Your Land."[58]

Notes

INTRODUCTION

1 Reynaldo Martinez to the author, Dec. 28, 2012.
2 Chris Hedges, *Death of the Liberal Class* (New York: Nation Books, 2010), 103.
3 Jefferson Cowie, *Stayin' Alive: The 1970s and the Last Days of the Working Class* (New York: The New Press, 2010), 43; and Sweetland, Comment in Support of Johnson-Humphrey at Crystal Springs Democratic Club, San Mateo Highlands, Mar. 5, 1968, box KK, Accession Number 1747 (hereafter Acc. 1747).
4 Monroe Sweetland, Autobiography, circa 1960, box 23, Acc. 1747; B. G. "Pete" Culver, *Leo Perlis, An Angel with the Union Label: A History of the AFL-CIO Community Services Program* (Farmersburg, IN: Jewett Publications, 1996), 46–47; and John E. Haynes, *Red Scare or Red Menace? American Communism and Anticommunism in the Cold War Era* (Chicago: Ivan R. Dee, 1996), 35. For an incisive critique of the national security state, see Ira Katznelson, *Fear Itself: The New Deal and the Origins of Our Time* (New York: LiveRight, 2013), 407–421.

CHAPTER 1

1 *Detroit News*, April 13, 1924. Also see Sweetland's memories of the event in Monroe Sweetland, Autobiography, 1960, Monroe Sweetland Papers, box 23, Acc. 1747, Oregon Historical Society Research Library, 4.
2 *Constantine Advertiser Record*, Aug. 20, 1924.
3 Jane Simon Ammeson, *St. Joseph County's Historic River Country* (Chicago: Arcadia Publishing, 2005), 19, 46, and 61; and United States Bureau of the Census, Fourteenth Census of the United States (1920), Population of Incorporated Places, Constantine Village, St. Joseph County, Michigan, 232, Table 51.
4 Monroe Sweetland, box 23, Acc. 1747; Susan Dingle to Monroe Mark Sweetland, May 2, 2002; photocopy, *Compendium and Biography of North Dakota* (Chicago: George A. Ogle and Company, 1900), 1215, both in box 8, Acc. 26165; and Aunt Olive to Monroe Sweetland, Mar. 15, 1982, photocopy from Rebecca Sweetland.
5 This brief family genealogy is derived from the following sources: George B. Goodrich, *The Centennial History of the Town of Dryden* (Dryden, NY: The Dryden Herald Steam Printing House, 1898), 84; Sweetland Family Genealogy, photocopy from Barbara Sweetland Smith; Our Mayflower Descent, box 12, Acc. 26165; George James Sweetland, Obituary, unpublished typescript, box 6, Acc. 1747; and Monroe Sweetland, box 23, Acc. 1747.
6 "All-Time Lettermen—Hobart and William Smith Colleges," campus.hws.edu/athletics/hobart/football/2007Guide/v.pdf; Sweetland, Obituary, box 6, Acc. 1747; John Armstrong, *The Way We Played the Game* (Naperville, IL: Sourcebooks, Inc., 2002), 7–8; and "Michigan High School Football Record Book," http://www.peschstats.com/FBMythical.htm.
7 "Fighting Sioux Men's Basketball, 2004," www.fightingsioux.com/fls/13500/pdf/mbb2004.pdf?DB_OEM_ID; Sweetland, Obituary, box 6, Acc. 1747; L. H. Gregory, "Greg's Gossip," *Oregonian*, Sept. 12, 1948, and July 24, 1953; and *Kalamazoo Gazette*, Aug. 5, 1953, clipping in box QQ, Acc. 1747.
8 Sweetland, Obituary, box 6, Acc. 1747. Monroe received his first-grade report card, signed June 29, 1916, from the Geneva Public Schools. See photocopy, first grade report, box PP, Acc. 1747.

9   http://www.constantinemi.com/home.php?page=historical_society, accessed Aug. 19, 2011;
     Ammeson, *St. Joseph County's Historic River Country*, 7–8; "St. Joseph County, History and Geography,"
     http://www.lmb.org/routes!.html#LMBMaps, accessed Aug. 19, 2011; and Martha Mitchell Bigelow,
     "Michigan: A State in the Vanguard," in *Heartland: Comparative Histories of the Midwestern States*, ed.
     James H. Madison (Bloomington: Indiana University Press, 1988), 37–38.
10   Bigelow, "Michigan: A State in the Vanguard," 38, 45–46; John C. Hudson, *Making the Corn Belt: A
     Geographical History of Middle-Western Agriculture* (Bloomington: Indiana University Press, 1994),
     13–20; and John Marvin, "St. Joseph County," http://www.stjosephcountymi.org/community/
     history/historical_firsts.htm, accessed Nov. 16, 2014.
11   Monroe Sweetland, box 23, Acc. 1747, pp. 4–5; Photocopies, Monroe Sweetland Diary, Mar. 4, June
     6–9, and Oct. 2, 1922, box 8, Acc. 01747; and Lloyd Crisp, draft of Chapter 1 (June 2003), "Childhood
     through High School: 1910–1926" (hereafter Crisp manuscript), 14–16, photocopy of original from
     Barbara Sweetland Smith. Crisp, a neighbor to the Sweetlands in the Eichler Highlands in San Mateo,
     California, from 1964 to 1972, renewed his acquaintance with Monroe in early 2003. Before his death
     in 2006 Crisp completed the first chapter of a prospective biography of Monroe.
12   Monroe Sweetland, box 23, Acc. 1747, p. 5; Crisp manuscript, 16; *Kalamazoo Gazette*, Mar. 19, 1958,
     photocopy in box 19, Acc. 1747; and Emily Comstock to Sweetland, undated, box 10, Acc. 26165.
13   Photocopies of report cards, in box PP, Acc. 1747; and Crisp manuscript, 16–19. For general details
     about the *Advertiser-Record*, see The Library of Congress, Chronicling America, http://
     chroniclingamerica.loc.gov/lccn/sn96076804/, accessed Aug. 23, 2011.
14   Monroe Sweetland Diary, Jan. 8 to June 30, 1926 (hereafter Sweetland Diary), entries for Apr. 22 and
     24, and May 14, 20, and 22, 1926 (Diary on loan to the author from Rebecca Sweetland); *Oregonian*,
     Apr. 28, 1985.
15   Sweetland Diary, May 10, 15–16, 23, 29, and 30, and June 10, 1926.
16   Ibid., Mar. 12, 18, 20–22, and 25, Apr. 10 and 14, 1926.
17   Various photocopy materials, courtesy of Jane Moe and Ruth Strawser, Constantine Township Library,
     Constantine, Michigan.
18   Eugene *Register-Guard*, April 19, 1959; Monroe Sweetland, Acc. 1747, box 23, pp. 5–6; Rick Harmon,
     Interview with Monroe Sweetland, Nov. 16, 1984, transcript in Research Library, Oregon Historical
     Society, Portland, Oregon (hereafter Sweetland Interview), 14; Crisp manuscript, 21; Sweetland Diary,
     Apr. 18, 1926; and Barbara Sweetland Smith e-mail to the author, July 22, 2012.
19   Crisp manuscript, 16–17. For a brief account of the *Chicago Defender*, see "Newspapers, *The Chicago
     Defender*," http://www.pbs.org/blackpress/news_bios/defender.html, accessed Oct. 3, 2012.
20   Monroe Sweetland, Acc. 1747, box 23, p. 6; Sweetland Interview, p. 9; and Sweetland Diary, 1922–
     1923, photocopies, box 8, Acc. 01747.
21   Monroe Sweetland, box 23, Acc. 1747, p. 5; and Sweetland Diary, June 1, 7–9, 1926.
22   Crisp manuscript, 23; and Sweetland Diary, June 28–30, 1926. For the history of Western State Normal
     School, see Western Michigan University History, http://www.migenweb.org/kalamazoo/
     westernnormalschool.html, accessed Oct. 3, 2012.
23   For Wittenberg College see Wittenberg University, History and Tradition, http://www4.wittenberg.
     edu/about/history.html, accessed Oct. 4, 2012.
24   Ibid.; Monroe Sweetland, box 23, pp. 6–7; and Sweetland Interview, 16.
25   Janet to "Honey," June 5, 1930, box PP, Acc. 1747.

CHAPTER 2

1   David M. Kennedy, *Freedom from Fear: The American People in Depression and War, 1929–1945* (New
     York: Oxford University Press, 1999), 85–87; and *Ithaca Journal*, Feb. 14, 1944, news clipping in box
     QQ, Acc. 1747.
2   Monroe Sweetland, box 23, p. 8, Acc. 1747.
3   Sweetland Interview, 23, and the *Cornell Daily Sun*, May 8, 1931. Also see the issue for May 14, 1931.
     Albert E. Arent graduated from Cornell Law School in 1935 and served in Franklin D. Roosevelt's
     administration in the Justice Department's new Civil Rights Section, where he was involved in efforts
     to expand federal oversight of civil rights cases. Among other significant activities, Arent was a founding
     member of Common Cause and the National Urban Coalition for Unity and Peace. See Arent's
     obituary, *Washington Post*, Nov. 4, 2006, http://www.washingtonpost.com/wp-dyn/content/
     article/2006/11/03/AR2006110301688.html, accessed May 27, 2013.
4   Sweetland Interview, 24–25; and Ralph Miliband, "Harold Laski's Socialism" (1995), https://www.
     marxists.org/archive/miliband/1995/xx/laski.htm, accessed Mar.21, 2015, and http://www.
     spartacus.schoolnet.co.uk/TUlaski.htm, accessed May 27, 2013.
5   Sweetland Interview, 25–26.
6   Ibid.; and Monroe Sweetland, box 23, p. 10, Acc. 1747.

7   Sweetland Interview, p. 29; W. P. Graham to Sweetland, Jan. 29, 1932; and *Challenge: Voice of the Syracuse Student Liberal Club*, vol. 1, no. 1 (Feb. 1932), vol. 1, no. 2 (March 1932), and vol. 1, no. 3 (May 1932), all in Monroe Sweetland Papers, box 1, Acc. 24845.

8   Sweetland Interview, 28; and Monroe Sweetland response to questions at a libel trial, summer 1960, both in box 23, Acc. 1747. Paul Porter went on to a distinguished career in public service. Porter was an administrator with the War Production Board during the Second World War, an adviser on labor affairs with the Allied Control Commission in Germany, and then headed various United States delegations dealing with the revival of the European economy. See, http://www.trumanlibrary.org/oralhist/porterpr.htm#19, accessed Feb. 15, 2010.

9   This summary discussion of the onset of the Great Depression is from Kennedy, *Freedom from Fear*, 1999), 85–87.

10   Joseph P. Lash, Interview, "The Student Movement in the 1930s," http://newdeal.feri.org/students/lash.htm

11   Norman Thomas (1884–1968), a graduate of Princeton University and ordained as a Presbyterian minister, became disillusioned with the violence of the First World War and joined the Socialist Party in 1917. He was the Socialist candidate for president six times between 1928 and 1948. See Frank Warren, "Norman Thomas," in *The Oxford Companion to United States History*, ed. Paul S. Boyer (New York: Oxford University Press, 2001), 778.

12   Sweetland Interview, 28–29; The *Challenge*, vol. 1, no. 3 (May 7, 1932), both in box 1, Acc. 24845; and Devere Allen, "V. Norman Thomas—Why Not?" *The Nation* (March 30, 1932), http://www.thenation.com/doc/19320330/allen, accessed Feb. 18, 2010.

13   "Wayside Poll Gives Roosevelt Big Lead," *New York Times*, Sept. 20, 1931, clipping in box 1, Acc. 24845.

14   Ibid.; *Constantine Daily Advertiser*, Sept. 23, 1931; Franklin D. Roosevelt to Mr. George M. Sweetland, Jr., Oct. 26, 1931, clipping and letter both in box 1, Acc. 24845; and Roosevelt to Sweetland, Feb. 4, 1932, box 9, Acc. 26165. In signing authorship for the poll, Sweetland used "George" rather than Monroe "to seem less partial."

15   Joseph P. Lash, Eleanor Roosevelt National Historic Site, Hyde Park, New York, http://www.nps.gov/archive/elro/glossary/lash-joseph.htm, accessed Feb. 19, 2010.

16   Monroe Sweetland, 11; Sweetland Interview, 35; and "Mary Fox Herling Collection, Papers (1914–1980), in http://www.reuther.wayne.edu/node/3812, accessed Feb. 15, 2010.

17   Monroe Sweetland, 11; Sweetland Interview, 35; and "George Clifton Edwards, Jr. (1914–1995)," in http://www.ca6.uscourts.gov/lib_hist/Courts/circuit/judges/edwards/gce-bio.html, accessed Feb. 15, 2010.

18   Monroe Sweetland, 11; "Paul Beecher Blanshard," in http://en.wikipedia.org/wiki/Paul_Blanchard, accessed Feb. 15, 2010; and Jeannette Hopkins, "Paul Blanshard and Mary Hillyer Blanchard: Fighters for Social Justice, 1892–1980 and 1902–1965," in http: http://www.harvardsquarelibrary.org/unitarians/blanshard.html, accessed Feb. 19, 2010.

19   Hopkins, "Paul Blanshard and Mary Hillyer Blanchard," in http://www.harvardsquarelibrary.org/unitarians/blanshard.html, accessed Feb. 19, 2010.

20   William Alan Hodson and John Carfora, "Stuart Chase, Brief Life of a Public Thinker: 1888–1985," http://harvardmagazine.com/2004/09/stuart-chase.html, accessed Feb. 19, 2010.

21   Monroe Sweetland, 11, box 23, Acc. 1747; Sweetland Interview, 34–35; *Student Outlook* (June 1933), box 1, Acc.1747; and *Cornell Daily Sun*, Oct. 24, 1932. Nearing, who lived to be one hundred years old, was one of America's great independent radicals and the author of numerous books. See Jean Hay, "The Personal Price of Free Speech, Scott Nearing: 1883–1983," http://www.jeanhay.com/OTHER/SCOTT.HTM, accessed Feb. 24, 2010.

22   A. Fenner Brockway to M. Sweetland, Jr., July 3, 1933, box 1, Acc. 24845.

23   Lash Interview.

24   Ibid.; and Robert Cohen, *When the Old Left Was Young: Student Radicals and America's First Mass Student Movement, 1929–1941* (New York: Oxford University Press, 1993).

25   Lillie Megrath, "L.I.D. Summer School, First Season," *Student Outlook* (Summer 1934), box 1, Acc. 24845. Roger Baldwin, the founder and longtime director of the American Civil Liberties Union, maintained a lifelong correspondence with Monroe Sweetland. George Marshall, brother to conservationist Bob Marshall, was an American economist, labor activist, and one of the founders of the Wilderness Society. See *Columbia College Today* (May 2001), http:www.college.columbia.edu/cct_archive/May01_obituaries.html, accessed Apr. 22, 2013. David Lasser founded the Workers Alliance of America in 1933 and later held various federal positions. See, http://www.cgpublishing.com/Author_Bios/david_lasser.html, accessed Feb. 25, 2010. George W. Streator was business manager and then managing editor of the *Crisis* (1933–1934), the publication of the National Association for the Advancement of Colored People. He later wrote for and edited trade-union journals. See, http://www.oac.cdlib.org/view?docId=tf5199p0j9;query=;style=oac4;view=admin#acqinfo-1.2.3, accessed Feb. 25, 2010.

26   "Agitate! Educate! Organize!" *Student Outlook* (Summer 1934), box 1, Acc. 24845.

27   Frazier participated in League activities during the mid-1930s and, after the Second World War, worked for the Department of Labor. See *New York Times*, July 14, 1997, http://www.nytimes.com/1997/06/14/nyregion/howard-frazier-85-promoted-world-peace.html?pagewanted=1, accessed Feb. 26, 2010.

28   Ibid.

29   George C. Sellery, *Some Ferments at Wisconsin, 1901–1947: Memories and Reflections* (Madison: University of Wisconsin Press, 1960), 61–62, 63–68; and Annual Report of Monroe M. Sweetland, Field Organizer, Dec. 27, 1935, box 10, Acc. 26165.

30   Ibid., 63–68; and Annual Report of Monroe M. Sweetland, Field Organizer, Dec. 27, 1935, box 10, Acc. 26165.

31   Cohen, *When the Old Left Was Young*, 31, 34, 42, 52–54, and 76.

32   Ibid., 361, n. 11; and Robert Cohen, online course materials, Student Activism in the 1930s, "FIGHT WAR! National Committee for the Student Congress Against War," December 27, 1932, pp. 1–4, in http://newdeal.deri.org/students/fw.htm, accessed March 4, 2010.

33   Cohen, *When the Old Left Was Young*, 79–86.

34   The hearings were chaired by Senator Russell Nye of North Dakota.

35   Lash interview; Cohen, *When the Old Left Was Young*, 79–88; "Agitate! Educate! Organize! *Student Outlook* (May 1934), 20; and "The Anti-War Movement of the Thirties," in http://www.virginia.edu/100yearslawn/papers/stambaugh/anti-war.html, accessed Mar. 2, 2010.

36   Cohen, *When the Old Left Was Young*, 36 and 38.

37   Thomas to Sweetland, Dec. 26, 1934, box 1, Acc. 24845.

38   Lash interview; and Cohen, *When the Old Left Was Young*, 137–139.

39   Jean Symes, "The Student L.I.D. Convention," the *Student Outlook*, vol. 3, no. 3 (Feb. 1935), 15, 17, in box 1, Acc. 24845.

40   Mary Fox to Sweetland, Aug. 22, 1935, and Memorandum to Board of Directors – re Amalgamation, both in box 23, Acc. 1747.

41   Monroe Sweetland, Statement on Amalgamation of SLID and NSL; and Fox to Sweetland, Aug. 22, 1935, both in box 9, Acc. 26165

42   Cohen, *When the Old Left Was Young*, 139–40.

43   Ibid., 140–41.

44   Ibid., 141–44.

45   Annual Report of Monroe M. Sweetland: Field Organizer, Dec. 27, 1935, box 10, Acc. 26165.

46   Monroe Sweetland, box 23, pp. 11–12, Acc. 1747; and Sweetland Interview, 37.

47   Lash Interview, 10.

48   Ibid., 11; and Cohen, *When the Old Left Was Young*, 170–171.

49   Lash Interview, 11; and Cohen, *When the Old Left Was Young*, 171–173.

CHAPTER 3

1   For Portland and Salem population numbers in the mid-1930s, see www.oregonlink.com/population_history.html, accessed Sept. 12, 2011.

2   Monroe Sweetland Biography, typescript in Monroe Sweetland Papers, box 23, Acc. 1747 (hereafter Sweetland Biography). For Minnesota's farmer-labor politics, see Richard M. Valelly, *Radicalism in the States: The Minnesota Farmer-Labor Party and the American Political Economy* (Chicago: University of Chicago Press, 1989). For the Canadian parallel to radical farmer-labor politics, see Seymour Martin Lipset, *Agrarian Socialism: The Cooperative Commonwealth Federation in Saskatchewan, A Study in Political Ideology* (1950; New York: Doubleday, 1968). Also see Paul Porter, "The Commonwealth Plan: A Suggested Platform for the Socialist Party," reprinted from *The World Tomorrow*, May 24, 1934, copy in box 10, Acc. 26165.

3   Monroe Sweetland, "The C.C.F.," *Student Outlook* 4 (October 1935), 9–10, box 11, Acc. 26165.

4   Lillie Sweetland to Joseph Lash, Feb. 17, 1936, box 10, Acc. 26165. The Oregon Committee for Peace and Freedom was linked to the long-standing Committee on Militarism in Education, with Norman Thomas one of its three cofounders in 1925 (Monroe Sweetland to Joseph Lash, Mar. 7, 1936, box 10, Acc. 26165). Harry Lane was educated at Willamette University where he received a medical degree. He practiced in Portland and gained renown as a public health advocate and progressive reformer. He served two terms as mayor of Portland and then the Oregon Legislature elected him to the U.S. Senate in 1912. His vote opposing American entry into the First World War gained him enmity at home and in Washington, D.C. In poor health, he died on May 13, 1917, en route to Oregon to recuperate. See Kimberley Jensen's entry in the *Oregon Encyclopedia*, http://www.oregonencyclopedia.org/, accessed Apr. 21, 2010.

5   Sweetland to Clarence Senior, Mar. 27, 1936, box 10, Acc. 26165. Salem is both the state capital and the Marion County seat. For an extended discussion of efforts to organize a farm-labor party in Oregon, see

Hugh T. Lovin, "Toward a Farmer-Labor Party in Oregon, 1933–38," *Oregon Historical Quarterly* (1975), 135–151.

6 There were several nationwide student strikes against war and militarism during the 1930s, with the largest taking place on April 22, 1936. The outbreak of the Spanish Civil War in the summer of 1936, according to Robert Cohen, "served as a wake-up call for a generation of student activists who had been lost in isolationist slumber." See Robert Cohen, *When the Old Left Was Young: Student Radicals and America's First Mass Student Movement, 1929--1941* (New York: Oxford University Press, 1993), 152–154.

7 Sweetland to Richard Neuberger, Mar. 7, 1936; and Sweetland to Hayes Beall, Apr. 3, 1936, both in box 10, Acc. 26165; and Cohen, *When the Old Left Was Young*, 92–93 and 134–136.

8 Monroe Sweetland to Mary Farquharson, Apr. 4, 1936, box 10; Dorothy Shoemaker to Sweetland, April 7, 1936, box 9; Lil Sweetland to Mary Shoemaker, Apr. 15, 1936, box 10; and Monroe Sweetland to Robert B. Shaw, June 1, 1939, box 9, all in Acc. 26165. Without committing himself to the task, Sweetland outlined a "minimum budget" for the petition campaign. See, Sweetland to Edwin C. Johnson, Apr. 23, 1936, box 9, Acc. 26165.

9 Sweetland to Comrade Snyder, May 30, 1936; Sweetland to Robert B. Shaw, June 1, 1936; and Sweetland to Ray Newton, May 12, 1936, all in box 9, Acc. 26165.

10 Nathalie Panek to Charles Royer, May 23, 1976, box JJ, Acc. 1774; and Sweetland to Edwin C. Johnson, June 1, 1939, box 9, Acc. 26165.

11 Sweetland to Johnson, June 13; and Johnson to Sweetland, June 20, 1936, both in box 9, Acc. 26165.

12 Sweetland to Johnson, June 13, 1936, box 9, Acc. 26165.

13 Sweetland to Jo and Herbert Abraham, June 13, 1936; and Sweetland to Hayes Beall, June 13, 1939, both in box 10, Acc. 26165. Sweetland first mentioned the juxtaposition of a peace policy versus preparedness in a letter to Ray Newton, May 12, 1936, box 9, Acc. 26165.

14 Sweetland to Edwin C. Johnson, July 4, 1939, box 9, Acc. 26165; and *Oregon Journal*, July 5, 1936, news clipping in box 9, Acc. 26165. The idea for a state bank was borrowed from the State of North Dakota which had (and still has) the only state bank in the nation. The Bank of North Dakota had its origins with the radical Nonpartisan League during the First World War when supporters of a state bank viewed it as a vehicle to offer low-interest loans to farmers. See, "Bank of North Dakota History," http://banknd.nd.gov/about_BND/history_of_BND.html, accessed June 1, 2010.

15 Sweetland to Edwin C. Johnson, July 4, 1936; Sweetland to Ed and Dorothy Shoemaker, July 15, 1936; Edwin C. Johnson to Sweetland, July 16, 1936; and Sweetland to "CME," July 21, 1936, all in box 9, Acc. 26165.

16 See Elizabeth Dilling, *The Red Network: A "Who's Who" and Handbook of Radicalism for Patriots* (Chicago: Published by the author, 1934). Robert Cohen argues that Dilling "ranks among the Right's most prolific critics of the student movement" during the 1930s. Her books were filled with "unreason and [racial] prejudice." See Cohen, *When the Old Left Was Young*, 271–273.

17 *Oregonian*, Oct. 31, 1936, news clipping and Sweetland note, in box 1, Acc. 27109.

18 *Oregonian*, Nov. 4, 1936, news clipping in box 9, Acc. 26165; and *Oregonian*, Nov. 11, 1936, news clipping in box 1, Acc. 27109.

19 Jill Hopkins Herzig, "The Oregon Commonwealth Federation: The Rise and Decline of a Reform Organization" (master's thesis, University of Oregon, 1963), 6–10; and Nathalie Panek to Charles Royer, May 23, 1976, box, JJ, Acc. 1747. Panek wrote a five-page assessment of the Oregon Commonwealth Federation for Royer, who was contemplating a book on the organization. Also see Sweetland to Albert Streiff, Mar. 8, 1936, box 12, Acc. 26165; and Streiff to Sweetland, Mar. 12, 1936, box 10, Acc. 26165.

20 Howard Williams was the national organizer for the left-wing Farmer-Labor Political Federation and responsible for Floyd Olson's successes in Minnesota gubernatorial elections. See Steven J. Keillor, *Hjalmar Peterson of Minnesota: The Politics of Provincial Independence* (St. Paul: University of Minnesota Press, 1987), 101, 105.

21 Sweetland to Howard Y. Williams, Mar. 17, 1936, box 10, Acc. 26165.

22 Sweetland to Howard Ohmart, Mar. 28, 1936, box 9, Acc. 26165.

23 For accounts of the Minnesota Farmer-Labor Party, see the Minnesota Historical Society's "History Topics, Farmer-Labor Movement, http://www.mnhs.org/library/tips/history_topics/100farmer.html, accessed June 6, 2010. For a biography of Maverick, see Richard B. Henderson, *Maury Maverick: A Political Biography* (Austin: University of Texas Press, 1970).

24 Minnie McFarland to Sweetland, June 30, 1936, box 9, Acc. 26165. Lovin, "Toward a Farmer-Labor Party in Oregon," 135, 141–144.

25 *Oregonian*, Nov. 9, 1936, news clipping in box 3, Records of the Oregon Commonwealth Federation, Special Collections and University Archives, University of Oregon Libraries, Eugene, Oregon (hereafter OCF Records); and Herzig, "The Oregon Commonwealth Federation," 1, 6.

26 The Townsend movement emerged as a national phenomenon in 1933 when a retired California physician, Francis Townsend, proposed a federal plan to provide pensions for people over the age of

sixty. See Abraham Holtzman, *The Townsend Movement: A Political Study* (New York: Bookman Associates, 1963).

27 Herzig, "The Oregon Commonwealth Federation," 8.

28 Oregon Commonwealth Federation, A Call To A Convention For Progressive Political Action, box 23, Acc. 1747; and Howard Costigan to Monroe Sweetland, April 17, 1937, box 19, OCF Records.

29 Herzig, "The Oregon Commonwealth Federation," 12–14, 17; and Program of the Oregon Commonwealth Federation, box 30, OCF Records.

30 Highlights of the Oregon Commonwealth Federation Program, adopted April 24–25, box 23, Acc. 1747; and Program of the Oregon Commonwealth Federation, box 30, OCF Records.

31 Herzig, "The Oregon Commonwealth Federation," 15.

32 See Robert H. Zieger, *The CIO, 1935–1955* (Chapel Hill: University of North Carolina Press, 1995); and Gary Murrell, *Iron Pants: Oregon's Anti-New Deal Governor* (Pullman: Washington State University Press, 2000), 169–170.

33 *Oregonian*, May 28, 1937, news clipping in box 3, Acc. 26165; and Sweetland to Governor Charles H. Martin, box 8, OCF Records.

34 Salem *Capital Journal*, May 11, 12, and 24, 1937, news clippings in box 3, Acc. 26165.

35 The quotation is in Murrell, *Iron Pants*, 157.

36 Murrell, *Iron Pants*, 155–156, 173; and W. B. Odale, untitled typescript, in box 3, Acc. 26165.

37 Kelly Loe, "Shall Oregon Labor Submit To Political Sterilization," May 27, 1937, box 11, Acc. 26165.

38 Ibid.; and Sweetland to Herman Michelbrook, Feb. 10, 1938, box 12, OCF Records.

39 *Oregon Commonwealth Federation News* (hereafter *Commonwealth News*), June 14, 1937, box 11, Acc. 26165; and Stephenson Smith to Harold Ickes, June 1, 1937, box 33, Oregon Commonwealth Federation Records, Special Collections and Archives, University of Oregon Libraries.

40 http://newdeal.feri.org/tva/tva10.htm, accessed June 11, 2010; and Herzig, "The Oregon Commonwealth Federation," 32–34.

41 *Commonwealth News*, June 14, 1937; Herzig, "The Oregon Commonwealth Federation," 38; Gus Norwood, *Columbia River Power for the People: A History of Policies of the Bonneville Power Administration* (Washington, D.C., 1981), 56–62; and William F. Willingham, *Army Engineers and the Development of Oregon: A History of the Portland District, U.S. Army Corps of Engineers* (Washington, D.C., 1983), 102–103.

42 Declaration, Adopted in Convention, Oregon Commonwealth Federation, Portland, Oregon, December. 19, 1937, box 3, Acc. 26165.

43 Oregon Commonwealth Confederation, Minutes of the Third Convention, May 7, 1938, box 5, OCF Records; and *Oregonian*, May 13, 1938.

44 *Oregon Daily Journal*, circa Apr. 13, 1938, news clipping in box 3, Acc. 26165; Sweetland to E. L. Oliver, May 2, 1938, box 13, OCF Records; and Herzig, "The Oregon Commonwealth Federation," 47–48.

45 *Capital-Journal*, May 19, 1938, news clipping in box 9, Acc. 26165. A militant member of the CIO, a communist, and resident of British Columbia, Prichett was president of the International Woodworkers of America from 1937 to 1940. See Timothy Kilgren, "Harold Pritchett: Communism and the International Woodworkers of American," http://depts.washington.edu/civilr/Harold_Pritchett.htm, accessed June 21, 2010.

46 The quotations are in Murrell, *Iron Pants*. 183–185.

47 Sweetland to Thomas Corcoran, June 6, 1938, box 13, OCH Records; and Floyd J. McKay, *An Editor for Oregon: Charles A. Sprague and the Politics of Change* (Corvallis: Oregon State University Press, 1998), 99–100. Sprague's note to Sweetland is quoted in a letter from Harry Kenin. See Kenin to Sweetland, Nov. 18, 1938, box 4, Acc. 1747.

48 Stewier resigned in January 1938, and Governor Charles Martin appointed little-known Medford attorney Alfred Reames to fill the position. Reames chose not to run in the primary election, leaving the field to Henry Hess.

49 Sweetland to Henry Rutz, Dec. 22, 1938, box 13, OCF Records.

50 New York senator Robert Wagner was the principal author of the National Labor Relations Act. For the stipulations in the National Labor Relations Act, see "The Wagner Act," http://www.civics-online.org/library/formatted/texts/wagner_act.html, accessed June 24, 2010. In his four successful presidential races, Roosevelt always ran ahead of his party in the American West, garnering 20 percent more votes than other Democrats running for office. See Richard White, "*It's Your Misfortune and None of My Own*": *A New History of the American West* (Norman: University of Oklahoma Press, 1991), 472–473. Oregon, a Republican state at the outset of the Depression, voted for FDR from 1932 to 1944.

CHAPTER 4

1 See James S. Olson, "Labor's Non-Partisan League," http://www.novelguide.com/a/discover/egd_02_00311.html, accessed July 5, 2010; and Marc Dixon, "The Politics of Union Decline: Business

Political Mobilization and Restrictive Labor Legislation, 1938–1958," www.Sociology.ohio-state.edu/classes/soc606/Martin/Marc%20Dixon.pdf, accessed July 5, 2010.

2 Jill Hopkins Herzig, "The Oregon Commonwealth Federation: The Rise and Decline of a Reform Organization" (master's thesis, University of Oregon, 1963), 49.

3 S. Stephenson Smith, "What Hit Oregon," *Black and White*, vol. 1 (July 1939), 6, copy in box 14, OCF Records, Special Collections and University Archives, University of Oregon Libraries; and Monroe Sweetland, "The Part Oregon Must Play in the New Deal Campaign," Oregon Commonwealth Federation dinner, Aug. 27, 1938, box 12, OCF Records.

4 Linda Gordon, "Dorothea Lange's Oregon Photography: Assumptions Challenged," *Oregon Historical Quarterly* 110 (Winter 2009), 589–590; *Oregon Statesman*, Oct. 23, 1938; and *New York Times*, Oct. 30, 1938, both news clippings in box 3, Acc. 26165, Monroe Sweetland Papers, Oregon Historical Society, Portland.

5 Richard Neuberger, "Who Are the Associated Farmers?" *Survey Graphic* 28 (Sept. 1939), 516–517; and Herzig, "The Oregon Commonwealth Federation," 50. The *Capital Journal* is quoted in Smith, *Black and White*, 6.

6 Nathalie Panek to Charles Royer, May 23, 1976, box JJ, Acc. 1747.

7 Salem *Capital Journal*, Oct. 18, 1938.

8 Elizabeth Balanoff, "Socialism and the Social Gospel," in http://www.religion-online.org/showarticle.asp?title=1908, accessed Aug. 2, 2010; Nathalie Panek to Sweetland, Oct. 8, 1938, Sweetland to Ray Newton, Aug. 16, 1939, both in box 10, OCF Records; and David M. Kennedy, *Freedom from Fear: The American People in Depression and War, 1929–1945* (New York: Oxford University Press, 1999), 425.

9 Richard L. Neuberger, "The New Germany," *The Nation*, Oct. 4, 1933. This was Neuberger's first publication in a national magazine.

10 Richard L. Neuberger, "Foes; 'Progressive,' Assert Its Supporters," the *Sun*, May 5, 1938, photocopy in box 3, Acc. 26165, Sweetland Papers.

11 Address of Monroe Sweetland to Annual Convention of the CIO, Feb. 11, 1940, box 12, OCF Records. There were mass defections from the American Communist Party following the Nazi-Soviet pact of 1939. See John E. Haynes, *Red Scare or Red Menace? American Communism and Anticommunism in the Cold War Era* (Chicago: Ivan R. Dee, 1996), 32–35.

12 Kennedy, *Freedom from Fear*, 425; Sweetland to Eli L. Oliver, Sept. 13, 1939, box 6; Minutes of the OCF Board of Directors, Sept. 16 and Oct. 15, 1939, box 1; Minutes of the Sixth Oregon Commonwealth Convention, Dec. 9–10, 1939, box 6; and Sweetland to E. L. Oliver, Dec. 12, 1939, box 10, all in OCF Records.

13 Panek to Royer, May 23, 1976, box JJ, Acc. 1747, Sweetland Papers; and Herzig, "The Oregon Commonwealth Federation," 73–75. The IWA originated with the AFL's United Brotherhood of Carpenters, a craft union. However, its members chose affiliation with the more progressive CIO and formed the International Woodworkers of America in 1937. See Walter Galenson, *The United Brotherhood of Carpenters: The First Hundred Years* (Cambridge: Harvard University Press, 1983), 252–263.

14 Galenson, *United Brotherhood of Carpenters*, 264–265.

15 *Labor Newdealer*, Dec. 8, 1939, and Jan. 19, 1940.

16 Jerry Lembke and William Tattum, *One Union in Wood: A Political History of the International Woodworkers of America* (New York: International Publishers, 1984), 65–68; and Sweetland Biography, 16.

17 Sweetland Biography, 16; and Portland *Oregonian*, Dec. 11, 1939.

18 Employment status of the civilian noninstitutional population, 1940 to date, ftp://ftp.bls.gov/pub/special.requests/lf/aat1.txt, accessed Aug. 9, 2010.

19 Sweetland to Cecil Owen, April 7, 1939, box 9, OCF Records.

20 Sweetland to Nan Wood Honeyman, Nov. 1, 1939, box 8; and Panek to J. C. Capt, Oct. 9, 1939, box 9, both in OCF Records.

21 Sweetland to Panek, Nov. 6, 1939, and Panek to Sweetland, Nov. 21, 1939, both in box 9, OCF Records.

22 Panek to Charles Royer, May 23, 1976, box JJ, Acc. 1747.

23 Sweetland to Mrs. Milner (ACLU), May 1937, box 12, OCF Records. For the De Jonge decision, see Isidor Feinstein, "The Supreme Court and Civil Liberties," *The Nation* (Feb. 6, 1937), 151–153; and "Facts of the Case," http://www.oyez.org/cases/1901-1939/1936/1936_123, accessed Sept. 30, 2010.

24 Sweetland to Roger Baldwin, Jan. 7, Feb. 1, Mar. 17, and April 3, 1941, all in box 12, OCF Records.

25 Copy of S.1620, National Health Act of 1939, Feb. 28; and Sweetland to Senator Robert Wagner, May 18, 1939, both in box 19, OCF Records.

26 Sweetland to Panek, June 2; and Sweetland to Barbara Armstrong, June 16, 1939, box 19, OCF Records.

27 Abraham Epstein founded the American Association for Social Security in 1927 to secure old-age pensions and unemployment and health insurance. See Guide to the American Association for Social Security Records, Kheel Center for Labor-Management Documentation and Archives, Cornell

University Library, http://rmc.library.cornell.edu/EAD/htmldocs/KCL05002.html, accessed Oct. 7, 2010.

28 Sweetland to Fred K. Hoehler, Dec. 20, 1940; and Sweetland to Abraham Epstein, Jan. 27, all in box 19, OCF Records.

29 Sweetland to Oliver Larson, Feb. 5; Sweetland to Senator Arthur Capper, Feb. 12; Abraham Epstein to Sweetland, Mar. 10, 1941; and *Social Security*, vol. 15, no. 4, April 1941, all in box 19, OCF Records.

30 Epstein to Sweetland, Apr. 4; and Sweetland to Epstein, May 3, 1941, both in box 19, OCF Records.

31 Sweetland to Arthur Priaulx, April 15, 1941.

32 Sweetland to James A. Farley, Sept. 14, 1939, box 12, OCF Records.

33 Wheeler, one of Roosevelt's most reliable progressive allies, began to turn away from the president's policies when he orchestrated a brilliant strategy to defeat Roosevelt's "Court-reform bill," a scheme to expand the members of the Supreme Court to assure decisions favorable to the administration. In the hands of critics, the president's proposal for judicial reform quickly morphed into "Court Packing." See Kennedy, *Freedom from Fear*, 331–333.

34 Sweetland to Burton K. Wheeler, Nov. 25, and Wheeler to Sweetland Dec. 2, 1939, both in box 10, OCF Records. For Wheeler's presidential aspirations, see *Minneapolis Morning Tribune*, Dec. 16, 1939, newsclipping in box 10, OCF Records.

35 Minutes of the Sixth State Convention of the Oregon Commonwealth Federation, Dec. 9 and 10, 1939, box 6; John Nelson to Sweetland, Dec. 17; Sweetland to Nelson, Dec. 28, 1939; Nelson to Sweetland, Jan. 9; and Sweetland to Richard Neuberger, Feb. 5, 1940, all in box 10, OCF Records.

36 Sweetland to Sidney Hillman, Apr. 5; and Hillman to Sweetland, Apr. 16, 1940, both in box 12, OCF Records.

37 Kennedy, *Freedom from Fear*, 456–457; Sweetland to Tex Goldschmidt, Aug. 10, 1940, box 12; and Sweetland to Panek, circa Aug. 1940, box 9, all in OCF Records.

38 Wallace to Sweetland, n.d., box 12, OCF Records. David Kennedy termed Roosevelt's choice of Wallace as running mate "a farewell bouquet" to progressives in both parties. His decision also revealed the sharp ideological divide in the Democratic Party between conservatives and liberals, with convention delegates engaging in a near mutiny until Eleanor Roosevelt delivered conciliatory remarks. See Kennedy, *Freedom from Fear*, 456–457.

39 Steve Smith to Sweetland, Oct. 19, 1940, box 10; and Sweetland to Smith, Election Night 1940, box 10, all in OCF Records.

40 Panek to Charles Royer, May 23, 1976, box 9, Acc. 26165. Solomon is quoted in Harry H. Stein, *Gus J. Solomon: Liberal Politics, Jews, and the Federal Courts* (Portland: Oregon Historical Society Press, 2006), 59.

41 David Epps to Sweetland, circa Nov. 1938, box 4, Acc. 1747; and Sweetland to Epps, Nov. 14, 1938, box 1, Acc. 24845. For the death of George Sweetland, Jr., see the typescript obituary of George J. Sweetland in box 6, Acc. 1747.

42 Nan Wood Honeyman to Sweetland, Nov. 30, 1937, box 8, OCF Records.

43 Sweetland to Honeyman, Dec. 4, 1937, box 8, OCF Records.

44 Lil continued to use her maiden name during most of the 1930s.

45 Sweetland to Honeyman, Dec. 4; Sweetland to Honeyman, Dec. 13, 1937; and Sweetland to Honeyman, Nov. 1 and Nov. 8, 1939, all in box 8, OCF Records. In all the hundreds of letters in the Sweetland collections, his remark about "mother's place is in the home" stands singularly alone.

46 Statement of Lillie M. Sweetland in Reply to Interrogatory, Regional Loyalty Board, San Francisco, California, File LB:GJP: HIL:jve, Oct. 9, 1952, personal documents on loan from Barbara Sweetland Smith (hereafter Sweetland-Smith documents); and Panek to Sweetland, circa early 1940, box 1, Acc. 24845.

47 The Wages and Hours Division was created when Congress passed the Fair Labor Standards Act in June 1938. See Alice Kessler-Harris, *In Pursuit of Equity: Women, Men, and the Quest for Economic Citizenship in 20th Century America* (New York: Oxford University Press, 2001), 104–105.

48 Ernie Norback, "Lil Megrath Sweetland," in Sweetland-Smith Documents (copies in possession of the author). After the Second World War, Ernest H. Norback (1913–2010) earned a law degree and enjoyed a long career specializing in various aspects of labor law. Obituary in the *San Jose Mercury News*, Mar. 30, 1910, http://www.legacy.com/obituaries/mercurynews/obituary.aspx?n=ernest-h-norback&pid=141291819, accessed Oct. 12, 2010.

49 Sweetland to S. Stephenson Smith, Sept. 7, 1940, box 10, OCF Records.

50 Sweetland to Hunter and Mary Scott, Sept. 5; and Hunter Scott to Sweetland, Oct. 1, 1940, both in box 10, OCF Records.

51 Lil to Monroe, Oct. 14, 1944, box QQ, Acc. 1747.

52 Honeyman to Sweetland, Jan. 31, 1938; Sweetland to Honeyman, Nov. 1, 1939, box 8; Sweetland to Eli L. Oliver, Jan. 18; and Mar. 28, 1941, all in box 9, OCF Records.

53 Rick Harmon, interview with Monroe Sweetland, June 18, 1985, transcription, 73–81.

CHAPTER 5

1   Roosevelt's Fireside Chat of Dec. 29, 1940, is quoted in David M. Kennedy, *Freedom from Fear: The American People in Depression and War, 1929–1945* (New York: Oxford University Press, 1999), 468–474.
2   Records of the War Production Board, Record Group 197 (hereafter RG 179), 1918–1947 (Bulk 1937–1947), 179.1, Administrative History, U.S. National Archives and Records Administration, www.archives.gov.
3   Policy Documentation File, Growth of Functions and Key Staff of Labor Division, box 44, Records of the War Production Board, RG 179, U.S National Archives and Records Administration. For the patriotic aspect of factory work, see Nelson Lichtenstein, *Labor's War At Home: The CIO in World War II* (Philadelphia: Temple University Press, 2003), xvii.
4   Lichtenstein, *Labor's War At Home*, 47–51; and Nelson Lichtenstein, *Walter Reuther: The Most Dangerous Man in Detroit* (Chicago: University of Illinois Press, 1995), 178.
5   Monroe Sweetland to Clyde Wade, July 12, 1941, box 1, Acc. 24845.
6   David Epps to Sweetland, Sept. 29; Leonie Brooke to Sweetland, Oct. 9; and Alice Barnett to Sweetland, Dec. 11, 1941, all in box 1, Acc. 24845. The *Oregonian* quote is in Leonie Brooke's letter.
7   Peeples to Sweetland, June 13, 1942; Sweetland to Marcella, June 13; Peeples to Sweetland, July 13, all in box 10, OCF Records; and Sweetland to "Dear Friends," Aug. 1, box 1, Acc. 24845.
8   Monroe Sweetland, Description of Duties, Office of Production Management file, box 23, Acc. 1747; and Salem *Capital Press*, July 14, 1941, newsclipping in box 22, Acc. 1747.
9   D. E. Nickerson to Sidney Hillman, July 14, 1941, box 23, OCF Records. Nickerson sent copies of the letter to AFL head William Green, Oregon senators Charles McNary and Rufus Holman, and Oregon congressmen James Mott, Homer Angell, and Walter Pierce. Also see the Portland *Oregonian*, July 16, 1941.
10   Ed Foss, "Protesting a Protest," *Oregon Journal*, n.d., newsclipping, box 22; Charles McNary to Sidney Hillman, July 16, 1941, box 23; Harry Kenin to Sidney Hillman, box 1; and Walter Pierce to Sidney Hillman, box 23, all in Acc. 1747.
11   The Office of Production Management Records are subsumed within the vast Records of the War Production Board, with the former only marginally recognizable in the larger holdings.
12   Carroll K. Shaw, *Field Organization and Administration of the War Production Board and Predecessor Agencies, May 1940 to November 1945*. Civilian Production Administration, Historical Reports on War Administration: War Production Board, Special Study No. 25 (Washington, D.C.: Government Publications, n.d.), RG 287, 9, 29, and 274.
13   Monroe Sweetland (circa. 1960), 19, box 23, Acc. 1747; Office of Production Management, news release, Aug. 21, 1941, box 1, Acc. 24845; and Labor in National Defense, Dec. 6 and 7, 1941, box 1, Acc. 1747.
14   Panek to Sweetland, Dec. 10, 1941, box 1, Acc. 24845; and Panek to Sweetland, circa early 1942, box 1, Acc. 24845 .
15   Sweetland to Ernest Norback, Jan. 5, 1942; Panek to Sweetland, Dec. 10, 1941, Jan. 9 and 16, all in box 1, Acc. 24845; and Panek to Sweetland, Jan. 22, 29, and one letter, circa early 1942, all in box 4, Acc. 1747.
16   Sweetland to Ruth Haefner, Feb. 2, 1942, box 10, OCF Records. The salary figure is in B. G. "Pete" Culver, *Leo Perlis, An Angel with the Union Label: A History of the AFL-CIO Community Services Program* (Farmersburg, IN: Jewett Publications, 1996), 55.
17   Sweetland Autobiography, box 23, Acc. 1747; Culver, *Leo Perlis*, 46–47; and John E. Haynes, *Red Scare or Red Menace? American Communism and Anticommunism in the Cold War Era* (Chicago: Ivan R. Dee, 1996), 35.
18   Culver, *Leo Perlis*, 46–47; and flyer, CIO War Relief Committee, box 33, OCF Records. Labor historian Robert H. Zieger remarked several years ago that historians seeking "to chart the course of the CIO finds himself or herself trekking literally from coast to coast and almost as literally from border to border—and, indeed, across borders." See Zieger, "The CIO: A Bibliographical Update and Archival Guide," *Labor History* 31 (1990), 424. The consensus is that the CIO War Relief Committee records are scattered through many CIO collections.
19   Elizabeth Fones-Wolf, "Labor and Social Welfare: The CIO's Community Services Program, 1941–1956," *Social Service Review* (Dec. 1996), 614.
20   Fones-Wolf, "Labor and Social Welfare" 613–617. The Lewis quotation is on page 617. By 1944 more than 4,000 CIO men and women represented the union on various policymaking agency boards. See Culver, *Leo Perlis*, 54–55.
21   Confidential Report of Monroe Sweetland, July 1, 1942, box 1, Acc. 1747.
22   Culver, *Leo Perlis*, 49–53. For a brief sketch of Livermore's career, see Mayor Richard M. Daley's tribute delivered to the Chicago City Council Dec. 2, 1998. A native of Buffalo, New York, Livermore headed the city's Board of Community Relations after the war, directed President Eisenhower's

antidiscrimination section of the Committee on Government Contracts, served as director of New York's Commission against Discrimination, and after 1959, headed Chicago's Commission on Youth Welfare. See Chicago Mayor Richard Daley's tribute in "Journal-City Council-Chicago" Dec. 2, 98, http://www.google.com/#hl=en&source=hp&biw=1276&bih=837&q=charles+p.+livermore&btnG =Google+Search&aq=f&aqi=&aql=&oq=charles+p.+livermore&gs_rfai=CuyuiMi7wTJCVG4Waiw OJm9ncAQAAAKoEBU_QnDN6&fp=b476d6d78058c141, accessed Nov. 26, 2010.

23   Foreign Relief Allocations, War Relief Committee Reports, box 12, John Brophy Papers, University Archives, The Catholic University of America (hereafter Brophy Papers).

24   Sweetland Biography, 19–20. For the Eighth Route Army, see *Encyclopedia Britannica*, http://www. britannica.com/EBchecked/topic/181256/Eighth-Route-Army. On the CIO purge of communist unions from the CIO, see Lichtenstein, *Labor's War At Home*, 135.

25   Ralph Blanchard to Sweetland, Nov. 5, 1943, box 1, Acc. 24845.

26   Like other CIO records, copies of the *CIO War Relief News* may be scattered in several collections. The Walter Reuther Library at Wayne State University holds one manuscript box titled, "War Relief Committee Publications." See http://www.reuther.wayne.edu/node/4726, accessed Nov. 24, 2010.

27   *CIO War Relief News*, vol. 1, no. 8 (Nov. 1943), 1, 6, box QQ, Acc. 1747.

28   Ibid., 7; and Phillip Murray to Sweetland, Mar. 7, 1944, box QQ, Acc. 1747.

29   Priscilla Yadad to Sweetland, Mar. 9, 1944, box 5; and Ethel Polk to Sweetland, June 8, 1944, box 5, both in Acc. 1747. Before Ethel Polk joined the CIO War Relief Committee, she was a secretary for the United Auto Workers-Works Progress Administration, Welfare Department in Detroit. See the Ethel Polk Papers, Special Collections, Walter Reuther Library, Wayne State University. James J. Lorence interviewed Polk for his book, *Organizing the Unemployed: Community and Union Activists in the Industrial Heartland* (Albany: State University of New York Press, 1996), 164–176. *International Woodworker* was published under the auspices of the CIO from 1942 to 1955 and the AFL-CIO from 1955 to 1987. It was published in Seattle in 1942 but moved to Portland the following year. See The Labor Press Project: Labor and Radical Newspapers in the Pacific Northwest, http://depts.washington. edu/labhist/laborpress/International_Woodworker.htm, accessed Nov. 30, 2010.

30   Charles Livermore to Sweetland, July 11, 1944, box 5, Acc. 1747.

31   Panek to Sweetland, April 20 and 28, 1944, both in box 5, Acc. 1747.

32   Ibid., Dec. 15, 1944.

33   Dyke Miyagawa to Sweetland, June 6, 1944, box QQ, Acc. 1747; and Dec. 11, 1944, box 5, Acc. 1747.

34   Panek to Sweetland, circa 1942, box 4, Acc. 1747. For Sweetland's commitment to pacifism, see Sweetland to Robert Zimmerman, circa August, 1940, box 12; Sweetland to Hunter Scott, Sept. 5, 1940, box 10; and Annual Report of Monroe Sweetland, Executive Secretary, Dec. 14, 1940, box 10, all in OCF Records. In his 1940 Annual Report to the Commonwealth Federation, Sweetland expressed the hope that the OCF was "determined now as always to make our weight count against being involved in the war." In this message to the convention, he urged OCF members "to devote ourselves primarily to the kind of national defense of our American democracy without which all of our pride of country will be the emptiest vanity." He then listed his personal criteria for national defense: security for senior citizens, opportunity for youth, freedom of speech and religion, democracy in industry, and protection for racial minorities.

35   Sweetland Biography, 20; and Sweetland to Roberta Blain, Nov. 8, 1943, box 1, Acc. 24845.

36   World War II Accomplishments of the American Red Cross: Historical Summary, http:///www. redcross.org/museum/history/ww2a.asp, accessed Nov. 26, 2010.

37   Vi's husband (and Mike's father), journalist Jake Shapiro, died of some unknown disease (as a civilian) early in the war. Phone conversation with Barbara Sweetland Smith, Nov. 23, 2009.

38   Panek to Sweetland, box 5, Acc. 1747.

39   Red Cross personnel stationed in the Central and South Pacific numbered 539 men and women in the summer of 1943. The agency also had on its payroll another 1,500 locally employed people. See Nyles I. Christensen to Richard F. Allen, Aug. 18, 1944, box 1580, Records of the American National Red Cross, RG 200, National Archives and Records Administration, College Park, Maryland.

40   Undated and unaddressed letter, box 4, Acc. 24845. Sweetland's letters to Lil invariably show signs of a censor's penknife. For a memo warning about safeguarding military information, see letter to Mr. Christensen, Dec. 3, 1943, box 1549, RG 200.

41   Monroe to Lil, n.d., box 4, Acc. 24845.

42   Sweetland to the *Woodworker*, draft manuscript, May 20, 1944, box 4; published version, newsclipping, the *Woodworker*, Feb. 21, 1945, box 5, both in Acc. 1747.

43   The *Woodworker*, Feb. 21, 1945.

44   The *Woodworker*, Oct. 4, 1944, news clipping in box 5, Acc. 1747.

45   Ibid.

46   Monroe to Lil, Aug. 14, 1944, box QQ, Acc. 1747.

47   Lil to Monroe, July 30, 1944, box QQ, Acc. 1747.

48 LeBaron Stinnett to Sweetland, Feb. 6, 1945, box QQ, Acc. 1747.

49 Monroe to Lil, Aug. 14, 1944, Acc. 1747. Lillian Smith, a Georgia native, published *Strange Fruit* in 1944, a novel about interracial love. See the *New Georgia Encyclopedia*, http://www.georgiaencyclopedia.org/nge/Home.jsp, accessed Jan. 13, 2009.

50 Monroe Sweetland, Notes from Projects of Services of ARC Field Director in 1944 and 1945 in the Marshall Islands and Okinawa (hereafter Notes), box 10, Acc. 26165.

51 Sweetland, Notes, box 10, Acc. 26165; Linda Tamura, "The Enemy's Our Cousin," *Columbia Magazine* (Spring 2006), vol. 20, no. 1, http://columbia.washingtonhistory.org/magazine/articles/2006/0106/0106-a2.aspx, accessed Dec. 6, 2010; and Joseph D. Harrington, *Yankee Samurai: The Secret Role of Nisei in America's Pacific Victory* (Detroit: Pettigrew Enterprises, 1979), 125.

52 W. A. Myers to Sweetland, Sept. 18, 1944; W. A. Myers to Sweetland, Sept. 18, 1944; and Sweetland to Myers, Oct. 2, 1944, all in box 5, Acc. 1747.

53 Monroe to Lil, late Dec. 1944, box QQ, Acc., 1747.

54 Lil to Monroe, Sept. 23, Oct. 9, and Oct. (n.d.), 1944, all in box QQ, Acc. 1747.

55 Ibid., Jan. 7, Feb. 15, late Feb., and Mar. 21, 1945.

56 Charles Livermore to Sweetland, Apr. 10, 1945, box QQ, Acc. 1747.

57 Ethel Polk to Sweetland, June 5, 1945, box QQ, Acc. 1747.

58 Laura Lacey, "Battle of Okinawa," http://www.militaryhistoryonline.com/wwii/okinawa/default.aspx, accessed Dec. 3, 2010; and Laura Lacey, "A Brief History of the Battle of Okinawa," http://www.sixthmarinedivision.com/Okinawahistory.htm, accessed Dec. 7, 2010.

59 Sweetland, "In the Thick of It," the *Woodworker*, n.d., news clipping, box 4, Acc. 1747.

60 Sweetland to Ralph Philip, May 1945, box 4, Acc. 1747.

61 Allen E. Kolb to American Red Cross Personnel, Aug. 15, 1945, box 1541; and Memorandum to all Red Cross Workers in the Pacific Theater, n.d., box 990, both in RG 200.

62 Monroe to Lil, July 5 and Lil to Monroe, July 24, 1945, both in box QQ, Acc. 1747.

63 Lil to Monroe, July 16, 1945, ibid.

64 Monroe Sweetland, "Hatred-Limited," unpublished manuscript, Oct. 24, 1945, box 2, Acc. 1747.

65 Ibid., 2

66 Ibid., 3–4.

67 Ibid., 5. Japan's Greater East Asia Co-Prosperity Sphere refers to Japanese Prime Minister Matsuoka Yosuke's announcement in 1940 that Japan's economy required regional resources to remain viable. See Bill Gordon, "Greater East Asia Co-Prosperity Sphere," http://wgordon.web.wesleyan.edu/papers/coprospr.htm, accessed Dec. 8, 2010.

68 Ibid., 11–12.

69 Roy H. Hewitt to Sweetland, Dec. 4, 1941, box 1, Acc. 24845; Gus Solomon to Sweetland, Dec. 31, 1941; Solomon to Sweetland, Nov. 27, 1944, all in box 4, Acc. 1747; Monroe to Lil, Dec. 12, 1944, box QQ, Acc. 1747; and Sweetland to Solomon, Dec. 15, 1944, box 4, Acc. 1747.

70 Panek to Sweetland, Nov. 15 and Dec. 16, 1944, and July 13, 1945, all in box 5, Acc. 1747. For Sweetland's enthusiasm for a newspaper in McMinnville, see Sweetland to Solomon, Dec. 15, 1944, box 4, Acc. 1747.

71 George Sweetland to Monroe, Aug. 6, 1944, Aug. 20 and undated 1945 letter, all in box QQ, Acc. 1747.

72 Monroe to Lil, Aug. 12 and Sept. 10, 1945, both in box QQ, Acc. 1747.

73 Monroe to Lil, Sept. 23, 1945, box QQ, Acc. 1747.

74 Monroe to Lil, Dec. 15, 1945, box QQ, Acc. 1747. In this letter, Sweetland discusses driving through Maryland on Wednesday evening, December 12. Monroe inherited several thousand dollars from his uncle Monroe Mark Sweetland, a lawyer and judge, who died in 1944.

75 Ibid.

CHAPTER 6

1 Snell, who was secretary of state, soundly defeated Charles Sprague, the Republican incumbent governor in the May primary. See Floyd J. McKay, *An Editor for Oregon: Charles A. Sprague and the Politics of Change* (Corvallis: Oregon State University Press, 1998), 146.

2 Sweetland to Wayne Morse, July 13, 1941; and Morse to Sweetland, July 19, 1941, both in box 6, Acc. 26165.

3 Morse to Sweetland, Jan. 25, 1944, box 6, Acc. 26165. The Ruth Washke quote is in Mason Drukman, *Wayne Morse: A Political Biography* (Portland: Oregon Historical Society Press, 1997), 121.

4 Nathalie Panek to Sweetland, April 7, 1944, box 5, Acc. 1747; and Drukman, *Wayne Morse*, 131.

5 Panek to Sweetland, July 5 and Aug. 2, 1944; Morse to Sweetland, Oct. 16, 1944, all in box 5, Acc. 1747; and Drukman, *Wayne Morse*, 135–141.

6 Sweetland Letter to the Editor, *Oregon Historical Quarterly* 96 (1995), 102.

7   Robert E. Burton, *Democrats of Oregon: The Pattern of Minority Politics, 1900–1956* (Eugene: University of Oregon Books, 1970), 89, 92–93.
8   *Molalla Pioneer*, Feb. 7, 1946.
9   Ibid., Feb 7 and 14, 1946. The proposal for a Columbia Valley Authority was based on the model of the Tennessee Valley Authority.
10 Ibid., Feb. 28, Apr. 4, 18, and 25, 1946.
11 Sweetland to Manley Wilson, Oct. 26, 1946; and Wilson to Sweetland, Oct. 31, 1946, both in box 25, Acc. 1747.
12 *Oregon Blue Book, 1999–2000* (Salem, Oregon), 298, 311–312, 327–328.
13 Dan Goldy to Sweetland, Oct. 31, 1946, box 24, Acc. 1747; and Lil to Monroe, n.d., box 8, Acc. "D."
14 Sweetland to "Dear Friends," Jan. 9, 1947, box 3, Acc. 1747. On the first anniversary of the publication of the *Molalla Pioneer*, Sweetland wrote an editorial to let readers know that he and Lil were "still in debt, and we will be for a long time." See *Molalla Pioneer*, Feb. 6, 1947.
15 News clipping, *Oregon City Enterprise*, Dec. 18, 1947, box 10, Acc. 26165; and Sweetland to "Dear Friends," Jan. 9, 1948, box 3, Acc. 1747.
16 Joella Werlin, Interviewer and Editor, *Convictions, Controversy and Unintended Consequences: Memoirs of Daniel L. Goldy, An Oral History* (hereafter *Memoirs of Daniel L. Goldy*) (Monmouth: Western Oregon University, 2003), 19.
17 Goldy to Sweetland, Dec. 13, 1947 and Dec. 31, 1947, both in box 24, Acc. 1747.
18 Goldy to Sweetland, Nov. 28, 1947 and Jan 6, 1948, both in box 24, Acc. 1747.
19 Sweetland to "Dear Friends," Jan. 9, 1947, box 3, Acc. 1747; Ward Schori to Sweetland, Feb. 3, 1947; and Sweetland to Schori, Feb. 9, 1948, both in box 8, Acc. 1747.
20 Sweetland to Goldy and C. Girard Davidson, Feb. 29, 1948, box 24, Acc. 1747; C. W. Barrett to Sweetland, Mar. 4, 1948; John W. Lewis to Sweetland, Mar. 12, 1948; and Sweetland to C. B. Barrett, Mar. 13, 1948, all in box, 3, Acc. 1747.
21 Sweetland to Sheldon Menefee, June 16, 1948, box 20, Acc. 1747; Goldy to Sweetland, April 13, 1948, box 10, Acc. 26165; Goldy to Sweetland, May 4, 1948, box 26, Acc. 1747; Davidson to Sweetland, May 11, 1948, box "Mystery"; and Goldy to Sweetland, June 25, 1948, box 24, last two letters in Acc. 1747.
22 Goldy to Sweetland, May 13, 1948, box 10, Acc. 26165; Goldy to Sweetland, June 15, 1948, box 24; and Sweetland to Menefee, June 16, 1948, box 20, both in Acc. 1747.
23 Goldy to Sweetland, June 17, 1948; Don Bomen to Sweetland, June 20, 1948; Sweetland to Goldy, June 21, 1948, all in box 3; and Goldy to Sweetland, June 25, 1948, box 25, all in Acc. 1747.
24 Sweetland to Hugh Ball, Feb. 20, 1945, box QQ, Acc. 1747. Also see the *Hood River News*, Mar. 16, 1945.
25 The Minidoka Relocation Center was located in unincorporated Hunt, Idaho, about seventeen miles north of Twin Falls.
26 Junkichi Hachiya to Sweetland, Mar. 13, 1945, box 3, Acc. 26165. The Hood River American Legion post gained national attention when it removed the names of sixteen local Japanese servicemen from the county's Roll of Honor late in 1944.
27 Sweetland to Arline "Mrs. Max" Moore, April 5, 1948, box 16, Acc. 1747; Ray T. Yasui to Sweetland, Sept. 5, 1948, box 25, Acc. 1747; and Sweetland to Harry K. Hondo, editor, *Pacific Citizen*, April 29, 1979.
28 *Oregonian*, Sept. 12, 1948.
29 The JACL did not achieve its objective until 1952 when Congress passed the Walter-McCarran Act. See *Pacific Citizen*, June 11, 1949, and June 17, 1950. Also see "Japanese Americans in the Columbia River Basin," Center for Columbia River History, http://archive.vancouver.wsu.edu/crbeha/ja/ja.htm, accessed Nov. 20, 2011.
30 *Oregonian*, Aug. 13, 1952.
31 Sweetland to Dan and Rusty, Oct. 11, 1948; and Goldy to Sweetland, Dec. 14, 1948, both in box 3, Acc. 1747.
32 Goldy to Sweetland, Dec. 14, 1948, box 3, Acc. 1747.
33 Sweetland to J. W. Forrester, Jr., Jan. 28, 1949, box 9, Acc. 26165.
34 Ibid.; and Sweetland to Davidson, Jan. 30, 1949, box 3, Acc. 1747.
35 Sweetland to Davidson, Jan. 30, 1949, box 3, Acc. 1747.
36 Walter May to Sweetland, Feb. 5, 1949, box 20; and Goldy to Forrester and Sweetland, Mar. 7, 1949, box 3, both in Acc. 1747; and Sweetland to John Hubach, May 8, 1949, box 2, Acc. 24845.
37 Democratic National Committee for Oregon, News Release, June 19, 1949; and Sweetland to Nathalie Panek, June 2, 1949, both in box 2, Acc. 24845. Panek was living in Philadelphia and working for the Transport Workers Union of America, a militant east coast labor organization. See Guide to Transport Workers Union of America: Records of Local WAG 234, The Tamiment Library and Robert F. Wagner Labor Archives, http://dlib.nyu.edu/findingaids/html/tamwag/twua_locals.html, accessed Mar. 14, 2011.

38   Werlin, interviewer and ed., *Memoirs of Daniel L. Goldy*, "Vita," n.p.; Goldy to John Ferguson, Oct. 12, 1950; Goldy to Ray Moe, Oct. 12, 1950, both in box 15, Acc. 1747; and Goldy to Ray Kell, Oct. 18, 1950, box 16, Acc. 1747.

39   Goldy to Sweetland, Dec. 29, 1947, box 24, Acc. 1747.

40   *Oregonian*, May 20, 1948, news clipping in box 21, Acc. 1747. When Sweetland was in the Marshall Islands, he wrote Wallace to express his disappointment when he learned that Wallace would not be Roosevelt's running mate in 1944. See Sweetland to Henry Wallace, July 23, 1944, box 1, Acc. 24845.

41   Panek to Sweetland, April 12, 1945, box 5, Acc. 1747.

42   James T. Patterson, *Grand Expectations: The United States, 1945–1974* (New York: Oxford University Press, 1996), 139, 155–156.

43   *Molalla Pioneer*, Dec. 25, 1947; and Goldy to Sweetland, Jan. 6, 1948, both in box 24, Acc. 1747.

44   Ancil Payne to Edward Gideon, Jan. 23, 1948, box 14, Acc. 1747; Hugh Sheehan to Sweetland, April 4, 1947; and Sweetland to Sheehan, Apr. 26, 1947, both in box 15, Acc. 1747.

45   Nelson Lichtenstein, *Walter Reuther: The Most Dangerous Man in Detroit* (Urbana: University of Illinois Press, 1995), 304; Chris Hedges, *Death of the Liberal Class* (New York: Nation Books, 2010), 103; and Patterson, *Grand Expectations*, 157. The Reuther quotation is in Patterson.

46   Bowles and Humphrey were running for the U.S. Senate from their respective states. Patterson, *Grand Expectations*, 151, 155–156; and Goldy to Sweetland, circa March 1948.

47   Hubert Humphrey to Sweetland, June 10, 1948, in box "Mystery," Acc. 1747; and Patterson, *Grand Expectations*, 148–150.

48   *Newport News*, Nov. 4, 1948. Truman won the 1948 presidential contest with 24,179,345 votes to 21,991,291 for Dewey, or 49.6 percent of the popular vote. In the Electoral College tally Truman had 303 electoral votes to Dewey's 189. See Patterson, *Grand Expectations*, 161. Dewey took Oregon with 50.1 percent to Truman's 46.6 percent of the vote. Sweetland to Acey Caraway, Nov. 17, 1948, box "Mystery," Acc. 1747.

49   Richard T. Mosher to Sweetland, Dec. 14, 1950; and Sweetland to Dear Sam, Jan. 12, 1951, both in box 2, Acc. 1747. The Oregon legislature approved and Governor Douglas McKay signed the bill into law in March 1949. The measure made it illegal for employers to discriminate on the basis of race or religion. See the *Spokane Daily Chronicle*, Mar. 19, 1949, http://www.news.google.com/newspapers?id=hDtYAAAAIBAT.

50   Sweetland to George Megrath, May 28, 1949, box 2, Acc. 24845; and Davidson to Sweetland, Dec. 18, 1950, box "Mystery," Acc. 1747. The reference to Lil's work with the Springfield public utility fight is in Sweetland to Panek, 2, 1949.

51   Sweetland to Ernest Norback, Apr. 26, 1951; and Norback to Sweetland, May 3, 1952, both in box 25, Acc. 1747.

52   Gordon Petersen to Lillie Megrath, Mar. 6, 1952, copy of letter loaned to the author by Barbara Sweetland Smith.

53   The Treaty of Peace with Japan, Signed at San Francisco, September 8, 1951, http://www.taiwandocuments.org/sanfrancisco01.htm; and Sweetland to Austin Flegel, Sept. 13, 1951, box 14, Acc. 1747. For Sweetland's contract with Alaska, see R. W. Marshall to Sweetland, Feb. 2, 1951, on loan from Barbara Sweetland Smith.

54   Sweetland to Nelson David, Dec. 12, 1952, box 14, Acc. 1747; W. L. Walker to Sweetland, Mar. 6, 1953; Sweetland to Lybrand, Ross Bros., and Montgomery, Mar. 31, 1953, both in box 20, Acc. 1747; and Sweetland to Nelson David, May 8, 1954, box 14, Acc. 1747.

55   Rick Harmon, interview with Monroe Sweetland, Feb. 15, 1986, transcription, 165–170.

CHAPTER 7

1   Monroe Sweetland to M. H. Chrisman, Feb. 15, 1948, box 14, Acc. 1747; and Sweetland, Toward The "Liberation" of Oregon: How An Effective Liberal Minority Deploys its Forces to Win Important Gains in Conservative Oregon, circa summer 1949, manuscript in box 10, Acc. 26165.

2   Sweetland to Arch Doria, June 22, 1948, box "Mystery," Acc. 1747; and Harry H. Stein, *Gus J. Solomon: Liberal Politics, Jews, and the Federal Courts* (Portland: Oregon Historical Society Press, 2006), 92.

3   Harry H. Stein, *Gus J. Solomon: Liberal Politics, Jews, and the Federal Courts* (Portland: Oregon Historical Society Press, 2006), 92; and Solomon to Sweetland, Jan 17, 1949, box 2, Acc. 1747.

4   Sweetland to William Boyle, June 29, 1949, box 2, Acc. 24845.

5   Sweetland to Nathalie Panek, June 2, 1949; and Sweetland to Panek, Oct. 16, 1949, both in box 2, Acc. 24845. For the recess appointment, see Stein, *Gus J. Solomon*, 104.

6   News clippings, *Oregonian*, Oct. 28, 1949, in box 2, Acc. 24845.

7   Solomon to C. Girard Davidson, July 18, 1949, box 2, Acc. 1747.

8   Sweetland to Warren Magnuson, July 18, 1949; Roger Baldwin to Sweetland, July 20, 1949; and Solomon to Sweetland, Aug. 3, 1949, all in box 2, Acc. 1747. "Pinky" refers to Josslin's nickname.

9   Ashley Greene to Sweetland, Aug. 18, 1949, box 2, Acc. 1747; and C. Girard Davidson to Sweetland, Oct. 10, 1949, box "Mystery," Acc. 1747.

10   Stein, *Gus J. Solomon*, 92–106.

11   Robert E. Burton, *Democrats of Oregon: The Pattern of Minority Politics, 1900–1956* (Eugene: University of Oregon Books, 1970), 103.

12   Burton, *Democrats of Oregon*, 105–111.

13   Ibid., 112–119.

14   A. Robert Smith to Sweetland, Nov. 5, 1959; and Sweetland to Smith, Nov. 24, 1959, both in box 6, Acc. 1747.

15   Nicholas Granet to Sweetland, Mar. 20, 1950; Walter Pearson to Fellow Democrats, Nov. 16, 1950, both in box 26; and Solomon to Sweetland, Nov. 21, 1950, box 23, all in Acc. 1747.

16   *Eugene Register-Guard* news clipping, Apr. 7, 1952, box 8, Acc. O1747.

17   James A. Wechsler, *The Age of Suspicion* (New York: Random House, 1953), 135.

18   The Truman Doctrine originated with the president's request to Congress for $400 million to underwrite economic and military aid to Greece and Turkey, with the proviso that it would aid those nations to fend off Soviet-sponsored communist insurgencies. See James T. Patterson, *Grand Expectations: The United States, 1945-1974* (New York: Oxford University Press, 1996), 128–129; and Paul S. Boyer, ed., *The Oxford Companion to United States History* (New York: Oxford University Press, 2001), 786.

19   Wechsler, *Age of Suspicion*, 215–216; Patterson, *Grand Expectations*, 129. For Joseph Rauh, see *The American National Biography On Line*, http://www.anb.org/articles/15/15-01307.html, accessed Oct. 30, 2012. For the ADA, see Boyer, ed., *Oxford Companion to United States History*, 34. For a critical comparison of the ADA and Henry Wallace's Progressive Party, see Max Lerner, "The Long March— An Appraisal of the New Liberal Movements," *PM*, Jan. 9, 1947, pp. 2–3, news clipping, box 15, Acc. 1747.

20   Monroe Sweetland to the Editor, the *Oregonian*, Jan. 1, 1950, typescript, box 25, Acc. 1747.

21   When Minneapolis voters overwhelmingly elected Humphrey to a second term as mayor, Sweetland applauded the event in a *Molalla Pioneer* editorial, "Hubert Humphrey—Minnesota's Rising Star." Humphrey's large margin of victory would make "political dopesters back East begin to take special notice."

22   Minnesota's Farmer-Labor Party had replaced the older Democratic Party by the 1920s as the most reform-minded Minnesota political organization. In the midst of the Second World War the party was renamed the Democratic Farmer-Labor Party (DFL). Hubert Humphrey, not yet the mayor of Minneapolis, worked behind the scenes to bring about the merger. Humphrey led the purge of communists from the DFL in 1948. See Steven J. Keillor, *Hjalmar Petersen on Minnesota: The Politics of Provincial Independence* (Minneapolis: University of Minnesota Press, 1987), 58–60, 79–80, 87–88, 158–163, and 235–240; and Richard M. Valelly, *Radicalism in the States: The Minnesota Farmer-Labor Party and the American Political Economy* (Chicago: University of Chicago Press, 1987), 1–3, 128–130, and 156–158. Also see John E. Haynes, *Red Scare or Red Menace? American Communism and Anticommunism in the Cold War Era* (Chicago: Ivan R. Dee, 1996), 120–121; and *Walter Reuther: The Most Dangerous Man in Detroit* (Chicago: University of Illinois Press, 1995), 186–193 and 250–269.

23   "Josslin Stand Stirs Protest," news clipping, Jan. 3, 1951, box 14, Acc. 1747.

24   Chester S. Williams to Sweetland, Feb. 20, 1951, box 25, Acc. 1747.

25   Sweetland to Adrian Fisher, Mar. 5, 1951; and Sweetland to Charles Murphy, Mar. 6, 1951, both in box 2, Acc. 1747. For an extended discussion of Truman's containment and anticommunism policies, see Patterson, *Grand Expectations*, 105–136

26   Karl Rolvaag to Sweetland, Oct. 5, 1951; Sweetland to Rolvaag, Oct. 10, 1951; and Rolvaag to Sweetland, Oct. 25, 1951, all in box 1, Acc. 1747.

27   Patterson, *Grand Expectations*, 179, 204, 263.

28   Sweetland to Mark Chamberlain, Dec. 5, 1952; and Sweetland to Chamberlain, Mar. 21, 1952, both in box 14, Acc. 1747. Roger Baldwin initiated the formation of the American Committee for the Protection of the Foreign Born (1933–1982) to defend the rights of foreign-born radicals. The committee came under increasing attack during the Cold War and was eventually listed as a "subversive" organization. See the "Historical/Biographical Note" of the committee's papers in The Tamiment Library and Robert F. Wagner Labor Archives, http://dlib.nyu.edu/findingaids/html/tamwag/acpfb.html, accessed Apr. 27, 2011. For the activities of the Oregon affiliate, see Michael Munk, *The Portland Red Guide: Sites and Stories of Our Radical Past* (Portland: Ooligan Press, 2007), 154–155, 163, and 159.

29   Chris Hedges, *Death of the Liberal Class* (New York: Nation Books, 2010), 103; Patterson, *Grand Expectations*, 263; and Ellen Schrecker, *Many Are the Crimes: McCarthyism in America* (Boston: Little, Brown, 1998), 412.

30   James W. Goodsell to Acey Carraway, Democratic National Committee financial director, Jan. 16, 1950, box "Mystery"; Granet to Editor, *Oregon Democrat*, Feb. 10, 1950; and Nicholas Granet, "Machine Politics," Summer 1950, circular, all in box 1, Acc. 1747.

31 Oswald West, "Sweetland Found To Be Sour," box 10, Acc. 1747. Someone had written beside West's name at the top of the document, "The McCarthy of the West." Another circular under West's name, "A Guide to Sweetland," made similar charges, with a listing of communist-front organizations that Sweetland supposedly was involved with. See Oswald West, "A Guide to Sweetland," box 24, Acc. 1747.

32 Leonard James to Oswald West, Mar. 31, 1952; and James to the Editor, Apr. 26, 1952, both in box 3, Acc. 1747.

33 Walter Pierce to Fellow Democrats, n.d., box 14; and Minnie McFarland to Fellow Democrats, box 3, both in Acc. 1747.

34 Text of address of Walter M. Pearson, Winston, Oregon, Apr. 18, 1952, box 3, Acc. 1747; and *Roseburg News-Review*, Apr. 19, 1952, news clipping, box 26, Acc. 1747.

35 *Oregonian*, Apr. 25, 1952.

36 Sweetland to Bob Klemsen, Nov. 7, 1952, box 16; and Oswald West to Sweetland, box 25, both in Acc. 1747.

37 Bob Frazier to Sweetland, May 21, 1952; and Sweetland to Frazier, June 2, 1952, both in box 14, Acc. 1747. Sweetland also sent a letter of appreciation to Robert Sawyer, publisher and editor of the *Bend Bulletin*, thanking him for his "generous endorsement," which helped with his campaign's decisive results in central Oregon. Sweetland to Sawyer, May 22, 1952, box 24, Acc. 1747.

38 *Oregonian*, Nov. 5 and 6, 1952; Sweetland to Bob Klemsen, Nov. 7, 1952, box 16, Acc. 1747; and Sweetland, "Bulletin," *Oregon Democrat*, May 19, 1952.

39 Jack Churchill to Sweetland, Nov. 13, 1952, box 14, Acc. 1747.

40 Sweetland to Churchill, Nov. 26, 1952, box 14, Acc. 1747.

41 Vi Gunther to Sweetland, Jan. 7, 1952, box 10, Acc. 1747; and Matthew J. Connelly Files, Papers of Harry S. Truman Staff Member and Office Files, Harry S. Truman Library and Museum, http://www.trumanlibrary.org/hstpaper/connellyhst.htm, accessed May 12, 2011.

42 Sweetland to Richard Nelson, Mar. 11, 1952, box 10, Acc. 1747.

43 Hubert Humphrey to Sweetland, box "Mystery"; and Vi Gunther to Sweetland, box 25, both in Acc. 1747.

44 Sweetland to John Despol, July 1, 1952, box "Mystery"; and Sweetland to Jack Arvey, July 2, 1952, box 2, both in Acc. 1747.

45 Sweetland to Hubert Humphrey, July 3, 1952, box "Mystery"; and Adlai Stevenson to Sweetland, July 7, 1952, box 15, both in Acc. 1747. Stevenson's "drooping Kansas sunflower" obviously is a reference to the Republican candidate, Dwight Eisenhower, who was a native son of Kansas.

46 *Oregonian*, July 20, 1952, news clippings, box 11, Acc. 26165; and the *Albuquerque Tribune*, July 21, 1952.

47 "Adlai Stevenson," Unitarian Universalist Association, Notable American Unitarians, http://www25.uua.org/uuhs/duub/articles/adlaistevenson.html, accessed May 17, 2011; and Patterson, *Grand Expectations*, 353–354.

48 Political Party Platforms, Democratic Party Platform of 1952, The American Presidency Project, http://www.presidency.ucsb.edu/ws/index.php?pid=29600#axzz1Mdw6LL9q, accessed May 17, 2011. Howe is quoted in Patterson, *Grand Expectations*, 353.

49 *Oregonian*, Aug. 3, 1952; and Sweetland to Stevenson, July 29, 1952, box 10, Acc. 1747.

50 Humphrey to Sweetland, Aug. 27, 1952, box 10; undated, untitled news clipping, box 25; Sweetland to Clayton Fritchey, Oct. 14, 1952, box 10, all in Acc. 1747 ; and *Oregonian*, Oct. 14 and 19, 1952.

51 *Oregonian*, Oct. 27, 1952; and Wilson W. Wyatt to Sweetland, Nov. 12, 1952, box 16, Acc. 1747.

CHAPTER 8

1 *Oregonian*, Nov. 7, 1952.

2 Ibid., Jan. 12, 1953; and Oregon Chapter, American Association of Social Workers, "Should the Names of Recipients of Public Assistance Be Made Public?" Feb. 13, 1953; Monroe Sweetland to Wesley Small, Mar. 2, 1953; and undated news clipping, all in box 19, Acc. 1747.

3 Pendleton *East Oregonian*, Jan. 19, 1953, news clipping in box 15, Acc. 1747; and *Oregonian*, Feb. 7, 1953.

4 Mrs. William A. Howell to Citizens Interested in Improving Public Assistance Programs in Oregon, Feb. 18, 1953; and Mrs. Mary L. Arnold to Sweetland, Feb. 27, 1953, both in box 19, Acc. 1747; and *Oregonian*, Feb. 27, 1953.

5 Sweetland to Wesley Small, Mar. 12, 1953, box 19; Sweetland to Phil Levin, Mar. 24, 1953, box 15, both in Acc. 1747; and *Oregonian*, Apr. 7, 1953.

6 *Oregonian*, Apr. 11, 17, and 18, 1953; and Sweetland to John J. Zimpelman, May 16, 1953, box 19, Acc. 1747.

7   James T. Patterson, *Grand Expectations: The United States, 1945-1974* (New York: Oxford University Press, 1996), 50–52; *Oregonian*, Feb. 17, 1953; Glen L. Jolley to Sweetland, Feb. 16, 1953; and Mrs. Floyd O. Neff to Sweetland, Feb. 20, 1953, both in box 19, Acc. 1747.

8   *Oregonian*, Mar. 15 and 20, and Apr. 23, 1953.

9   Edwin C. Berry to Sweetland, Apr. 14, 1949, box 10, Acc. 1747; and Monroe Sweetland, "My Stake in Civil Rights: A Panel Discussion," Portland Bethel Church, Aug. 25, 1950, box 25, Acc. 1747.

10 *Oregonian*, Jan. 20, 1953; and Lafe Compton to Sweetland, Feb. 13, 1953, box 19, Acc. 1747.

11 Oregon State Hotel Association, Oregon Motor Court Association, Oregon Licensed Beverage Association, and Portland Independent Hotel Association, Testimony to the Oregon State Legislature in Connection with Senate Bill No. 169, n.d., box 19, Acc. 1747.

12 Sweetland to Gene Rossman, Mar. 12, 1953, box 19, Acc. 1747; and *Oregonian*, Feb. 16 and Mar. 13, 1953.

13 *Oregonian*, Apr. 13, 19, and 24, 1953.

14 Ibid., Apr. 24 and 25, 1953; Edwin C. Berry to Sweetland, Apr. 27, 1953, box 19, Acc. 1747; and *Oregonian*, July 3, 15, 18, and 20, 1953.

15 *Oregonian*, Mar. 15 and 24, 1953.

16 Sweetland to Steve Forrester, May 15, 1953, box 1; and Sweetland to Reginald Zalles, Oct. 22, 1953, box 20, both in Acc. 1747.

17 Rick Harmon, interview with Monroe Sweetland, Feb. 15, 1986, transcript, 170–180; Lillie Sweetland to Herbert E. Hawkes, Mar. 1, 1955, box 6, Acc. 1747; and *Oregonian*, Mar. 26, 1954. Mills College awarded Barbara one of its eight freshman scholarships. See the *Oregonian* June 17, 1954.

18 Violet M. Gunther to Sweetland, Sept. 2, 1953, box 20, Acc. 1747; and C. Girard Davidson to Sweetland; and Davidson to RLW, both Apr. 26, 1954, box 12, Acc. 26165.

19 *Milwaukie Review*, Mar. 25 and Apr. 1, 1954.

20 Annie Chambers to Monroe Sweetland, June 18; and Sweetland to Chambers, June 29, 1954, both in box 6, Acc. 1747.

21 *Oregonian*, Jan. 20 and Feb. 13, 1954; Sweetland to Wayne Morse, Feb. 18, 1954, box 6, Acc. 1747; and Clark Hansen, "The Making of the Modern Democratic Party in Oregon: An Interview with Howard Morgan," *Oregon Historical Quarterly* 95 (Fall 1994), 368–385. For Morgan's anecdote about the shaving mirror, see page 281. Hess, who had served as a state senator in the late 1930s, defeated Democratic governor Charles Martin in the 1938 primary election and then lost to Republican Charles Sprague the following November.

22 *Oregonian*, Mar. 6, 1954.

23 Ibid., Mar. 10 and June 15, 1954.

24 Ibid., May 24, 1954. All the Democratic candidates attacked President Eisenhower's natural resource policies and supported a federal dam in Hells Canyon on the Snake River. See Robert E. Burton, *Democrats of Oregon: The Pattern of Minority Politics, 1900–1956* (Eugene: University of Oregon Books, 1970), 128.

25 *Oregonian*, Oct. 10 and 17, 1954; and Burton, *Democrats of Oregon*, 129–130.

26 *Oregonian*, Oct. 29, 1954.

27 Howard Morgan worked with Ken Rinke, Green's chief campaign operative, to discredit McCall by planting falsehoods and clandestinely raising suspicions about his character. One series of incidents involved riding the elevators at Portland's Meier and Frank store during the weekly "Friday Surprise" sales speaking loudly about McCall's money problems, that his personal finances were in disarray, and that he could not be trusted. See Brent Walth, *Fire at Eden's Gate: Tom McCall and the Oregon Story* (Portland: Oregon Historical Society Press, 1994), 100–102.

28 Portland *Oregon Journal*, Nov. 4, 1954; news clipping on loan from Barbara Sweetland Smith; and *Oregonian* Nov. 4, 1954.

29 *New York Times*, Nov. 7, 1954.

30 Hansen, "An Interview with Howard Morgan," 368–385; and *Oregon Democrat* 22 (Nov. 1954), 5, cited in Burton, *Democrats of Oregon*, 132.

31 Eleanor Forrester to Sweetland, Nov. 6, 1954, box 2, Acc. 24845. Bud Forrester was now publishing and editing the Pendleton *East Oregonian*.

32 Cornelius C. Bateson to Sweetland, Nov. 10, 1954, box 2, Acc. 24845; and H. R. Glascock, Sr. to Sweetland, Dec. 14, 1954, box 6, Acc. 1747.

33 Nathalie Panek to Sweetland, Nov. 4, 1954; Sweetland to Panek, Nov. 11, 1954, both in box 9, Acc. 26165.

34 Lil Sweetland to Barbara Sweetland, Nov. 11, 1954, copy in possession of the author.

35 Hansen, "An Interview with Howard Morgan," 379–381.

36 Ibid., 382.

37 Monroe Sweetland, "Letter to the Editor," *Oregon Historical Quarterly* 96 (Spring 1995), 102–104.

38 Dear Sirs, unsent letter to the *Oregon Historical Quarterly*, circa late 1994, box 7, Acc. 24845.

39   The *U.S. News and World Report* article is cited in the *Oregonian*, Nov. 17, 1954.
40   Mervin Shoemaker, "Morse's Label for Today: Independent Democrat," *Oregonian*, Nov. 18, 1954; Wayne Morse telegram to Sweetland (with copy of separate telegram to Morgan), Nov. 19, 1954; and *Oregonian*, Nov. 19, 1954. There was a substantive difference between the Sweetland and Morgan relations with Morse. The former had been corresponding with Morse since the late 1930s, and their families were acquainted as well. Sweetland and Morse regularly exchanged holiday greetings and news about their children. Morgan became acquainted with Morse only after he was elected state Democratic chair.
41   *Oregonian*, Dec. 11, 1954.
42   Sweetland to H. R. Glascock, Dec. 14, 1954, box 6, Acc. 1747; *Oregonian*, Feb. 18, 1954; and *Oregon Statesman*, Feb. 20, 1955, news clipping in box 17, Acc. 1747.
43   Mason Drukman, *Wayne Morse: A Political Biography* (Portland: Oregon Historical Society Press, 1997), 218; and Sweetland to Porter, Oct. 26, 1954, box 20, Acc. 1747; and Sweetland to Porter, Dec. 14, 1954, box 17, Acc. 1747. As for the acerbic Morgan, Drukman notes that during the 1956 election campaign there were complaints "that Morgan had become increasingly high-handed in his style of leadership" (235).
44   In a letter to Barbara in the spring of 1955, Lil, who was leaving for the east coast to visit sister Vi, regretted leaving "the paper which I passionately love (really!) and worry about like a cat with her first batch of kittens." See Lil to Barbara, May 24, 1955, letter on loan from Barbara Sweetland Smith.
45   Morse to Sweetland, Jan. 4, 1955, box 17, Acc. 1747; and author's interview with Rebecca Sweetland, Sept. 25, 2012.

CHAPTER 9

1   *Oregonian*, Jan. 1, 1955.
2   Ibid., Dec. 31, 1954; and Jan. 6 and 8, 1955.
3   Eugene *Register-Guard*, Jan. 9, 1955, news clipping in box 17, Monroe Sweetland Papers, Acc. 1747, Oregon Historical Society, Portland, Oregon; *Oregonian*, Jan. 21, 1955; and Sweetland to Sam Haley, Jan. 18, 1955; and *Oregonian*, Jan. 29, 1955, both in box 17, Acc. 1747.
4   Richard L. Neuberger to Sweetland, Feb. 8, 1955; Sweetland to J. R. Forrester, Feb. 14, 1955; and Sweetland to E. B. MacNaughton, Feb. 14, 1955, all in box 15, Acc. 1747.
5   *Oregonian* Jan. 29 and Feb. 18, 1955; and *Oregon Statesman*, Feb. 18, 1955, copy in box 17, Acc. 1747.
6   Sweetland to American Civil Liberties Union, Feb. 23, 1955; and Alan Reitman to Sweetland, Feb. 28, 1955, both in box 2, Acc. 1747.
7   *Oregonian*, May 26, 29, and May 4, 1955, clippings in box 17, Acc. 1747.
8   *Oregonian*, Apr. 19, 1955; Robert Prigmore (and thirteen other signers), Important Bulletin, Apr. 21, 1955; and Fred J. Yoder to Sweetland, Apr. 19, 1955, both in box 19, Acc. 1747.
9   Mrs. Howard Fetz, Jr., to Sweetland, Apr. 21, 1955; Sweetland to All Who Wrote me Concerning HB 483, Apr. 27, 1955, both in box 17, Acc. 1747; and History of Oregon's Land Use Planning, Oregon Department of Land, Conservation and Development, http://www.oregon.gov/LCD/history.shtml, accessed Dec. 2, 2011.
10   *Oregonian*, Feb. 12, 1955; and Savannah Lewis to Sweetland, n.d., box 3, Acc. 24845.
11   *Oregonian*, Mar. 19, Apr. 15, and May 8, 1955.
12   Gordon Swope to Sweetland, Feb. 25, 1955; Martin Rostvold to W. W. Chadwick (cc. to Sweetland), Feb. 28, 1955, both in box 17, Acc. 1747; and *Oregonian*, Mar. 13 and May 8, 1955.
13   G. Bernhard Fedde to Sweetland, Feb. 17, 1955; Sweetland to Fedde, Mar. 2, 1955, both in box 17, Acc. 1747; and *Oregonian* Feb. 13 and Apr. 17, 1955.
14   *Oregon Journal*, Mar. 2, 1955, news clipping; and Sweetland to Mrs. Ross E. Green, Mar. 29, 1955, both in box 7, Acc. 1747.
15   Unsigned, undated copy of letter to Arthur H. Bone, box 32, Acc. 1747; and *Oregonian*, April 17, 19, 21, 23, 25, 26, 27, and May 8, 1955.
16   Sweetland to Honorable Harry S. Truman, May 1, 1952, box 14, Acc. 1747; and H. E. Childs to Sweetland, Dec. 18, 1952, box 19, Acc. 1747.
17   Sweetland to *Oregon Journal*, Mar. 31, 1955, box 16; Sweetland to Stephen E. Epler, May 15, 1953, box 19; and Brief for A Four-Year State College for Portland, box 19, all in Acc. 1747. Sweetland to Epler, Feb. 16, 1955, box 3, Acc. 24845; and *Oregonian*, April 10 and May 8, 1955.
18   Sweetland to Mr. and Mrs. John Gunther, Nov. 7, 1954, box 9, Acc. 26165.
19   *Oregonian*, Oct. 14, 1955.
20   Ibid.; C. Girard Davidson to County Democratic Chairmen, with a copy to Howard Morgan, Oct. 14, 1955, box 3, Acc. 24845; and Mason Drukman, *Wayne Morse: A Political Biography* (Portland: Oregon Historical Society Press, 1997), 235.
21   *Oregonian*, Jan. 16, 1956.

22 Ibid., Nov. 20, 1955; and Sweetland to Panek, Jan. 17, 1956, in box 31, Acc. 1747.

23 Philip A. Levin to Mrs. Fern Davenport, March 7, 1956; Keith Burns to Dear Friends, June 26, 1956; and Campaign Statement, n.d., all in box 31, Acc. 1747.

24 Sweetland to Roy Reuther, Aug. 24, 1956; and Philip A. Levin to Paul Mills, Feb. 27, 1957, both in box 31, Acc. 1747.

25 Sweetland Secretary of State Committee, News Release, Sept. 5, 1956, and undated News Release, both in box 31, Acc. 1747.

26 *Oregonian*, Oct. 6, 1956.

27 Typescript of the *Capital Journal* editorial, Oct. 9, 1956, box 24, Acc. 1747; and "George Putnam," http://id.mind.net/~truwe/tina/putnam.html, accessed Dec. 14, 2011.

28 "Hatfield vs. Sweetland," typescript, *Oregon Statesman*, Oct. 11, 1956, box 24, Acc. 1747.

29 *Milwaukie Review*, Nov. 1, 1956; and *Coos Bay Times*, Nov. 2, 1956, photocopy in box 31, Acc. 1747.

30 *Milwaukie Review*, Nov. 8, 1956; *Oregonian*, Nov. 8, 1956; and *Oregon Labor Press*, Nov. 23, 1956, news clipping, box 31, Acc. 1747.

31 Sweetland's statement was quoted in the *Oregonian*, Nov. 8, 1956; also see Sweetland to Clackamas County Papers, n.d., box 31, Acc. 1747.

32 *Oregonian*, Oct. 8, 1956; and N. C. Nilsen to Sweetland, n.d., box 31, Acc. 1747. Sweetland remarked that "Hatfield's television advertising was extremely effective during the last month." Sweetland to William L. Josslin, Dec. 27, 1956, box 31, Acc. 1747.

33 Sweetland to Rudie Wilhelm, Dec. 21, 1956; and Sweetland to Our Republican Colleagues, Jan. 2, 1957, both in box 34, Acc. 1747.

34 *Capital Journal*, n.d., photocopy in box 34, Acc. 1747; and *Oregonian*, Jan. 14, 22, 25 and 26, 1957.

35 *Oregonian*, Feb. 6 and Mar. 26, 1957.

36 *Oregonian*, April 4, 1957.

37 BLM managed some 2.5 million acres of timberland, all of it in western Oregon. Referred to as the O & C lands, the timber was part of the original grant to the Oregon and California Railroad. Under the O & C formula, 50 percent of timber receipts were distributed to the county in which the timber was harvested. See Elmo Richardson, *BLM's Billion-Dollar Checkerboard: Managing the O & C Lands* (Santa Cruz, CA: Forest History Society, 1980).

38 *Oregonian*, April 16 and 28, 1957.

39 *Oregonian*, May 5, 1957.

40 Ibid., Mar. 1 and 13, 1957; Sweetland to Dean Morey, Apr. 17, 1957; and Sweetland to My Fellow Legislators, Apr. 25, 1957, both in box 34, Acc. 1747.

41 *Oregonian*, May 10, 15, 17, and 22, 1957.

42 Ibid., May 24 and 26, 1957.

43 Ibid., Feb. 15 and 25, 1957.

44 John R. Churchill to Sweetland, Mar. 1, 1957, box 6, Acc. 1747; *Oregonian*, Mar. 3, 1957; and Stan Federman to Becky [Sweetland], Dec. 11, 1989, box 9, Acc. 26165. The occasion for Federman's letter involved preparations for Monroe's ninetieth birthday. John "Jack" Churchill purchased the *Oregon Democrat*.

45 Oregonian, July 28, Aug, 4, and Sept. 4, 1957. Sweetland acknowledged that the campaign cards and folders were in the trunk of the Olds.

46 *Oregonian*, July 29 and Oct. 11, 1957.

47 Governor Robert D. Holmes' Administration, Oregon State Archives, http://arcweb.sos.state.or.us/pages/records/governors/guides/state/holmes/index.html, accessed Jan. 10, 2012.

48 *Oregonian*, Nov. 20, 1957, and Jan. 2, 3, 4, 16, and May 17, 1958.

49 Ibid., May 29, Oct. 18 and 28, 1958.

50 Richard Neuberger to Sweetland, July 7, 1958; and *Oregonian*, Oct. 24, 1958.

51 *Oregonian*, Nov. 6, 1958.

52 Ibid., Oct. 25, Nov. 5 and 6, 1958.

53 Oregonian, Oct. 12, 1958; Rebecca Sweetland to the author, Jan. 12, 2012; and author's interview with Rebecca Sweetland, Sept. 25, 2012.

CHAPTER 10

1 Source: Lil Sweetland to Monroe Sweetland, n.d., no title, box 23, Acc. 1747. Stan Federman, who would soon become business manager of the *Milwaukie Review*, recalls that Hatfield and Sweetland liked each other, "and the two remained on friendly—if cautious—terms throughout their lives." Federman to the author, Feb. 2012.

2 *Oregonian*, Jan. 13 and 16, 1959.

3 Ibid., Jan. 13, 1957.

4   Ibid.; B. A. Green to Sweetland, Jan. 29, 1959; Sweetland to Green, Jan. 30, 1959; Beatrice B. Reed to Sweetland, Feb. 4, 1959; Sweetland to Reed, Feb. 6, 1959; W. A. Franklin to Sweetland, Feb. 11, 1959; and Sweetland to Franklin, Feb. 20, 1959, all in box 7, Acc. 1747; and *Oregonian*, Mar. 20, 1959.

5   School Support "Must," Sweetland Tells PTA, Mar. 5, 1959; and Jean L. Roth to Sweetland, Mar. 11, 1959, both in box 7, Acc. 1747.

6   Mrs. Kenneth Marks to Sweetland, Mar. 11, 1959; Sweetland to Anna Pratt, Mar. 14, 1959; Stella Chlopek to Sweetland, Mar. 18, 1959; and Sweetland to Chlopek, Mar. 27, 1959, all in box 7, Acc. 1747.

7   *Oregonian*, Mar. 24, 1959.

8   Ibid.

9   Ibid., May 10, 1959.

10   Don Pence to Sweetland, Feb. 26, 1958, box 34, Acc. 1747.

11   Harry Brer to Sweetland, Feb. 20, 1959; Sweetland to Brer, Feb. 25, 1959; Charles Segar to Sweetland, Feb. 24, 1959; and Sweetland to Leslie A. Pickett, Feb. 25, 1959, all in box 3, Acc. 1747; and *Oregonian*, Feb. 2 and Mar. 22, 1959.

12   H. A. Catlin to Sweetland, Mar. 6, 1959; Virginia Kletzer to Sweetland, Mar. 9, 1959; Joseph L. Thimm to Sweetland, Mar. 13, 1959; Sweetland to Thimm, Mar. 27, 1959; Barbara Barrett to Sweetland, Mar. 16, 1959; Margie R. Lee to Sweetland, Mar. 17, 1959; and A. R. Watzek to Sweetland, Mar. 18, 1959, all in box 7; and Jean Lewis to John R. Richards, Sept. 14, 1959; Richards to Lewis, Sept. 19, 1959; and Lewis to Sweetland, Sept. 21, 1959, all in box 6, Acc. 1747.

13   *Oregonian*, May 7, 8, and 10, 1959.

14   Memorandum on State Senator Monroe Sweetland, Dec. 30, 1959, box 3, ACC. 1747; "Educators Pay Tribute to Monroe Sweetland," news clipping, box 13, Acc. 1747; and *Oregonian*, Mar. 17 and 19, 1960. Anticipating a busy election season, Sweetland concluded a contract with Stan Federman to oversee the business side of the *Milwaukie Review* while he was campaigning. See *Milwaukie Review*, Oct. 28, 1959.

15   *Oregonian*, Oct. 30, 1960.

16   Sweetland to The Editor, Feb. 20, 1960, box 4, Acc. 24845; Eugene *Register-Guard*, Apr. 21, 1960, news clipping in box 13, Acc. 1747; and Dodd to Katz, Apr. 30, 1960, box 4, Acc. 24845.

17   See the following sources: "Richard Lewis Neuberger," *Biographical Directory of the United States Congress*, http://bioguide.congress.gov/scripts/biodisplay.pl?index=n000053, accessed May 13, 2013; and William G. Robbins, "Richard Neuberger (1912–1960)," the *Oregon Encyclopedia*, http://www.oregonencyclopedia.org/entry/view/neuberger_richard_1912_1960_/, accessed May 13, 2013.

18   Eugene *Register-Guard*, May 4, 1960, typescript in box 34, Acc. 1747; and Sweetland Defends Role of Government, June 7, 1960, box 13, Acc. 1747.

19   *Oregonian*, July 17, Aug. 10 and 29.

20   Medford *Mail-Tribune*, Oct. 21, 1960; and Eugene *Register-Guard*, Oct. 21, 1960, both news clippings in box 13, Acc. 1747.

21   *Oregonian*, Oct. 15, 1960; and *Oregon Statesman*, Oct. 12, 1960, news clipping in box 13, Acc. 1747.

22   Monroe Sweetland—His Real Record, box 12, Acc. 1747.

23   *Milwaukie Review*, Oct. 27, 1960. See Ancil H. Payne, HistoryLink.org, http://www.historylink.org/index.cfm?DisplayPage=output.cfm&file_id=5679, accessed Feb. 18, 2012.

24   See Ancil H. Payne, HistoryLink.org, http://www.historylink.org/index.cfm?DisplayPage=output.cfm&file_id=5679, accessed Feb. 18, 2012.

25   Ibid.

26   Howell Appling, news release, July 12, 1959, box 32, Acc. 1747.

27   *Oregonian*, Nov. 10, 2012; and John M. Swarthout, "The 1960 Election in Oregon," *Western Political Quarterly* 14 (Mar. 1961), 361–362.

28   No title, box 8, Acc. 1747.

29   *Milwaukie Review*, Nov. 11, 1960.

30   Nathalie Panek to Sweetland, Nov. 16, 1960, box 21, Acc. 1747.

31   *Portland Reporter*, Nov. 1, 1960; *Oregon Journal*, Nov. 5, 1960, news clippings, both in box 12, Acc. 1747; and The Americanist Research and Defense Fund, Portland, n.d., box 12, Acc. 1747.

32   Sweetland to Norman Thomas, Jan. 1, 1961; Sweetland to James Carey, Jan. 1, 1961, both in box 23, Acc. 1747; and Howard Friedman to Paul Meyer, Jan. 27, 1961, box 4, Acc. 24845.

33   Panek to Sweetland, Feb. 13, box 23; and Feb. 16, 1961, box 22, both in Acc. 1747.

34   Panek to Sweetland, June 20, 1961; and *National Review*, July 1, 1961, news clipping, both in box 22, Acc. 1747.

35   *Oregonian*, Aug. 24 and Sept. 19, 1961; *Portland Reporter*, Sept. 18, 1961, news release in box 12, Acc. 1747; and *Milwaukie Review*, Sept. 21, 1961.

36   *Oregon Journal*, Jan. 4, 1963, news clipping in box 9, Acc. 26165; and Stan Federman to the author, Feb. 2012.

37   *Milwaukie Review*, Dec. 31, 1960.

38 Sweetland to Manakkal Sabhesan Venkataramani, June 30, 1961, box 23, Acc. 1747; and Stan Federman to the author, Feb. 2012.
39 Hubert Humphrey to Sweetland, May 4, 1959; and John F. Kennedy to Sweetland, May 11, 1959, both in box 4, Acc. 24845; Theodore Sorensen to Sweetland, May 18, 1959; and Sweetland to Sorensen, June 6, 1959, both in box 6, Acc. 1747.
40 Vi Gunther to Sweetland, June 15, 1959, box 4, Acc. 24845.
41 Humphrey to Sweetland, June 15, 1959, box 4, Acc. 24845. Humphrey sent copies to ADA officials Joseph Rauh and James Loeb.
42 Walter H. Dodd to Sweetland, Aug. 3, 1959; and Sweetland to Dodd, Aug. 21, 1959, both in box 4, Acc. 24845; O. Charles Press to Sweetland, Aug. 4, 1959; and Sweetland to Press, Aug. 18, 1959, both in box 6, Acc. 1747.
43 *Oregonian*, Aug. 4–5, 1959; and Kennedy to Sweetland, Aug. 6, 1959, box 4, Acc. 24845.
44 Joseph S. Miller, *The Wicked Wine of Democracy: A Memoir of a Political Junkie, 1948–1995* (Seattle: University of Washington Press, 2008), 123–125; and Joseph S. Miller to Sweetland, Oct. 26, 1959, box 6, Acc. 1747.
45 Miller to Sweetland, Oct. 26, 1959; Sweetland to Miller, Nov. 4, 1959, both in box 6, Acc. 1747; and *Oregonian*, Nov. 8, 1959.
46 Mason Drukman, *Wayne Morse: A Political Biography* (Portland: Oregon Historical Society Press, 1995), 325–326.
47 Sweetland to Kennedy, June 4, 1960, box 4, Acc. 24845.
48 James T. Patterson, *Grand Expectations: The United States, 1945–1974* (New York: Oxford University Press, 1996), 336–339; Lewis B. Stewart to Sweetland, July 19, 1960; and Sweetland to Stewart, July 25, 1960, both in box 3, Acc. 1747.
49 Sweetland to Vi Gunther, July 21, 1960; Jonathan Marshall to Sweetland, Aug. 4, 1960, both in box 32, Acc. 1747; and Nelson L. Jones to Sweetland, July 23, 1960, box 3, Acc. 1747.
50 *Milwaukie Review*, Nov. 10, 1960. The newspaper predicted a Kennedy victory in Oregon and the nation. See the issues for Oct. 6 and Nov. 3, 1960.
51 C. Girard Davidson to G. Mennen Williams, Dec. 7, 1960, box 22, Acc. 1747.
52 Sweetland to Arthur Schlesinger, Jr., Dec. 8, 1960; Sweetland to Ted Sorensen, Dec. 12, 1960; and Sorenson to Sweetland, Dec. 19, 1960, all in box 22, Acc. 1747.
53 Wayne Morse to Sweetland, Jan. 6, 1961; Sweetland to Edith Green, Jan. 26, 1961, both in box 23, Acc. 1747; and *Milwaukie Review*, Jan. 8, 1961.
54 Sweetland to Humphrey, Jan. 26, 1961; Sweetland to Green, Jan. 26, 1961; Sweetland to Howard Morgan, Feb. 2, 1961, all in box 23, Acc. 1747; Simeon Booker, "Tough Man for a Tough Job: George L. P. Weaver," *Ebony* (Nov. 1961), 55–62; and *Oregonian*, Jan. 26, 1961.
55 N.d., no title, box 23, Acc. 1747. Stan Federman remembers Lil being "mad as hell" when Monroe failed to secure a federal position, Federman to the author, Feb. 2012.
56 *Oregonian*, Feb. 6, 1961. Federman contends that Green was "one tough lady with a lot of DC clout." Although Sweetland had always supported her, he believes that it may have been personal—"Green always demanded instant worship." Federman to the author, Feb. 2012.
57 Sweetland to George Weaver, Feb. 26, 1961; Morse to Weaver, Mar. 20, 1961, both in box 22, Acc. 1747; and Sweetland to Morse, Mar. 22, 1961, box 23, Acc. 1747.
58 George Edwards to Sweetland, Mar. 31, 1961, box 22, Acc. 1747.
59 *Oregonian*, Jan. 10, 1961; and John M. Swarthout, "The 1960 Election in Oregon," *Western Political Quarterly* 14 (Mar. 1961), 355, 361–362. Voters elected Democrat Maurine Neuberger to succeed her husband Richard, who died the previous March.
60 *Oregonian*, Jan. 13, 1961.
61 Bob Crosier to Sweetland, Jan. 30, 1961; Emil Abramovic to Sweetland, Feb. 13, 1961; and Richard Rosekang to Sweetland, Feb. 14, 1961, all in box 7, Acc. 1747.
62 Cecil Posey to Sweetland, April 8, 1961; Lynn Johnson to Sweetland, April 10, 1961; and Pearl J. Cleaver, Apr. 29, 1961, all in box 7, Acc. 1747.
63 *Oregonian*, Apr. 23, May 1, 2, 5 and 12, 1961.
64 Mrs. John R. Catlin to Al Flegel, Mar 1, 1961; Sweetland to George Morrison, Apr. 11, 1961; and Sweetland to Al Ullman, Feb. 15 and Mar. 20, 1961, all in box 3, Acc. 1747.
65 *Milwaukie Review*, May 11, 1961; and Clackamas Community College, History, http://www.clackamas. edu/inside.asp?content=0200-08, accessed Jan. 31, 2012. Several other community colleges— Southwestern (Coos Bay), Clatsop (Astoria), and Blue Mountain (Pendleton)—were already offering classes before Clackamas Community College.
66 *Bend Bulletin*, April 8, 1961.

CHAPTER 11

1   Lillie Sweetland to C. Girard Davidson, Mar. 1, 1957, box 24, C. Girard Davidson Papers, University of Oregon Collection 162, Special Collections and University Archives, University of Oregon, Eugene (hereafter Davidson Papers).

2   Sweetland to Jack Olds, Sept. 3, 1957; and Ancil Payne to Sweetland, May 15, 1959, both in box 24, Davidson Papers. For information about Davidson's company, see Davidson, C. Girard (Crow Girard), 1910-Northwest Digital Archives, http://socialarchive.iath.virginia.edu/xtf/view?docId=davidson-c-girard-crowe-girard-1910--cr.xml, accessed Apr. 12, 2012.

3   Payne to Sweetland, May 25, 1959, box 24, Davidson Papers.

4   Payne to Sweetland, Oct. 20, 1959; and Draft Agreement between Milwaukie Publishers & Printers, Inc. and Stan Federman, Nov. 23, 1959, both in box 24, Davidson Papers.

5   Stan Federman to Sweetland, May 2, 1960, box 24, Davidson Papers.; George Sweetland to Dear Roe, Feb. 2, 1946, box PP, Acc. 1747; and Federman to the author, February 2012.

6   Federman to Davidson, July 14, 1962, box 24, Davidson Papers. Clark, according to Federman, arrived on the newspaper scene in about 1959 with lots of capital and published a shopper out of Portland with an extensive reach on the east side of the Willamette. He had a large advertising staff that gave competitive fits to weekly newspapers. Federman to the author, Apr. 21, 2012.

7   Federman to Davidson, July 14, 1962, box 24, Davidson Papers.

8   News Release, Sept. 4, 1962; Front Page Statement for *Review* and *Shopper*, Sept. 1962, typescript, both in box 2, Acc. 1747; and *Oregonian*, Sept. 16, 1962.

9   Sweetland to Manakkal Sabhesan Venkataramani, June 30, 1961, box 23, Acc. 1747; Barbara Smith e-mail to the author, Mar. 13, 2012; and author's interview with Rebecca Sweetland, Sept. 25, 2012.

10 George Azumano to George Somekawa, June 26, 1961; John Kenneth Galbraith to Sweetland, June 23, 1961; and Sweetland to Galbraith, July 1, 1961, all in box 23, Acc. 1747.

11 George Somekawa to Sweetland, Oct. 6, 1961, box 23, Acc. 1747; and *Milwaukie Review*, July 27 and Aug. 3, 1961. Also see Eugene Burdick and William Lederer, *The Ugly American* (NY: W. W. Norton, 1958), a fictional story about Americans in Southeast Asia.

12 Typescript, "Asia Calling," Djakarta, Indonesia, July 29, 1961, box 23, Acc. 1747.

13 Ibid.

14 Ibid.

15 Ibid. Lumumba's assassination on January 17, 1961, only seven months after Congolese independence, was linked to the covert work of the CIA.

16 *Milwaukie Review*, Aug. 24, 1961.

17 Ibid., Sept. 7, 1961.

18 Ibid., Sept. 14, 1961.

19 Ibid., Sept. 28, 1961.

20 Ibid., Sept. 21 and 28, and Oct. 12, 1961.

21 *Oregonian*, Oct. 29, Nov. 5, and Dec. 11, 1961; and *Milwaukie Review*, Dec. 21, 1961.

22 *Milwaukie Review*, Jan. 18, 1962.

23 Robert Delson to Mrs. [Alexa] Bernard Saunders, June 17, 1964, box 5, Acc. 24845; Early History, n.d., box 8, Acc. 26165; and Alexander Shakow to the author, Mar. 20, 2012. For the background to the Asia Society, see http://asiasociety.org/about/mission-history, accessed Mar. 19, 2012.

24 Wendy Sorensen to Sweetland, Feb. 26, 1962; Sweetland to John C. Clutter, Mar. 24, 1962; and Sweetland to George Curran, Apr. 11, 1962, all in box 11, Acc. 26165.

25 For Guy Pauker's role as CIA operative, see George McT. Kahin, *Southeast Asia: A Testament* (New York: Routledge Curzon, 2003), 156; and Guy J. Pauker, "The Rise and Fall of the Communist Party in Indonesia," United States Air Force Project Rand, March 1969, www.dtic.mil/cgi-bin/GetTRDoc?AD=AD0684526, accessed Mar. 20, 2012.

26 Sweetland to Carl Slater, Mar. 25, 1962; Alexander Shakow to the author, Mar. 20, 2012; and Robert Delson to Sweetland, May 15, 1962, both in box 11, Acc. 26165. There is also the likely possibility that income from the *Milwaukie Review* supported his work until the newspaper's sale in September 1962.

27 Sweetland to Louis Bial, June 5, 1962; Bial to Sweetland, June 9, 1962, both in box 11, Acc. 26165; Indonesian-American Society of the United States, Meeting of the Board of Directors, June 17, 1962, box 13, Acc. 26165; and the *Christian Science Monitor*, n.d., news clipping in box 9, 1962. The articles of incorporation were placed on file with the State of New York.

28 Sweetland to Jesse Tapp, June 30, 1962, box 11, Acc. 26165; and Sweetland to Keith Burns, Aug. 8, 1962, box 23, Acc. 1747.

29 Sweetland to Shakow, Aug. 26, 1962, box 11, Acc. 26165.

30 Shakow to Sweetland, Dec. 24, 1961, box 8, Acc. 24845.

31 *Oregonian*, Feb. 8, 1963; and Sweetland to His Excellency Sukarno, Apr. 16, 1963, box 9, Acc. 1747.

32 Lil to Barbara, May 13, 1963, box 5, Acc. 24845.

33 The Chevy Greenbrier Van was a Corvair model, built between 1961 and 1965.

34 Sweetland to Vernon Neigenfind, May 31, 1963, box 9, Acc. 1747; and Sweetland to Alexa Saunders, June 2, 1963, box 5, Acc. 24845.

35 McT. Kahin, *Southeast Asia*, 156.

36 Lil to Far-away family and friends, June 26, 1963, box 5, Acc. 24845.

37 Ibid.; "CIA's Covert Indonesia Operation in the 1950s Acknowledged by U.S.," *Los Angeles Times*, Oct. 29, 1994, http://articles.latimes.com/print/1994-10-29/news/mn-56121_1_state-department, accessed Mar. 14, 2012; Bruce Vaughan, "Indonesia: Domestic Politics, Strategic Dynamics, and U.S. Interests," Congressional Research Service, www.fas.org/sgp/crs/row/RL32394.pdf, accessed Mar. 13, 2012; and Stieg Aga Aandstad, *Surrendering to Symbols: United States Policy Towards Indonesia, 1961–1965* (Oslo, Norway: Stieg Aga Aandstad, 2006), 25–30.

38 Aandstad, *Surrendering to Symbols*, 28–29.

39 Sweetland to Wilson Wyatt, July 11, 1963, box 9, Acc. 1747.

40 Sweetland to Michael Morris, Oct. 1, 1963; and Sweetland to Arthur Schlesinger, Oct. 28, 1963, both in box 9, Acc. 1747.

41 Sweetland to Saunders, June 28, 1963; Sweetland to Saunders, Nov. 7, 1963, both in box 5, Acc. 24845; and Sweetland to Zarin Zain, Nov. 14, 1963, box 9, Acc. 1747.

42 John Fitzgerald Kennedy—In Memoriam, Bandung, Nov. 28, 1963; and Sweetland to Dan Inouye, Dec. 7, 1963, both in box 9, Acc. 1747.

43 Sweetland to Zarin Zain, Nov. 14, 1963; The Standing of Journalism, Oct. 1963, box 5, Acc. 24845; and Hungry Teachers Cannot Teach, n.d., box 9, Acc. 1747.

44 Lil to Nanna, Dec. 27, 1963, box 5, Acc. 24845.

45 Ibid.; and Sonny Sarjadei, A Farewell to Mr. Monroe Sweetland, box 9, Acc. 1747.

46 Sweetland to Dear Friends, Mar. 28, 1964, box 12, Acc. 1747; the *Portland Reporter*, undated news clipping, box 9, Acc. 26165; Sweetland to Frank Coffin, June 1, 1964, box 12; Morgetan Setiawrip to Sweetland, Oct. 7, 1964, box 9, both in Acc. 1747; and (illegible signature) to Sweetland, Sept 8, 1964, box 12, Acc. 26165.

47 Indonesian-American Reactions to Each Other, 1964; and Sweetland to the Editor, *San Francisco Chronicle*, typescript, Apr. 20, 1965, both in box 12, Acc. 1747.

48 David Ransom, "Ford Country: Building an Elite for Indonesia," in *The Trojan Horse: A Radical Look at Foreign Aid*, ed. Steve Weissman (Palo Alto: Ramparts Press, 1975), 10, http://www.cia-on-campus. org/internat/indo.html, accessed Mar. 13, 2012; Ralph W. McGehee, *Deadly Deceits: My 25 Years in the CIA* (New York: Sheridan Square Press, 1983), 57–58; Aandstad, *Surrendering to Symbols*, 208–211; and John Bresnan, *Managing Indonesia: The Modern Political Economy* (New York: Columbia University Press, 1993), 11–12.

49 Aandstad, *Surrendering to Symbols*, 208–211; Ransom, "Ford Country," 10–11; Dennis Small, "Ghosts of Genocide: The CIA, Suharto, and Terrorist Culture," http://www.converge.org.nz/abc/prsp25.htm, accessed Mar. 13, 2012; McGehee, *Deadly Deceits*, 57–58; William Blum, *Killing Hope: U.S. Military and C.I.A. Interventions Since World War II* (Monroe, ME: Common Courage Press, 2004), 194–195. Paul F. Gardner, *Shared Hopes, Separate Fears: Fifty Years of U.S.-Indonesian Relations* (Boulder, CO: Westview Press, 1997), 213–224, attributes full blame to the PKI for initiating the coup.

50 Ken Conboy, *Intel: Inside Indonesia's Intelligence Service* (Djakarta: Equinox Publishing, 2004), 51–53; and *Oregonian*, Mar. 12, 1967.

51 Sweetland to George W. Friede, Dec. 31, 1970, box 9, Acc. 1747.

CHAPTER 12

1   Monroe Sweetland to *Wall Street Journal*, Feb. 26, 1964; Sweetland to Robert Bush, Mar. 23, 1964; and Sweetland to James McCaskill, July 14, 1964, all in Box 3, Acc. 01747.

2   *Oregonian*, Dec. 23, 1964; Lorraine V. Lee to Sweetland, Dec. 4, 1964; Roy Archibald to Henry Kono, Sec. 18, 1964, both in box 5, Acc. 2845; and Reynaldo Martinez to the author, Dec. 28, 2012.

3   For the NEA's membership in 1964, see *NEA Handbook, 1966–67* (Washington, D.C.: National Education Association, 1966), 370.

4   James T. Patterson, *Grand Expectations: The United States, 1945–1974* (New York: Oxford University Press, 1996), 542–547 and 569–571. Rebecca Sweetland remembers the family moving in the midst of a major snowstorm in northern California. Sweetland to the author, Apr. 24, 2012.

5   George W. Jones to Sweetland, Dec. 6, 1961, box 23, Acc. 1747.

6   Sweetland to William G. Carr, Jan. 4, 1962; and Carr to Sweetland, Jan. 10, 1962, both in box 23, Acc. 1747.

7   Carol F. Karpinski, *"A Visible Community of Professionals": African Americans and the National Education Association During the Civil Rights Movement* (New York: Peter Lang, 2008), 137–139.

8   Patrick J. Groff, "The NEA and School Desegregation," *Journal of Negro Education* 29 (Spring 1960),
     181–186; Gloria Stewner-Manzanares, "The Bilingual Education Act: Twenty Years Later," *NCBE* (Fall
     1968), 1–2; and NEA Actions in the Civil Rights Field: A Chronology, box 0302, ms. 2266, National
     Education Association Records (hereafter NEA Records), Special Collections, Gelman Library,
     George Washington University.

9   NEA Actions in the Civil Rights Field; and The NEA and Civil Rights: Recent History and Present
     Status, both in box 0302, ms. 2266, NEA Records.

10   Sweetland to Roy Wilkins, Apr. 22, 1965, box KK, Acc. 1747.

11   Sweetland, "A Major Obligation of a Professional Organization," box KK, Acc. 1747.

12   Barbara Sweetland Smith, In Memoriam, Our Dad; and Reynaldo Martinez, Monroe Sweetland
     Eulogy, both Sept. 30, 2006, copy in the author's files; and Martinez to the author, Dec. 28, 2012. A
     cache of missing files complicates the effort to document Sweetland's significance in shaping the
     nation's first bilingual education legislation. In the huge trove of material in the Sweetland collections at
     the Oregon Historical Society, the most notable missing papers during his ten years with NEA are those
     associated with bilingual education. When Sweetland retired in 1975, he left a "voluminous" file related
     to bilingual education in Burlingame, California, that was to be shipped to the Washington office. Those
     materials are missing from the NEA Records at George Washington University. See Roy Archibald to
     Bob Harmon, July 17, 1975, box JJ, Acc. 1747; and Kyle Conner e-mail to the author, Apr. 7, 2010. The
     surviving Sweetland correspondence related to bilingual education cited in this chapter is from
     Reynaldo Martinez's files.

13   Guadalupe San Miguel, Jr., *Contested Policy: The Rise and Fall of Federal Bilingual Education in the United
     States, 1960–2001* (Denton: University of North Texas Press, 2004), 7–10; and A. Bruce Gaarder, The
     "Federal" Role in the Education of Bilingual Children, box 9, Acc. 26165. Also see Rachel F. Moran,
     "The Politics of Discretion: Federal Intervention in Bilingual Education," *California Law Review* 76
     (Dec. 1988), 1249; and John Skrentny, *The Minority Rights Revolution* (Cambridge: Harvard University
     Press, 2002), 189.

14   Adelberto Guerrero to Angel Noe Gonzales, Sept. 13, 2003, photocopy in the files of Reynaldo
     Martinez, Incline Village, Nevada (hereafter Martinez files).

15   *Association of Mexican-American Educators, Inc.*, vol. 2 (Mar. 1966); Philip Montez to All Members, May
     13, 1966; and Call to Convention, Mexican-American Educators, Long Beach, California, May 27–29,
     1966s; Burlingame the *Advance Star*, June 12, 1966; and Sweetland to Jack Rees, June 1, 1966, all
     photocopies in Martinez files.

16   Skrentny, *The Minority Rights Revolution*, 186–189; and Testimony of Monroe Sweetland, Field
     Hearing, Committee on Education and Labor, U.S. House of Representatives, Los Angeles, box KK,
     Acc. 1747.

17   Southwest Council of Foreign Language Teachers, "Our Bilinguals: Social and Psychological Barriers.
     Linguistic and Pedagogical Barriers," Nov. 13, 1965, http://www.eric.ed.gov/ERICWebPortal/
     contentdelivery/servlet/ERICServlet?accno=ED019899, accessed Apr. 26, 2012.

18   Guerrero to Gonzales, Sept. 13, 2003.

19   *The Invisible Minority: Para No Vencibles* (Washington, D.C.: Department of Rural Education, National
     Education Association, 1966), v–vii and 5–9. During his tenure with NEA, Sweetland was fond of
     making reference to Thomas Jefferson.

20   Ibid., 9–18.

21   San Miguel, Jr., *Contested Policy*, 13–14.

22   Photocopies of the news reports were all from Southwest newspapers, obviously the work of Sweetland.
     See Robert M. Isenberg and Lewis R. Tamblyn to NEA-Tucson Survey Committee, circa Sept., 1966,
     Martinez files.

23   The news clippings are in the Martinez files.

24   Sweetland, Illiterate in Both Languages, box kk, Acc. 1747.

25   San Miguel, Jr., *Contested Policy*, 14; and Skrentny, *The Minority Rights Revolution*, 491–492.

26   California Teachers Association, *Education Service News*, Nov. 21, 1966, photocopy in Martinez files;
     Gilbert Sanchez, "An Analysis of the Bilingual Education Act, 1967–68" (Ph.D. dissertation, University
     of Massachusetts, 1973), 50–51; and Dean E. Triggs to Roy Archibald, Nov. 16, 1966, box 9, Acc.
     26165.

27   Elinor Hart, ed., "The Spanish-Speaking Child in the Schools of the Southwest," *New Voices of the
     Southwest* (Washington, D.C.: National Education Association, 1966), 1, 12–14; Guerrero to Gonzales,
     Sept. 13, 2003, Martinez files; and Martinez, Monroe Sweetland Eulogy, Sept. 30, 2006, copy in the
     author's files.

28   San Miguel, Jr., *Contested Policy*, 14; Ninetieth Congress, 1st Session, S.428, pp. 1–11, photocopy,
     Martinez files; and Sanchez, "An Analysis of the Bilingual Education Act," 75.

29   Sweetland to Harry Simmons, Jan 13, 1967, copy in Martinez files.

30   *Congressional Record*, vol. 113, no. 47, Mar. 23, 1967, and no. 50, Apr. 5, 1967, photocopies of both in
     Martinez files. After the first day of hearings, Gilbert Sanchez (who was there) made two observations:

the U.S. Office of Education opposed S.428, and no Mexican Americans testified. See Sanchez, "An Analysis of the bilingual Education Act," 67.

31 Bilingual Education, Hearings before the Special Subcommittee on Bilingual Education of the Committee on Labor and Public Welfare, U.S. Congress, Ninetieth Congress, First Session, on S428 (Washington: Government Printing Office, 1967), 1–2.

32 Ibid., 95–100.

33 Ibid., 102–111.

34 Bilingual Education Programs, Hearings before the General Subcommittee on Education of the Committee on Education and Labor, House of Representatives, Ninetieth Congress, First Session, June 28 and 29, 1967 (Washington: U.S. Government Printing Office, 1967), 302–304.

35 Ibid., 306–310.

36 See Ursula Casanova, "Bilingual Education: Politics or Pedagogy?" in Policy and Practice in Bilingual Education: Extending the Foundation, ed. Ofelia Garcia and Colin Baker (Avon, England: Multilingual Matters, 1995), 15–17.

37 National Education Association, Minutes of the Legislative Commission Meeting, May 29, 1967, box RR, Acc. 1747; and San Miguel, Jr., Contested Policy, 15–16.

38 San Miguel, Jr., Contested Policy, 15–16; Skrentny, The Minority Rights Revolution, 204–205; Sanchez, "An Analysis of the Bilingual Education Act," 55; Elementary and Secondary Education Amendments of 1967, Conference Report, 90th Congress, 1st Session, Report No. 1049, United States, Congress. House of Representatives, 37–41, copy in Martinez files; and Patrick Cox, Ralph W. Yarborough: The People's Senator (Austin: University of Texas Press, 2001), 232–235.

39 Moran, "The Politics of Discretion," 1264–1265.

40 Sweetland to Bernard Rapoport, June 14, 1968, box 12, Acc. 26165; "Affecting Eternity," Excerpts of a speech by U.S. Senator Ralph W. Yarborough, July 5, 1968, National Education Association Convention, box 13, Acc. 26165; and Ralph Yarborough, address to the NEA convention, Proceedings of the National Education Association 106th Annual Meeting, Dallas, Texas, July 5, 1968, box 0809, MS2266, NEA Records.

41 This information is in NEA News, West Coast Regional Office, Jan 31, 1969, box 13, Acc. 26165.

42 NEA News Release, West Coast Regional Office, Feb. 14, 1969, box 13; and Sweetland to Ernest Garcia, Apr. 14, 1969, box 12, both in Acc. 26165.

43 Congressional Record, Apr. 22, 1969, box 13, Acc. 26165; Sweetland to Federal Legislative Committeemen, NEA West Coast Regional Office, Nov. 27, 1973, box OO, Acc. 1747; and Jeffrey W. Kobrick, "The Compelling Case for Bilingual Education," Saturday Review (Apr. 29, 1972), 54–58, photocopy in box OO, Acc. 1747.

44 John C. Molina, "ESEA Title VII Bilingual Education: State of the Art," Linguistic Reporter (Nov. 1973), 4, box OO, Acc. 1747; and Skrentny, The Minority Rights Revolution, 211, 222, 225, and 228. Alan Cranston was also involved in the reauthorization of the Bilingual Act in 1970. See Cranston to Sweetland, Aug. 17, 1970, box 6, Acc. 24845.

45 Sweetland to Paul J. Fannin, Jan. 13, 1971. box RR, Acc. 1747; Arthur G. Cisneros to Carmen Leon, Feb. 17, 1972, box OO, Acc. 1747; Ronald Reagan to Honorable Members of the Senate, Aug. 25, 1972, box OO, Acc. 1747.

46 Rosenfield is quoted in Skrentny, The Minority Rights Revolution, 337; and Joseph M. Montoya, "Bilingual Education," Washington Post, Oct. 22, 1974, box 9, Acc. 26165.

47 Duane E. Campbell, Choosing Democracy: A Practical Guide to Multicultural Education, 4th Edition (Boston: Allyn and Bacon, 2010), cited in D. E. Campbell, "Bilingual Education Attacked," http://www.education.com/print/attacks-bilingual-education/, accessed Apr. 25, 2012; and Skrentny, The Minority Rights Revolution, 339.

48 San Miguel, Jr., Contested Policy, 87–91; James Crawford, "Obituary: The Bilingual Ed Act, 1968–2002," Rethinking Schools 16 (Summer 2002), http://rethinkingschools.org/archive/16_04/Bill64.shtml; and Arizona Daily Star, May 1, 2011, http://azstarnet.com/news/local/article_23696f63-d039-52b8-b32d-75e3faae6dc0.html.

49 Sweetland to Dirck Brown, Nov. 13, 1967, box MM, Acc. 1747.

50 Sweetland to Rosalyn Hester, June 18, 1971, box OO, Acc. 1747.

51 Oregonian, Mar. 24 and 26, 1963, Jan. 8–9, 1954, and Jan. 1 and Mar. 25, 1955.

52 Excerpts from the Testimony of Monroe Sweetland to the California General Assembly, Jan. 1968, box LL, Acc. 1747.

53 Ibid.

54 Sweetland to George Moscone, Feb. 15, 1968; and Moscone to Sweetland, Apr. 15, 1968, both in box LL, Acc. 1747.

55 Sweetland to Richard Batchelder, Jan. 16, 1968, box LL; and Sweetland to Dirck Brown, Jan. 29, 1968, box MM, both in Acc. 1747.

56 Sweetland to Douglas Cater, July 12, 1968, box MM, Acc. 1747.

57   Sweetland to Seymour M. Lipset, Aug. 8, 1968, box MM, Acc. 1747; Minutes of the NEA Legislative
      Commission Meeting, Sept. 22–23, 1968, NEA Records, Gelman Library, George Washington
      University, ms. 2266, box 1323; Sweetland to Edmund Muskie, Dec. 5, 1968, box RR, Acc. 1747.
58   Sweetland to Muskie, Dec. 8, 1968, box RR, Acc. 1747; Sweetland to John A. Blatnik, Jan. 16, 1969; and
      Blatnik to Sweetland, Jan. 29, 1969, both in box LL, Acc. 1747.
59   Les Francis e-mail to the author, Nov. 28, 2009.
60   Sweetland to George Moscone, Jan. 27, 1969, box LL, Acc. 1747; and Sweetland to Dirck Brown, Jan.
      27, 1969, box MM, Acc. 1747.
61   A National Campaign to Lower the Voting Age—The Youth Franchise Coalition—A Statement of
      Purpose, box 2258, MS 266, NEH Records; and Sweetland to Frank Karelsen, Feb. 14, 1969, box MM,
      Acc. 1747.
62   Sweetland to Prime Minister George Wilson, Feb. 13, 1969; Sweetland to Secretary of the Parliament,
      New Zealand, Feb. 13, 1969; Bob Ruby, assistant to Governor Forest Anderson (MT), Jan. 31, 1969;
      Victor Atiyeh to Sweetland, Feb. 17, 1969; and Edward Fadeley to Sweetland, Feb. 18, 1969, all in box
      LL, Acc. 1747.
63   Sweetland to Sherie D. Holbrook, Feb. 26, 1969; and Sweetland letter to *San Francisco Chronicle*, Mar.
      7, 1969, typescript, both in box LL, Acc. 1747.
64   Testimony of Monroe Sweetland to the California Assembly Hearings on Lowering the Voting Age,
      Apr. 9, 1969, box KK, Acc. 1747.
65   "Backlash Hits Move to Cut Voting Age," May 6, 1969, unidentified newspaper photocopy, box MM,
      Acc. 1747.
66   *San Francisco Examiner*, Sept. 15, 1969, photocopy in box LL, Acc. 1747.
67   Sweetland to the Editor, *San Francisco Examiner*, Sept. 16, 1969, typescript in box LL, Acc. 1747.
68   Testimony of Monroe Sweetland before the Assembly Committee on Elections and Constitutional
      Amendment, Dec. 3, 1969, box LL, Acc. 1747.
69   Sweetland to Edmund Muskie, Feb. 24, 1969; Sweetland to Robert Finch, May 22, 1969; C.F. Hall
      (British Embassy) to Sweetland, Mar. 6, 1969, all in box LL, Acc. 1747; and Sweetland to Senate
      Committee on Codes and Constitutional Amendments, Aug. 14, 1949, box MM, Acc. 1747.
70   Clay Myers, "Thoughts in Favor of the 19-Year Old Vote," Jan. 1970, both in box LL, Acc. 1947; and
      Oregonian, undated photocopy, box LL, Acc. 1747.
71   Earl Blumenauer to Sweetland, May 8, 1970; and Sweetland to Blumenauer, May 22, 1970, both in box
      LL, Acc. 1747.
72   *Oregonian*, May 27, 1970; *San Francisco Examiner*, June 2, 1970, photocopy in box LL. Acc. 1747; and
      New York Times, June 23, 1970, photocopy in box MM, Acc. 1747.
73   *San Francisco Chronicle*, June 23, 1970, photocopy in box MM, Acc. 1747.
74   Sweetland to Ted Kennedy, June 24, 1970, box RR, Acc. 1747; Sweetland to George Chaplin, editor,
      Honolulu Advertiser, Sept. 3, 1970, box LL, Acc. 1747; and Harris Survey, Sept. 7, 1970, box MM, Acc.
      1747.
75   *Washington Post*, Dec. 22, 1970, photocopy in box MM, Acc. 1747; and *Oregonian*, Dec. 22, 1970. For a
      biography of Justice Hugo Black, see Howard Ball, *Hugo L. Black: Cold Steel Warrior* (New York: Oxford
      University Press, 1996).
76   Sweetland to Clay Myers, Feb. 2, 1971, box LL, Acc. 1747.
77   Amalia Toro to Sweetland, Feb. 24, 1971, box LL, Acc. 1747.
78   *New York Times*, Mar. 24, 1971, photocopy in box PP, Acc. 1747; and *Oregonian*, Mar. 24, 1971.
79   *Oregonian*, Mar. 24, May 12, June 8, 11, and 12, 1971; and *New York Times*, June 28, 1971, photocopy in
      box PP, Acc. 1747.
80   John Wilson, "Fourth of July Celebration—July 4, 2011," Les Francis e-mail to the author, Aug. 7, 1911;
      and Francis to the author, Nov. 28, 2009 (including a segment of his memoir).

CHAPTER 13

1   Sweetland to A. Robert Smith, June 30, 1964; David Aberle to Sweetland, June 29, 1964; and Sweetland
      to J. K. Stranahan, Aug. 7, 1964, all in box 12, Acc. 1747.
2   *Oregonian*, July 4 and 5, 1964.
3   Ibid., July 4, 5, and 6, 1964.
4   Charles Porter to Dear Delegate, July 7, 1964, box 12, Acc. 1747.
5   *Oregonian*, Aug. 12, 1964.
6   *Convention News*, no. 2 (Aug. 17, 1964), box 34, Acc. 1747; and *Oregonian*, Aug. 24, 1964.
7   *Portland Reporter*, Aug. 24, 1964, photocopy in box 34, Acc. 1747; and *Oregonian*, Aug. 24 and 26, 1964.

8   James T. Patterson, *Grand Expectations: The United States, 1945–1974* (New York: Oxford University Press, 1996), 554–557; and *Oregonian*, Aug. 26, 1964. The only African American among the Oregon delegation, alternate delegate Gustava Thompson, did not agree with Sweetland.

9   Patterson, *Grand Expectations*, 558–561; and Lyndon Baines Johnson to Sweetland, Oct. 1964, box 10, Acc. 1747.

10 Testimony of Women Strike for Peace before the Democratic National Convention, Aug. 18, 1916; and For Immediate Release, "Norman Thomas Urges Foreign Policy Shifts, Aug. 17, 1964, both in box 34, Acc. 1235.

11 Maurine Neuberger Biography, Oregon History Project, http://www.ohs.org/the-oregon-history-project/biographies/Maurine-Neuberger.cfm.

12 Ibid.

13 Lorna Marple to Sweetland, Feb. 21, 1965, box NN, Acc. 1747. For Lorna Marple, see Guide to the Lorna Marple Papers, Special Collections, University of Washington Library, http://digital.lib.washington.edu/findingaids/view?docId=MarpleLorna0411.xml, accessed July 6, 2012.

14 Mike Katz to Sweetland, Jan. 7, 1966, box NN, Acc. 1747; *Oregonian*, Jan. 18, 1966; and Sweetland to Ambassador Lambertus M. Palar, Jan. 16, 1966, box RR, Acc. 1747.

15 *Oregonian*, Feb. 2 and 6, 1966.

16 Thomas R. Noe to Sweetland, Jan. 31, 1966, box KK, Acc. 1747; and Nathalie Panek to Sweetland, Feb. 1, 1966, box KK, Acc. 1747.

17 *Eugene Register-Guard*, Feb. 2, 1966; and Robert B. Frazier to Sweetland, Feb. 11, 1966, box NN, Acc. 1747.

18 *Oregonian*, Feb. 6 and 18, 1966.

19 Arthur H. Bone to Robert Duncan, Feb. 13, 1966; and Bone to Sweetland, Feb. 21, 1966, both in box NN, Acc. 1747.

20 *Oregonian*, Feb. 23, 25, and Mar. 1, 1966.

21 Sweetland to Duncan, Mar. 3, 1966, box NN, Acc. 1747.

22 Stan Berger, for *ADA World*, Sept. 1966, typescript in box KK, Acc. 1747.

23 *Oregonian*, April 11, 2011. Mapes notes that there were several variations of the quotation, but its general sentiment spoke to Duncan's views on Vietnam.

24 *Oregonian*, Nov. 6 and 10, 1966.

25 Sweetland to Mark Hatfield, Nov. 18, 1966; and Sweetland to Tom McCall, Nov. 18, 1966, both in box KK, Acc. 1747.

26 Patterson, *Grand Expectations*, 678–681.

27 Ibid., 678–685.

28 Sweetland to Joseph Rauh, Jr., June 5, 1967, box KK, Acc. 1747.

29 Sweetland, Comment in Support of Johnson-Humphrey at Crystal Springs Democratic Club, San Mateo, Highlands, March 5, 1968, box KK, Acc. 1747.

30 Ibid.

31 Joseph L. Rauh, Jr., to Lil and Monroe Sweetland, April 23, 1968, box KK, Acc. 1747.

32 Sweetland to Bernard Rapoport, June 14, 1968; and Sweetland to Leonard Nicoloric, Aug. 6, 1968, both in box 12, Acc. 26165.

33 Panek to Sweetland, Sept. 7, 1968, box 12, Acc. 26165. There are no surviving letters or documents in the Sweetland collection indicating his reactions to the most tumultuous political convention of the twentieth century.

34 Carl Solberg, *Hubert Humphrey: A Biography* (Saint Paul: Minnesota Historical Society Press, 1984), 340–346; and *Time*, July 17, 1968.

35 Jefferson Cowie, *Stayin' Alive: The 1970s and the Last Days of the Working Class* (New York: The New Press, 2010), 78; and Haynes Johnson, "1968 Democratic Convention: The Bosses Strike Back," *Smithsonian Magazine* (August 2008), www.smithsonianmag.com/history.../1968-democratic-convention.ht, accessed July 18, 2012.

36 Solberg, *Hubert Humphrey*, 370–385, 407.

37 Ibid., 407.

38 Rick Harmon, interview with Monroe Sweetland, Oct. 27, 1987, Tape 27, side 1, Research Library, Oregon Historical Society, Portland, Oregon.

39 Solberg, *Hubert Humphrey*, 422–425; and Sweetland to Bill Connell, Nov. 17, 1971, box 6, Acc. 24845.

40 Solberg, *Hubert Humphrey*, 421–436; and Robert G. Kaufman, *Henry M. Jackson: A Life in Politics* (Seattle: University of Washington Press, 2000), 223–236. For the Wechsler quotation, see pp. 223–224.

41 *Daily Astorian*, Nov. 11, 1974, photocopy; and Sweetland to the editor, *Daily Astorian*, Dec. 3, 1974, both in box 6, Acc. 24845.

42 Howard Costigan to Sweetland, Mar. 22, 1975, and July 10, 1975, both in box 5, Acc. 24845.

43 Kaufman, *Henry M. Jackson*, 309, 318, and 335–336.

44 Sweetland to Duncan, Mar. 3, 1966, box NN, Acc. 1747.

EPILOGUE

1   Norman Lubeck was a graphic-arts designer who worked for NEA's Burlingame office as early as 1964. See http://www.eric.ed.gov/PDFS/ED015736.pdf, accessed Aug. 8, 2012.

2   Photo Album. A Presentation to Monroe Sweetland on the occasion of his retirement, Hyatt House Hotel, Burlingame, California, May 17, 1975, on loan to the author from Rebecca Sweetland. A letter from Sweetland to Roy Archibald on the last page of the album expressed his appreciation for "the time and talent you put into my retirement festivities.... The whole scheme of the evening was memorable— but the t.l.c. evident in the projected cartoons by Norm Lubeck was the high-point of the event."

3   Rebecca Sweetland to the author, Aug. 6, 2012.

4   Ray Yasui to Sweetland, June 13, 1979; Yukio Kawamoto to Sweetland, June 18, 1979; Homer Hachiya to Sweetland, June 21, 1979; and Alan K. Ota, *Oregonian*, May 5, 1980, all in box JJ, Acc. 1747.

5   Koe Nishimoto to Mr. and Mrs. Sweetland, June 4, 1980, box JJ, Acc. 1747.

6   Rick Harmon, interview with Monroe Sweetland, Oct. 27, 1987, tape 27, side 2, Research Library, Oregon Historical Society; Monroe Sweetland to Jose Luis Corona, June 11, 1983, box 8, Acc. 01747; and Rebecca Sweetland to the author, Aug. 7, 2012.

7   Ancil Payne to Sweetland, Aug. 16, 1985, box 9, Acc. 01747.

8   Monroe to Lil, May 7, 1944, box QQ, Acc. 1747; and Harmon interview, Oct. 27, 1987, tape 27, side 2.

9   Monroe to Lil, May 7, 1944, box QQ, Acc. 1747; Harmon interview, Oct. 27, 1987, tape 27, side 2; Sweetland to John D. McSweeney, Oct. 16, 1961; Sweetland to Mrs. McFarlane, Nov. 13, 1961; and Sweetland to Mr. Magsamen, Nov. 16, 1961, all in box 23, Acc. 1747.

10 Harmon interview, Oct. 27, 1987. Although Western Wilderness Products was Sweetland's most significant business venture of its kind, the information in his papers is limited.

11 Sevie Allen to Sweetland, Dec. 8, 1985, box 12, Acc. 26165.

12 Patrick A. Cox to Sweetland, July 19, 1994; and Sweetland to Cox, Oct. 26, 1994, both in box 1, Acc. 01747. There is another document in the Sweetland files suggesting a case of theft from his business. A city attorney in East Los Angeles sent Sweetland a document, "Re: People v. John Mueller," in which he was named as a victim. See Office of City Attorney, East Los Angeles, California to Sweetland, n.d., box 8, Acc. 01747.

13 M. J. Stauffer to Sweetland, June 19, 1984; and Sweetland to Stauffer, June 25, 1984, box 8, Acc. 01747.

14 Richard Williams to Sweetland, n.d., box 7, Acc. 01747; and Brian to Sweetland, June 29, 1995, box 11, Acc. 26165.

15 Western Wilderness Products, Dried Floral Products, Mar. 1, 1991, box 8, Acc. 01747.

16 Terri Marconi to California Employment Development Department, Feb. 24, 1992; Employer's Quarterly Federal Tax Return, Mar. 26, 1992; State of California, Employment Development Department, Notice of Assessment for period ending Mar. 31, 1989, Statement Date, Sept. 15, 1992; Western Wilderness Products, Oct. 1992, Federal Taxes; Marconi to California Employment Development Department, Dec. 11, 1992; and Marconi to Sweetland, Feb. 24, 1993, all in box 8, Acc. 26165.

17 Author's interview with Rebecca Sweetland, Sept. 25, 2012; and Rick Harmon interview with Monroe Sweetland, Oct. 27, 1987, transcript pp. 403–404.

18 Sweetland, draft letter with no name, Jan 14, 1993, box 7, Acc. 01747.

19 Sweetland to Corri Pollock, May 1, 1994, box 8, Acc. 01747.

20 Nathalie Panek to Sweetland, Sept. 2, 1972; and Jim Patton to Sweetland, Sept. 20, 1972, both in box KK, Acc. 1747.

21 Nathalie and Jim Patton to Dearest Family and Closest Friends, Nov. 13, 1972, box KK, Acc. 1747.

22 Ibid.

23 Panek to Sweetland, Sept. 16, 1973, box KK, Acc. 1747; James B. Carey: A digital collection, Bob Golon, "Biography of James B. Carey," http://www.rci.rutgers.edu/~smlr/library/james_carey/biography.htm, accessed Aug. 14, 2012.

24 Panek to Sweetland, May 27, 1974, box KK, Acc. 1747. Arthur Burns was chairman of the Federal Reserve from 1970 to 1978.

25 Panek to Sweetland, Apr. 1, 1975; Jim Patton to Sweetland, Mar. 23, 1978; both in box 6, Acc. 24845; and David Panek to Sweetland, Aug. 25, 1992, files on loan from Rebecca Sweetland.

26 For a sample of Federman's columns, see *Oregonian*, July 8 and Dec. 27, 1972, and Sept. 18, 1977.

27 *Oregonian*, Feb. 19, 1986.

28 Circular Letter to Friends, n.d., box 9, Acc. 26165; and *City Club of Portland*, photocopy in box 8, Acc. 01747.

29 Sweetland to Barbara Boxer, Aug. 10, 1995; and Sweetland to Paul Simon, Sept. 28, 1995, both in box 1, Acc. 01747. Packwood resigned from the Senate in 1995.

30 Sweetland to Leon Panetta, Sept. 28, 1995, box 1, 01747.

31 Charles Porter to Sweetland, June 16, 1996, box 1, Acc. 01747; and William G. Robbins, "Charles O. Porter (1919–2006)," *Oregon Encyclopedia of History and Culture*, http://www.oregonencyclopedia. org/entry/view/porter_charles_o_1919_2006_/, accessed July 16, 2012.

32 Lisa Bentley to Sweetland, Sept. 4, 1996; and Sweetland to Bentley, Sept. 21, 1996, both in box 1, Acc. 01747.

33 Sweetland to Mike Tassone, Sept 6, 1995, box 1, Acc. 01747. For Captain Jack, see "A Brief History of the Modoc War," National Park Service, U.S. Department of the Interior, www.nps.gov/labe/ planyourvisit/upload/MODOC%20WAR.pdf, accessed Aug. 17, 2012.

34 Tassone to Sweetland, Sept. 4, 1996, box 1, Acc. 01747.

35 Sweetland to Tassone, Sept. 6, 1996, box 1, Acc. 01747.

36 Tassone to Sweetland, Jan. 14, 1997, box 1, Acc. 01747.

37 Rebecca Sweetland to Dear Dad, Feb. 21, 1997, document on loan from Rebecca Sweetland.

38 *Clackamas Review*, Aug. 14 and 28, 1998, clippings on loan from Rebecca Sweetland.

39 Stan Federman to Rebecca Sweetland, Dec. 11, 1989, box 9, Acc. 26165.

40 Author interview with Verne Duncan, Aug. 27, 2012; and *Oregonian*, Mar. 26, 1998.

41 *Oregonian*, Mar. 26, 1998.

42 *Northwest Labor Press*, vol. 99, no. 2 (Apr. 3, 1998), box 2, Acc. 01747; and *Oregonian*, Mar. 26, 1998.

43 "Monroe Sweetland for State Senate," campaign brochure in box 2, Acc. 01747.

44 Keith Burns to Libby Solomon, Feb. 3, 1993, box 7, Acc. 24845.

45 Ibid., Myron B. Katz to Judith Ramaley, Feb. 6, 1993, box 13, Acc. 26165; and *Oregonian*, June 10, 1995, photocopy in box 8, Acc. 26165. For the endowment figures, see Katrina Ratzlaff to Sweetland, Feb. 25, 1997, box 1, Acc. 01747; Dan Bernstein to Sweetland, Nov. 28, 2001; Teresa Vrivlo to Sweetland, Mar. 2005, both in box 3, Acc. 01747; and Becky Hein e-mail to the author, Aug. 24, 2012.

46 Myron B. Katz to MacNaughton Awards Committee, Sept. 7, 1994, document on loan from Rebecca Sweetland; and e-mail, Jann Carson to the author, Aug. 21, 2012, notes on the ACLU Awards Dinner Program.

47 Monroe Sweetland Appreciation Banquet invitation, Nov. 8, 1997; Charles O. Porter to Democratic Friends, Nov. 5, 1997; and Daniel Bernstein to Monroe Sweetland, all in box 12, Acc. 26165.

48 "Top 10 Reasons Monroe Sweetland is a Revered Democrat," box 12, Acc. 26165.

49 Josie Villamil Tinajero to Sweetland, Dec. 3, 1993; e-mail, Adalberto Guerrero to Angel Noe Gonzales, Sept. 13, 2003; Guerrero to Sweetland, Oct. 1, 1993; and Gonzales to Tinajero, Sept. 24, 1993, all in box 7, Acc. 01747.

50 Senator Harry Reid, "Honoring Monroe Sweetland," *Congressional Record*, vol. 150, No. 10 (Feb. 2, 2004), Senate, from the *Congressional Record* online through the Government Printing Office, www. gpo.gov, accessed Aug. 22, 2012.

51 Author's interview with Bob Davis, Mar. 17, 2011.

52 Author's interview with Mike Katz, Nov. 2, 2010.

53 Author's interview with Fred Neal, Mar. 8, 2012.

54 Rick Harmon, interview with Monroe Sweetland, Oct. 27, 1987, Tape 27, side 1, Research Library, Oregon Historical Society, Portland, Oregon.

55 At his memorial service, Mike Katz referred to Sweetland as "eternally optimistic." Copy of Katz's remarks in the author's possession.

56 Reynaldo Martinez to the author, Dec. 28, 2012.

57 Author's interview with Rebecca Sweetland, Sept. 25, 2012.

58 Copies of the remarks of the following individuals are all in the author's possession: Mike Katz, Kate Sweetland-Lambird, Earl Blumenauer, and Barbara Sweetland Smith.

Index